DISRUPTION

DISRU

POTOMAC BOOKS | *An imprint of the University of Nebraska Press*

PTION

Inside the Largest Counterterrorism
Investigation in History

AKI J. PERITZ

Library of Congress Cataloging-in-Publication Data
Names: Peritz, Aki, author.
Title: Disruption: inside the largest counterterrorism
investigation in history / Aki J. Peritz.
Description: [Lincoln, Nebraska]: Potomac Books,
an imprint of the University of Nebraska Press,
[2021] | Includes bibliographical references and
index.
Identifiers: LCCN 2021022964
ISBN 9781640123809 (hardback)
ISBN 9781640125049 (epub)
ISBN 9781640125056 (pdf)
Subjects: LCSH: Terrorism—Prevention—
International cooperation. | Aeronautics,
Commercial—Security measures—International
cooperation. | Suicide bombings—Prevention—
International cooperation. | Intelligence
service—International cooperation. |
BISAC: POLITICAL SCIENCE / Terrorism
Classification: LCC HV6431 .P466 2021 |
DDC 363.325—dc23
LC record available at
https://lccn.loc.gov/2021022964

Set in Minion Pro.

Never doubt that a small group of thoughtful, committed citizens can change the world; indeed, it's the only thing that ever has.

—*Apocryphally attributed to Margaret Mead*

CONTENTS

ILLUSTRATIONS

MAJOR CHARACTERS

OVERT CONSPIRATORS

Rashid Rauf	Birmingham native in Pakistan who would eventually become the Overt mastermind
Mohammed Yasar Gulzar	Rauf's childhood friend who fled to Pakistan following Rauf's uncle's murder
Abdulla Ahmed Ali	Walthamstow resident and Overt's London ringleader
Assad Sarwar	High Wycombe resident and Overt quartermaster
Tanvir Hussain	Ali's second-in-command and avid cricketeer
Waheed Arafat Khan	One of the potential suicide bombers
Ibrahim Savant	One of the potential suicide bombers
Umar Islam	A convert to Islam and potential suicide bomber
Waheed Zaman	A university student and potential suicide bomber

OTHERS

Mohammed Patel	Owner of the Islamic Medical Association (IMA)
Mohammed Hamid	Al-Koran bookstore owner, a.k.a. "Osama bin London"

Cossor Ali (Anwar) — Abdulla Ahmed Ali's wife
Dawood Khan — Abdulla Ahmed Ali's oldest brother
Dhiren Barot — Al Qaeda operative who tried to attack London's Underground and carparks
Mohammed al-Ghabra — London-based jihadist with connections to multiple plots
Anwar al-Awlaqi — Leading English-speaking al Qaeda propagandist
Abdul Rauf — Rashid Rauf's father
Mohammed Saeed — Rashid Rauf's uncle
Mohammad Sidique Khan — The 7/7 attack's ringleader
Muktar Said Ibrahim — The 7/21 attack's ringleader

PAKISTAN-BASED TERRORISTS

Osama bin Laden — Founder and leader of al Qaeda
Ayman al-Zawahiri — Osama bin Laden's deputy
Masood Azhar — Founder of Jaish-e-Mohammed (JeM) and Harkat ul-Mujahidin (HUM)
Abu Ubaydah al-Masri — Senior al Qaeda bombmaker
Khalid Sheik Mohammed — The 9/11 attacks' mastermind
Hamza Rabi'a — Al Qaeda's operational commander
Hafeez Saeed — Head of Lashkar-e-Taiba
Marwan al-Suri — An al Qaeda bombmaker and trainer

BRITISH OFFICIALS

Tony Blair — Prime Minister
John Reid — Home Secretary
Eliza Manningham-Buller — Security Service (MI5) Director General
John Scarlett — Secret Intelligence Service (MI6) Chief
Peter Clarke — Head of SO15, Metropolitan Police
Andy Hayman — Asst. Commissioner for Specialist Operations, Metropolitan Police

U.S. OFFICIALS

George W. Bush   President

Fran Townsend   Assistant to President Bush for Homeland Security and Counterterrorism

Juan Zarate   Deputy Assistant to the President and Deputy National Security Adviser for Combating Terrorism

Michael Chertoff   Department of Homeland Security (DHS) Secretary

Michael Hayden   CIA Director

Stephen Kappes   CIA Deputy Director

Larry Pfeiffer   Chief of Staff to CIA Director Hayden

Jose Rodriguez   CIA National Clandestine Service Director

Robert Mueller   FBI Director

Scott Redd   National Counterterrorism Center (NCTC) Director

Andy Liepman   NCTC's Director of Intelligence

PAKISTANI OFFICIALS

Pervez Musharraf   President

Ashfaq Parvez Kayani   ISI Director-General

Azmat Hayat Khan   ISI Deputy Director-General

ABBREVIATIONS

3MPO   Sec. 3 of the Maintenance of Public Order Ordinance (Pakistan)
ACCOLC   Access Overload Control (UK)
ANPR   Automatic Number Plate Recognition (UK)
BAA   British Airports Authority
CBRN   Chemical, Biological, Radiological and Nuclear
COBR   Cabinet Office Briefing Rooms (UK)
CPS   Crown Prosecution Service (UK)
CTC   CIA's Counterterrorism Center (U.S.)
DHS   Department of Homeland Security (U.S.)
FATA   Federally Administered Tribal Areas (Pakistan)
GCHQ   Government Communications Headquarters (UK)
HMP   Her Majesty's Prison
HMTD   Hexamethylene triperoxide diamine
HUA   Harakat ul-Ansar
HUM   Harakat ul-Mujahidin
HUMINT   Human Intelligence
ISI   The Inter-Services Intelligence Directorate (Pakistan)
IMA   Islamic Medical Association
IOC   International Olympic Committee
JEM   Jaish-e-Mohammed
JTAC   The Joint Terrorism Analysis Centre (UK)
KSM   Khalid Sheikh Mohammed
LeT   Lashkar-e-Taiba
Met   The Metropolitan Police (UK)

MI5   The Security Service (UK)

MI6   The Secret Intelligence Service (UK)

NCTC   National Counterterrorism Center (U.S.)

NSA   National Security Agency (U.S.)

ODNI   Office of the Director of National Intelligence (U.S.)

PDB   President's Daily Brief

SIGINT Signals Intelligence

SO15   Counter-Terrorism Command of the Metropolitan
        Police (UK)

SVTC   Secure Video TeleConference

TATP   Triacetone Triperoxide

TPIM   Terrorism Prevention and Investigation Measures (UK)

TSA   The Transportation Security Administration (U.S.)

TSOC   The Transportation Security Operations Center (U.S.)

TVP   Thames Valley Police (UK)

UAV   Unmanned Aerial Vehicle

AUTHOR'S NOTE

Thank you for reading this book. A few housekeeping notes: writing about a global terrorist conspiracy and the desperate race to stop it means a fair amount of bureaucratic language has wormed its way into the text. That said, in order to make the narrative more accessible to a general reader, I've tried to eliminate as many acronyms and unfamiliar terms from these pages as possible.

For the sake of clarity, I've chosen to call Great Britain's Security Service "MI5" and the Secret Intelligence Service "MI6," as these are how these organizations are often referred to in public discourse. Complicating matters is that in CIA cables, MI5 is often termed as the "British Security Service" (BSS), which means absolutely nothing outside of classified agency traffic. In any case, for the intelligence purists among the readers of this book, please note the URL for the Security Service is www.MI5.gov.uk; the Secret Intelligence Service website is www.MI6.gov.uk.

I sometimes use American verbiage to explain British terminology. This includes occasional references to a "cellphone" when a Brit means "mobile"; "train station" for "railway station"; "apartment" instead of "flat," etc.

Due to my previous employment, this book was submitted to and cleared by the CIA Publication Review Board prior to publication.

Apologies in advance: despite my best efforts, errors have inadvertently snuck into the text. There are also some events that remain unknowable because everyone involved was either killed, died, or is serving a sentence in a maximum-security lockup. I've tried to be as honest as I could in recreating the events in these pages, with as much first-hand documentation as was available.

Finally, as I've worked on this book for over the course of several years, I was able to include many formerly classified documents from the British and American governments. This is however not the universe of all that is known about the subjects and the investigations, and so there remain still-buried secrets. I've unearthed what I believe is the lion's share for this book, but there are still a few jewels securely locked away in classified databases and in people's minds.

One day they will be known.

But not today.

DISRUPTION

1

The Killer beside You

You didn't notice your killer in the seat next to you on the flight to New York City.

Indeed, no one paid much attention to the twitchy young man with the trimmed goatee and thick London accent. He breezed through security, flashing his British passport before wandering over to the gate and easing his way into a black-backed airport chair. On that day, two hundred thousand other passengers and their baggage passed in and out of security at London Heathrow Airport with no problem.

He was one of tens of thousands of people that afternoon milling about the terminal with plans to fly from Europe to North America. You both had economy class tickets for American Airlines flight no. 131 from Heathrow to John F. Kennedy International Airport. The London to New York City route was the most popular long-haul in the world; some sixty flights crossed the Atlantic Ocean daily from one English-speaking metropolis to the other. If you added up all the passengers annually, the airlines moved some three million souls across the dark waters each year without much of a hitch.

The man, like you, had already had a bite to eat before heading out for the airport. It was going to take almost nine hours to reach the Big Apple; looking at your watch, you hoped to get some shuteye on the flight before the wheels touched down on the tarmac. As you killed time playing with your phone, he stared passively at the monitor next to the gate, waiting for the flight to begin boarding. Together you entered the airplane and played Tetris with your bags in the overhead bins. You dutifully buckled your seatbelt as the monitors began to play the preflight safety instructions for the widebody passenger jet. You absentmindedly thumbed through the in-flight magazine *American Way* instead of focusing on what might happen in the event of a water landing. You weren't sitting in an exit row, so you and your seatmate didn't have a special conversation with one of the stewards. You took a sip from the water bottle you brought with you—air travel can be so dehydrating.

After takeoff, the flight staff passed out drinks and pretzels, higher-end treats for those in the business and first classes. Some people were already feeling the effects of sleeping pills. The "fasten seatbelt" sign had been turned off. A businesswoman nearby was enjoying a lonely gin and tonic behind the glow of her laptop. A little blonde boy in the back was squealing; it was his first time in an airplane. It was dark out there, some five miles above the ocean.

Around midflight, the man sitting beside you reached under the seat in front of him and fished out a small bag. You found it a bit odd, how he kept peeking inside it during the early part of the flight, repeatedly examined the contents. Without offending his personal space, you could see a sports drink and other assorted junk. If you were an especially sharp-eyed observer, it might have crossed your mind that the drink's orange tint was a bit off—a little too orange or perhaps not orange enough—but maybe that was due to the airplane's dimmed lighting.

He suddenly rose and said he was headed toward the lavatory by the wing, all the while examining his wristwatch. You moved your legs to allow him to pass. He mumbled a "thank you" and headed down the aisle. Absentmindedly, you also checked the time; it read 9 p.m., on the dot.

◆

Your aircraft did not immediately disintegrate from the onboard explosion. Instead, the blast resulted in a compression of the surrounding air, creating an internal shockwave.[1] The shock load—the pressure created by the explosion's front—ripped a large, gaping hole in the side of the aircraft.

The cabin immediately depressurized. Subzero temperatures and a half ton of pressure surged in to fill the void. The air, traveling almost at the speed of sound from the inside of the aircraft to the outside, caused everything not strapped or bolted down to be sucked from the flapping, gaping wound. As large sections of the plane started ripping off, the pilots donned oxygen masks, tried to establish crew communications, checked the cabin altitude and rate, and attempted to descend to a lower altitude.

The bomb had exploded in the bathroom near the wing, and the aircraft flipped and began to dive. Twisted pieces of airframe, fabric, plastic, Plexiglas, passengers, and the odd piece of luggage descended earthward.

Desperately punching in "7700" on their transponders—the squawk code for "EMERGENCY"—the pilots hoped any air traffic control and government officials monitoring these communications would take notice. The main civilian voice frequency of 121.5 MHZ, also the emergency frequency, heard a stream of garbled, sickly static; sounds that originated as "MAYDAY MAYDAY MAYDAY."

At five miles up in the air and falling fast, passengers and aircrew still alive were rendered unconscious. The last things you would have experienced: a flash of light, the sudden murderous expansion of air pressure, the acrid singe of explosives, and the violent contraction of steel and plastic. The jet, cruising over the North Atlantic at 35,000 feet at 470 knots (540 miles per hour) with 240 passengers and 11 crewmembers, took approximately two and a half minutes to hit the water.

Then a deep, eternal silence.

◆

Most people look up in the air and see blues and grays, white clouds and haze, but pilots and air traffic controllers see the globe as an interlocked, interconnected series of highways in the sky. Along the way, there are waypoints where airplanes either manually or automatically check in with air control, but there are also areas of dead space over the open ocean.

Airline companies have an operations center—like a NASA control room—that monitors their fleet. Each plane has an assigned dispatcher who would have been among the first to know that something had gone wrong. Likewise, officials within the Transportation Security Administration (TSA) command center—a squat, large, anonymous building located near Washington DC's Dulles International Airport, now known as the "Freedom Center"—similarly found their attention directed to the unfolding event.

One by one over the course of a few hours, commercial aircraft disappeared from the air traffic computer screens across multiple command-and-control centers. Secure lines rang with frantic airline and government employees trying to determine whether this was some systemic computer malfunction—or something worse.

In a scenario like this, "the blips," recalled TSA acting deputy administrator Tom Blank, "would go away" as they fell from the sky into the ocean.[2] "It'd be damned difficult," Blank said, "to organize the response."

◆

In a town northwest of London, a man in his twenties named Assad Sarwar was lounging on the couch at his parents' home, looking around for the remote control. His mother had just finished cleaning up the kitchen and retired to her bedroom. Finding the remote, Sarwar glanced at the clock on the wall, nine in the evening, and flipped on the television.

BBC cut into its regularly scheduled program forty minutes later. The announcer shifted his focus down from the teleprompter to an off-screen piece of paper in his hand: "We interrupt this broadcast to bring you breaking news. I'll caveat this now, this is coming from the wires, they are quoting an unnamed official at Transport Security saying that there's been some sort of accident on a passenger airline—"

Sarwar's eyes widened as he took a deep breath.

The announcer paused, his hand on his earpiece, and then continued. "We've received word that a passenger aircraft has gone down, another passenger airplane has had a mishap over the Atlantic—" The announcer struggled to clarify whether the two news items were referring to the same plane or to two different ones.

A faint smile crept over Sarwar's face. In his mind's eye, he imagined his friends, with whom he had lunch with several days beforehand. They were scheduled to be on a plane flying somewhere over the Atlantic, or maybe even Canada, at this hour. He flipped the channel, where the announcer intoned, "cursory details coming to us at Sky News; a shipping vessel off the coast of Greenland reported seeing a bright light and an explosion in the sky—"

He imagined television sets with the same news flickering on in the houses up and down the street. "In the last few moments, we received word of a third plane from London Heathrow airport had some sort of mechanical failure over the Atlantic Ocean, reports are still coming in, but it appears a third plane has been—"

◆

Key decision makers from across the political and national security communities were pulled from meetings, dinners, and photo ops, as their security teams hustled them into secure areas for top secret briefings. Presidents and prime ministers called emergency sessions of their national security staff. Data from across the globe ricocheted over secure lines and the vast data fiber optic cables that stretch from North America to the UK and across the European continent. Intelligence was patchy and scrambled.

Flights across the Atlantic were immediately shut down. Tens of thousands of angry, frightened individuals mobbed airports across Europe and the U.S. Asian nations were alerted that something was terribly wrong in American airspace; flights over the Pacific—a much larger expanse of water—were likewise grounded as soon as possible. Relatives begged, cried, and tried to squeeze information from helpless airline representatives. Voices rose; riot gear and chemical irritants were handed out as a precaution in case things spiraled out of control.

As the big flight boards flipped the full line of upcoming arrivals and departures to "cancelled," the media speculators, social media vultures, insurance adjusters, lawyers, and damage control consultants descended. In every great tragedy, there is also always great opportunity to make money.

The assumption was a 9/11-style attack was underway. The militaries of the world were placed on highest alert. The massive steel gates that guarded the North American Aerospace Defense Command and elements of Northern Command inside a mountain near Colorado Springs clanged shut.

◆

The news came in first as a trickle, and then in an avalanche. The first sketchy reports were from ships reporting seeing bright flashes and large booms as crippled aircraft started falling from the sky. The welcomes of friends and family waiting for the arrival of some two thousand travelers and crew aboard the ill-fated flights turned into plaintive wails, echoed on television sets across the United States and Europe. The twenty-four-hour news channels broadcast each whiff of a rumor over and over again.

Everyone on television instantly became an airlines/terrorism pundit, and the airwaves and the internet overflowed with speculative nonsense. Conmen set up fake fundraisers by the dozens to extract money from the well-meaning. Conspiracy theorists pumped garbage into the public discourse, claiming the attack never happened or that everyone onboard was a "crisis actor." Savvy, shameless, and unscrupulous politicians would not wait long to further their goals to restrict immigration and promote Islamophobia.

In High Wycombe, Sarwar was still glued to his television. His thoughts were again interrupted by the television announcer. Another plane. And another. This went on throughout the evening. Sarwar stayed up all night, watching and listening before finally passing out on the couch in the wee hours of the morning.

◆

The Transportation Security Operations Center (TSOC) was a cavernous, windowless room of beige walls crammed with people, computers, and large displays of the current flights over American airspace. This would become the central clearing house for incoming information about the unfolding event. TSOC also served as the hub for multiple government agencies concerned with airspace security, and the unfolding disaster sent a lightning bolt through the room. It would be unlike anything any of these individuals had experienced, even those who had worked on 9/11.

TSOC alerted TSA headquarters, a facility located near the Pentagon, just across the Potomac River from Washington DC. Someone, with real or perceived authority, then made the command decision to ground or divert all flights in American airspace—thousands of civilian aircraft—while his or her British and Canadian counterparts did the same. Surveillance aircraft took off from bases across the eastern seaboard. As a precaution, the U.S. Air Force also scrambled fighter jets over all the major urban areas along the East Coast. Boston, Washington DC, and New York City had military planes in the air within minutes of receiving the go-ahead. The secretary of defense considered giving shoot-down orders to the pilots. However, unlike on 9/11, the civilian aircraft were exploding in midair, not being used to target buildings, making the pilots' ultimate mission unclear.

All along the Atlantic rim, from the Commonwealth of Virginia up through Canada, Greenland, Ireland, and Great Britain, coast guards and navies would be immediately placed on the highest alert. The U.S. Coast Guard deployed the vast majority of its available vessels for a rescue effort. Some were equipped with cranes designed to pick up whatever wreckage or survivors might be bobbing on the high seas.

The Coast Guard also prepared to assist the U.S. Navy dive teams. However, its vessels weren't designed to travel offshore at any great length and cannot safely operate in the choppy, swirling waters of the North Atlantic. In any case, by the time anyone arrived to where the airplanes had fallen from the sky, much of the evidence was already at the bottom of the ocean.

◆

First responders have three objectives at a crime scene: secure and protect the scene; institute authority and jurisdiction; and establish firm boundaries to determine the outer area of the blast.[3]

It was dark work. The first people on the location where your plane had hit the Atlantic would notice the smell of jet fuel on the water's surface. This particular "crime scene" was enormous, given the flight arc of passenger planes. Multiple widebody aircraft—each weighing almost three quarters of a million pounds worth of cargo, fuel, passengers, and structural components[4]—went down mostly over international waters. First responders found debris floating on the surface for hundreds of miles around. Depending on the current, some of it would eventually drift toward the shoreline.

Establishing jurisdiction over such a massive case was a logistical nightmare. American and Canadian planes were on the target list, and neither the United States nor Canada (or Great Britain, for that matter) ceded complete control over the investigation. Incompatible procedures, papered over during the best of times, quickly came to the forefront. Who or what organization from which country would secure the site? Handle the evidence? Document the wreckage? A million different points of bureaucratic arcana would rise to the surface. Eventually, the United States of America, with its overwhelming resources, would establish dominance.

As it became clear that some terrorist group had downed the planes, the national security talking heads on every news channel began citing Lockerbie to highlight the challenges that such an attack would cause investigators. That was because when agents of the Libyan state smuggled a bomb onto a New York-bound Boeing 747 in December 1988, the plane exploded over Scotland, a process that took two and a half minutes before large portions of the wreckage landed throughout the countryside. Some parts fell eighty miles away in northern England.[5] The explosion at 31,000 feet disbursed parts of the plane and its 259 unlucky passengers and crew over the town of Lockerbie and killed 11 people on the ground. The "crime scene" itself was spread across some 845 square miles—an area almost twice the size of the City of Los Angeles—and all of it needed to be meticulously catalogued for an eventual trial.[6] This effort was complicated by the looters and souvenir hunters who descended immediately upon the wreckage, metal detectors in hand, altering the crime scene.[7]

Of course, the plane you were on blew up over the ocean rather than over land, so much of the critical evidence—that is, the cockpit voice recorders and the flight data recorders, also known as "black boxes"—were not expected to be recovered for months. After all, when an Air France flight departing from Rio de Janiero for Paris crashed in the middle of the Atlantic in June 2009, it took a few days for the Brazilian Navy to reach the wreckage site.[8] It took search teams another two years to locate the cockpit voice recorder.[9]

◆

What is acceptable risk? People exist in a fragile, interconnected world and confront all sorts of negative phenomena every second of existence. Taking a risk could be described as making a decision when information is inadequate and outcomes are uncertain.[10] People make choices all the time, as do groups and nations. As the world's transportation, financial, trade, health, and communication systems become more integrated, an individual action in one domain can and will come barreling into others. There is no benevolent guiding hand that will right the course if events go awry, no single agent or government agency keeping things from going off the rails. A wrench thrown into one system will affect all the others. And it has become harder to game out all hundreds of thousands of variables. The globalized world has paradoxically become more uncertain.[11]

Across American airspace, over forty-four thousand flights are handled across 5.3 million square miles every year, almost all without a hitch.[12] One billion passengers fly to and fro, all without injury or death. More people perish every year on American roadways than in the air; thirty-seven thousand men, women, and children, enough to populate a town. Annually, there are 1.25 million deaths on the road across the globe, about the population size of Dallas, Texas, or Birmingham, England.[13]

Commercial aviation remains the safest way to travel from point A to point B. The industry has been the beneficiary of public interest, government regulation, and technological advances. Fatalities in the air nowadays are less than half of what they were in the 1980s, despite the exponential growth in commercial aviation.[14] When an in-flight accident occurs, trained investigators thoroughly examine the causes to prevent it from happening again.[15] In the planes and on the ground, developments in navigation systems, early warning devices, and engines offer ever increasing assurances. The pilots are also generally better trained than they were a generation ago.

Still, there is a peculiar terror in air travel. Traveling at great distance through the sky, held aloft by a rattling machine guided by laws of physics most people don't understand, can be frightening. Being in a confined space with dozens of people, recycled air, and a pint-sized bathroom raises the blood pressure. Routinely placing one's life, and the lives of one's family members, in the hands of strangers sitting behind a locked, reinforced door can seem nonsensical. And, of course, airplane tragedies never fail to grip the headlines.

When something goes wrong on a flight, statistics become utterly meaningless. And in your heart, you also know there are always quirks, mishaps, and vulnerabilities in the system. Planes crash.

◆

Beyond the direct human tragedy, a massive shutdown of the U.S. eastern seaboard and most of the European continent to air traffic caused economic spasms throughout the globe.

The airline industry would be the hardest hit. Flight disruptions, whether caused by man-made or natural assailants, have the potential for tremendous impact. Pan American Airlines suffered a devastating blow from the bombing over Lockerbie, accelerating the company's decline, bankruptcy, and dissolution a little over two years later. 9/11 caused over $30 billion (in 2001 dollars) in insured losses, surpassed only by the devastation of New Orleans and the Gulf Coast in Hurricane Katrina during the Bush era.[16] For years afterward, domestic air travel didn't bounce back to pre-attack levels; another massive terror operation in the skies would have crippled the industry.[17] Between 2001 and 2006, TWA, US Airways, United Airlines, Air Canada, Aloha Airlines, Northwest Airlines, and Delta Air Lines had all declared Chapter 11 bankruptcy for a host of reasons—and if people stopped flying in record numbers because of the possibility of another major attack, most of these companies would have gone belly-up for good. Finally, in the worst blow to date, the worldwide airlines industry lost a whopping $84 billion in just half a year during the global coronavirus pandemic of 2020, shedding millions of jobs in the process, and only avoided collapse due to direct government financial assistance.[18]

With most of the evidence at the bottom of the North Atlantic, it would take weeks or months to figure out what exactly happened. First by government edict and then by consumer confidence, planes would be relegated to their hangars. With imperfect information, the TSA might impose new security directives—billed as "temporary enhancements of security," according to former senior TSA official Chad Wolf, who eventually rose to become an acting Department of Homeland Security secretary.[19]

And what if another plane blew up in midair over the waters soon afterward? After all, al Qaeda tried to destroy a plane midflight three months after 9/11. Had that attack been successful, how confident would anyone have been about stepping into the air? What would the pilots and stewards think? Would they be comfortable going to work without proper precautions? Would you? Every day planes don't fly generates significant financial losses for their companies. These losses would ripple through adjacent industries for years afterward, making losses on 9/11 seem manageable by comparison. If, say, United Airlines ceased to function, one million jobs could eventually vanish in its undertow. And that's just one company.

Without the airline companies, the U.S. tourism industry—which generated hundreds of billions of dollars and employed millions of Americans—would be devastated. Duty free and the travel retail industry—which in 2017 generated almost $70 billion globally—would be wrecked.[20] If insurance rates became too high to service both the surviving airlines and airports, then no plane would take off from American airspace. The government would have to step in. Economies would contract; unemployment would soar. And of course, the timing of the attack could have shoved America—and the world—into another Great Depression.

It would have been a dramatic, grisly victory for a few warped souls.

◆

You jolt awake as the steward gently shakes you to let you know dinner is about to be served. For a few terrifying seconds, you have trouble processing the fact that the nightmare you so vividly watched play out was just that, a nightmare.

Luckily for you and hundreds of your fellow travelers, history took a different path. The twitchy young man and his coconspirators never materialized on your flight. Some may argue this was the work of fate or some higher power. But that is ultimately unknowable. What we do know is that thousands of anonymous men and women desperately tried to prevent this tragedy from unfolding. They mostly, but not fully, succeeded.

This is as much their story as it is that of the men with the warped worldview who plotted death and carnage on an almost unthinkable scale.

Don't worry. Everything in this story turned out fine, more or less. Enjoy the flight.

2

Baker's Boy

On Wednesday, April 24, 2002, at 4 a.m., Mohammed Saeed, a paunchy, gray-bearded fifty-four-year-old deliveryman finished his work in the dark early morning hours in East Birmingham. This was his normal routine, driving his van around town. He headed home after a long day that stretched into the night.

It was a bit after four in the morning as he cut the engine to his vehicle and turned off the headlights near his modest terraced home in the working-class community of Washwood Heath in East Birmingham. His wife and two children were inside. Half asleep himself, he opened the vehicle door and saw his doorstep dimly illuminated by the nearby windows and the almost full moon. Saeed then saw movement on the street—a silhouette was walking quickly toward him. Startled, he tensed, suspicious of crime in the predawn darkness, but relaxed as light passed across the stranger's face. The man was young, with sad eyes and the wisp of a black beard. Saeed knew him well.

Saeed was not, however, expecting a blade. The nighttime visitor savagely struck the deliveryman, stabbing him twenty-eight times in a ferocious assault.[1] Saeed fell to the pavement while the attacker continued his murderous task. Satisfied with his handiwork, the assailant then fled down the street and disappeared into the night. Bleeding profusely from his torso and chest, clothes in tatters, Saeed staggered back and collapsed on his doorstep.[2] Fading in and out of consciousness, he was rushed to a nearby hospital, where he died.

The West Midlands Police, which had jurisdiction over the homicide, were baffled. This was a particularly savage crime, but the victim was neither wealthy nor had any particular enemies. The killer left his wallet. The murder took place on Clodeshall Road, a residential sidestreet just off the commercial Alum Rock Road.

In the hours and days that followed, police distributed posters throughout the neighborhood and the city, asking for help. They picked up a woman in her fifties and two teenage boys in the neighborhood of Ward End, to the east, hoping for a lead but released them shortly afterward. Detectives canvassed local mosques, searching for people who heard Saeed cry out, or who had seen the attacker vanish into the darkness. It stood to reason some of the more pious residents of the predominantly Muslim neighborhood would have been making their way to one of the nearby mosques for early morning prayers. But no one reported seeing or hearing anything.

Suspicions soon turned inward, to the murder victim's family. The nature of the murder—a "frenzied" knife attack with multiple stab wounds, in the words of the investigators—was terrifyingly intimate and particularly gruesome. The killer would have smelled his victim. He would have felt him falling to the pavement. There would have been blood, viscera. There would have been a grimy weapon—and a motive.

◆

Let's back up a bit. The journey that brought Saeed and his extended family to East Birmingham was set in motion forty years earlier, during the early 1960s. This was because Pakistan needed to tame a river.

In 1960 Pakistan signed a treaty with archrival India to divide control over the rivers that flowed from Tibet and the Himalayas in order to quench the subcontinent's thirst. The mighty Jhelum River flowed from the southeastern end of the Kashmir valley from the Pir Panjal mountain range, through Srinagar and Punjab, to finally merge with the Chenab River hundreds of miles south. It was one of those waterways that Pakistan now formally controlled.

Map 1. Pakistan. Created by Erin Greb Cartography.

Pakistan then began construction on a massive development on the Jhelum, which later became known as the Mangla Dam. This structure would eventually become the seventh largest water infrastructure project in the world, with the reservoir's contours visible in satellite imagery.

A marvel of engineering, the Mangla Dam generated power and provided a stable source of water for thirsty crops and tens of millions of people. But in the process of building it, Pakistan also caused massive environmental and social havoc. It chewed up pristine valleys and green mountains, destroyed ancient natural habitats, and submerged houses, villages, and eons of history. Some of the finest rice paddies in Pakistan disappeared under the water, as did fields of millet and wheat. The Mirpur district of Pakistani-controlled Azad Kashmir bore the brunt of the ecological and civilizational damage, as two hundred and fifty villages sank beneath the reservoir.[3]

The city of Mirpur, population some one hundred thousand, was partially submerged under the "Mangla Lake," obliging the residents to create a new city altogether. Today, holidaymakers can see the crumbling edifices of "old Mirpur" revealed when the waters of the reservoir occasionally recede. In order to relieve pressure for the tens of thousands of people displaced by the dam's construction, Pakistan allowed many of its citizens to emigrate. Numerous Mirpuris took up that opportunity, leaving the subcontinent for Great Britain.

These Kashmiris from Mirpur joined the postwar Pakistani immigrant community in Britain, adding their brains, backs, and hands to factories, foundries, and manufacturing plants. They drove cabs, cleaned streets, staffed hospitals, opened chip shops, and helped to construct vast swaths of postwar British society. According to the British government, by the 2000s, about 60 percent of the million-plus British citizens of Pakistani descent were from the Mirpur district.[4] The tightknit Birmingham neighborhoods of Alum Rock, Sparkhill, Sparkbrook, and environs welcomed the Kashmiri influx. About 15 percent of the million residents of Birmingham considered themselves Kashmiri. Many also brought their close-knit families, social hierarchy, intense cultural identity, religious conservatism, and vestiges of Kashmir's simmering conflict back home.

Among the Kashmiris who landed in industrial Birmingham were Mohammed Saeed, his sister, and his sister's husband, Abdul Rauf.

◆

Abdul Rauf left his speck of a village of Haveli Beghal in Pakistan-controlled Azad Kashmir, settled in Birmingham, and opened Oriental Bakeries on Belchers Lane in the Bordesley Green area of the city.[5]

This section of town was central to the local Kashmiri community, and Rauf's bakery serviced local groceries and markets with South Asian delicacies. He prayed at the Masjid Tayyabah, the two-story terraced house converted into a mosque on the corner of Coleshill and Rogers Roads, near the family's home.

Friends and others described Abdul Rauf as "polite," "unobtrusive," and "very devout."[6] He hailed from a line of religious judges in Mirpur, which gave him an elevated status within the community in both Kashmir and Birmingham. He and his wife Salma taught local girls the Quran in a small structure in their backyard.[7] He had five children of his own.

But there appeared to be a different side to the low-key, unobtrusive baker, namely, a deep connection to the struggle in his place of his birth. He formed and registered a charity called Crescent Relief to assist those "suffering from financial hardship, sickness, or distress," with a particular focus on refugees and displaced persons from Azad Kashmir and Pakistan. Despite its noble aims, Ishfaq Ahmed, who ran the Kashmir International Relief Fund, claimed the group was really set up to raise money for those fighting against Indian rule in Kashmir. "Crescent Relief was just a front for financially supporting the Kashmir insurgency," he later told a British court.[8]

Furthermore, Abdul Rauf reportedly had connections to a number of individuals who were neither unobtrusive nor tranquil. Given his position in the community, he rubbed shoulders with some of the foremost purveyors of Kashmiri jihadist activity as they passed through Britain. It's odd, given the post-9/11 perspective, that these firebrands could freely travel to Great Britain, call for violent jihad, raise funds, and meet tens of thousands of British citizens.

Hafiz Saeed (no known relation to murder victim Mohammed Saeed), the leader of the Pakistan-based terrorist group Lashkar-e-Taiba (LeT), reportedly spoke at the Rauf family's mosque and stayed at their house while he sojourned in Birmingham in the 1990s.[9] During a 1995 tour of Britain, Saeed stopped in Birmingham to give a speech in which he termed Indians "Hindu dogs" and told his audience, "Let's all rise up for jihad."[10] Saeed had founded LeT in 1987, along with Abdullah

Azzam, who would soon thereafter found al Qaeda with a Saudi multimillionaire named Osama bin Laden.

Abdul Rauf also reportedly had a connection with Masood Azhar, a charismatic man of five foot two with a golden tongue who serviced the jihad in Kashmir. In 1993, Azhar, then in his midtwenties, traveled around Great Britain and gave over three dozen speeches to crowds in the thousands. "The youth should prepare for jihad without any delay," he cried. "They should get jihadist training from wherever they can. We are also ready to offer our services."[11] Azhar, much like Hafiz Saeed, wanted to turn the Indian presence in Kashmir into a religious conflagration between Hindus and Muslims—and he did so on behalf of Pakistan's formidable intelligence service, the Inter-Services Intelligence Directorate (ISI). He had a magnetic way of speaking, drawing all manner of people to the pro-Pakistan, but not pro-independence Kashmiri cause. Older women reportedly would hand family jewelry and gold chains to Azhar at the end of his talks to use as he saw fit. Everywhere he went, people would introduce him as a veteran of the conflict in Afghanistan against the Soviet Union as he walked with a pronounced limp from unspecified wartime exploits. His reported time fighting the Red Army and his ability to turn words into religious fire earned him the title "Hazrat"—the "respected one."[12]

What most people didn't know was that he was actually wounded by friendly fire. One night outside of the Afghan town of Khost in 1988, Azhar stepped out of his dugout to urinate. Unfortunately for him, he had forgotten his unit's password, and in the darkness, the sentry opened fire, hitting him in the leg.[13] Luckily for the wounded Azhar, his father, Allah Baksh Sabir Alvi, was an important Deobandi scholar connected to the ISI in the Pakistani city of Bahawalpur, and he was medically evacuated from Afghanistan to recuperate.

Physical combat may not have personally suited Azhar, but he nevertheless excelled at fundraising and drawing new recruits to the battlefield. On Christmas Day 2000, a man drove a car full of explosives and detonated it in front of an Indian army barracks in Srinagar, killing nine; this attacker, Mohammed Bilal (a likely pseudonym), was supposedly from Birmingham, acting on behalf of Azhar's militant group.[14] Young, impressionable men in the city heard about this exploit. According to one radical preacher eventually expelled from Britain, two thousand British citizens eventually went abroad to join armed organizations in the pre-9/11 era.[15]

In Adrian Levy and Catherine Scott-Clark's *The Meadow*, they noted that when Azhar visited Birmingham on his 1993 fundraising tour, he reportedly stayed with the Rauf family.[16] It was during that time the Rauf patriarch asked Azhar to chat with his "rootless teenage son, Rashid Rauf, who he said was in need of a mentor."[17]

◆

Abdul Rauf's son, Rashid, was born in Pakistan on January 31, 1981 and was brought to Great Britain before he turned one.[18] The boy had sad brown eyes and grew up in the Rauf's strict religious home on St. Margaret's Road, Ward End. His best friend was another kid from the South Asian diaspora, Mohammed Yasar Gulzar.[19] Several months younger than Rashid—he was born on August 5, 1981—Gulzar was affectionately also known as "Yak" or "Yaks."[20] The boys lived within walking distance of each other. Gulzar lived with his parents and his siblings Asad, Nasar, and Nazia in a tidy split-level on Caldwell Road, Alum Rock, not too far from Bordesley Green, where the Rauf bakery was located. Gulzar's family was not part of the great Mirpuri exodus, as his family was from Chokar Kalan, a village in Gujrat, Punjab. While Rauf's family were quite engaged in politics both at home and abroad, Gulzar's family generally kept to themselves.[21]

Rauf attended Washwood Heath High School and Gulzar the nearby Saltley School, about a mile away from each other.[22] Washwood Heath gained some unwelcome notoriety during this time after a teacher berated his students after the school's choir sang a number of Christmas songs and carols. "Who is your God?" he reportedly claimed after leaping to his feet during a rehearsal. "Why are you saying Jesus and Jesus Christ? God is not your God—it is Allah."[23] It's possible that Rauf was in attendance when this incident occurred.

Despite attending different schools, Rauf and Gulzar were thick as thieves. Both boys liked playing cricket and football and spent much of their free time in local parks. Gulzar was a common face around the bakery, where the young Rashid helped his father by delivering baked goods. As their father grew older, Rauf and his younger brother Tayib took over the day-to-day business operations. Together, they distributed sweet delicacies in a battered white van around to the markets around town.[24]

Neighbors suggested Rauf was a hard-working, nose-to-the-grindstone kind of teenager. He was the responsible son who kept the family bakery going and dutifully attended religious services. However, like his father, he had another side to his personality. Some former classmates remembered him as a bully, with a violent edge. Others suggested Rauf might have been friends with or somehow otherwise connected with a local gang.[25]

After high school, both Rauf and Gulzar began studies at the University of Portsmouth, on England's south coast. Gulzar, despite being described as a lousy student, had enrolled in a computer science program and found accommodation in Portsmouth's Langstone Flats, off Furze Lane in the Student Village.[26] For his part, Rauf moved into 49 Queen Street in another part of Portsmouth. The university was known as a pleasant place to spend four years to study but also to kick around a ball, drink, and meet pretty girls in the city's fantastic pubs. However, it appears Gulzar and Rauf did not indulge in these earthly pursuits, because they fell in with Tablighi Jamaat, a large Islamic missionary movement based in South Asia that sought to bring its adherents back to a simpler, more austere version of Islam.

Tablighi Jamaat was an offshoot of the Deobandi movement, the preferred religious-ideological school of the Taliban in Afghanistan. Its missionary calling, combined with a socially conservative worldview, often pulled into its orbit those yearning for identity and purpose. The group encouraged an outwardly "Muslim" appearance; in this case, this meant growing beards with no moustache. Rauf and Gulzar quickly became far more interested Tablighi Jamaat than their studies, attending meetings in Portsmouth sometime in 2000.[27]

Gulzar traveled to Pakistan that year and returned to England a changed man. What he did and with whom he met in South Asia remains unknown, but what was clear was that he returned a far more devout Muslim than he had been beforehand. He grew out a long, dark beard and became far more somber in personality than what he had been in high school. His sudden seriousness made him stand out from other young men in East Birmingham; one high school acquaintance recalled that when he ran into some wayward teenagers from the neighborhood, he'd yell at them to "do something with our lives and encourage us to get a job if we didn't have one already."[28]

But a newfound religious outlook didn't keep Rauf and Gulzar from landing in trouble. In February 2002, Portsmouth cops busted them at a local internet café using fake credit card numbers ordering a satellite phone, a GPS map receiver, and a number of cartography-related CDs.[29] Just several months after 9/11, they were also looking at websites for an American aviation firm. They were "cautioned" for this fraud, which meant police made a note, but this crime wouldn't impact their permanent record unless they were caught again.

◆

While Rauf's and Gulzar's willingness to engage in petty crime and membership in Tablighi Jamaat could be viewed as youthful pursuits, the pair would soon emerge as key persons of interest in a much more serious crime: the April 24 murder of Rauf's uncle, Mohammed Saeed.[30]

Police began operating under a theory that Rauf and Gulzar had murdered Saeed together. It appeared there might have been an eyewitness from one of the local mosques, or perhaps a family member confessed. But why? The generally accepted narrative was the killing occurred over a marriage proposal gone sour, or a difference in money or politics. A countertheory was the slaying was an honor killing due to a supposed sexual transgression.[31]

Their involvement unproven and motivation unclear, the police interest nonetheless spooked Rauf and Gulzar. Police knocked on the Gulzar family home's front door several times between May and August 2002, but each time the family member who answered said they had no idea where "their boy" had gone.[32] Finally in September, several months after the murder, the police arrived at the family doorstep with a search warrant, demanding to see Gulzar. They were then informed that he had long since left for Pakistan.

◆

As they stepped off the plane in Islamabad, Pakistan, the young fugitives encountered a wet heat very different from the cool Midlands springtime. They faced few official problems after landing at the airport; Rauf was a dual UK/Pakistan passport holder, so he easily slid through immigration and customs. Gulzar used his British passport.

The pair then trekked south for four hundred kilometers to Raiwind, on the southern outskirts of Lahore. This was Tablighi Jamaat's headquarters in Pakistan. Although normally a town of forty thousand, the gated city of Islamic missionaries ballooned to half a million people during Tablighi Jamaat's annual gathering. It was easy for two young men running from a British murder charge to shed their identities and disappear into the pulsing throng of hundreds of thousands of worshippers, all dressed in white clothing and skullcaps.

In Raiwind, it is possible, though unproven, that the two young British citizens made connections to important people in the country. At that time, the Pakistani military allowed its personnel to take leave from official duties in order to perform missionary work with the group.[33] Tablighi Jamaat certainly had friends in high places: A number of senior military officers were members, as then-president Mohammad Zia-ul-Haq had allowed the group to preach and proselytize within the Pakistan Military Academy during the 1980s.[34] When al Qaeda struck New York City and Washington DC on 9/11, the ISI director-general at the time, Lt. Gen. Mahmud Ahmed, was actually a closeted Tablighi Jamaat adherent. After his retirement from the military, he publicly embraced the group.[35]

The duo parted ways in Raiwind. The powers-that-be eventually sent Gulzar to the northern district of Swat, in what is now called Khyber-Pakhtunkhwa. He also journeyed to the city of Abbottabad, where a few years later, Osama bin Laden would build a compound and take up residence. There, Gulzar claimed he preached for some fifty days—he could speak both Punjabi and Urdu—after which he visited his paternal grandmother in the village of Samlotha, near the Mangla Dam's massive reservoir. Until the summer of 2004, Gulzar spent time with family, splitting time between his grandmother's village, where he claimed he stayed until she died a year later, and his mother's extended family's town of Choha Khalsa, about an hour away.[36]

Unlike Gulzar, Rauf didn't head to his family's village, where his father was held in high regard. During this time, no one recalled him ever stopping to visit his grandmother, his aunt, or any other extended family members in the area.[37] Neither did he travel to Mirpur or Muzaffarabad, the two largest cities in Azad Kashmir.

Instead, he sought to take up arms against the Americans in Afghanistan. Soon after arriving, Rauf linked up with Amjad Farooqi, whose connections with al Qaeda were well-known on both sides of the border. With Farooqi's assistance, Rauf transited across rough mountain paths in and out of Afghanistan multiple times, meeting with militants and terrorist operatives working both sides of the border.[38] At some point, Rauf also likely trained at a militant camp in or near Kashmir.[39]

◆

The year 2002 was a confusing time for both established and aspiring jihadists. America's overwhelming firepower had routed al Qaeda and the Taliban in Afghanistan in a matter of weeks the winter before, and the battered, dispirited remnants of their forces fled across the rocky border to Pakistan. These jihadists were in disarray following this retreat over the mountains. In the moment of their greatest need, in stepped the "Kashmiri" militants in Pakistan, providing their fleeing comrades-in-arms with networks, safehouses, and isi-protected camps in Pakistan. These fighters were also given assistance by the Pakistani state itself, which had long nurtured the Taliban faction during the 1990s civil war in Afghanistan in order to consolidate its influence over its neighbor.[40]

Rauf was one of numerous eager jihadist wannabes from Britain and elsewhere who headed to Afghanistan during those muddled times. With little military experience, many likeminded individuals met their end quickly against a combination of American airpower, special operations forces, and CIA capabilities. The smart and lucky ones, like Rauf, instead bided their time and stayed off the target lists. Several years into the war, MI5 estimated that some four thousand British nationals had traveled to Afghanistan for military training.[41]

Eventually, Rauf headed in the completely opposite direction toward a mentor from his teenage years. His destination was the city of Bahawalpur, over seven hundred kilometers to the south, in southern Punjab.

◆

Bahawalpur, a hardscrabble city of four hundred thousand souls, lies south of the Sutlej River. It is only twenty miles from the Cholistan desert, a windswept land that sprawls into Sindh and then across an invisible line that demarcates Pakistan from India. This city briefly made international headlines in August 1988 when Pakistan's President Zia, the U.S. ambassador Arnold Raphel, and other senior Pakistani military officers took off in a military C-130 plane from the airport that mysteriously exploded midflight. There's a heavy security presence in the city; the Pakistani army's XXXI Corps is garrisoned in the southern part of town, where the officers are tasked with countering threats from India and working on their swing at the Bahawalpur Golf Course.[42]

There's only one other major industry in town: the ISI-founded Jaish-e-Mohammed (JeM),[43] an anti-Indian terrorist group founded and operated by Masood Azhar, the traveling firebrand who Rauf's father had hoped would provide his teenage son with direction. Azhar took the now twentysomething Rashid Rauf under his wing.

◆

In the years since Azhar and Rauf last met, Azhar and his various organizations had greatly expanded their horizons. This included helming another ISI-backed group, Harakat ul-Mujahidin (HUM), a component of the larger jihadist umbrella group, Harakat ul-Ansar (HUA). By the time Rauf arrived, HUM was one of Pakistan's premier jihadist groups. After al Qaeda bombed U.S. embassies in Kenya and Tanzania in 1998, the Americans struck a terrorist training camp in Afghanistan in an unsuccessful effort to kill Osama bin Laden. While they didn't kill the al Qaeda chief, American cruise missiles nevertheless managed to kill twenty Kashmiri militants—and several Pakistani handlers.[44]

Shortly after his successful fundraising circuit in Britain in the mid 1990s, Azhar snuck into India-controlled Srinagar under a false identity. Indian forces soon arrested him and chucked him into the high-security Kot Balwal prison in Jammu, a facility designated to incarcerate Pakistan-sponsored separatists.[45] There, Azhar reportedly later claimed under interrogation that he had worked in the early 1990s with Somali groups fighting U.S. forces on the streets of Mogadishu.[46] HUA reacted to Azhar's arrest strongly, first taking hostage and then murdering several Western backpackers in Kashmir in mid-1995 to compel India to free him. That effort failed.

Then, on Christmas Eve 1999, HUM operatives hijacked Indian Airlines flight 814 leaving Kathmandu bound for New Delhi. One of the hijackers was reportedly Azhar's brother, Ibrahim.[47] Indian intelligence also believed another brother, Abdul Rauf Asghar, masterminded the operation.[48] After a series of stops on runways across India, Pakistan, and the United Arab Emirates, the plane reached its final destination in Taliban-controlled Kandahar, Afghanistan. There, the hijackers demanded several men from Indian custody, most notably Masood Azhar. India capitulated to the hostage takers' demands, and its foreign minister Jaswant Singh flew to Kandahar to negotiate the handoff. Singh later asserted in his memoirs that the hostage takers deliberately landed in Afghanistan so the ISI could stage-manage the hijacking's end.[49] The foreign minister further noted Pakistan's intelligence agency funded and exerted some degree of control over both the hijackers and their Taliban hosts.

On the last day of the millennium, Azhar limped onto the cool, cracked tarmac of the Kandahar Airport a free man, received by Mullah Akhtar Mohammed Mansur, who would eventually become the leader of the Taliban.[50] Osama bin Laden, another honored guest of the Taliban, separately hosted a victory dinner for the now-freed terrorist chief.[51] Despite Islamabad's solemn statements stating Azhar would never return to Pakistan, he nonetheless returned home to Bahawalpur within a week to a hero's welcome. He then gave a rousing speech to ten thousand people, proclaiming, "I have come here, because this is my duty to tell you that Muslims should not rest in peace until we have destroyed America and India!"[52]

It remains quite curious how significantly al Qaeda, other jihadist groups in the region, and the Pakistani state consistently protected Azhar and continued to guarantee his safety. An unrepentant killer, Azhar soon founded JeM, again with significant ISI assistance. As Pakistani journalist Ahmed Rashid recalled in *Descent into Chaos*, "With ISI officers by his side," Azhar toured the country giving rousing speeches. At one rally in Karachi, Azhar cried, "Marry for jihad, give birth for jihad and earn money for jihad till the cruelty of America and India ends."[53] Following the 9/11 attacks, Pakistan reluctantly declared JeM a terrorist organization after the United States placed significant pressure on Islamabad to do so. Despite its official illegality, Azhar continued to freely travel around the country denouncing India and the United States; for instance, Ahmed Rashid recounted that he once met Azhar at an army-run mosque in 2003 within the Lahore Cantonment.

Like other groups operating under ISI sponsorship, JeM began to grow and expand its violence. Less than a month after 9/11, on October 1, 2001, the group detonated a truck bomb in front of the main entrance of the Jammu and Kashmir State Legislative Assembly complex. The subsequent firefight between security forces and JeM operatives lasted several hours and killed thirty-eight people.

Ten weeks later, on December 13, JeM and LeT struck the Indian parliament building in New Delhi, killing twelve. It remains doubtful these groups would have launched such a spectacular, complex attack against India's legislative body without ISI's knowledge, acquiescence, or approval. An enraged India deployed troops to its border with Pakistan, with the appropriate military buildup on the Pakistani side. Maybe it was coincidence, but at that very moment, U.S. Special Operations Forces and the U.S. Air Force were battering al Qaeda to a pulp in the Tora Bora cave complex just over Pakistan's border with Afghanistan. With the Pakistani military distracted by the aftermath of the Indian parliament attack, bin Laden, al Qaeda, and the rest were able to melt away into Pakistan.

◆

Rauf traveled along National Highway 5 on the scrubland outskirts of Bahawalpur to the gates of JeM's formidable Madressatul Sabir and Jama-e-Masjid Subhanallah mosque and seminary campus.[54] He had arrived at the next chapter of his destiny.

Once inside and ensconced in his Bahawalpur sanctuary, Rauf did quite well for himself. Within about a year, he had changed his name to "Khalid" and married Umatul Warud Saira in May 2003.[55] She was several years his senior, an old maid by conservative Pakistani standards. It was likely there was back-and-forth between their families in Pakistan and Great Britain during this time agreeing to the terms of the marriage. It remains unclear who played the matchmaker.

Rauf's new bride was the daughter of Ghulam Mustafa, the founder of the JeM-operated Darul Uloom Madina madrassa in town. Locals called the compound a school for jihadi fighters; the facility provided room and board for five hundred students. This facility was notable for its horse stables, since riding is mentioned in the Quran as a particularly noble means to wage jihad.[56] Through this marriage, Rauf became brother-in-law to Masood Azhar, as the JeM chief had married another of Mustafa's daughters.

Rauf and his wife eventually had two children, but his real passion was cultivating the dense web of jihadists who operated in both Pakistan and Afghanistan. Through these ties, he eventually met Abu Faraj al-Libi, a Libyan al Qaeda operative with a terrible skin condition on his face who would later become a senior member of the group. More importantly, Rauf connected with Abu Ubaydah al-Masri, a longtime Egyptian jihadist explosives expert. He had a long, checkered career all over Europe, spending time in London in the 1970s, fighting in Bosnia in the 1990s, and later claiming asylum in Germany.

In turn, Abu Ubaydah saw something special in Rauf, a kindred spirit who felt comfortable in the West and knew how to evade authorities. He could speak about the necessity to fight the unbelievers and then thirty seconds later talk about who was up and who was down in the Premier League. Abu Ubaydah would become Rauf's teacher in the dark, unforgiving art of bombmaking. Without his guidance, Rauf would never have been the man he was about to become.

3

Triple A

Walthamstow is the largest urban area in the London Borough of Waltham Forest, in East London. Despite the name, London's eastward expansion during the Industrial Revolution and the arrival of the steam locomotive in the 1870s consumed much of the forest and marshland that gave the area its name.[1] What woodland remained exists in Epping Forest to the west, along the banks of the Rivers Roding and Lea as they flow into the Thames to the south. The area is a tightly compacted series of glazed tan brick and cracked-plaster terraced houses stretching for miles in every direction; these in turn are bisected by dozens of residential streets and commercial districts. It crackles with the lively, striving immigrant bustle of an East London exurb; uniformed children of a hundred creeds and colors can be seen skipping along the sidewalk after school. Pubs dot the streets, as do pizza joints, hardware stores, clothing shops, minimarkets, and mosques; they are often full after work, catering to the needs of the area's quarter million inhabitants.

There are several major landmarks around Walthamstow, which in the early 2000s included a famous but now shuttered greyhound racetrack. The first is a grouping of municipal buildings called the Waltham Forest Town Hall complex. The complex includes the Waltham Forest Council building, a 1940s-era Portland stone structure with a green oxidized clock tower and a large, once-majestic fountain spritzing streams of water from an underpowered pump hidden underneath its concrete base. To the building's east is the Walthamstow Assembly Hall, whose concrete cornice in those days announced *Fellowship Is Life and Lack of Fellowship Is Death*. In front is the neoclassical granite Walthamstow War Memorial to "Our Glorious Dead," with a sharply shaped stone woman, head bowed, resting on the structure. Bowing to the inevitable need for vehicle space, the buildings are abutted by two car parks.

Just west of the Council offices is the refurbished childhood home of textile designer William Morris, a leader of the Victorian-era British Arts and Crafts movement. From his heyday and into modern times, the walls of many respectable English homes and hotels bore his bright floral patterns; his home has since been reconsecrated as a local arts center and textile museum. Behind the stately mansion lies a lovely patch of greenspace—the tidy, pleasant Lloyd Park, named after the penny dreadfuls publisher Edward Lloyd. The park provides local families a green respite at the outer edge of the metropolis. All in all, it's a generally pleasant place to live.

One Walthamstow resident, Abdulla Ahmed Ali,[2] did not see the beauty and history and bustle around him. Instead, he headed down a different, darker path.

◆

Abdulla Ahmed Ali was born in the borough of Newham, London, near the north bank of the River Thames on October 10, 1980, to a middle-class Pakistani family.[3] In his childhood school photos, Ali is a sweet-looking boy in a uniform and a striped necktie. His parents, like many British Pakistanis of the era, emigrated to Great Britain in the 1960s. Ali was one of eight children—six brothers and two sisters, in a household that was moving up in the world. All but two of his siblings graduated with a university degree.[4] The family was also somewhat socially conservative and religiously observant, although not ostentatiously so. Beyond their mosque, the family writ large wasn't involved in public activities of much consequence.

Ali struggled with a slight speech impediment—from childhood, he wrestled with certain sounds, like *r* and *s* and *f*. He continually worked

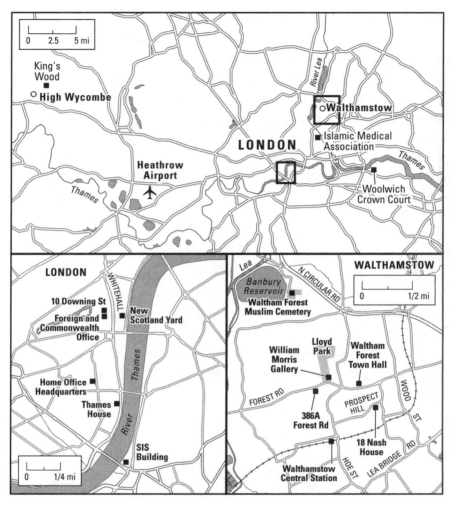

Map 2. London. Created by Erin Greb Cartography.

on fixing his lisp, but when he became nervous, his tic would again come tumbling from his mouth.[5]

Soon after his birth, his family moved back to their hometown of Jhelum, Pakistan, a transport hub along the Grand Trunk Road along the eastern bank of the Jhelum river. When little Ali went for a stroll along the waters, he might have walked past St. John's, a large brick church erected a few years following the 1857 Indian Rebellion. Inside, carved into its marble lectern, were the names of the thirty-five British soldiers killed in this area during the insurrection. Even though the building had fallen into disuse in recent decades, it still retained a cross atop its spire in this overwhelmingly Muslim city, a symbol of Britain's former dominion in this part of the world. The Mangla Dam was also less than an hour away by car, another hulking reminder of why so many locals left in the first place.

The family lived in Jhelum for several years before returning to Great Britain and settling in Walthamstow in East London. Ali attended Chapel End Primary School in Walthamstow and Aveling Park Secondary School from 1992 to 1997. As he entered his teenage years, however, his view of the world began to grow dim. He felt Muslims the world over were being abused; images of skeletal Bosnians behind barbed wire during the 1990s were seared into his mind. The brutality of conflict during the first Gulf War against Iraq filled his brain as well. By the late 1990s, he reportedly fell in with some older kids and started watching videos about Afghanistan under Taliban rule. One of his secondary school teachers reminisced, "He thought the Taliban had created a model society in Afghanistan . . . He was always trying to persuade other people that Islam was the path to follow."[6]

At the age of fifteen, he became involved with the missionary group Tablighi Jamaat—the same group Rashid Rauf and Mohammed Gulzar connected with some years later in Portsmouth. Ali would later call the group and its activities a "boy scout, but more of in a religious environment kind of thing."[7]

Ali grew to be a charismatic ruffian, a keen debater with a sharp tongue. He graduated from high school and then attended City University in London, earning a computer systems engineering degree. He also became increasingly politically active; his eldest brother Dawood, over a decade his senior, was already involved with various groups such as the Anti-War Coalition and various Islamic charities. Ali followed in his footsteps, attending demonstrations and handing out leaflets for conferences.

Ali's petitioning was often directed toward Home Secretary David Blunkett, who had championed several controversial national security measures following 9/11. These included allowing the British government to detain without trial foreign nationals suspected of terrorism offenses.[8] To further his goals, Ali would also try to collect signatures. Oftentimes, he'd cruise the Queens Street mosque on the suggestion of his older brother. "When you go to the mosque, you'll see your friends," Dawood would say. "Try to get as many signatures as you can."[9] Another time, a young woman from the Anti-War Coalition approached Ali and asked if he wouldn't mind leafleting his mosque's prayer hall—the journalist Robert Fisk was coming to speak. He obliged, leaving pamphlets at the Masjid e Umer.[10] He also reportedly was involved with al-Muhajiroun, a British militant Salafist group, during his undergraduate days.[11]

Ali completed his university degree in September 2002. One day, while he was attending his home mosque on Queen's Road in Walthamstow, an older man named Mohammed Patel handed him a leaflet describing his charity organization, the Islamic Medical Association (IMA). The group collected money, clothing, blankets, milk, canned foods, and other goods for those caught in the crossfire following the American invasion of Afghanistan. As it turned out, Dawood already knew Patel from working together in Bosnia and Kosovo in the mid- to late 1990s.[12] Hearing of Ali's interest in the organization, Dawood gladly introduced his brother to Patel, who convinced Ali and his father to fill up the family car with old clothes to donate them at his shop at 19 Chatsworth Road in Clapton.

After accepting their castoffs on behalf of faraway Afghans, Patel, seeing a potential source of free labor, casually mentioned that his organization desperately needed help managing its donations. Its storefront, a dilapidated two-story facility in East London, operated on a shoestring. Patel made a pitch to get Dawood to volunteer, but he already had a full-time job as an IT technician. On the other hand, Ali wasn't fully employed at the time. "Here's a young man with some spare time on his hands," said Dawood. "He can help you."[13]

Soon, Ali was sorting clothing at the IMA's shop several evenings a week. Besides Ali, there were usually ten to fifteen volunteers sorting through dozens of donation bags. Their main task was to place these clothes into forty-foot containers to ship to Pakistan, en route to Afghanistan. Very often they would receive "donations" in terrible shape—some people viewed the IMA as a dumping ground for unwanted, stained, and ripped clothing—so the volunteers would simply chuck the detritus into the rubbish bin.

Groups of people were always coming and going, rotating in for one shift or a hundred. Being a charismatic guy from the neighborhood, Ali drew in some of his circle of friends to help him sort clothes and do odd jobs for the charity. These included Tanvir Hussain, a fun-loving, not-particularly-religious cricketer from Blackburn with a large, off-center nose. Hussain had three siblings and never really held a steady job, but once worked part-time at a National Health clinic treating sexually transmitted diseases.[14]

Ali roped in Arafat Waheed Khan, another Walthamstow local and his friend from primary school. Born in Gujranwala, Pakistan, Khan came to Britain as an infant. Tanvir Hussain, whom Arafat Khan met at Waltham Forest College in the late 1990s, recalled he was a "very easy-going guy" and was "always joking around, having fun."[15] He liked clubbing, smoking weed, and chasing pretty women, and hung out at Shout Bar in Ilford.[16] His father came to Britain with his brother in the vast 1960s-era emigration and was very Western-oriented, so much so that his family gave each other presents and enjoyed a turkey dinner every Christmas.[17] Khan was actually the one who first introduced Ali to Tanvir Hussain, and the two hit it off immediately.

There was Ibrahim Savant, whom Ali knew from school. Ibrahim, the son of an Indian architect and an English mother, was a trumpet player and Walthamstow native. He converted to Islam in the late 1990s and then grew out his beard.[18] He was also friends with Khan, who also introduced him to Tanvir Hussain.[19]

While sorting out the clothing castoffs of dozens of families across East London, Ali met Umar Islam, a former Rastafarian born "Brian Young" who converted to Islam and changed his name around the year 2000. Another young man, a decade younger than the rest, was Adam Khatib, the teenage son of immigrants from Mauritius. He was Ali's youngest brother's best friend.

Finally, Ali became friends with Assad Ali Sarwar. He was a distant connection of Mohammed Gulzar, but unlike most of the others who volunteered at the IMA, he didn't live in East London.[20] Rather, he lived in High Wycombe, between London and Oxford, with his parents. He too was of Kashmiri heritage, although he was born in Great Britain. The people who knew him didn't think much of his academic abilities; in the last few years, he had withdrawn or flunked out of at least two different universities. He found his studies—first in sports science, then in earth science—beyond his mental capacities.[21] But his inability to finish a degree didn't mean he didn't pay attention.

◆

Ali spent a fair amount of time at the IMA, rising in the management chain to become a trusted member of the organization. He spent enough time at the office to eventually meet the proprietor of the nearby al Koran bookstore, a crack-addict-turned-Islamic-street-preacher named Mohammed Hamid, who would swing by the charity on a regular basis. While it's not clear how Hamid—who styled himself "Osama bin London"—interacted with the IMA volunteers, he was certainly involved with the organization. In late 2001 he took seven containers of medical supplies from the Karachi seaport up through Pakistan and into Taliban-controlled Kandahar. When he went on trial on terrorism-related charges several years later, he casually mentioned he took the shipment on behalf of the IMA.[22]

Ali's role continued to expand to encompass designing websites, writing leaflets, and collecting donations at area mosques. However, he felt compelled to do more for the cause. By January 2003, the IMA wanted volunteers to travel to Pakistan to deliver and administer its aid along the border. Ali volunteered for this mission, despite having no experience or particular source of income to fall back upon in Great Britain.

Misgivings about his finances aside, he flew from London to Karachi, the financial and industrial capital of Pakistan. He hadn't been back since he was a boy. Karachi in January was dry and warm—the monsoon rains had disappeared a few months beforehand, and the humid season had not yet begun. The breeze coming off the Arabian Sea cooled Ali's body, and the sun was a welcome change from grim, overcast London.

He stayed in Karachi for a few weeks, linked up with his friend Umar Islam, the former Rastafarian, and spent a few days with him idling around town. Islam was still using the name "Brian Young" on his passport, his old identity not yet fully subsumed into his new one. He too was in Pakistan on the IMA's behalf.

Ali also met with Mohammed Altaf, a project manager for another charity called Doctors Worldwide, a generally well-regarded organization that performed medical work in underserviced areas. The IMA and Doctors Worldwide had cooperated in the past, and the two men flew to the city of Quetta, an hour's flight north. Quetta is a rough-and-tumble, mud-and-cement, socially conservative city situated at the foot of soaring mountains covered in Pashtun juniper trees. Over a million people lived there, a pastiche of tribes and ethnicities; Baluchis, Pashtuns, Brahuis, Hazaras, Sindhis, Muhajirs, and Punjabis coexist uneasily in a frontier-like atmosphere that explodes every so often into murderous violence. The heavy scent of *sajji*, a local delicacy of coal slow-roasted leg of lamb, chili-infused goat-feet, and *kadi kabab* (a goat stuffed with rice, almonds, and raisins) would waft through the streets. These delicacies were favored dishes of the hard-edged Afghan men who prowled the streets, black mascara applied around their flinty eyes. They were the city's most recent arrivals. Following the U.S. invasion of Afghanistan, the Taliban's surviving senior leadership had comfortably regrouped in Quetta and was launching the insurgency back into Afghanistan from Pakistani soil—with the ISI's knowledge and blessing.

Ali arrived in Quetta and ran into another familiar face, Assad Sarwar, who was also working for the IMA.[23] But soon Sarwar left town on a personal trip to visit his family's village in Jammu, India. Ali then made his way to Chaman, the large border town abutting Afghanistan. This was Achakzai territory, part of the larger Pashtun Zirak Durrani tribe, whose lands extended from Quetta to Kandahar; some members own compounds that straddle the international border in order to thwart local custom regulations.

It was a dangerous road, but Ali arrived at his destination unmolested. After arriving, he observed convoys of trucks hauling supplies and fuel through the heavily defended Friendship Gate, bound for NATO troops beyond the border. He also saw thousands of Afghan refugees fleeing by foot in the other direction; men, women, and unsmiling children with their meagre belongings trying to escape the violence, the wrenching human consequence of war and a concurrent three-year drought.

When Ali arrived at one of the thirteen refugee camps near Chaman to deliver the IMA's donations, he was shocked by what he witnessed. "There's loads of people everywhere," he later recalled. "It's so mucky, smelly, loads of kids running round crying, really like appalling conditions. Lots of arguing, kind of chaotic . . . I don't think anything can prepare you for something like that."[24] The smell around the camp was dreadful; with no formal toilets or sewers, thousands of people were forced to defecate outside of their flimsy tents.

The young man with a university degree and middle-class British upbringing struggled with the abject plight of these refugees. When he went to the camp, which was run by the Médecins Sans Frontières, it was wintertime. He shivered while wearing a thick jacket and two sweaters, knowing the Afghans he met were mercilessly exposed to the elements, clothed in rags. He was in good health, but many of these refugees were maimed, legless, armless, scarred, and burnt as a result of the fighting that took place in Afghanistan over the last generation.

The camps by Chaman were home to almost seventy-five thousand people, overwhelmingly ethnic Pashtuns from northern Afghanistan. They were fleeing vengeful Uzbeks and Tajiks, who accused them of supporting the Taliban.[25] Many had been traveling along dirt paths and steep mountain ravines for up to two months before arriving at the squalid, overcrowded, unsanitary camps within Pakistan proper.[26]

The mortality rate in these facilities was sky-high—and the children died first. There were funerals almost every week for the little ones who perished from malnutrition, dysentery, or other otherwise easily treatable maladies. In their grief, mothers ripped their hair out and would scream in Pashto at the other volunteers. Ali didn't understand what they were saying, but the Pakistanis who did would translate: the women blamed the volunteers for their suffering, as if it were they who had torn out their hearts.

"Emotionally," Ali would later recount, "it was very straining."[27] When he was alone, Ali would weep. Despite this psychic toll, he stayed for another couple of months, into the springtime.

On his return trip to Quetta, Ali was attacked by another ancient scourge of this rough area of the world: bandits. He had been traveling with another charity group, Mercy Malaysia, when a group of armed men ambushed his convoy. NGO workers were easy pickings along the remote, thinly policed roads in Baluchistan. These do-gooders were also usually unarmed and wouldn't fight back. They were lucky; the bandits didn't kill anyone but only relieved them of their money and other items. The shaken group of volunteers filled out the requisite forms at the first police station they encountered, but the local cops were powerless to confront the mountain outlaws. Ali then contacted the British High Commission for a replacement passport. He received it on February 26, 2003, and then left the area some time thereafter. He had had enough; he left the border and then made his way to Jhelum to visit family.

◆

Ali returned to Britain that April. At the tender age of twenty-two, still living at home and without a real job, Ali nevertheless decided he wanted to find a wife. He asked his mother for help. "My son's looking to get married," she told her contacts in the community. "Do you know any suitable girls?"[28]

Eventually, Ali's mother found someone she deemed suitable. "Are you interested?" she asked him, passing on a photo and the biography of a young woman named Cossor Anwar. She lived with her family on Albert Road, a tidy house in a tidy part of Walthamstow lined with cherry blossoms that showered pink petals onto the pavement every springtime. "Yes, I'm interested," Ali responded. Like Ali, Cossor was born in Great Britain, but by coincidence her family also hailed from Jhelum.

They were married within a few months, and she moved into his family's house on Banbury Road, in a quiet subdivision by the Banbury Reservoir and the River Lea. It was a tight fit with Ali, his new wife,

Ali's brothers, sisters, and parents crammed into one house. Everyone was living on top of each other, and something had to give.

Ali and Cossor's marriage immediately began to run into problems. She later described moving in with her new in-laws as "culture shock," as her new husband's family was far more socially conservative than her own. Within a short time of the wedding, they were fighting. Ali had an idea of what a good Muslim wife should be and tried to bend his new bride to his will. For example, Ali wanted Cossor to wear a veil when walking outside. When she refused, he bit her on the cheek, calling it a "love bite" so she'd remember to cover herself when she left the house. Ali also beat her; one time he reportedly left the marks of his fingers across her face, causing her to flee to her parents' home on Albert Road.[29] Together, Cossor and her parents went to the nearby police office and filed a report, but at the last minute, she declined to press domestic abuse charges and returned to her husband.[30]

Eventually, the couple found a spot at 18 Nash House, a ground-floor one-bedroom in a four-story L-shaped council home, sandwiched between Prospect Hill and Church Hill Road. Finally, the two of them could spread out a bit. Ali eked out a living doing odd jobs for his property developer brother, overseeing the workmen who put up drywall, fixed the plumbing, and repainting damaged walls in his units around town. He also began working at the tiny Covent Garden branch of The Link, a mobile phone store.

◆

Around this time, Ali picked up several audio tapes featuring Anwar al-Awlaqi, a New Mexico-born preacher who had increasingly turned to militancy. Awlaqi traveled to London and preached at the Masjid and Madrasah al-Tawhid in Stratford in 2002 and 2003, a few miles from Ali's charity work in Clapton. While it's not certain, it's possible Ali, looking for direction in his life, stopped in on one of Awlaqi's talks.

Ali liked the American's way of constructing a worldview that gave meaning to his feelings of insecurity, bafflement, and irritation about the world around him. Awlaqi was adept at speaking to the disaffected Muslim in the West in a way that began to lead many, step-by-step, to accept violence in the name of the faith. As Ali explained, Awlaqi expanded his mind. "The way he explains and talks is really good," Ali later recalled, "and obviously it's like when you like an author in a book, you want more books from that same author."[31]

Awlaqi was in many respects the Pied Piper for the new generation of extremist thought. He successfully packaged jihadist ideas to generate maximum impact. He was a runaway hit among certain circles; his sermons, mostly in English, were viewed hundreds of thousands of times on YouTube, the French site Dailymotion, and other social media platforms. Even now, it's not hard to find his words online.

◆

Cossor became pregnant. Ominously, one of the early scans indicated the fetus had trouble opening his hand from a clenched fist. The fetus also had clubbed feet, an indication of something more serious. As the pregnancy progressed, the doctor informed the couple about a life-threatening condition that caused abnormalities in the heart and other organs, called Edwards syndrome.[32] One of Ali's older brothers had Down syndrome, so there were concerns about genetic challenges complicating the baby's future.

Despite this serious health challenge, Ali, his cricketeer friend Tanvir Hussain, and a few other close relatives nevertheless left to make a pilgrimage in Saudi Arabia for a month. Cossor was in her second trimester during this time. Alone, pregnant, the health of her fetus in doubt, she moved back into her in-laws' house by the reservoir, from which she had only escaped a few months before.

Ali's family responsibilities were expanding greatly, but after he returned from Mecca, he penned these mysterious words in a March 2004 will: "We know with full certainty that we are going to die so let us aim high and strive for the best death, i.e., *shahada* [martyrdom], and let us do the most pleasing deed to Allah and make the greatest sacrifice, fight with our life, tongue and wealth in the path of Allah."[33]

Ali nonetheless had to attend to his family. Soon after his time in Saudi Arabia, he and Cossor went to see a specialist at King's Hospital. It was apparent the fetus was in serious jeopardy. A scan telegraphed further danger—there was too much amniotic fluid in the womb. A doctor at the hospital finally pulled Ali aside and said, "We have to ask you this question, and don't take it the wrong way, but do you want to consider terminating the baby?" Shocked, Ali replied, "No, that's not something that I would do. Whatever happens, we'll get through it and stick by the baby."

The baby was born several weeks premature on the last day of March; he went straight from the birthing room to the intensive care unit. The identification bracelet only classified the newborn as "Boy of Anwar Cosser," misspelling Cossor's name. The machines kept his little lungs moving, but the lack of brain development complicated his growth. In retrospect, the baby's little hands weren't opening or closing because the area of the brain that controls movement hadn't developed. The part of his brain that controlled his breathing hadn't grown correctly either.[34]

Over the next few weeks, the baby's condition worsened. Cossor became increasingly despondent, watching her child hover between life and death. A consultant at the ICU in the hospital again pulled Ali aside to a room, saying, "I know it's difficult, but we have to put this to you: it doesn't look like his breathing's getting any better." The baby's lungs were failing. "Do you want to turn the machines off?" As a parent, it was his decision. He asked a religious scholar about his predicament, who replied, "You're not allowed to do that. Even with a one percent chance you're not allowed to take that life. You've got to keep trying." And so the pumps remained on.

Cossor was sent home to recover; she was still fragile from the pregnancy and an emotional wreck from all that had transpired. One night, the phone rang. The hospital was calling with the message no parent wanted to hear: "Something has happened." By the time Cossor and Ali arrived, medical staff were trying to resuscitate the baby. His little lungs had completely given out and he died shortly thereafter.

Physically and emotionally spent, Cossor stayed inside the flat for days at a time, crying in bed. She was trapped inside with an abusive husband, memories of a dead child, and dimming hope for things to get better. Eventually fed up with the situation, Ali suggested going to

Pakistan to visit her ailing grandmother. She reluctantly said yes, and off they went, in the summer of 2004.

At this point, Rashid Rauf and Abdulla Ahmed Ali's paths had not crossed. Gulzar had disappeared entirely. The others were floating around the outskirts of London. But fate would bring these men together soon enough.

4

Recruits

South Africa Airways flight no. 277 from Mumbai touched down with a screech of the tires in Johannesburg on May 24, 2004. Into the hot and thin-aired arrivals terminal of Johannesburg International Airport emerged Mohammed Patel, the man theoretically in charge of the London-based IMA, which had sent Ali to Pakistan the year before.[1] Tagging along was his new fiancée, Sakina Bhamjee, holding an Indian passport. Both Patel and Bhamjee had visitor visas, but they had unofficially come to South Africa to start a telecom business.

Patel was a serial entrepreneur, although an unsuccessful one. Among other endeavors, he had founded a telecommunications business in Great Britain that never came to fruition. His South African startup would prove unsuccessful as well. Living a threadbare existence, Patel eked out a living as a freelance mechanic in the working-class Brixton neighborhood of Johannesburg, living in the shadow of the 778-foot Brixton Tower that dominated the skyline.

◆

On June 19, 2004, Mohammed Gulzar arrived in Johannesburg from Pakistan on South African Airways flight no. 65. Despite the West Midlands Police open warrant regarding Saeed Mohammed's unsolved murder, he transited using his real name and authentic British passport.[2] There were no red flags raised in either Pakistan or

South Africa; on this occasion, the long arm of the British lawman was not long enough.

Gulzar told immigration agents that said he was in South Africa for a holiday; like Patel, he overstayed his allowed time. Johannesburg's various bureaucratic institutions didn't make the connection that this man was abusing local hospitality; authorities issued him a provisional driver's license and an identity card soon afterward. Strangely, Gulzar's license was for a residential house in Mayfair, but his identity card was for a light industrial area in Ophirton off Booysens Road, a ten-minute drive to the southeast.

◆

Patel and Gulzar overlapped in Johannesburg only for a short period. Three days after Gulzar touched down on South African soil, Patel was back in London. On Friday, August 6, he was a curious onlooker to a fiery speech by Abu Hamza al-Masri outside the Finsbury Park Mosque.

Abu Hamza, a goonish figure known for having a hook for a hand, had been the mosque's imam during the time when "shoe bomber" Richard Reid, "9/11 twentieth hijacker" Zacarias Moussaoui, and a whole host of other scoundrels passed through its doors. Eventually the Charity Commission, which regulated charities in England and Wales, demanded his removal from the post and that the mosque be shut. Undeterred, Abu Hamza gave speeches just outside the mosque's brick and metal gates, calling for jihad and whatever violent hate-filled ramblings he had put together in the previous week.

The "sermon" Patel attended was one of Abu Hamza's last performances; by the end of the month, Abu Hamza found himself inside of a police lockup, arrested on multiple terrorism offenses. Britain eventually extradited him to the United States where American authorities provided him with a lifetime in prison without parole.

There was another man in the crowd for Abu Hamza's August 6 sermon, a young Eritrean immigrant named Muktar Said Ibrahim. He had recently received his British citizenship but had already drunk from the poisoned chalice of violent jihad. He spent the previous May Day bank holiday in rural Cumbria on a "camping" trip designed to prepare men to attack Americans in Afghanistan. Organized by the IMA's neighbor, the self-styled "Osama bin London," Mohammed Hamid, the camp equipped attendees with paintball guns with which to "train" against U.S. troops.[3] They were obviously in over their heads.

Despite his lack of actual military training, Ibrahim was fired up and ready to fight. On December 11, 2004, he drove with his two friends, Shakeel Ismail and Rizwan Majid, to the airport for a one-way trip to Pakistan. The two other twentysomethings had both worked at Mohammed Hamid's bookstore over the last few years; one had even been Hamid's assistant.[4] They had an inkling the British Security Service, more commonly known as MI5, was watching them. This paranoia happened to be well-founded, since MI5 was indeed surreptitiously surveilling their driver, an Iraq-born cabbie suspected of facilitating the travels of British nationals to the deserts of Iraq and the mountains of Afghanistan.[5]

Authorities stopped the trio at Heathrow Airport. The men possessed a significant amount of cash that they planned on providing to the Taliban; they explained the money away by telling their skeptical interrogators they were flying to Pakistan to attend a wedding. As further cover, they produced a bogus wedding ring purchased especially for the trip. Ibrahim also provided authorities a mobile number that corresponded to a "pay-go" number; that number had been registered to the Syria-born London jihadist Mohammed al Ghabra a few days beforehand. Al Ghabra had attended HUM training and had been fundraising on that terror group's behalf in Great Britain. He had also met with al Qaeda's Abu Faraj al-Libi and had stayed with him in 2002.[6] MI5 believed al Ghabra had arranged the trio's travel to Pakistan through a trusted intermediary.[7]

The young men were in temporary custody for so long that they missed their flight to Pakistan.[8] While British authorities surmised they were being fed a pack of lies, they had little with which to hold the trio. They had clean records. They hadn't committed any crime. So, they were allowed to catch a flight the next day to Islamabad, and to the war beyond.

Soon after the trio's arrival in Islamabad, officers from the ISI dropped by Majid's family's house where they had been sleeping off jet lag to inquire why they were in the country. British authorities must have tipped off their counterparts. The three again repeated their cover story of attending a wedding and, again, showed the local authorities the wedding ring. After a bit more conversation, the authorities left, having decided they had bigger fish to fry than these young Londoners.

◆

Rashid Rauf had been busy. After marrying and connecting to a pre-eminent jihadist family, he and the ISI-backed JeM were branching out. Through blood, kinship, and ideological brotherhood, they were merging their talent with their al Qaeda comrades in arms. Rauf traveled up and down the length of Pakistan, from the windswept plains of Punjab to the mountains of the Federally Administered Tribal Areas (FATA), the semiautonomous mountain region that hugged Afghanistan in the northwestern corner of the country. During this time, Rashid Rauf assumed the role of a shepherd for British jihadis eager to join the fight. Each UK citizen flowing through Pakistan wanting to fight Americans presented an opportunity for the enterprising Rauf, but also a danger; any one of these men could be a Secret Intelligence Service (MI6) informant. He knew he had to be both careful and discreet.

Rauf heard through the grapevine about the arrival of Muktar Ibrahim, Shakeel Ismail, and Rizwan Majid. Rauf knew these Brits had zeal for jihad in their hearts but lacked street smarts. He figured if they were foolish enough to "train" using paintball guns in firearms-unfriendly Great Britain, the authorities might already be tracking them. Thus, Rauf took his merry time, waiting awhile before contacting the men.

After deciding they were clean, Rauf rang Majid's family on the telephone. Once he made the connection, he advised the trio about basic countersurveillance techniques. He believed someone could be watching—the Pakistanis, the Americans, the British—so they continued the fiction of attending a wedding. After keeping up the pantomime for a few days, Rauf arranged onward travel for the group into the tribal lands.

When the men took the roundabout path to the heights of the tribal highlands, it was far colder than what they had expected. The soft boys of England were chilled to the bone. Perhaps they should have shown up in the springtime, and not in the dead of winter.

They were brought to a drafty compound away from prying eyes, a grim, unfinished slice of real estate of mud and brick, surrounded by a high wall.[9] The wind howled through the mountains and the darkness came on quickly. Their heads ached from the high altitudes. The food was rough and basic. Since plastic sheets served as window coverings, the chill penetrated the room where they slept. They couldn't get their hands to stop shaking from the cold; they wore the sweaters, jackets, hats, and gloves that they had brought to keep themselves from freezing. Bathing was achieved by dousing one's body in an ice bath. They pissed into a hole in the ground.

Al Qaeda's trainers seemed in no particular hurry to do their jobs; they'd show up in the late morning, provide instruction, and disappear by early lunchtime. In between their sparse training, Ibrahim and his friends had little to amuse themselves with. Sometimes they'd try to do sets of push-ups and sit-ups, or run limply around the compound, but the bitter cold dampened their spirits. Every so often, they'd be allowed to dismantle an AK-47, but they weren't allowed to fire it lest it draw the interest of the neighbors, who might report it to—well, it was never certain. There were spies everywhere. Of course, the men were forbidden to leave the compound. All in all, it was a miserable experience.

But in the mountains, they began to learn how to construct bombs. One of their first instructors was none other than Abu Ubaydah al-Masri, who had taken Rashid Rauf under his wing some time before.

◆

An explosion is the rapid release of energy from a small volume of material, an almost instantaneous chemical change from solid to liquid to gas. The detonator causes a small transfer of explosive power that, in turn, ignites a larger explosive. The released energy creates a shock wave that radiates out in the blink of an eye. For suicide attackers, ball bearings, screws, nuts, nails, and other metal objects are glued or stitched within the explosive vest that they wear. The detonation then propels these fragments outward at a high velocity. In many cases, it's not the explosive but the shrapnel that devastates human flesh.

It can also be a devil for an amateur bombmaker to build an effective explosive. Chemicals and their spirits are finicky beasts; make them too hot or too cold and they fizzle instead of fire. Bombs explode prematurely. Many times, they don't go off at all. A novice bombmaker thus benefits from a competent instructor to guide him. But, even with expert guidance, things sometimes don't work out as planned. And experience can be an unforgiving teacher.

Fresh recruits to the global jihad generally began their explosive tinkering on inert devices. But on one winter's day, al Qaeda's trainers played fast and loose with basic safety protocols. Ibrahim's friends from London, Shakeel Ismail and Rizwan Majid, were huddled over 300 g test devices they had recently constructed from scratch. Ibrahim was standing slightly off to the side, along with Abu Ubaydah.

Ismail or Majid then dropped something, sparked something, or touched two live surfaces together. There was a flash and a bang; the duo bore the brunt of the resulting explosion, their efforts to kill American troops in Afghanistan coming to an abrupt end. Remarkably, Ibrahim and Abu Ubaydah remained unscathed, despite standing close by to the blast.

Abu Ubaydah seemed unperturbed and took the sudden deaths of his new recruits in stride. Mishaps occured in this business all the time. Bombmakers were expected to lose a finger, or a hand, sometimes more. No matter; there would be other recruits. If anything, their deaths were a waste of British passport holders.

Ibrahim felt differently about the accident. Watching friends perish for no divine purpose came as a shock to him. They were there in the mountains of Pakistan to train, fight, and die for a great cause. Now his friends were dead before they could make the jump into Afghanistan.

After they had cleaned up Ismail and Majid's remains, Abu Ubaydah sat the shaken Brit down and gave him another option. By then, Ibrahim knew the rudimentary elements of bombmaking, such as building detonators made of triacetone triperoxide (TATP). Instead of dying for the glory of jihad on the Afghan battlefield, would he instead consider returning to the United Kingdom? He could be of much more use in the West.

Still shaken over the premature deaths of his friends, Ibrahim eventually returned to Islamabad. While waiting for his return flight back to Europe, he met Rauf again. The Birmingham exile wanted to talk about next steps. Yet for one reason or another, the two didn't click; Rauf found the Londoner a bit standoffish. Maybe his coolness was because Ibrahim had just experienced the visceral consequences of what awaited him at the end of the road.

After one of their discussions, Rauf finally asked Ibrahim about what he learned up north. Like a student caught unprepared for a surprise quiz, Ibrahim hedged. He tried to convince Rauf that his ability to build bombs had advanced sufficiently to allow him to build explosives independently and without mistakes. Rauf wasn't convinced.

Although no grand plot was hatched during those days in Islamabad, in the back of his mind, Rauf knew what lay in store for Ibrahim once he returned the United Kingdom: fiery death during a martyrdom operation, or a long prison sentence. He hoped it would be the former. Therefore, Rauf convinced Ibrahim to record a suicide tape to be released on the news and online. Rauf understood terrorism was political theater. The packaging and repackaging of this content was oftentimes more important and longer lasting that the attack itself. He also knew the operatives in charge of online content—dubbed "the media brothers"—would want something ready to disseminate in case something on the other side of the world went boom.

Before long, their time together came to an end. Ibrahim had to take a flight home since his visa was expiring. Before parting ways, Rauf crafted a rudimentary communications plan with Ibrahim, using code words to discuss plans. Ibrahim wasn't altogether ready to leave Pakistan and his new social support structure, but he knew that if he missed his return flight—as would be the case for his two hastily buried friends—he might attract unwanted attention. He had to fly home to London and pretend as if nothing had happened.[10]

One of the first things Ibrahim did when he arrived back in London was ring Rauf. "I'm safe," he told his new associate. They promised to talk again. Following this conversation, Rauf was however unable to connect with Ibrahim again to help guide him on his path to martyrdom. What Ibrahim didn't quite realize at the time was that building bombs was harder than it looked in the movies, or even in the freezing mountains of Pakistan.[11]

Unbeknownst to Ibrahim, Rauf and Abu Ubaydah had another, more competent, crew working independently on a separate plot. And, unlike Ibrahim and his hapless friends, they were far better students.

5

Ali's Evolution

Ali and Cossor buried their infant son in England and then flew to Karachi. They first visited one of Ali's cousins, then made their way to their families' homes in Jhelum. They stayed there for about a month, but Ali had more pressing issues on his mind beyond caring for his wife.

Ali knew he was destined for something big, but the specifics of the plan remained unformed. He needed more time and training. So, Ali told Cossor he was going back to work in the camps on the border, as he had done in the past. But that was a lie; instead, he was readying himself to fight in the butcher's backroom of Afghanistan.[1]

Ever the talent scout, Rauf contacted Ali after conducting his usual long-range surveillance. Ali's previous experience in the refugee camps provided great cover for action. Rauf eventually facilitated Ali's northbound travel to the FATA to meet Abu Ubaydah al-Masri at an al Qaeda camp. There, Ali learned basic weapons training and the like, preparing him for a trip across the mountainous border to fight with al Qaeda and the Taliban against the Americans. If Abu Ubaydah was involved in his training, it is likely that Ali also received a course in bombmaking from one of the best instructors in the region.

The lifespan of a foreign-born al Qaeda fighter in Afghanistan against the relentless might of the American military was a short one. If he was lucky, he'd be able to commit two or three attacks before his name went up on a military or CIA PowerPoint slide deck with his passport photo attached. Then, the pressure would be on to "remove him from the battlefield"—that bloodless bureaucratic phrase that meant he should be killed or captured, usually the former. And more often than not, he would then be "removed" in one way or another.

In some of the downtime at the camp, Ali confided in Rauf that he never wanted to return home. He wanted to fight, kill, and die a martyr in Afghanistan.[2] But both Rauf and Abu Ubaydah saw something special in the twenty-four-year-old Ali. During his training, Ali was patient, smart, and thoughtful. He was a serious, but not overbearing student who could convince others to follow his command. But he could be charismatic and funny too. It was obvious to Rauf and Abu Ubaydah this new recruit could be better utilized than as just another martyr in the graveyard of empires.

In short, Rauf and Abu Ubaydah saw a leader.[3]

◆

When a man finds his life's mission, his whole outlook changes. It's a bit like falling in love. He becomes far more thoughtful and focused. He feels it in his bones.

In the mountains of northwestern Pakistan, Ali was evolving. No longer was he an aimless twentysomething, latching onto whatever cause came his way. He had found his mission. Rauf sensed it too. He had had his own awakening some time before. A few years later, Rauf wrote, "a big change came over [Ali's] temperament when he first came and when he left."[4]

Al Qaeda had little problem maintaining a pipeline of recruits who wanted to blow themselves up against a checkpoint, or walk into a hotel with an explosive belt. By this point, the terror group had made its calling card well known the world over. But identifying Western passport holders with a level of smarts, dedication, and sophistication was a far more difficult endeavor. Ali was a diamond in the rough. Over mutton-and-naan conversations with Rauf in the mountains, Ali became a different man, a man with purpose. How his evolution would manifest itself was still a gray smudge in the distant future. But he was now part and parcel of the grander jihadist enterprise, one they hoped would change the world.

Ali returned to his sad wife in Jhelum to await further instructions. But just because Ali was quickly becoming an asset for al Qaeda didn't mean he kept a particularly low profile. Toward the end of his time in Pakistan, he received a number of calls from his friend Muktar Ibrahim, who was probably in the country too. It was risky and stupid to connect in this way, given the CIA's and MI6's scrutiny of telephonic relationships between two British passport holders in Pakistan. The walls of the CIA's Counterterrorism Center (CTC) were covered with minutely detailed link charts connecting the communications of young men like Ali and Ibrahim.

At some point, Rauf, Abu Ubaydah, or some other security-minded Islamist finally told these terrorist wannabes that cellphone tracking was the standard way the Americans or the Pakistanis could locate, and then kill, them. By then, the vulnerabilities from using mobile and satellite phones were well known among the jihadist community. Bin Laden himself famously hadn't used a satellite phone since the mid-1990s since he was plainly aware the Americans and others exploited technical means to monitor and then geolocate the caller.[5] Many other brothers fell because they carried around a trackable communications device in their pocket. This was not even a technology exclusive to the Western powers; Moscow killed Chechen insurgent leader Dzhokhar Dudayev in April 1996 by homing in on his satellite phone.[6] Yet eager jihadists kept bringing these devices into areas where they shouldn't. The veteran fighters were rightly paranoid about their operational security, for they knew one slipup could lead to disaster.

Another technical evolution compounded this threat. On June 19, 2004, a missile fired from an unmanned aerial vehicle (UAV) struck a Taliban commander, Nek Muhammad. Muhammad had a few months beforehand fought Pakistani troops around the village of Wana, in South Waziristan. Following the firefight, he signed a truce with his Pakistani adversaries, then immediately renounced it. Pakistan wanted him dead since he had killed sixty of its soldiers. Nek Muhammad had been speaking over a satellite phone with a journalist before sitting down to a late dinner. Around ten in the evening, he and four other men were still enjoying their meal when a missile streaked from the blackened sky and incinerated all five, leaving a six-by-six-foot crater. His dubious legacy was that he was the first, or one of the first, in a long line of men to die in such a manner.

So Ali and Ibrahim ceased calling each other on the phone. In retrospect, it didn't seem to matter, since neither man was on anyone's radar.

◆

Upon their return to Great Britain several months later, in December 2004, Ali and Cossor passed through immigration and customs in both in Pakistan and the United Kingdom with no hassle. The young couple, tired and worn out from a long flight in coach class, returned to their ground-floor council flat and settled back into their humdrum routine.

Ali's household suffered another tragedy. While in Pakistan or right after returning, and less than a year after losing her first child, Cossor suffered a miscarriage. She spent much of her time cloistered away again in their one-bedroom flat, hidden away by her overbearing husband with his secret double life.

Ali eventually found a job with his cricket-loving friend Tanvir Hussain selling commissions for mobile phone contracts. He received £20 per contract; if he sold more than twenty contracts per month, he received £30. Ali turned on the charm, of course. He also returned to assist his brother in the real estate business. Through these efforts, he made enough money to cover his family's expenses.

Neither of the couple were avid readers. Only a few chosen books were in their flat; paperbacks extolling the virtues and necessities of jihad. First, *The Lofty Mountain* by Abdullah Azzam, the cofounder of LeT and al Qaeda and "mentor" of Osama bin Laden. The book describes the life and death of a jihadist in 1980s Afghanistan, as well as a battle where fifty mujahideen fought scores of Soviet and communist troops. This particular tome was translated, republished, and sold in Islamic bookstores across Great Britain in the early 2000s; despite Azzam's death-by-car-bomb in 1989, the copy Ali had contained a eulogy for a jihadist killed by the Americans at Tora Bora, thus linking the jihad of old with the present struggle.[7] The other was *Milestones* by Sayyid Qutb. Written while on death row in Egypt, this slender work was probably the most influential book about Islamist global revolution in the modern era. As Lawrence Wright would later muse in *The Looming Tower*, "The international Salafist uprising might have occurred without the writings of Sayyid Qutb or Abdullah Azzam's call to jihad, but al Qaeda would not have existed."[8] There's nothing wrong with either book, of course—Qutb's works have been published many times over. But it seemed strange that both books found a place in a household of nonreaders.

Ali linked up with his friend Assad Sarwar, who was now working for the Royal Mail. Muktar Ibrahim also started calling him on the telephone. Despite being told to lay low, Ibrahim couldn't resist calling Ali. It remained unclear whether Ali knew about the young refugee's plans for a history-changing event, or if Ibrahim had kept his mouth shut. Also, things were also finally looking up for Ali and Cossor in the confines of 18 Nash House; by the spring of 2005, they had conceived another baby.

Walthamstow's cherry blossoms bloomed and fluttered to the ground as spring became early summer. But Ali knew he was needed elsewhere; his training was incomplete. Thus, he concocted a tale for his family about how he wanted to start a business in Pakistan by buying real estate or working in the compressed natural gas business. He told his brother that his ideas would be profitable, since "you don't need as much money to buy a property and you can build like something you would consider a mansion here, in Pakistan you could build it for like £50,000 or £60,000."[9] But his family, already involved in the local real estate market, remained skeptical about his plan. Ali had scant business experience and little capital to invest. More importantly, he had a habit of dropping off to South Asia to do who knows what for months at a time. Great Britain was their home, where their family and their neighbors had flourished. It was their land of opportunity, not Pakistan. "Look, you need some substance," said one of his brothers.

"Do a proper feasibility study. Come back with some facts and figures, some more detail, and then we can consider it."[10]

In late May 2005, Ali applied for a six-month visa to visit Pakistan; he received it at the end of the month. On June 6, he left his pregnant wife to fend for herself yet again and flew back to South Asia. Tagging along with him was his brother's friend Adam Khatib, several years his junior.

Of course, Ali didn't bother to develop a comprehensive business plan or draft a proper feasibility study. He had little interest in founding a real estate business or property management firm. Instead, Ali flew to Pakistan to meet his comrades in arms. By the end of the year, Ali returned to the United Kingdom at Rauf's command to build a list of targets across Britain to strike simultaneously.[11]

Unbeknownst to Ali, Rauf had already set into motion two other plots.

6

Incident on the Tube

Tony Blair was in a mood—diplomatically, he was "not happy."[1] The British prime minister had just spent two days inside a series of five-star hotel suites and government facilities in Singapore to lobby for London to host the Olympic Games. Alongside footballer David Beckham, he wooed the members of the International Olympic Committee (IOC) in a last-ditch effort to snatch the golden prize from France or Spain, considered the far better candidates. He was also trying to advocate for Britain without committing any sort of diplomatic faux pas. The whole affair was "really horrible stuff," he later recalled, as he was forced to be "competitive without appearing to be" and try to "maintain dignity while begging."[2]

Still queasy, he spent the next thirteen hours in the air returning to Britain, finally touching down in Edinburgh to host his own Group of Eight (G8) meeting. This annual meeting of the world's richest nations (plus Russia) was supposed to tackle global issues. This year, the meeting was to focus on Africa and climate change. By 2005 the 9/11 attacks and mass protests at previous gatherings convinced the G8 member states to host these meetings in out-of-the-way venues that were more easily secured. Thus the meeting took place in Scotland at Gleneagles, a magnificent 850-acre luxury hotel and golf resort with a two–Michelin star restaurant. President George W. Bush had arrived via helicopter, accompanied in the Scottish rain by First Lady Laura Bush and their daughter Jenna.[3] U2's Bono was there among the elite, too.

As the dignitaries arrived in Scotland, the IOC announced London would indeed host the Olympics, winning with a squeaker vote of fifty-four to fifty over Paris on the final ballot. This was just in time for a jet-lagged but meticulously dressed President Jacques Chirac of France to arrive on British soil.

The G8 atmosphere was convivial on July 6, 2005, although not without the usual trifling controversy. The French president had trashed British cuisine a few days earlier to Russia's Vladimir Putin and Germany's Gerhard Schroeder. At the dinner, the Elvis Presley-loving, political gadfly–turned–accidental Japanese prime minister Junichiro Koizumi, asked Chirac over the appetizers, "Hey, Jacques, excellent British food, don't you think?" Koizumi then proceeded to needle the French leader with the same line during each subsequent course.[4] President Bush was also recovering from a minor incident earlier that day; while waving to the Scottish riot cops, he had accidentally steered his bike into a policeman.[5]

The next day was Thursday, July 7. Heavy rains made their way across Scotland and England that morning. By 8:30 a.m. Blair and Bush had wrapped up a short press conference; Bush discussed his so-called Freedom Agenda and downplayed his mishap with the officer from the day before.[6] The two leaders then went to their separate meetings; Blair met with Communist Party General Secretary Hu Jintao of China in the press office to discuss climate change and the particulars of coal production. Fifteen minutes into the formal meeting, Blair's gray-curled chief of staff, Jonathan Powell, handed him a hastily scribbled note.

Incident on the Tube. Possible casualties.[7]

Blair quickly explained the note to Hu. A few minutes later, Powell returned with more information.

There was one more explosion.

The prime minister took his leave of the Chinese leader. On the way back to his hotel suite, Blair and Powell ran into Bush and his entourage in the hallway. The U.S. president already knew something had happened, but he had little information to give or to provide.

The two middle-aged men looked at each other. Bush simply asked, "Terrorist attack?"

"Could be an accident." But in their hearts, they both knew the answer.

Early reports of something terrible on the Underground began filtering onto the television channels. Blair made his way up to his hotel suite and contacted the British home secretary, Charles Clarke. Clarke had taken over the role after David Blunkett—the recipient of Ali's letters and petitions—resigned the previous December in a scandal concerning his fast-tracking a visa renewal for an ex-lover's nanny.

"How many casualties?" the prime minister asked.

"I can't tell."

"Deaths?"

"Bound to be, I'm afraid."

"How many?"

"Don't know."[8]

Meanwhile, from his own hotel suite, Bush contacted Fran Townsend, his assistant for homeland security and counterterrorism, on her phone. Townsend was a no-BS workaholic fireplug who loved to work out and use nautical terminology. It was a bit after four in the morning on the East Coast of the United States, and Fran had just woken up to prepare for an early-morning workout.

The president asked, "What's going on? What's happening?"

Groggily, she replied, "I don't know, Mister President. I'm just out of bed."

"Turn on the TV."

The thought raced through her mind that it was never a good idea for the boss to know more about something than you did, especially on your topic of expertise. She found the remote control and turned on the television—to chaos in London.[9]

Her counterpart Juan Zarate, the deputy national security advisor for combating terrorism, also received the call in the wee hours and was likewise told of the attack. Zarate and deputy national security adviser J. D. Crouch drove to the White House from their homes and made their way to the Situation Room on the ground floor; Secretary of Homeland Security Michael Chertoff was elsewhere. They knew they had to put a plan in place before the morning rush hour began on the East Coast, just in case there was a second prong to the attack. Across the secure system, they contacted the president and breathlessly began to update him on the events of the last hour.

After connecting with President Bush, they hurriedly started on their brief. Bush told everybody, "Stop. Calm down. I've talked to Blair."

The president proceeded to brief his subordinates about what was happening in the United Kingdom. Bush then told them what he was advising the prime minister to do. Zarate vividly recalled the president was clearly in charge, a voice of composed reason.[10]

◆

The reports kept coming in. There were near-simultaneous attacks around 8:50 in the morning on the Circle Line tunnel between Aldgate and Liverpool Street stations, the Circle Line by Edgware Road, and the Piccadilly Line tunnel between Russell Square and King's Cross. In the confined spaces of the London Underground, the cars quickly filled with smoke. The floors near the blast were blackened and filled with obscenely twisted pieces of machinery and victims.

A large percentage of the police force were commuting to work on public transport themselves when the bombs exploded. Steve Dryden, a senior officer with the London Metropolitan Police, better known as the Met, was on the Piccadilly line—he first thought it was a power surge within the system.[11] Some of the other members of SO15, the Met's Counter Terrorism Command, were already in the office, watching Sky News reporters on the scene of the stricken tube entrances. Jonathan Evans, a longtime MI5 official promoted to deputy director the week before, was already at his Thames House headquarters when he received word of unexplained but coordinated explosions on the Underground around 9:20 a.m., with more possibly to come.[12] The train system shut down, stranding tens of thousands of commuters in the inky darkness of the tunnels, punctuated by the flickering emergency lights in the bowels of London.

About half an hour later, the top floor of the no. 30 double-decker bus in Tavistock Square, traveling east on its lumbering route from

Marble Arch to Hackney Wick, exploded. The bus was loaded with commuters forced aboveground when the Underground was shuttered. The flash of white, the searing heat, and the outward force of the blast were powerful enough to rend the roof, fiberglass seats, and steel doors apart. Blood splattered at least ten meters up into the air, splashing the cement sign of the nearby British Medical Association. One victim, Miriam Hyman, had just spoken to her father minutes before, telling him she was safe before alighting upon the ill-fated bus at Tavistock Square.[13]

Fifty-two members of the public were murdered and over seven hundred were injured. The dead were a cross-section of the metropolis; they included a hairdresser from Herefordshire, an Iran-born medical officer, an accountant from Poland who had just arrived in the city several weeks prior, and a cleaner from Ghana. Ateeque Sharifi, a refugee who fled from Afghanistan after the Taliban murdered his parents, died in the explosion nearest to King's Cross.[14] Jamie Gordon, a thirty-year-old about to be married, died because he had spent the night in the city with a friend. The dead were Christians, Muslims, Jews, Hindus, and the unchurched. Regular folks: mothers and fathers, sisters and brothers, coworkers, lovers, and strivers.[15]

The divine algorithm made it all so unfair and cruel; it was random chance who lived, who died, who alighted from the bus at the last stop before the explosion, who spent a few more minutes in the shower before work and then caught the fatal train, who awoke earlier than usual and who didn't.

Still, many others survived, even those in close proximity to the attackers. One woman, Cynthia Chetty, sat very near the explosion on the Circle line and somehow survived serious injury.[16] Professor John Tulloch was in the same car sitting three feet away when the bomb went off. He survived because a piece of luggage absorbed much of the blast. A photograph of his blackened, bloodied, bandaged head became an iconic image of that terrible day.[17]

Londoners experienced the unfolding terrorist operation in waves. Shimon Taylor from Ilford, Essex, traveled daily across much of London to her work in Hammersmith, in the western part of the city. Her commute took over an hour. Like most days, she left the house at 6:30 in the morning, took the rail to Liverpool Street station, changed to the Circle tube line, and arrived at her desk by eight o'clock sharp. It was just a regular day at the office, a stone's throw from the River Thames.

Out of the blue, she received a text from an ex-boyfriend. "Are you okay?" She ignored it and went back to work.

A few minutes later, her mother called with the same, agitated question: "Are you okay?" Shimon reassured her mother and, as she did, a colleague turned on the office television. Scenes of carnage filled the screen.

In a quiet but urgent voice, her mother told her, "I can't reach your sister."

Shimon's younger sister had been commuting into London. She was somewhere deep within the system when the explosions went off. Her phone wasn't responding; the lines were jammed. Frantically, mother and daughter joined the tens of thousands of people trying to locate their loved ones caught underneath the ground.

Several terrible hours later, Shimon and her mother found out her sister had survived, unscathed.[18] She had been on the Circle line near the Liverpool Street a few minutes before a bomber stepped into the second car of an eastbound train.

◆

Mobile phone traffic surged, almost crashing the system. Vodafone's and O2's cellular networks received three hundred thousand calls every fifteen minutes, a 1,000 percent increase from regular usage.[19] Communication was spotty not just for civilians but also for the authorities. MI5, with many of its employees commuting by public transportation, was directly affected; its landline network almost collapsed from officers calling out, and their distressed families calling in, as they watched the attack unfold on their television sets.[20]

The London Ambulance Service, the London Fire Brigade, the City of London Police, and the Met also all relied to varying degrees on the mobile network to communicate with each other, and back to their control rooms. The British Transport Police had a specialized terrestrial trunked radio police radio system to talk with each other, but other emergency services lacked access.

No one had much idea what was happening. Maybe more bombers were in play. Rumors spread like wildfire.

Complicating matters, the City of London Police—a separate force from the Met—unilaterally activated the last-resort "Access Overload Control" (ACCOLC) system around noon, shutting down telephone networks to everyone except those with special communications capabilities. The ACCOLC system created a one-kilometer dead zone around the Aldgate East tube stop; the zone stretched from Shoreditch High Street station in the north, Whitechapel station and the Royal London Hospital in the northeast, past the Liverpool Street stop in the northwest, and all the way south beyond the Tower of London to the Thames. This was the most congested section of the largest city in Europe, and now no one could communicate in that zone unless they had an ACCOLC-enabled mobile phone.[21] Confoundingly, the City of London Police took this action without informing all the other police forces and emergency services, which were all operating within the blast sites. Steve Dryden, now in the office and dealing with the immediate fallout, noted, "That really didn't help."[22]

◆

The United Kingdom had no idea this attack was coming. No one had caught a whisper of the conspiracy or had come across in a meaningful way the perpetrators who went on to kill on July 7. The terror operation was planned and executed right under their very noses.

In retrospect, someone should've assessed an operation like this was coming down the pike. The largest terrorist strike on European soil had just occurred the previous March, when a jihadist cell simultaneously bombed passenger trains during rush hour in Madrid, murdering 193 people and wounding two thousand others. Still, several weeks before the London attacks, the Joint Terrorism Analysis Centre (JTAC), the British intelligence community's one-stop shop for terrorism issues, had lowered the threat level from the third most dangerous, "Severe General" to the fourth, "Substantial."[23] As MI5 director-general Dame

Eliza Manningham-Buller later said, JTAC believed the aggressive efforts against these terror groups over the past few years had blunted their capabilities and did not expect a terror operation on the British mainland. A subsequent Parliamentary inquiry found

> The main reason given in the JTAC report for the reduction in the UK threat level was that there was no intelligence of a current credible plot to attack the UK at that time (i.e. a group with established capability and current intent). The report noted that the threat level had been maintained since August 2004 on the back of concerns, arising from intelligence and investigations, that attack planning "might" be going on. *At this time, however, there was no firm intelligence of attack planning.* By May 2005 the investigative leads that had previously been a cause for concern had been followed up and discounted.[24] (emphasis added)

"It turned out," Manningham-Buller wistfully noted later, "wrongly."[25] After all, "shoe bomber" Richard Reid, who had tried to smuggle and detonate explosives in his footwear a few months after the 9/11 attacks, and the individuals implicated in two attempted attacks in Tel Aviv in 2003 were British citizens. Perhaps it was a bit of a failure to think creatively about who might want to carry out a lethal operation, and how they might do so. This deadly strike against London's transportation system quickly became known by its date: the 7/7 attacks.

◆

The U.S. intelligence community had an intimate counterterrorism relationship with its British cousins, as close as lips and teeth. Had there been indications of a terrorist cell on allied soil, this intelligence would have been passed along immediately. In a question-and-answer session with reporters later that day, Homeland Security Secretary Chertoff revealed the United States was caught off-guard as well:

QUESTION: Was there any intelligence stream or chatter in the months before this to indicate that something like this was afoot, or did the London bombings take us completely by surprise?

CHERTOFF: I'm not aware of any specific intelligence that suggested this was going to take place.[26]

U.S. president George Bush had brought a large security and foreign policy team to Scotland that morning, but like everyone else, he found information was scant and confusing. From their perch at the G8, Stephen Hadley and the rest of the White House staff were watching television but also communicating back to Washington DC.[27]

Across the Atlantic Ocean, watch officers in walled-off facilities were scrambling to figure out what just happened as well. CIA's Operations Center, situated within a large conference-like room within its headquarters, provided 24/7 alerting and warning communication.[28] Staffed mostly by younger employees willing to do shift work and older employees "voluntold" to serve, this center began to receive updates from abroad. U.S. embassy and other U.S. government employees took the same public transportation system to work. The chaos on the street personally affected them too.[29]

When rush hour started breaking across the Eastern Seaboard, from Maine to Florida, and then spread across the North American continent, the U.S. government needed to be ahead of the curve. As Townsend, responsible for the White House's response to homeland security threats, later recounted, "Transport was always our Achilles heel since they're generally free-flowing, open architecture systems. If you shut them down, then nothing works."[30] What should government officials and the police be looking for, and where should they be looking? How did the bombers behave, and what did the explosives actually look like? These were questions that lacked concrete answers as rush hour began across the United States. Thankfully, there were no bombers that day in America.

By the afternoon, London picked up the pieces; the Underground eventually reopened for business and the markets self-corrected. The night before the attack, the FTSE 100 closed at 5,229.6, then lost over 200 points as the news of the operation broke. By the closing bell on the next day, those losses were shrugged off and the FTSE rose to 5,232.2. Hilton Hotels indicated no major cancellations throughout London in the aftermath.[31] The British and larger world economy were unshaken in a meaningful way. Despite the carnage, it simply wasn't the devastating blow that the jihadists had hoped for.

◆

American and British intelligence and security officers may have been blindsided, but terrorizing Britain had been in the works for some time. Pakistani President Pervez Musharraf recalled that 9/11 mastermind Khalid Sheikh Mohammed (KSM) himself recruited and tasked a Pakistani national, Naeem Noor Khan, a.k.a. "Abu Talha al-Pakistani," to consider conducting attacks on the subway system in London. "Security at the underground stations," according to the former Pakistani president quoting the terrorist operative, "was virtually nonexistent except for cameras, and it would be easy to carry bags onto the train."[32] He continued, "Thus KSM suggested using not suicide bombers but operatives who would carry small backpacks, get off the trains, leave the backpacks on the platforms, board the next train, and activate the bombs after they were a safe distance away."[33]

But Rashid Rauf and the main bombers—Mohammad Sidique Khan (also known as MSK) and Shehzad Tanweer—viewed the operation differently. Martyrdom was always the point.

◆

Sidique Khan, thirty years old at the time of his death, was at least upon first glance a seemingly ordinary British citizen of Pakistani heritage from Beeston, outside the industrial city of Leeds. Father to a growing family—he and his wife had one daughter and another on the way—he worked as a special needs teacher's aide. He worshipped at a Tablighi Jamaat mosque in Dewsbury, south of Leeds.[34] He also taught martial arts at a place called the Hamara Centre, where it appears he first met the twenty-two-year-old Tanweer and eighteen-year-old Hasib Hussain.[35]

In spite of his family and job, in June 2001 Sidique Khan and another British friend, Waheed Ali, traveled to Pakistan to fight. After landing in Islamabad from Great Britain, they were met by Khan's uncle at the airport, who was waiting for them with his van.[36] The transport vehicle was owned by HUM—Masood Azhar's ISI-backed group. By this time, Azhar—Rashid Rauf's future brother-in-law—was safely back in Pakistan after India released him following the Indian Airlines hijacking, and had already founded his new terror outfit, JeM.

After a three-hour drive north on the N35 highway, Sidique Khan and Waheed Ali arrived at a HUM training camp. There, the two men shot AK-47s, fired rocket propelled grenades, and generally made things explode.[37] The hot war on the other side of the border had cooled down somewhat; the 9/11 attacks and subsequent American invasion remained in the future. The two men wanted to link up with the Taliban front lines, then battering the Northern Alliance in its last strongholds up in the north of Afghanistan; HUM facilitated these connections into the warzone.

They had fire in their guts but their delicate internal plumbing wasn't up to the task. Both Sidique Khan and his friend were struck down with bowel-shattering diarrhea. Plus, the Taliban fighters—hardened, sinewy men with gimlet eyes—thought these English men with their soft hands and fat complexions were too physically weak to make it very far. Thus, they were ordered to stay behind. Ali did, and served as a cook. Sidique Khan persevered and made it into Afghanistan proper, but didn't see any fighting. Both eventually gave up and returned to their marshmallow lives in the West.[38] When they touched down on British soil, it was September 5, 2001.

Six days later, al Qaeda launched its audacious attacks in New York City and Washington DC, killing almost three thousand people. In the following weeks, Sidique Khan watched his erstwhile Taliban comrades' fighting positions quickly crumple under the awesome power of the U.S. Air Force. The fighters and families he knew were fleeing along the same mountain passes in the opposite direction he had trod only a month prior as they were routed on the ground by the Northern Alliance, CIA, and U.S. Special Operations Forces.

Already well down his path toward the darkness since his abortive effort with HUM and the Taliban, Sidique Khan was further infuriated by Tony Blair's full-throated support of the U.S. invasion of Iraq over a year later. Sometime in late 2003, he drove one hundred thirty miles from his home to a meeting space above a closed shop in Dudley, a grim industrial town west of Birmingham. There, he, Shehzad Tanweer, and their teenage friend Germaine Lindsay sat spellbound by an American orator and his call for global jihad. The men took careful notes of what this man, Anwar al-Awlaqi, had to say. Over the course of the evening, Awlaqi held court, pouring poison into the ears of his audience. "Muslims," he rhapsodized, "will never experience peace unless jihad is established because the harm of the enemy can only be stopped through jihad. No peaceful means will deliver that."

At the time, Awlaqi was not on the authorities' radar, and this meeting would not have been noted except for the fact that an MI5 asset decided on his own to check out this rising star from America.[39] The asset, Aimen Dean, later informed MI5 that Awlaqi held his audience in the palm of his hand. He told his handler, "Everybody in that room has the potential to become a suicide bomber."[40] MI5 belatedly began monitoring Awlaqi's speeches throughout Great Britain, as well as some of their participants. But they missed the participation of Sidique Khan, Tanweer, and Lindsay completely.

Sidique Khan flew back and forth to Pakistan again that year and made further connections with a group of men who would later be busted in a conspiracy the authorities codenamed Crevice. This plot, which involved six hundred kilograms of ammonium nitrate fertilizer in a storage depot, was disrupted by the largest operation that MI5 and the police had carried out up until that date. It had ramped up from a routine investigation to a full-blown national emergency in under three weeks.[41] Sidique Khan knew the perpetrators and appeared on the periphery of the operation, but he never became a person of interest himself. Years later, authorities conducted a review of a forty-five-minute audio recording made after MI5 placed a probe within a suspect's car. The people in the car—including Sidique Khan—spoke in heavily Yorkshire-accented English, Urdu, Punjabi, and Arabic. The review revealed Sidique Khan was more involved in the conspiracy than first understood, but the cops who originally transcribed the conversation could neither fully understand nor interpret what was being said.[42] Remarkably, Sidique Khan's only transgression, attending a militant training camp in Pakistan, was not illegal. Britain finally made it a criminal offense in 2005.

Once back home in the UK, Sidique Khan and Shehzad Tanweer nonetheless took precautions to outwardly mask their violent fundamentalism. They didn't know if there'd ever be a series of knocks and "Police!" yelled against the door before a battering ram and black uniforms busted through and dragged them away. So they wore Western outfits, went to the movies, and ate in restaurants. That said, it wasn't clear local law enforcement had a granular appreciation for what was, and what was not, considered pious behavior among the Islamists. But it turned out all their efforts at subterfuge were unnecessary: no one was watching them.

Sidique Khan and his small circle must have been shaken on August 3 after authorities raided and shut down a cell in Luton, thirty miles north of London on the River Lea. That operation, codenamed Rhyme, involved a possible radiological bomb and limousines filled with gas canisters to be detonated in London's underground parking garages. The main plotter, Dhiren Barot, a.k.a. "Issa al-Hindi," was an India-born convert to Islam who fell in with Kashmiri militant groups in Pakistan, and who was then was quickly redirected by al Qaeda to return to the West. After another terrorist in Pakistani custody positively identified him, British authorities half a world away breached Barot's front door. Rhyme, like Crevice before it, had absorbed the authorities' full attention.[43]

Rauf knew all about these events in Great Britain, since Sidique Khan told him about them during his trip to Pakistan in November 2004. There, he was ready to give his life to fight the Americans and their Afghan allies. Sidique Khan didn't personally know Rauf when his plane touched back down in Pakistan, his third trip in four years. But he had no particular desire to come back alive, despite being married with a young daughter. He was leaving Britain to die.

Just before he left the UK that November, he made a video. Holding a camcorder in his left hand while holding his baby in his right, he said in between kissing his little girl:

> I just wish I could have been part of your life, especially these growing up . . . these next months, they're really special with you learning to walk and things. I just so much wanted to be with you but I have to do this for our future and it will be for the best, *Inshallah* [God willing] in the long run . . . But most importantly I entrust you to Allah and let Allah take care of you.
>
> And I'm doing what I'm doing for the sake of Islam, not, you know, it's not for materialistic or worldly benefits.[44]

But Sidique Khan's story didn't end there. He arrived with Tanweer in Pakistan, but it so happened another British national named "Umar" told Rashid Rauf the duo had arrived in the country. Umar then provided Rauf with Sidique Khan's mobile number; and like he did with Ali, Rauf eventually made a telephone call.

Sidique Khan and Tanweer did not head straight for the border; instead, they took a detour to Samundari, a town in Punjab thirty miles southwest of the city of Faisalabad.[45] Tanweer had family there, and let Rauf know he'd be in the area. Rauf, ever cautious with new recruits, waited for a bit before meeting them in person.

The men finally met in Faisalabad, far away from most of Tanweer's large family. But not entirely; Tanweer's family had a driver shuttling them around who might inform the family of the duo's real intentions. Rauf had a simple idea; after they met and got into the family car, he turned up the radio, the latest bhangra beats masking their words from the man sitting in the driver's seat.

Very quickly, Rauf came to like Sidique Khan and Tanweer. They told Rauf of their interest in fighting the unbelievers in Afghanistan. Sidique Khan likely also told Rauf about his aborted effort a few years beforehand to fight with the Taliban. They even told him about Umar, who had made the initial connection. It turned out Rauf had refocused Umar from his path toward martyrdom in the mountains of Afghanistan—just like he was in the process of turning Abdulla Ahmed Ali around—so he could commit an attack in Britain. Umar apparently then got cold feet and disappeared once he returned to the West; Sidique Khan filled Rauf in on his whereabouts.[46]

Rauf thought Sidique Khan and Tanweer had much to offer the cause. After bidding farewell to the family in Samundari, the trio made their way north to Islamabad, where Rauf then helped them secure transit to the tribal areas. It was wintertime and bitterly cold in the mountains, but they pressed on. Upon their arrival, Rauf introduced the men to "Hajji," the bombmaker Abu Ubaydah al-Masri.

Like Muktar Ibrahim and Abdulla Ahmed Ali, both of whom were in play, Abu Ubaydah saw in Sidique Khan and Tanweer real potential and asked them to return to Britain. It took a mere six days for these two to decide to forego certain death in Afghanistan. They arrived in Pakistan on November 18, and by November 26, Sidique Khan's wife wrote in her diary, "S [Sidique Khan] rang—good news!—back by Feb?"[47]

In the camps, Sidique Khan and Tanweer were smart, dedicated students. They paid attention to the trainings and their teachers appreciated their meticulousness to their craft. They even took a specialized module from a Syrian bombmaker and sometime al Qaeda money mule named Marwan al-Suri, who lived in the Bajaur Agency with his family. He taught them how to build explosives made from hydrogen peroxide—al Qaeda's calling card.[48] A little over a year later, Pakistani soldiers would kill al-Suri at a military checkpoint.[49]

Back home, on January 17, 2005, the West Yorkshire Police Special Branch received information that a man named "Saddique [redacted]" had gone to Afghanistan for extremist reasons with another friend named Imran; "Saddique" lived in the Batley area; near Soothill, a village southwest of Leeds.[50] The police officers couldn't find any other hits in their databases. This nondescript information likely came from a local informant, and not a tearline from the U.S. National Security Agency (NSA) or CIA. The local Special Branch kicked it up to MI5 several weeks later, but the Security Service likewise could generate no further information. Nothing could corroborate any of this intelligence, despite the receipt of an additional note on March 1, likely from the same source.[51]

Such is the nature of fragmentary intelligence that doesn't fit into any preconceived understanding of a plot or a terror cell. The head of MI5, Dame Manningham-Buller, later explained, "In order to get on the 'essentials' list you needed to be doing something which suggested you were involved in some form of life-threatening activity . . . we had not got to that point with Mohammad Sidique Khan."[52] The information was filed away, only to be resurrected after the attack.

◆

The newly empowered Sidique Khan and Tanweer returned to Islamabad and taped their martyrdom videos—a splotchy, poorly lit affair. The duo did so reluctantly, since they didn't know where the tapes would end up, but Abu Ubaydah insisted they do so before they left Pakistan. Still, the two were confident and eager to return home to the United Kingdom. Rauf thought this was going to be the big score; he even considered flying back to Europe and joining them in the operation.[53] He then had second thoughts, since he was still wanted for questioning in connection with his uncle's murder. Even though the knifing was now almost three years in the past, he remained the prime suspect. In any case, Rauf couldn't get clean travel documents and thus chose to remain in Pakistan.[54]

Rauf remained in touch with his operatives over the phone. Boiling down hydrogen peroxide to the requisite levels needed for an explosive was challenging enough in the mountain climes of Pakistan, and no one was watching them there. This chemical process was far more difficult to pull off in Britain. Nevertheless, the duo had help; back home, Sidique Khan and Shehzad Tanweer were now joined by two others, Germaine Lindsay and Hasib Hussain. Lindsay was nineteen years old and Hussain was eighteen.

Even with additional manpower, the cell still couldn't generate the right chemical composition for their bombs. They also needed space to build their weapons. To avoid their parents and friends, they moved from property to property, finally renting a flat from a chemistry graduate student from Egypt across the street from the Leeds Grand Mosque. The group didn't stick out in the unremarkable student area, where renters and young people were constantly coming and going. They also installed a commercial-grade refrigerator in the unit to keep the chemicals cold and stable.[55]

But their bodies were exuding unmistakable signs that something was going terribly wrong in their lives. Their skin and hair began to lighten considerably from continued contact with the hydrogen peroxide mix. At one point, some of their family members noticed and remarked about their changed appearance; they blew them off by saying they were going swimming, and the chlorine from the pool was making their hair color lighter.[56] They then wore shower caps while mixing the chemicals to minimize the transformation.

Rauf continued to walk them through the bombmaking process, offering advice over a series of emails, phone calls, and text messages. It was 2005; Rauf used the Yahoo! Messenger function to guide and troubleshoot the cell's efforts.[57] Sidique Khan was paranoid they were being monitored by the NSA or its British counterpart, the Government Communications Headquarters (GCHQ), as they built their bombs and were getting ready to execute their plan.[58] But it turned out that no one was watching them at all.

The primary target for the men was the Gleneagles hotel complex in Scotland, where Blair, Bush, and the rest of the G8 were meeting. But they soon realized they wouldn't be able to penetrate the numerous rings of security surrounding the facility. There were too many guards and too many guns. They wouldn't get very far or inflict many casualties. They then decided the London Underground transportation network was a far easier target to strike.

On July 6, Shehzad Tanweer played cricket with some of his friends into the evening. Hasib Hussain slept in that day, and then around 2:30 p.m. came downstairs to his family kitchen in pajamas and had a bowl of cereal. He left an hour later to meet up with his coconspirators. The nineteen-year-old Germaine Lindsay had been recently kicked out of his own home by his wife, a British convert to Islam, who had found text messages from another woman on his phone. What Mohammad Sidique Khan did during his final night on earth remains unclear.

Sidique Khan, Tanweer, and Hussain hopped into a rented light blue Nissan Micra early the next morning, and headed south from Leeds for London. Rauf had instructed them to leave the tops off the containers of their explosives since the chemicals could otherwise overheat.[59] Rauf later wrote, "With the blessings of Allah I think it rained on the day of the attacks which means the weather was cooler."[60]

Sidique Khan had stopped to fill up his car on the way, bought some snacks at the petrol station, argued with the cashier over the change, then looked directly into the CCTV camera. Was there a hint of a smile on his face, knowing this videotape would become a piece of evidence?

They then connected with Lindsay, who arrived in a red Fiat Brava. For some reason, Lindsay had left a 9 mm handgun inside the car. The men met outside the Luton railway station, which serviced the nearby Luton airport. They opened the trunks of their cars and removed large backpacks, as if they were headed for a camping trip.

The quartet, now weighed down by their packs, entered the station, past whatever minimal or nonexistent security existed within, and headed to the platform for the King's Cross Thameslink. It was 7:40 in the morning when the train arrived. The four men entered.

There was a delay up the line, so the train arrived a bit later than expected at King's Cross, at 8:23 a.m. The station was packed with morning commuters. The King's Cross St. Pancras Underground station was one of the busiest and biggest connective hubs to the entire system, where six lines—Piccadilly, Hammersmith & City, Northern, Metropolitan, Victoria, and Circle—came together as a part of the city's beating transport heart. Twenty million–plus souls passed through its doors on their way to work every year. The men embraced each other for the last time and then went their separate ways, their rucksacks full of concentrated hydrogen peroxide upon their backs.

In less than half an hour, Sidique Khan, Tanweer, and Lindsay were all dead, blown to pieces, along with scores of other Londoners. At 9:47 a.m., so too was Hussain, the roof of the no. 30 bus ripped off and the rear portion devastated, along with thirteen other people. White-clad forensic investigators would find pieces of victims days later in a nearby park hundreds of feet away.[61]

◆

Almost two months later, on September 1, a dead man sprang back to life. Or at least, a video emerged on Al Jazeera of Mohammad Sidique Khan, claiming credit for his actions. He said:

> I and thousands like me are forsaking everything for what we believe. Our driving motivation doesn't come from tangible commodities that this world has to offer. Our religion is Islam—obedience to the one true God, Allah, and following the footsteps of the final prophet and messenger Muhammad . . .
>
> Your democratically elected governments continuously perpetuate atrocities against my people all over the world. And your support of them makes you directly responsible, just as I am directly responsible for protecting and avenging my Muslim brothers and sisters.
>
> Until we feel security, you will be our targets. And until you stop the bombing, gassing, imprisonment and torture of my people we will not stop this fight. We are at war and I am a soldier.[62]

Two months later, on November 16, al Qaeda's number two, the longwinded Egyptian medical doctor Ayman al-Zawahiri, released a video of his own, taunting the British and the Americans. He gloated about the July 7 attacks, calling them "the blessed raid" that took the battle to the enemy's own soil.[63]

Rauf was undoubtedly pleased with his handiwork. The execution of the operation was flawless. And unbeknownst to the intelligence and law enforcement agencies on both sides of the Atlantic, now all on high alert, he had another trick up his sleeve.

7

Bang/Fizz

Abdulla Ahmed Ali found out about the 7/7 attack like everyone else—on television. He had departed for Pakistan the month before and was in the benevolent company of his al Qaeda comrades. He was no longer attempting to wage jihad in Afghanistan; instead, he was learning to build bombs similar to the ones Sidique Khan and Tanweer had just deployed. Concentrated hydrogen peroxide explosives were quite powerful, as was now plainly apparent. He knew it had been important to pay close attention to his teachers and show the chemicals proper respect. Images of the shredded double-decker bus in central London covered in a tarp appeared on television and in every newspaper on the globe, no doubt sparking dreams in Ali of even greater devastation by his hand.

Likely contented by the success of his men in London, Rashid Rauf left for the tribal areas until he could be sure that no one was looking for him.[1] Pakistani law enforcement was largely nonexistent in those areas, and so he believed he could generally remain safe, or at least safer, in that general territory.

Unknown to Rauf, even in the immediate aftermath of the bombings he had just orchestrated, the name "Rashid Rauf" was on no one's target list.

◆

In the hours and days following the attacks, authorities scrambled to find bits and pieces of perishable data. The killers hadn't bothered to hide their tracks. By the evening of 7/7, police had discovered among the debris some articles with the names of "Sidique Khan" and "Mr S Tanweer" near the Aldgate station, where Tanweer had killed seven people plus himself during the morning rush hour. Hasib Hussain's family had called the police hotline on 7/7 reporting him missing, unaware he had blown himself up on a bus earlier that morning.

By the next day, Sidique Khan's Barclaycard was found at the Edgware Road crime scene—linking him to both sites. Hasib Hussain's driver's license was found at Tavistock Square, and very quickly he, Sidique Khan, and Shehzad Tanweer were identified as traveling to London together. Five days later, on July 12, police raided all their family homes, as well as their bombmaking factory in Leeds. The factory was more or less intact when authorities busted the door down. On that day, they also found Germaine Lindsay's car, which had been towed away from the carpark in Luton, and began to connect him to the 7/7 attacks as well. All manner of evidence such as identification cards, phone records, and thousands of hours of CCTV footage were further scoured for clues.

The British way of working, as positively noted by at least one Pakistani spy chief, was a "calm" no fuss, a get-to-work attitude.[2] In a crisis, there wasn't much time for finger-pointing. Still, some members of law enforcement were angry at MI5 over the attack; they viewed it as a systemic failure. The feelings were sometimes mutual, with MI5 members questioning the abilities of their Met counterparts.[3]

Since the 9/11 attacks, the Met was thinking about what actions its officers could take when confronted with a suicide attacker armed with a bomb. Codenamed Operation Kratos, the protocol was to have armed officers essentially sneak up on a suspected suicide attacker and then shoot him in the head.[4] The rationale was to immediately incapacitate an attacker without warning him or otherwise giving him a chance to set off hidden explosives. But this plan appeared half-baked. When Detective Ira Greenberg, NYPD's liaison to the Met at the time, was briefed on this tactic with other senior British officers, he offered serious reservations about its effectiveness. As an American cop, Greenberg had far more experience with firearms than his Met counterparts, and had even used his service weapon in the line of duty. During the meeting, he asked, "'So, has anybody in the British police ever shot anybody?' And they're all looking at me like I had four fucking heads." He pressed further. "'Has anybody in this room ever seen what happens after someone gets shot on the street?'" Greenberg knew the pandemonium that could erupt after cops killed a suspect on the street without warning. The briefers insisted that "after we shoot the guy in the head, we're going to flood the area with police officers with baseball caps that say 'Police' on them."[5] Such was the totality of the plan.

On 7/7 the head of the Met's Special Branch, Janet Williams, was in Washington DC for routine meetings with her American counterparts. By being in the United States, she helped bring the British network directly into the American law enforcement and intelligence communities face-to-face, cop-to-cop, in real time.[6] The silver-haired, square-jawed, mafia-fighting FBI director Robert Mueller dropped into London for a personal briefing and to provide high-level American assistance in the days following the attack. Andy Hayman, who ran the Met's SO15, recalled the men on Mueller's security team were so large that they all couldn't quite fit in Scotland Yard's elevators—Hayman spent the ride staring into one of Muller's security detail's enormous chest.[7]

Steve Dryden was appointed to lead the Met's forensic investigation, now codenamed Theseus. From his workstation on one of the upper floors of Scotland Yard, he and his team tried to make sense of the hundreds of thousands of bits of data surging in from multiple locations. This was a time-consuming, delicate operation with major political ramifications, and little room for error.

Many sets of eyes were watching Dryden. Juan Zarate at the White House noted, "We and the Brits were all over the remnants of the plot and the precursors."[8] Indeed, in the first week following the attack, Dryden received a strange request from the FBI's Met liaison. This man requested the authority to move his seat to directly behind Dryden's workspace and computer terminal to watch everything that came in—and everything Dryden did.

He told the American to bugger off.[9]

The Americans were mostly concerned about a copycat attack in the United States. New York City mayor Michael Bloomberg quickly announced the police would start searching random bags across subways in the five boroughs and the Long Island Rail Road as people entered the turnstiles. Mayors of other cities like Washington DC, Atlanta, Boston, and Salt Lake City considered this precaution but ultimately decided not to implement the costly, personnel-intensive effort.[10] These warrantless "random" searches created their own problems. While a federal court ruled they were constitutional, and the police maintained that its efforts were race- and ethnicity-neutral, New York City nonetheless settled a case in 2009 after police stopped a Brooklyn hospital manager of Kashmiri heritage twenty-one times.[11]

◆

While the investigation remained ongoing in intelligence and law enforcement spaces in both London and Washington, the British public moved on. The undamaged sections of the Underground had long since reopened to passengers. Things ambled back to the status quo. American newspapers shifted focus; a Supreme Court nomination replaced the bombing scene above the billfold of the *New York Times* and the *Washington Post*. The British broadsheets still paid attention to the investigation's particulars, as well as the softer human-interest stories, but even so, other stories quickly competed for space.

The immediate crisis over, SO15's Andy Hayman went home to Essex for a long-scheduled dental appointment.[12] He was in the chair on the morning of July 21.

Reports started filtering into police stations in a bit before 12:30 p.m.: an explosion on the Hammersmith & City line at the Shepherd's Bush station, an explosion on the Northern line at the Oval station. Several minutes later, around 12:45 p.m., there was another report of an explosion on the Victoria line at Warren Street. About an hour later, while the Underground was shuttered for the second time in as many weeks, there were reports of an explosion on a bus in East London.

The police and security services were in the dark, again. The fearsome global counterterrorism capabilities of the Western world had again failed to catch an al Qaeda cell in a European capital. Not anticipating a follow-up attack fourteen days later indicated a failure to learn the lessons from the Spanish experience. In April 2004, less than a month after the Madrid bombings, operatives from the same network had tried to destroy a train using explosives similar to the March attack. They left a bag with a cable and explosives on a rail line near Seville. Thankfully, they botched the job.[13]

◆

On the ninth floor of an unremarkable cement edifice in an unexceptional suburb existed a nondescript, one-bedroom council flat. 58 Curtis House, near the train tracks and North Circular ring road, and catty-corner to a primary school, served as the unassuming workshop with a nefarious purpose. This was where Muktar Said Ibrahim, with his confederates Ramzi Mohamed, Yassin Omar, Hussain Osman, and "Manfo Kwaku Asiedu" (an alias) decided to build their bombs.

Ibrahim learned his bombmaking skills in similar camps as the 7/7 bombers, using the same chemical precursors, and likely the same design. After his two friends had accidentally killed themselves, Ibrahim kept working to perfect his skills before leaving from Pakistan when his tourist visa ran out. Unlike Sidique Khan and Tanweer, who had been mentored by Marwan al-Suri, another "brother" in the camps taught Ibrahim the craft.[14]

Their bombs consisted of concentrated hydrogen peroxide mixed with chapati flour that would burn and explode when ignited by a detonator. A detonator could be made, as Ibrahim had learned in the mountains, from the volatile TATP chemical compound by mixing hydrogen peroxide with acetone. Both items could be distilled from paint thinners.[15]

Ibrahim and his cell first placed the chemical/chapati flour mix, now a grayish, unstable sludge, into a plastic tub and then put into a rucksack. It weighed about eleven to thirteen pounds. They inserted five grams of TATP into a tube, the curled cover of an A4 notebook that they sealed with tape. The men then took a flashlight bulb and taped it into the base of the tube. Stringing two thirty-inch wires, they attached them to the plastic tub. Ibrahim carefully punctured the bulb's glass near the metal rim; he then placed a small amount of TATP within the bulb itself so that it would touch the filament. Finally, Ibrahim hooked up the wires to a 9 volt battery with a snap connector, so when it was time, the wires would heat the TATP, making it explode within the glass bulb. This reaction would set off the rest of the TATP within the tube, thereby setting off the rest of the charge.

To increase the bombs' lethality, the plotters taped a large number of nuts, screws, washers, and other metal objects to the top of the tub so they would fragment and kill anyone who didn't perish in the explosion itself. Slitting the backpacks, they ran the wires from within the bags and into their clothes. Then each wearer could use the snap connector to bring the wires together, complete the circuit, and set off his bomb. The victims wouldn't see anything and even if they did, they'd be dead before they could stop him.[16]

Ibrahim was paranoid someone was watching him; he shaved his beard after coming home and was worried all the time, according to his housemate.[17] He knew that Rashid Rauf and Abu Ubaydah had his martyrdom video that he had recorded before leaving Pakistan, but didn't know what was happening with it.[18] It was a piece of evidence for a crime not yet committed, and it was in the hands of strangers. Furthermore, as Sidique Khan came to independently realize, building bombs in Britain was more challenging than building them in the tribal areas of Pakistan. The altitude was different, as were the dangers from the police and the intelligence services.

Without consistent contact, the cell at Curtis House appeared to be an independent operation from the 7/7 attack. Rauf left the final targeting decisions in the hands of his men on the ground. Ultimately, all Rauf could do was wind up his toy soldiers, point them in a general direction, and hope for the best. Ibrahim and his cell nonetheless decided a sequel to the successful martyrdom operation was the best bet for a big bang. They even planned a bus bombing. What they didn't know at the time was that the only reason why Hasib Hussain didn't blow up in the Underground was because of a faulty battery, which he fixed before striking a bus.

July 21 was a Thursday. Late that morning, Ibrahim, Ramzi Mohamed, and Yassin Omar left Mohamed's no. 14 flat in Block K of the Peabody Estate in Dalgarno Gardens and squeezed into Mohamed's tiny blue Fiat Punto with their rucksacks full of explosives. The trio drove south, past Kensington Palace and Hyde Park, and parked on the other side of the river, near the tube station in Stockwell.

Mohamed then called Hussain Osman and Manfo Asiedu, idling at a grassy treelined area named Little Wormwood Scrubs. They were trying to synchronize their efforts by having bombs arrive from both the north and south of London. On his own, Osman walked the twenty-five minutes to the Westbourne Park station, which serviced both the Circle line as well as the Hammersmith & City line, which had been hit two weeks earlier.[19]

Ibrahim, Omar, and Mohamed split up, although they each entered the Stockwell station around the same the time. Ibrahim decided to take the Northern line for his terminal ride. Omar headed to Victoria, and Mohamed, who cheekily wore a shirt with "New York" emblazoned on the front, stepped on the Northern line headed toward the urban core.

Ibrahim headed toward the City, exiting at Bank station. He then alighted upon the no. 26 bus, and, like his predecessor, took a spot on the top deck. Sometime after one in the afternoon, as the bus passed the intersection of Shoreditch High Street and Hackney Road, he snapped the connector into place.[20]

Bang—fizz.

It was as if a large firecracker had gone off in his backpack. It was loud and messy, but no fire, metal, or death. The TATP detonator had indeed fired, but the main charge hadn't. The windows on the upper deck blew out from the pressure, and the backpack had ripped open and was now oozing pungent yellowish goop; the hydrogen peroxide was dribbling all over the bus floor.[21] But there was no large explosion. Ibrahim was surprised to realize that he wasn't in heaven, but still sitting on public transport on Earth surrounded by stunned, increasingly terrified, and finally enraged passengers all around him. Ibrahim should've paid more attention to his lessons in Pakistan.

He fled from the bus.

On the Northern train headed toward the City, Mohamed readied to deploy his charge. While in the tunnel, barreling toward the Oval stop, he noticed a woman sitting with a young child in a stroller. He thought about it for a second, then positioned his rucksack laden with explosive and shrapnel in their direction so they would absorb the blast's full impact. He then clicked his detonator into place.[22]

It fizzled.

In the panic that ensued, Mohamed got off at Oval and fled, yelling, "This is wrong, this is wrong!"[23] He headed toward Brixton and down a number of side streets. Along the way, he dumped his New York shirt, as well as the battery and connector.

As the Victoria line train approached the Warren Street station, Omar, like his compatriots, snapped his connector into place. A foul-smelling liquid began to ooze from the hole from the backpack and splashed over the floor of the car.[24] In the confusion, he too ran.

Meanwhile, Osman had entered the Westbourne Park station, where he took a Hammersmith & City line train, headed toward Hammersmith along the River Thames. In this area, the tracks ran above ground, and sunny West London passed by. On a train trestle between Latimer Road and Shepherd's Bush stations, he detonated his explosives.[25] His bomb too was a dud, and he only heard a large crack and then nothing more. His fellow passengers stared at him, eventually realizing that this man had just tried to murder them all.

In the minute or so that it took the train to pull into the Shepherd's Bush station, Osman squeezed between the steel and fiberglass C-Stock carriage—poetically forged in Rashid Rauf's neighborhood factory in Washwood Heath—and jumped onto the tracks. He then plunged into the backyard of a private house, hurting himself in the thigh. He ditched his wires in the garden, climbed into an open window, went out the front door, and headed north. A bystander on the street saw this strange man running around and started chasing him, but Osman managed to give him the slip.

Osman then boarded a bus traveling south to Wandsworth, south of the Thames. From there, he called his partner Yeshi Girma and her brother Esayas, who gave him a lift to the beachside city of Brighton.[26]

Esayas provided Osman a new SIM card for his mobile, which he used to phone Mohamed several times over the next day, unintentionally creating digital breadcrumbs for the police to eventually follow.

Manfo Asiedu, the fifth bomber, lost his nerve to kill. Once his coconspirators left him alone with his thoughts within Dalgarno Gardens, he yanked the battery out of his bomb, rendering it theoretically inert, and then dumped it in a wooded area. Both his rucksack and battery were found a few days later. He went to the police four days afterward and spun an incoherent fable about how he wanted to assist in the investigation. The cops eventually placed him under arrest.

◆

The largest manhunt in modern British history was on. As far as the police and MI5 knew, the suicide cell was regrouping and planning another strike. Everyone knew how high the stakes were to locate and neutralize them in an effort hurriedly termed Operation Vivace. Echoes of 7/7, which had only happened two weeks earlier, played through everyone's mind. Prime Minister Blair oversaw the government's emergency planning committee in the Cabinet Office Briefing Rooms (COBR) at 70 Whitehall.

By two in the afternoon of the twenty-first, the police sent experts down into the Underground to test for signs of chemical, biological, radiological, and nuclear material. By 3 p.m., the broader public was asked for help in the investigation; ports, airports, and police forces around the country were put on alert.[27] The Met deployed all of its Automatic Number Plate Recognition (ANPR) vehicles to collect intelligence on cars and trucks across the region, although the force had little idea which of the two-plus million vehicles on London's tens of thousands of streets, alleys, and squares were relevant to the hunt.[28] At Shepherd's Bush, a large crane removed the stricken car from the aboveground tracks and brought it to a secure facility for further examination.

The police were naturally jittery after the second coordinated suicide attack on London's transportation in two weeks. At one point, New Scotland Yard was locked down for half an hour because there was concern that a suicide bomber was in the neighborhood.[29] When someone reported a man with wires protruding from his jacket, armed response stormed University College Hospital near the Warren Street tube station. It turned out to be a false alarm.[30] Another local police unit spotted a man carrying a backpack and clad all in black walking toward the prime minister's Downing Street residence. In public and at gunpoint, the cops surrounded the man and forced him to remove his bag and place his face down onto the street. They cuffed him and took him away. It was another false alarm.[31]

◆

Many Londoners took this latest brush with carnage in stride. One such resident was a sharply dressed computer programmer named James Hutton, who had recently moved to the Shepherd's Bush area from Melbourne. Hutton lived with a group of Australians in a redbrick terraced house on Pennard Road, around the corner from the station. He was at his office building commodities-trading software when the news of the attack began to circulate. Seeing the news on his screen, Hutton walked to his colleague's desk and muttered an expletive. His colleague nodded silently. After the initial shock subsided and it was apparent nobody had been seriously hurt, everyone returned to their desks; the company's software wasn't going to write itself.

Hutton was not alone in moving along. The FTSE never shut down, closing 6.4 points higher that day than it had when it opened that morning. Closed temporarily, the Northern and Victoria lines opened the day after the bungled suicide strike.

When Hutton returned home later that evening, he discovered the police had cordoned off his street because it ran parallel to the tracks that had been attacked several hours beforehand. Hutton and his Australian flatmates, now unable to access their home, found themselves drawn to an impromptu street party nearby. Just outside of the security cordon, a large man with dreadlocks stood astride the roof of a large white van pumping out bass beats. The neighbors, all facing similar obstacles, were out dancing. Pints of beer magically appeared. The mood was festive, fun, and felt exactly right to Hutton—a defiant middle finger to the terrorists. Around one in the morning, the police gave the all-clear and the partiers returned home. The next morning Hutton woke to a uniformed officer stationed outside his house when he left for work. He thanked the cop for his service.[32]

◆

It was not all street parties and festivities in London. In a tragic series of cascading errors and misinterpreted intelligence, British cops operating under Kratos rules killed a twenty-seven-year-old electrician named Jean Charles de Menezes a day later, mistaking him for a suicide bomber on the Underground. Per the guidelines, armed police shot him point-blank seven times in the head and once in the shoulder as he entered a Northern train at the Stockwell tube station.[33] What made little sense was the suspect they were searching for was dark-skinned and from East Africa, but de Menezes was light-skinned and from Brazil. The police on the scene likely knew within seconds that they had gunned down the wrong person. Now the Met, already dealing with a massive manhunt, had the killing of an innocent to handle. It was a tragedy for the victim and his family, and a public relations disaster for the authorities.

◆

Following the botched attack, the trolls and thugs came out to wreak havoc. Someone tried to burn down the home of Germaine Lindsay— the 7/7 bomber who struck the Piccadilly line—in Buckinghamshire. On the morning of July 22, someone called the East London Mosque, one of the largest mosques in Europe. A receptionist picked up.

"Is that the East London mosque?" It was a calm, male voice with an English accent.

The receptionist responded, "Yes."

"There's a bomb in your building; you have half an hour to evacuate."

At the adjoining the London Muslim Centre, a hundred children were studying; they had to flee for their lives. It turned out to be a hoax, just like the sixteen other threatening calls the mosque had received since the 7/7 attacks.[34] Five other mosques, as well as two Sikh gurdwaras, were also vandalized throughout the country in the days following the botched operation.[35]

Back at Thames House, MI5 deputy director Jonathan Evans recalled a feeling of mounting frustration beginning to permeate the senior staff. Their robust security apparatus had failed them twice in two weeks. "We were already feeling under the cosh and wondered, 'Have they got wave after wave to throw at us?'"[36] These cells operated completely under the noses of everyone who prided themselves on keeping their home and hearth safe. "With new threat intelligence each week, we asked ourselves, 'Can we cope?'" Evans mused. More ominously: "Are we running out of troops?"[37]

◆

The failed suicide bomber Hussain Osman, also known as "Hamdi Isaac," fled London after jumping from the train and made his way to Brighton on the coast. Inexplicably, he left Brighton on the twenty-third and returned to the capital via train. It was strange behavior on his part; he was meandering back into the lion's den after barely escaping it. At that point, the police had released the first grainy CCTV photos of the would-be killers on television and in the newspapers; every cop in Britain was looking for him, as were the American and other European intelligence services. Still, his curiosity about the fate of the others in his cell must've gotten the better of him, as he called one of the other failed bombers to talk about what had transpired. He also called his girlfriend's sister while on the train.[38]

By chance, he saw an acquaintance, twenty-three-year-old Ismael Abdurahman, waiting for a train at the Clapham Junction railway station after work.[39] The two men hadn't seen each other in several years. After hugging, they both took the train headed toward Vauxhall. When Abdulrahman arrived at his station, Osman said he was getting off as well since he had to tell him something important. As the two men walked under the tracks and through the then-seedy Vauxhall Pleasure Gardens, Osman confided that he was in trouble with the police. He said, almost sheepishly, that he had stolen some money and the cops were looking for him. Could he help an old friend?

They arrived at Abdurahman's flat, a squat dark-brown brick edifice by the tracks; once inside, Osman flipped on the television. The top story on the news was naturally the attempted bombing the day before. As the announcer discussed the early rough sketches and CCTV images of the suspects, Osman insisted the people involved were "good men." When the television flashed to the fourth photograph, Osman pointed to the screen and exclaimed, "That's me!"[40]

His friend didn't believe him at first, but Osman insisted the grainy black-and-white screenshot was indeed him. He showed Abdurahman the injury he sustained on his thigh during his escape from the train. On and on Osman went, discussing the justification for striking public transport.[41] From his belongings, he produced the *Daily Star* tabloid to show his friend; there, he revealed the identity of the other three bombers. Osman informed his increasingly bewildered and scared friend that there were supposed to be five bombs, not four.

Abdurahman inexplicably didn't inform the police. It was never clear whether he was paralyzed from fear or sympathetic to Osman's cause. Regardless of his feelings, Abdurahman did nothing, instead giving Osman a key to the apartment so he could go out to obtain some money. He also lent him clothing.[42] Osman spent two days at his flat, during which he told Abdurahman about how they prepared the bombs, and about the videos that were to be released once the operation was complete. Meanwhile, Abdurahman continued to go to work as an administrative assistant at a solicitor's office.

In the morning of Tuesday, July 26, as Abdurahman was readying for work, Osman informed his host that he was going to travel to Paris. They left the flat together around eight in the morning and walked to a bus stop. Osman took the bus headed to Waterloo station; Abdurahman returned home. About an hour later, Osman called to report that he was Paris-bound on the Eurostar. He had taken the passport of one of his brothers, Abdul Waxid Sherif, so he could easily evade security, just in case.[43] Abdurahman, now realizing what a terrifying situation he had just been in, immediately shut off his phone. Osman called him again but received no answer.[44]

The police had already begun to unravel the conspiracy. Based on their ongoing investigation, they sent an undercover surveillance officer to Abdurahman's area. On the morning of the twenty-sixth, now five days after the attack, CCTV recorded the two men ambling toward a bus stop. Eventually the police determined Osman was one of the bombers, but how was Abdurahman connected to him? They dropped by his flat after he returned from work the next day and brought him to the Kennington Road Police Station, near the Imperial War Museum.[45]

There were sticky questions about why Abdurahman hadn't turned Osman in immediately to the authorities—and why he had sheltered, fed, clothed, and accompanied him. It didn't help Abdurahman's case when the police produced CCTV footage of him meeting with Whabi Mohamed, the brother of the man who tried to blow up a Northern line train, near Vauxhall Station. The footage showed Abdurahman giving a bag to the brother that contained a digital camera and an envelope containing a suicide note.[46] The two interviewing officers, Detective Constables Vernon and Stewart, eventually arrested him on July 28.[47] The police charged him on August 3 with assisting Osman's escape and failing to disclose information after the bombings. In 2008 he was sentenced to ten years imprisonment for his role, although the sentence was reduced to eight upon appeal. He was released in 2011.

From Paris, Osman took a train to Rome, where another one of his brothers sheltered him. Osman tried a few more times to call Abdurahman. This sense of obligation led to his undoing; since he used the same mobile phone continuously to connect with Abdurahman, police were able to trace Osman with almost pinpoint accuracy.[48] By the next day, Abdurahman was cooperating with the police, who handed the case over to their Italian counterparts. Italian police arrested Osman in Rome on Friday, July 29.

◆

After fleeing the tube, another failed bomber, Yassin Omar, contacted his seventeen-year-old fiancée Fardoza Abdullahi for help—they had only been engaged four days prior and she was already pregnant, though they didn't know it at the time.[49] The next day, Friday the twenty-second, the pair made their way to Golder's Green Coach station in the northwest of the city; he was covered in a head-to-toe burka in order to mask his identity. Unlike Osman, he fled north to Birmingham, where he thought he could hide. But the police, who were tracking his mobile phone, were not far behind.

Omar's family was naturally distressed because his face was plastered all over the television and the internet. They had no idea that his fiancée had already deposited him at the bus station and that he was headed north into the West Midlands.[50]

Five days later, armed police bashed in a door around 5:15 in the morning and found the hapless Omar standing in the bathtub, fully clothed, with a backpack.[51] The officers thought he might try to detonate some hidden explosives, so they fired a taser into his chest and forcibly removed the bag. They took the stunned Omar and bundled him into the waiting police van.

◆

Muktar Said Ibrahim had spent significant effort training to build explosives in Pakistan, gathering a cell of men of East African heritage, collecting bombmaking components throughout metro London, and preparing his team for deployment. Then the operation fell apart literally at the last moment.

The cell's primary mistake was that its hydrogen peroxide was concentrated to only 58 percent, not the 70 percent-plus necessary to finish the job. The fifteen grams of TATP blew up—creating the series of bangs across London—but didn't set off the intended larger explosions.[52] Maybe it wasn't Ibrahim's fault, since it was difficult to adapt the plan for the summery sea-level environment and determine the exact concentration without specialized instruments or a confident guiding hand.

Rashid Rauf's, for example.

Still, in the early days of the investigation, the police didn't know who the cell's ringleader was. No matter: Muktar Said Ibrahim's parents recognized their son on television, and then called the police. By the afternoon of July 29, now a week after the botched operation, Ibrahim and Ramzi Mohamed were back at Mohamed's place in Dalgarno Gardens. They hadn't gone far or tried to escape the country. They had no plan, nor had they developed one in the eight days since their bungled attack. It was also the final meeting point for the conspirators, and a short walk to Little Wormwood Scrubs, where one of them had dumped his explosives.

Police were concerned that the two men might try to blow themselves up as law enforcement approached the front door of flat no. 14. This wouldn't have been without precedent, as the 2004 Spanish train bombers had prepped for similar circumstances in the Madrid suburb of Leganés. When the Spanish special police unit stormed the apartment after a siege, the cell set off explosives, killing police officer Javier Torronteras as well as the cell's members.[53] Vandals later desecrated the officer's grave, dug up his coffin, and set his corpse on fire.[54]

In Dalgarno Gardens, the streets were sealed off, and helicopters circled overhead. Men in body armor and balaclavas entered the security cordon. Snipers took up positions around the property. In the intervening time, the media had been tipped off to the siege. Television crews and reporters appeared upon the scene, as well as dozens of curious onlookers beyond the barricades. The midday operation was broadcasting into millions of televisions in Britain and around the world.

The British police learned from their Spanish counterparts' experience. They told Ibrahim and Mohamed to come out with their hands up.

"Come out, this is the police!"

Nothing.

They tried again: "Mohamed, come out with your hands up!"

Nothing.

"Why won't you come out?"

Finally, a reply from inside. "I'm scared," said a man's voice. "How do I know you won't shoot me?" It wasn't clear whether it was Ibrahim or Mohamed responding to the police.

According to a witness who later recounted the conversation, a cop replied, "That was a mistake."[55] Everyone knew what that meant: the accidental killing of Jean Charles de Menezes on the tube had occurred the previous week, and it was still all over the news.

Meanwhile, by 12:10 p.m., a Metropolitan Police firearms commander, codenamed Whiskey Alpha, led a team to the front of the flat and blew the door off of its hinges. Everyone wanted Ibrahim and Mohamed to surrender peacefully, but the team was trained and capable of using maximum force if required.[56] There was little information about the flat itself, and there was concern the rooms might be wired for detonation. And the suspects had again gone silent. Police were yelling at them from both the from and rear of the apartment, but neither Ibrahim nor Mohamed were responding.[57] The police kept trying, but warning them: don't come out with any clothes on, since the cops assumed they may try to conduct a suicide attack on the officers themselves.

To compel compliance, the police fired a nonlethal cs gas canister into the front window of the small flat around 12:37, a half hour after the door was removed. Still nothing. They fired another canister. By 1:34 p.m. the police put another cs canister into the back of the flat, through the balcony.

That did the trick. Three minutes later, Ibrahim emerged and then Mohamed, stripped down to his underpants, with their hands up into blue skies of summery London. They had inhaled the gas; their reactions were caught on camera and broadcast all over the world. The masked police, guns drawn, forced the seminaked, spitting men into white evidence suits and hustled them away.

The siege was over. The suspects were taken down successfully, with no injuries. The *Sun* tabloid the next day splashed a photo on its front page of the bare-chested, confused-looking Ibrahim with the all-caps headline, "GOT THE BASTARDS."

The bombs of July ultimately didn't have the impact that Rashid Rauf and his colleagues in Pakistan had hoped for. They needed to come up with a much bigger plan. Something that would kill more people and would shake the infidels to their roots.

◆

On October 5, 2005, the first cabinet minister to brief the prime minister in the hour after the bombings, British home secretary Charles Clarke, appeared on the *Charlie Rose* television show to discuss what he had learned.[58] Sporting a billowy pinstripe suit with a clashing purple striped shirt, Charlie Rose introduced the home secretary, another rumpled, middle-aged man in an ill-fitting blazer. Neither seemed to have successfully combed their hair for television. As they sat together around a well-worn circular table on a blackened set, the home secretary didn't mince words. "What we know now is that there were at least four people who actually committed the explosions themselves," Clarke said. "They were people who were British, who were brought into this terrible, nihilistic act by a set of events which we don't fully understand. Some of them traveled abroad to countries far away. That they planned it. They prepared it beforehand. They did a trial run a few weeks before they actually did the thing itself. At least one of them felt so strongly about it that he prepared a video explaining his hostility to everything we stand for and why he did it."

Rose said, "Mmmhmm."

Clarke continued, "There's a massive trail of forensics and also of telecommunications networks, which we have still not bottomed out, of exactly what were the national relations that existed, and how did that operate. And there's a lot of issues still to go. It was deeply shocking to people who knew them, their families, their friends, because—"

Rose interjected: "It was a stunning thing to have these people say."

"It was extraordinary. It wasn't simply that it was surprising that they were British-born. That was surprising to some. But it's obvious to even the families and indeed the wider communities of people who knew them that they weren't people who people thought were likely to commit this kind of act."

"Middle class?"

"Middle class, a bit less well off than that, but basically well-educated, not coming to it from poverty."

"And the rage wasn't born out of poverty."

"No, that's right, and I think it's the same if you look at 9/11 and look at other events . . . You're talking about an alienation, however you describe it, from our form of society, which took them down certain routes."

Pointing at his guest across the table, Rose countered, "Alienation influenced by what? By certain clerics? By what?"

Clarke offered a philosophical perspective: "I describe it as firstly a nihilism, rather like the late nineteenth century, people who wanted to destroy all the things about our society, whether it's democracy, free media, et cetera. Also then almost like some of those cults that we know about of people who got drawn into this destructive kind of force. Now, we don't know the precise inferences on these people. You have to say that there are people about, clerics of various kinds, who seduce people towards that kind of action. And we're trying to take action to deal with that."

8

The Rosewater Solution

Rashid Rauf was in the tribal areas of Pakistan on July 21, with limited connectivity to the outside world. Only after Ibrahim's name percolated through the media did he realize it was his crew of East Africans who had tried, and failed, to devastate London's transport system.[1]

Rauf knew his fingerprints on the plot would soon be discovered; he had now orchestrated two separate operations in Britain. With Ibrahim and his cell in custody—unlike Mohammad Sidique Khan and his colleagues—someone might mention his name. Despite his precautions, Rauf was raising his profile considerably, and someone was likely to tie these activities back to him.

Notoriety had a steep price. Senior al Qaeda members were increasingly being found, fixed, and finished, including his friend and mentor Amjad Farooqi, whom Pakistani police had killed the year before. The head of al Qaeda's external operations, Abu Faraj al-Libi, was in American custody, en route to Guantanamo Bay. KSM was likewise detained in a black site.

More importantly for Rauf, the July events and capture of Ibrahim's cell would generate new hurdles for future operatives trying to procure the basic bomb precursors. He rightly figured the police would be on the lookout for large purchases of hydrogen peroxide. Western operatives would have to be more careful about buying these chemicals.

They'd have to buy in much smaller quantities, so as not to attract too much attention.

Rauf, Abu Ubaydah, and others knew they would have to change their game plan. They surmised Ibrahim was confessing in police custody. They were now concerned the British and the Americans would be on the lookout for people transiting to and from Pakistan, and their international network of spies and informants would let them know who was where. Any new recruits looking to sign up with the jihadis would have to come to Pakistan, receive the training, and then swiftly leave. "We would now send back brothers quickly," Rauf wrote, "and not keep them for a long time."[2] Rauf still retained the British passports of Shakeel Ismail and Rizwan Majid, who had blown themselves to pieces in a training camp the year before, at his home in Bahawalpur.[3] Maybe those would come in handy.

Jihadist groups had little problem sourcing precursor chemicals inside Pakistan through their own networks. They could then build these explosives far away from nosy neighbors concerned about acrid smells and the occasional explosive mishap. But they knew it was far more difficult to do so in a Western city.

Rauf and al Qaeda's technical operatives therefore developed a novel solution: why not send concentrated hydrogen peroxide to their cells in the West via the mail? He and his colleagues could purify the explosive chemicals to the right percentage, thereby avoiding the error that condemned Ibrahim and his men to spend their lives in prison. They could then ship the premade product overseas marked in bottles marked as "rosewater," a common product throughout South Asia.[4]

The next hurdle for Rauf and his colleagues was to move these rosewater bottles into onto an airplane without detection. He personally researched the machines used in airports to detect explosives. Solid explosives were relatively easy to identify in international airports; they showed up as something nefarious and would set off alarms. But, according to Rauf's research, liquids were far easier to smuggle onto airplanes.

And then the light bulb went on.

"It would be possible to take concentrated hydrogen peroxide on board," Rauf later surmised. And so "the thought came to our mind: would it be possible to detonate the hydrogen aboard an airplane?"[5]

◆

Abdulla Ahmed Ali and Assad Sarwar had missed the July explosions in their hometown by a matter of weeks and experienced the aftermath like most people—on television and on the internet. Their disappointment palpable, they understood the shortcomings of the concentrated hydrogen peroxide explosive/TATP detonator mechanism. They were nevertheless being trained—like Mohammad Sidique Khan, Shehzad Tanweer, Muktar Ibrahim before them—in the dark arts of bombmaking.

◆

On October 8, 2005, at 8:50 in the morning, a sudden, abrupt movement deep in the earth between the Indian and Eurasian tectonic plates caused a massive 7.6 magnitude earthquake. Its epicenter was centered several miles north of the city of Muzaffarabad, the capital of Azad Kashmir in Pakistan. This densely populated area was smashed to pieces. Hundreds of thousands of buildings, including many government facilities, collapsed.[6] Seven thousand schools were destroyed; thousands of children were crushed at their desks. Rock and mud swallowed whole villages. Bridges, roads, houses, and people disappeared under the debris. Government estimates put fatalities between seventy-five to one hundred thousand people. Millions were suddenly homeless, during the holy month of Ramadan.

The impact was felt throughout the region. In Islamabad, one of the capital's first modern high-rise residences, the ten-story Margalla Towers, collapsed, killing seventy.[7]

The earthquake also set off devastating landslides throughout the region. Eighty million cubic meters of earth and rocky debris fell from a mountainside, traveled almost a mile downward, killed everything in its path, and dammed two tributaries of the Jhelum.[8] A thousand people died this way, swallowed by rivers of mud and rubble.[9] The only access road into Panjakot in the Neelum River Valley, the earthquake's epicenter, was washed away for forty-seven days. In the mountains of Kashmir and beyond, the freezing temperatures then killed untold scores more in the days and weeks ahead across the merciless highlands; the subsequent sickness felled many more.

Despite the massive natural disaster in one of the most militarized places on earth, the Pakistani military failed to competently assist the millions of people digging through tons of rubble to save their loved ones. The military, the real center of coercive power in Pakistan, prioritized the rescue and evacuation of its own personnel.[10] The Pakistanis even spurned an offer of Indian Army helicopters—critical machinery that would have doubled the search-and-rescue capacity to reach rural, roadless areas—unless Pakistani pilots flew them.[11]

Compounding this tragedy, the government of Pakistan delegated much of the responsibility to assist the Kashmiris to the "charitable" wings of militant groups. LeT played an active role in relief efforts in and around Muzaffarabad, running a field hospital that reportedly performed twenty operations a day.[12] The militant organization also provided the on-the-ground manpower to distribute food and goods, working with international organizations such as the World Food Programme, the World Health Organization, the United Nations Children's Fund, and the Red Cross. It was even helping uniformed NATO troops in Pakistan cross otherwise impassable rivers.[13] These groups set up nationwide appeals for funds to help the suffering people of Kashmir and made quite a bit of money doing so. Some of that money, earmarked by regular Pakistanis to help their fellow countrymen, likely found its way back into extremist activities.

American troops were there too. The U.S. military deployed a c-17 transport aircraft to Islamabad within forty-eight hours, with ninety thousand pounds of medicine, food, water, and blankets. At one point, twelve hundred U.S. troops were providing much-needed aid in Pakistan—alongside groups like the al-Rasheed Trust, which the United Nations noted raised money for JeM and al Qaeda.[14] Rashid Rauf's compatriots in the now-officially-banned JeM paused cross-border suicide attacks into India-controlled Kashmir in order to provide food, water, and medicine to stricken areas. They also planned to build or rebuild schools and mosques in shattered villages, thereby extending their reach and indoctrinating the students with their ideology.

The prime minister of devastated Azad Kashmir had LeT's leader, Hafiz Saeed, come to his official residence in Muzaffarabad to personally thank him for his organization's assistance. Later on, the prime minister donated one hundred thousand rupees from his own pocket to the organization.[15]

LeT and others jihadist groups used their efforts to plant further roots in the region. They opened militant camps in and around the city, funneled 75 percent of their fighters through training there, and sent them on to fight and die in Kashmir and elsewhere.[16] These jihadist groups also likely recruited children orphaned by the earthquake and its aftereffects to serve as their new generation of fighters.

◆

During the maelstrom of grief and misery brought on by the earthquake, Abdulla Ahmed Ali was at his family's home in the city of Jhelum, 150 miles south of the quake's epicenter. The ground moved even there. He didn't know if the training camps had been struck, but given his previous background in aid work on the Afghan border, he felt he had to help. He linked up with the Pakistan Islamic Medical Association, a wing of another jihadist outfit the ISI helped found to fight India in Jammu and Kashmir. The group was even rumored to have provided medical assistance and escape routes to al Qaeda operatives following the 9/11 attacks.[17]

Ali later claimed it was his experience assisting during the earthquake relief efforts that curdled his mind toward America and Britain, that U.S. and British foreign policy were the real roots of all the Muslim world's agony.[18] His feelings were a confused mishmash of fact and falsehood, legitimate grievances about Iraq and Afghanistan vying with fanciful flights of conspiracy. But this was untrue, as he had been meaning to wage jihad for a very long time beforehand.

Back home in Walthamstow, Ali's wife Cossor went into labor on December 4, 2005, and brought a healthy, sweet baby boy into the world. It was a blessing, given the problems she'd had in the recent past with carrying a child to term. But she was on her own in the hospital, because her husband wasn't there.

He was in Pakistan with his real family.

9

Glimmers

January 19, 2006. The most hunted man in the world broke the silence that he had kept for over a year. It was just an audio recording, but the voice was unmistakably his: "My message to you is about the wars in Iraq and Afghanistan and how to end them," he said. "I did not intend to speak to you about this because this issue has already been decided. Only metal breaks metal, and our situation, thank God, is only getting better and better, while your situation is the opposite of that."

Osama bin Laden wanted to remind the world he was still in charge of the global jihad. He was sanguine about his organization's efforts to strike deep into the heart of the West: "The mujahideen, with God's grace, have managed repeatedly to penetrate all security measures adopted by the unjust allied countries." Specifically, bin Laden offered, "The proof of that is the explosions you have seen in the capitals of the European nations who are in this aggressive coalition. The delay in similar operations happening in America has not been because of the failure to break through your security measures."

Finally, he ended on an ominous note. "The operations are under preparation and you will see them in your homes the minute they are through, with God's permission."[1]

He only offered glimmers of information, and nothing concrete. In the United States, intelligence analysts weighed whether it was a direct message that something big was underway, or merely the posturing of a media-savvy adversary. Bin Laden's message was certainly suggestive and "the delay in similar operations" was a concerning phrase.

An intelligence officer's first obligation is a "duty to warn." The CIA's analysts, sitting in bland cubes in windowless Sensitive Compartmented Information Facilities, drafted and submitted the first finished pieces of intelligence to the White House in an attempt to contextualize what little scraps of information they had. There was certainly reason to be concerned.

Bin Laden's recording offered encouragement to his operatives feeling mounting pressure from the West. The month before, the United States killed al Qaeda external operations chief Hamza Rabi'a, who had been developing plots in both Britain and America. The Hellfire missile that struck the house where he was staying in Miram Shah in North Waziristan now rendered him permanently incapable of executing on his vision.[2] Afterward, one Pakistani official told the press not to examine the specifics of Rabi'a death too closely, gamely noting, "Comments on media reports that it was a Predator strike would invoke sovereignty issues. Let's enjoy the fact that al Qaeda has lost another key person."[3]

Al Qaeda's external operations chiefs were often "rendered to justice" quickly. This was especially so since Pakistan deployed its gunships into the tribal areas, complementing the stepped-up U.S. missile strikes. But, with yet another external operations chief dead, others stood up, willing to take his place. There was no let up. The shadow war ground on.

◆

By the turn of the new year, President Bush and CIA director Porter Goss issued orders to "flood the zone"—to reinvigorate the hunt for bin Laden and crush al Qaeda's cells operating worldwide. At the beginning of his tenure, Goss, a former Republican congressman from Florida and chairman of the House Permanent Select Committee on Intelligence, forced out a number of senior agency officials. His underlings—derisively termed "the Gosslings"—immediately started demoting and firing other senior CIA officers, including Robert Grenier, a longtime case officer who served as both the agency's top man in Islamabad following the 9/11 attack and head of the CTC.[4]

Grenier's replacement at the CTC, "Roger," was a tall, bearded, chain-smoking workaholic convert to Islam. While "Roger's" identity has been documented in the press over the years, it will not be included here. Roger became the living embodiment of the "find-fix-finish" ethos of hunting down and killing terrorists. He basically lived in his office; his desk was occupied long after most CIA employees had gone home and the cleaning crews were buffing the hallway floors. Not one to waste time, upon confirming a plot Roger directed his officers to "smoke those motherfuckers," according to one senior agency official.[5]

There certainly was reason to be concerned. But few questions about the nascent conspiracy could be adequately answered—because the terrorists hadn't figured it out themselves.

◆

April 27, 2006, was a new moon. A young man arrived at a business park in the tidy village of St. Clears in Wales, a short drive to the home overlooking the Tâf estuary where the poet Dylan Thomas once lived. The young man, who went by Jona Lewis, entered the premises of Health Leads UK Ltd, a modest operation that specialized in homeopathic medicines and natural supplements. Lewis said he was gathering goods to open a small health food shop in the seaside English city of Bristol and needed to purchase some items to get the business off the ground.

From within his coat pocket, Lewis produced a handwritten list—tampons, panty shields, salts, sulfuric soap, and a whole host of other items. Sandwiched between the health products was something a bit off: four bottles of hydrogen peroxide at 35 percent strength, in 500 ml bottles.[6] This was about the amount of liquid found in a single-serving bottle of soda. Health Leads had four bottles in the shop for £16.75 each. The cashier helpfully placed the bottles in a series of brown cardboard tubes so they wouldn't break in the car. Lewis paid for his goods in cash and left the business park, heading back on the M4 highway.[7]

Of course, the health foods business in Bristol wasn't real, and neither was "Jona Lewis." Rather, it was the thick-faced Assad Sarwar who had concocted the identity and the fable. He told his friends he wasn't interested in carrying out a martyrdom operation himself, but he showed a knack for procurement and logistics. He surmised he would attract the authorities' attention if he bought too much hydrogen peroxide in one place without a particularly good reason, so he diversified his purchasing across multiple wholesalers. The police would much later find an identical white 500 ml bottle from Health Leads in a heavily wooded area near his home. But that wouldn't be for months.[8]

◆

While Sarwar was commandeering supplies in Wales, Ali was home in East London with his wife and infant son. He had spent the better part of six months in Pakistan and had missed the birth of his boy by a day. Still, his obligations as a father remained secondary to his primary mission.

On Rauf's instructions, Ali returned to his regular ways and tried not to create a fuss or raise the authorities' suspicions. He was to keep his dress strictly in a Western manner and not attend mosques known to espouse "radical" views. Al Qaeda's own manuals recommended its operatives to maintain a low profile in the West so as to not arouse law enforcement attention.[9] He would also see his cricketeer friend Tanvir Hussain and have him over to his home to drink tea and smoke shisha.[10]

Rauf knew public transit was passé; he wanted to dream bigger. Still, as with 7/7 and 7/21, Rauf left it to Ali to pick his possible targets. He trusted his cell to carry out the mission in the way they saw fit.[11]

During this time, Rauf and the teenage Adam Khatib were also exchanging emails. Khatib, who was using the handle "charminhardnut," had been arrested for a driving infraction in the springtime. Rauf, in code, told Khatib to get his affairs in order lest he wreck the whole operation. "What on earth gave u an idea about callin off the marriage!!" Rauf wrote, with the understanding that the word "marriage" had to do with the attack. "i would never do that . . . u dont need to wait any longer i think the wedding will be quick especially now dad is ok with it!!!!!"[12]

◆

At this point, another man entered the scene. Waheed Zaman, a scruffy, bearded student at London Metropolitan University, was the fifth of six children. He hailed from a long line of men who fought for the Crown. His great-grandfather was killed in the first World War, his grandfather served with the Indian Army in the second, and his father had worked for the army.[13] He was the president of his university's Islamic Society and a Liverpool football fan, and he held a weekend job at the world-famous Hamleys toy store in Soho. He lived in a socially conservative household on Queen's Road near the Walthamstow Cemetery. His was not a terribly cheerful home—his family had recently forced two of his older sisters into unhappy arranged marriages.[14] His sister Nagina later recalled he was "quite a caring, kind-natured individual, a 'gentle giant.'"[15]

While at university, Zaman began traveling down a dark path. He believed the Iraq war had nothing to do with Saddam Hussein or the search for weapons of mass destruction. Zaman thought it was more about securing oil fields for the United States, and to a lesser extent, for Great Britain.[16] The scandalous images of American troops mistreating Iraqi prisoners that emerged from the Abu Ghraib prison further radicalized Zaman, or so he claimed. As a Muslim, he was affected by the prisoners' nudity and humiliation. General Stanley McChrystal, the commander of the U.S. Joint Special Operations Command, knew this spark of discontent could be fanned into something much more useful for terror groups. He mused, "In my experience, we found that nearly every first-time jihadist claimed Abu Ghraib had jolted him into action."[17]

What pushed Zaman over the edge was a widely circulated letter from a "Sister Fatimah" that proliferated throughout the internet. Reportedly written by an incarcerated Iraqi woman being held at Abu Ghraib, it detailed horrible rapes, tortures, and murders occurring within the prison walls. Zaman took Sister Fatimah's words, rumored to be written in her own blood, to heart:

My mujahideen brother in the path of Allah, what can I say to you?
    I say to you: Our wombs have been filled with the children of fornication by those sons of apes and pigs who raped us. Or I could tell you that, they have defaced our bodies, spit in our faces and tore

up the little copies of al-Quran that hung around our necks . . . With me are thirteen girls, all unmarried. All have been raped before the eyes and ears of everyone. They wouldn't let us pray. They took our clothes and would not let us get dressed . . .

As I write this letter, one of the girls has committed suicide. She was savagely raped. A soldier hit her on her chest and thigh after raping her. He subjected her to unbelievable torture. She beat her head against the wall. She beat her head against the wall of the cell until she died. Until she died. For she could not take anymore, even though suicide is forbidden in Islam. But I excuse that girl. I have hope that Allah will forgive her, because He is the most Merciful of all.

Brothers, I tell you again . . .

Fear Allah!

Kill us with them so that we might be at peace.[18]

It didn't seem to matter to Zaman that the incendiary "Sister Fatimah" letter wasn't real, because it confirmed his already congealed impressions of the war. Had he looked closer, he would have noticed the letter lacked specifics, such as Sister Fatima's real name, where she was from, her tribe's name, the names of the other prisoners, descriptors of her captors, and the location of her prison within Abu Ghraib. The letter was even dated December 17, 2004, over a year after the Abu Ghraib scandal broke in the press, several months after the pictures of abuse had emerged the previous April, and months after the Pentagon study detailing the behavior had been made public.[19] It was likely crude but effective al Qaeda propaganda.

Zaman began to hang around the wrong people, who introduced him to others who shared similar beliefs. He was good friends with Ibrahim Savant and Umar Islam, with whom he chatted frequently about world events and politics. Zaman and Islam even took a local martial arts class together.[20] Rounding out the cast of characters, he knew the charismatic Ali from evenings at the mosque for Friday prayers and was friendly with Ali's two younger brothers.[21]

From these friendships, a cell would emerge.

◆

Spring turned to early summer; the blossoms in Walthamstow's cherry trees bloomed and then drifted to the pavement. Ali and Cossor's son turned six months old, almost ready to eat solid foods. By May, however, Ali and Assad Sarwar found themselves recalled to Pakistan. Sarwar had ditched his passport and put in an application for a brand new one prior to his trip; Ali used his own. This caught his wife and her family by surprise. Cossor's grandfather, Nazir Ahmed, mused, "We didn't understand what the hurry was and why he needed to go."[22]

Rauf, with Abu Ubaydah's help, had finally overcome certain technical hurdles for their explosives, and it was imperative to show his men how to use them. He also wanted Sarwar to bring him a "voice changer" in order to mask his voice on the telephone, which Sarwar obligingly purchased after his return to the UK.[23]

Around this time, British authorities began to take an unexpected interest in Ali's comings and goings. On his way to Pakistan on May 18, Ali was extensively queried at the airport about his travels abroad. He played it cool, like Muktar Ibrahim and so many others had done before him. The authorities eventually relented and allowed Ali to board his plane to South Asia. Ali nonetheless knew there was something odd about this encounter; he had never been questioned like that leaving the country before. Perhaps it was all the entry and exit stamps from Pakistan? He didn't know.

The authorities were suspicious about something, but nobody was sure whether Ali was really up to no good, or if he was just a person who went back and forth from Pakistan annually. The British and Americans didn't have access to Ali once he landed in Pakistan, and in any case he hadn't done anything that would allow local authorities to detain him once he landed in Islamabad. Thus, London sent a note to the ISI to keep tabs on Ali's comings and goings. However, the recipients of this message did not view Ali or the request as particularly important, farming it to someone down the totem pole in Islamabad. Someone else could stop Ali and check his luggage.

As luck would have had it, the Pakistanis tasked to handle Ali were friendly with his extended family. Thus, in the spirit of friendship, they tipped him off about the Pakistani spy agency's interest in his travels and then let him vanish from the airport. Ali then slipped unmolested into the tribal areas for further training.[24] Years later, when one CIA analyst who worked on this case heard how easy it was for Ali, a person of significant interest with suspected ties to al Qaeda, to flit through a major airport and shake surveillance, he exclaimed, "Oy, Pakistan!"[25]

Once Ali was safely in the camp, Rauf let them know about some bad news. Around the same time Sarwar had been buying the first of the hydrogen peroxide in Wales, a Pakistani helicopter strike blew to pieces one of Rauf's senior comrades, a soft-spoken Egyptian known as Abdulrahman al-Muhajir. The mud-brick compound he was working from was leveled; nine other people were killed.[26] Al-Muhajir had a multimillion-dollar price on his head because he had been involved in al Qaeda's bombings of the U.S. embassies in Kenya and Tanzania in 1998. More importantly to the assembled men, he ran a lab in the tribal areas where he had been experimenting with a new type of hydrogen peroxide bomb with a pepper-activated detonator.[27] That particular type of explosive now was not going to be available for use.

The cautious Rauf then briefed Ali on new communications codes for chatting with his London cell and stymying local surveillance. Rauf would now be known as "Jamil" or "Jameel" and Mohammed Gulzar was to be known as "Arif." He was trying to minimize the blowback, or at least confuse anyone who may be reading the email traffic. Around this time the email address J4mood@yahoo.com was established; the time was in GMT and the country that it claimed to use was the United States, but the IP address linked back to Islamabad. It wasn't the only one—within thirty minutes of establishing J4mood, Rauf created the address RSTUPL@yahoo.com.[28] Ali gave it a try, linking the two emails together on June 6—he sent no message, but want to ensure the emails worked.

They did.[29]

♦

Around the same time back in Britain, a new, disturbing case had emerged. Fragmentary intelligence indicated a chemical weapon was being transported from house to house throughout East London. The information suggested there might be a biological component in addition to the chemical elements, and that it could be detonated remotely.

The intelligence suggested the bomb was in a residence in a densely packed, heavily immigrant neighborhood of Forest Gate, southeast of Walthamstow.[30] The police decided to storm the property. It was on a tight residential street, which made it difficult for police vehicles to maneuver. Due to the chemical nature of the threat, the firearms team had to also put on bulky chemical, biological, radiological, and nuclear (CBRN) suits before entering the police vans. They all had learned the hard lessons of the Madrid bombing aftermath, now two years in the past; the cell could detonate after cops breached the front door in order to kill as many officers as possible.

The Met decided to take down the house at 46/48 Lansdown Road, Forest Gate in the early morning hours of June 2. The police assumed there would be few civilians on the street who would complicate the operation or alert the perpetrators. However, it slipped the planners' minds that it was a Friday morning, when many in the neighborhood would be awake heading to mosques for the morning call to prayer.[31] Around 250 officers, enough to blanket the whole small street and surrounding areas, moved in.

After securing the perimeter, the cops kicked down the flimsy front door. Police in their awkward CBRN suits entered, weapons at the ready. The eleven occupants of the house—two brothers along with their sisters, parents, and others—were fully awake. Twenty-three-year-old Mohammed Abdul Kahar bounded down the staircase, thinking burglars had broken into the family home. As he came down the stairs, a heavily suited police officer fired his weapon, striking Kahar in the shoulder. Police then handcuffed him, dragged him from the building, and placed him on the pavement.[32] Both the wounded man and his brother, Abul Koyair, were arrested and hauled to Paddington Green Police Station, the high-security facility for individuals suspected of terrorism offenses.[33]

Complicating matters, the two properties were in the middle of being renovated into one large unit, and the wall separating the two homes had been removed. This construction job had rendered the whole structure, along with the surrounding homes, unstable and unsafe. The Met thus had to evacuate the neighbors before turning the whole property upside down for the bomb. The press had caught wind of the high-profile operation and turned it into a media circus. Adding to the frenzied atmosphere, some of the officers searching the property for evidence were wearing their unfamiliar CBRN suits inside out.[34]

Over the next few days, forensic teams tore apart the building, ripped up the back garden, and emerged with bags of evidence. The two properties were stripped to their studs.

They found—nothing.

No chemical precursors like hydrogen peroxide, no explosive manuals, no biological agents. The whole operation, codenamed Volga, was a dud. It was a very embarrassing, very expensive, and very dry hole. The Met soon released the detained brothers, and eleven days later, Assistant Commissioner Andy Hayman bowed to the obvious error, publishing a statement that the police "caused disruption and inconvenience to many residents in Newham and more importantly those that reside at 46 and 48 Lansdowne [sic] Road. I apologise for the hurt that we may have caused."[35] The community was angry; hundreds of people joined a street protest two weeks after. One carried a sign "Police brutality never makes us feel safer" while another said, "How can we trust you if you see us all as terrorists?" The family of the Brazilian man killed by the police in the aftermath of 7/21 joined the protest.

♦

One person missing out on the protests was Mohammed Gulzar. He was still in South Africa.

By August 2005, Gulzar had obtained a fake South African passport under the alias "Altaf Ravat." South Africa had developed a notorious reputation during this time as a place to generate high-quality false identification papers, even passports. Radio Frequency Identification chips, commonly inserted into legitimate travel documents as safeguards against falsified documents, hadn't reached South Africa yet.

Gulzar developed this new identity, generating a MasterCard credit card with Standard Bank, which added legitimacy to his falsified papers.

Adopting his "Altaf Ravat" alias, Gulzar crossed the South African border with Botswana on August 13 at the Kopfontein border crossing, two hundred miles northwest of Johannesburg. He then returned to the South African side, a Botswanan passport stamp in the pages of his passport.

Three days later, on August 16, he used his fraudulent, but stamped, passport to apply for and receive a single-entry visa to enter Pakistan. By September 28, Gulzar/Ravat was back in Pakistan for a six-month visit.[36] He finally left Pakistan on March 21, 2006, but in the departure lounge of the Islamabad airport, he met a woman, Zora Siddique (or "Siddiqui"). She was a divorcée four years older than Gulzar. Gulzar/Ravat returned to South Africa, and Siddique flew on to Belgium.

Back in South Africa, he ditched the fake passport with the Pakistani stamp and generated another fraudulent South African passport with the same Ravat name. Repeating his success at validating his fake papers, on June 13, 2006, he drove the three and a half hours to the Oshoek-Ngwenya border crossing with Swaziland, east of Johannesburg. The border guards stamped it and he crossed the border unquestioned and unmolested, then immediately returned to the South African side.[37]

Siddique arrived in Johannesburg on June 29. Despite having met only once before, Siddique and Gulzar married the next day. The 200-rand marriage certificate indicated the bridegroom's name was "Altaf Ravat," not "Mohammed Gulzar."[38]

A few weeks later, thanks to their travel agent at Top Holidays in Pretoria, Gulzar and his new bride flew to Mauritius and spent three days and two nights at the Blue Lagoon Beach hotel, in the town of Blue Bay. It was on the breezy, less developed southern part of the island, a drop-dead gorgeous piece of real estate in the Indian Ocean.

Zorra and Gulzar took room 60 at the hotel. They checked in under her name but paid with his fake name's credit card for almost 4,200 rand. They made phone calls from their room to a UK mobile number and ordered room service.[39] Pear juice, soft drinks, and red wine—strange, given Gulzar's supposed religious missionary status and stern Islamic bent, which forbade him from drinking alcohol.[40]

After two nights in paradise, on July 18, the couple flew to London. Gulzar booked a roundtrip flight from South Africa to Mauritius, then to Great Britain, and then back to South Africa via the same route on the first of August. But he had no intention of returning to the tip of the continent.

Gulzar was going home.

10

The Dilemma

Barring an unforeseen violent weather pattern, gate delay, or airplane malfunction, a flight from Pakistan to the UK took a little over eight hours, longer if there was a stopover in Dubai or Frankfurt or Amsterdam. Over a quarter of a million British citizens made the roundtrip trek annually, mostly to visit relatives or do a little business.

As the clouds parted to reveal the verdant English expanse on June 24, Abdulla Ahmed Ali ruminated on his recent trip. It had been a productive one; he had met with Rauf to go over preparations for the operation, picked up various odds and ends, and spent quality time with the master bombmaker, Abu Ubaydah al-Masri. Abu Ubaydah's eyes had by then taken on a yellowish tint, and his face was becoming a mess of crimson, spidery blood vessels. Unbeknownst to Ali or anyone else, the bombmaker would be dead by the following December from an untreated case of Hepatitis C. Ali's visit to Pakistan would likely be his last; the operation's pieces were beginning to fall into place.

With the knowledge of explosives rattling around in his brain, he had much weighing on his mind as the wheels touched down on British soil and the plane rolled to the gate. He did his best to mask his concern as he exited the plane and headed for immigration control with the rest of the passengers. It would take about an hour, perhaps an hour and a half to clear the airport.

◆

Other people also had weighty matters on their minds during that golden hour. They had a little less than sixty minutes to determine Ali's destiny—and their own as well.

Officials in the nonpublic area of the airport quickly located Ali's baggage. Carefully opening it, they found among his dirty clothes and miscellaneous effects a large number of low-quality batteries made for the Pakistani domestic market. Strange items to bring home from South Asia, as the United Kingdom did not suffer from a shortage of batteries.

On a prior trip from Pakistan, Ali had also brought several containers of the Tang orange drink mix home to London. How the authorities knew this was a mystery, given that he had come home the previous December and no police efforts had been spun up at the time.[1] Of course, like batteries, powdered drinks were also widely available across Britain. These items, however, held the potential for havoc: the citric acid in Tang, when mixed with concentrated hydrogen peroxide, could create a devastating homemade explosive. British officials knew the 7/7 bombers used devices that were a mixture of hydrogen peroxide and flour. If properly deployed, they surmised, Tang could create a similar or larger explosion.

As Steve Dryden at the Met explained, Ali's return from Pakistan was the event that jumpstarted the police investigation.[2] It was the moment when Ali's otherwise normal-seeming behavior warranted more serious attention. Of course, someone had noticed him sometime beforehand, but the police had not yet been notified of MI5's interest. While he was now in the sights of law enforcement, it nevertheless remained unclear how he fit into Britain's larger jihadist community.

Counterterrorism is a delicate balancing act between collecting intelligence and taking decisive action. There is a mindset, particularly in the aftermath of attacks like 7/7, that upon identifying a terrorist efforts should be taken to neutralize the threat they pose. Security services fail if a suicide attacker boards the plane or arrives unscathed at an embassy checkpoint. Capturing or killing one terrorist means they'll be stopped from carrying out the next attack. The threat of death or incarceration also obliges terrorists to spend a fair amount of time, money, and effort planning for their safety instead of plotting further strikes.

Yet a tactical success may also result in a serious strategic setback. Had the authorities taken action against Ali at the airport, it may have resulted in a short-term disruption of some as-yet mysterious plot. More importantly, it would have left the rest of the conspiracy intact. Furthermore, the arbitrary use of police powers against an individual would betray the democratic ideals the police and intelligence community fight to protect, while also confirming the warped perceptions that Ali and others had of the countries in which they lived. As such, direct action would have to wait and the labor-intensive process of investigation would have to begin.

◆

In 2006, passengers flying into Heathrow encountered two lines for passport control. Marked by the large overhead yellow-and-black signs, the first line was for European Union, European Economic Area, British, and Swiss nationals; the other was for everyone else. As a UK passport holder, Ali walked across the grim industrial carpeting to the first queue, which moved much more quickly than the second. He stood there, bleary-eyed, shifting from one foot to another, absentmindedly listening to the low din of other grumbling, frazzled passengers while he waited for immigration control to call him.

At the desk, the border official examined his passport. The official was a foot and a half away from the al Qaeda operative, separated by only a desk of compressed particleboard and his computer screen. He asked a few questions, stamped his papers with a perfunctory *thunk-thunk*, and then waved him on. On to baggage pickup, customs—nothing to declare—and out into a splendid, fast-fleeting, postcard-perfect summery London day.

Ali exited Heathrow unmolested and none the wiser. Everything had been carefully reassembled in his luggage as to appear untouched. Ali and his baggage reentered Britain more or less the way they entered the plane, several thousand miles to the east. And after passing through the large sliding doors that separated the secure sections of the airport from the public area, Ali disappeared from sight.

◆

Authorities had taken a small gamble, figuring Ali was a smaller pawn in a larger chess game. In CIA National Clandestine Service director Jose Rodriguez's memoirs, he asserted, "The Brits originally learned of the plot by finding that one of the plotters had traveled from the UK to meet with a known al-Qa'ida operative in Pakistan."[3] But British authorities had questioned Ali *before* he had left for Pakistan on this trip, not afterward. Therefore, the exact tipoff that jumpstarted the investigation into Ali versus any of the other thousands of travelers on that particular route was likely from evidence discovered on the mobile phones used by other terrorists. No doubt 7/21 ringleader Muktar Said Ibrahim's phone was thoroughly examined for information about other plotters. He after all had called both Rauf in Pakistan and Ali in Britain in short order.

In a 2016 independent review of terrorism legislation presented to Parliament, one tantalizing line from the report emerged: "Bulk acquisition data enabled MI5 to identify the formerly unknown leader of a further cell in the UK."[4] Yet if this were the end of the story, American and British intelligence services would have trumpeted this as proof that large-scale data-mining helped thwart a terror plot following former CIA employee Edward Snowden's massive leak of top-secret information in mid-2013. But both London and Washington declined to do so, suggesting they were using somewhat different capabilities to direct their focus upon Ali and his friends.

◆

Two days afterward, Ali wrote an email to Rauf, noting, "It will take a few days. Then I'll start trading. I'll send you my new number as soon as I get it."

Also: "Tariq is cool. I saw him and he is ready to trade as well."[5]

Rauf replied a few days later. "Nice to know Tariq is good. Any news on your friend that was supposed to come to me?" On the same day, Assad Sarwar, who was still in Pakistan, established a hotmail.com email address, TANVMSD. Another email address, M4JLD4, was created the next day, and its user sought to contact Sarwar at the previous address. Rauf was well aware of the dangers of connecting electronically; to try to minimize this threat, he set up different email addresses to converse with different people, so if one was compromised, the others would remain operational.[6]

Sarwar responded, "I will be going home in six days. I will leave you a number once I get there." True to his word, he left Pakistan on July 7, six days after sending this email.

◆

London was in the middle of a heatwave that had settled upon the British Isles, setting records unseen since scientists began recording monthly temperatures in the year 1659. It was also abnormally bright and sunny.

Ali had very plainly started picking up supplies. On June 30, he and Tanvir Hussain went to a Maplin's Electronics store to purchase a multimeter and a 1.6 volt bulb. Ali also placed an order for three dozen light bulbs. On July 4 Ali emailed Rauf: "Listen dude, when is your mate gonna bring the projectors and the taxis to me? I got all my bits and bobs. Tell your mate to make sure the projectors and taxis are fully ready and proper I don't want my presentation messing up."[7]

"Projectors" and "taxis" were code for equipment. Like Sidique Khan before him, Ali needed some guidance from his handler in Pakistan. Also, he mentioned: "Hey, my mate half Guji one, he's up for the gig as well. Is it okay if we put him in? I believe he's ready to be promoted."

"Half Guji" referred to Tanvir Hussain, who once played cricket for the Gujerati Metropolitan Cricket League and was so proud of it that he put it on his CV.[8] He convinced the Indian players from Gujarat that he, a man of Pakistani heritage, was actually "half Guji."[9]

Ali also wrote, "My black mate said he's cool with the rehearsal, trial run." He was talking about Umar Islam. Sometimes Ali referred to the ex-Rastafarian formerly known as "Brian Young" as his "black mate,"

"Kala" (the word "black" in Urdu), and "n——," although Ali never called Umar the latter nickname to his face.[10]

Finally, the individual who provided a video camera was willing to work: "He is a top guy with experience in the field and tried doing a big job before but things did not work out."[11]

Rauf soon replied, "I will get the projectors and the taxi as soon as I can. Can you let me know if Aro want some as well."

Aro was Arafat Khan, Ali's friend from school. Rauf knew who he was, even in Pakistan. Indeed, he knew who most of these men were. He continued, "Can you let me know if Aro wants some as well. About your friend that sent the camera. Half Guji seems okay too but I will confirm and let you know. I don't think it should be a prob."[12]

Ali replied on July 5: "Half Guji is well up for it. I told him he must do X, Y, Z and he's done it straight away so he's well up for it. Ask Paps where exactly I should send my n—— for the rehearsal, which studio?"

◆

The first recorded police surveillance of Ali also occurred on that day, July 5. Unbeknownst to Ali, his return on the twenty-fourth set into motion a flurry of bureaucratic activity behind the scenes as the investigation against him began to take shape. Profiles would have been set up, warrants written, and countless briefings made.

Unlike in the movies and on television, surveillance is a rare and precious commodity that is used sparingly. Not only is it an expensive and a resource-heavy endeavor but also every opportunity must be carefully weighed against countless others. A deployment against a potential terrorist suspect may mean the same resource is unavailable to follow, say, a Russian intelligence officer meeting a contact stealing state secrets, or a criminal gang engaged in smuggling guns and narcotics. As a result, the amount of work that goes into deploying a surveillance team is significant in order to ensure maximum return. Photos of the target will need to be sourced, a rough pattern of life must be established, subject's vehicles and addresses noted—all before beginning an aggressive observation.

While not always the smoothest, the relationship between the police and intelligence community remains a symbiotic one; neither can fulfil their mission to protect the country and the public without the other. In Great Britain, MI5 has primacy over covert counterterrorism investigations. However (unlike in countries like the United States) it lacks the power to detain or to prosecute an individual. Instead, those powers reside with the police. In training, the relationship is best explained with the analogy of driving a car: at this stage of the investigation, MI5 is in the driver's seat, but the police are sitting beside them, reading the map and providing guidance on opportunities to gather evidence for a future prosecution in court. When the investigation arrives at a point where action is required, the roles are flipped: the police take the wheel, but MI5 remains in the car to provide guidance and support, as intelligence is turned into evidence, and opportunities are identified to identify any new subjects of interest.

As is often the case, the surveillance wasn't exciting, at least at first. At eleven in the morning, the surveillance team watched Ali depart his home at 18 Nash House with his wife and child and enter a red Citroën, parked on Church Hill Road. His family then drove to Tesco superstore in the Galleons Reach Shopping Park, near the London City Airport. At Tesco, he used a mobile phone. The surveillance squad took a number of photos, but the officers didn't want to edge too close to the suspect, and so the images were all at an odd angle. After an hour in the supermarket, the three drove off.[13]

That was basically it. While all this sounds somewhat dull and unglamorous, even these first few hours proved to be valuable. For example, surveillance conclusively placed Ali behind the wheel of a red vehicle. The observed phone call was likely and subsequently matched with phone records in order to determine who was on the other end of the line. A file would have then been opened on that person to determine his potential connection to a wider terrorist network. Finally, if the phone call itself was intercepted, those investigating would now have a conclusive voice match for Ali.

Yet there was a lot of activity occurring completely outside of police surveillance. Ali's friend Tanvir Hussain walked into a branch of Barclays

Bank and asked for an application for a "career development loan" for £8,000. This was the maximum amount one could borrow from the bank for this sort of activity. In his application, Hussain wrote the purpose of the loan was to pay for a two-year, full-time IT essentials distance learning course provided by Multi-Training Centre, at 185 Canal Road, Small Heath, Birmingham. Hussain said he was in a hurry; he told the bank that the two-year course started that day, so he needed the money to pay his tuition. His arguments were accepted, and he received the loan.[14]

Two days beforehand, Arafat Khan—about whom Rauf and Ali had exchanged emails—had applied to Barclays Bank for a similar loan of £8,000 for an IT essentials course with the Multi-Training Centre. The address for the coursework was the same that Tanvir Hussain provided in Birmingham. That, too, was approved by the bank; Khan got his money.[15]

But there was no "Multi-Training Centre" at 185 Canal Road, Small Heath, Birmingham. In fact, there was no "Canal Road" at all in Birmingham. Of the other possibilities in Rauf's hometown, "185 New Canal Street" was a scruffy-looking carpark; "Canal Lane" housed a scrap yard behind a brick wall tipped with barbed wire; and "Canal Court" was a pleasant residential subdivision in the far southwest. It was hardly a coincidence that Tanvir Hussain and Arafat Khan both used the same address and excuse to generate quick funds.

There was other financial trickery afoot. On the same day Ali touched down in London from Pakistan, a young man named Nabeel Hussain (no relation to Tanvir Hussain) applied to HSBC Bank for a personal loan of £25,000. He said he needed the money because he was getting married. The bank, however, rejected Nabeel Hussain's application. He then moved on to Barclays. On July 18, Barclays Bank sent a Career Development Loan Information and Application Pack to Hussain, who partially completed the form requesting to borrow the maximum amount of £8,000.[16] Yet for one reason or another, he never finished the application.

◆

The next day, July 6, Ali was out again, driving about in his Citroën. The police surreptitiously followed him to Nottingham Road into the southern reaches of Walthamstow. London was bathed in radiant sunshine, and Ali, wearing a gray T-shirt, produced a white grocery bag from the back.

Tanvir Hussain, a resident of 14 Nottingham Road, entered Ali's car along with another bearded man in his midforties named Mohammed Shamin Uddin. Uddin was a squat, affable Bangladeshi bodybuilder known in the community for two things: running a local gym and suffering neurological damage after a thief struck him in the head with an iron bar.[17] Ali remained in the driver's seat, Tanvir Hussain got into the passenger seat, and Uddin jumped into the back. They headed south on the A112 road and pulled off near the Leyton tube station, to the office of the Eagle Mini-Cars, a private car hiring organization. Hussain popped out, entered the office, then came out holding a brown envelope. Off they went around the corner to B&Q, a popular home improvement store.

There, the men wandered through the cavernous aisles of tools and floor lamps, slabs of drywall, tiles, paints, and flooring solutions and past the friendly store attendants clad in bright orange aprons. They didn't buy anything that seemed out of the ordinary—two grip clamps, a screwdriver, a utility knife, and a can of WD40. Although nothing they purchased required portable power, the cops overheard them discuss the size of batteries. They wrote it down, like everything else. No one knew what any of it meant.[18]

It was now pushing into three in the afternoon. They drove to Uddin's home address on Cazenove Road. They chitchatted for a bit, and Uddin then left the car and entered the house. Ali and Tanvir continued on to YS Communications, a shop that dealt in communication devices. The officers tailing them remained outside since it was a small store in Stoke Newington High Street—and they'd be spotted immediately if they followed. But they remained tantalizingly close by; an officer was near enough to overhear Hussain exclaim to Ali, "Good deal that," when they exited the store. Beyond that, the men were quiet, and headed back to Uddin's house. Ali then quickly left.

With Ali parting ways with Uddin and Tanvir at Cazenove Road, the team had to make a choice; they couldn't split up and couldn't call in reinforcements on such short notice. They decided to stay with the original target: Ali and his Citroën. He drove back to his flat, where he picked up his wife and infant son and took them both to a local outpost of the now-defunct department store chain, British Home Stores.

But before they departed the department store parking lot, Ali felt like something was askew. His hackles were up, and he took a very long, hard look in his rear-view mirror. Scanning the horizon, Ali was looking for something out of place. He mumbled something to his wife, who looked over her shoulder as the car turned onto the Hoe Street thoroughfare on their way home.

Ali didn't know it at the time, but he stared almost directly at the surveillance officers who had been tailing him all afternoon.[19]

11

Rendezvous in Lloyd Park

Rauf was the kind of person who wished to be kept informed of his subordinates' activities. He wanted to make sure his men were in place throughout greater London. So he wrote to Ali on July 9: "I should be getting in touch soon. Thanks for the number. No worries about Aro. About the gig for your n—— rapper mate, I'll let you know when I call."[1]

Rauf was contacting Sarwar pretty regularly, but Sarwar took his time in writing back. And he was off doing other things besides buying chemicals. Rauf sent a note to his burner email on July 9: "I have tried to phone you. I assume you have gone."[2]

A few hours later, Rauf sent a more brusque, insistent note: "No news from you at all. Please get in touch."[3]

Rauf knew the authorities would eventually catch on, even if the July bombings gave him confidence he could stay two steps ahead of them. He kept pinging Sarwar to make sure he knew what he was doing; he didn't want another operation to fizzle at the last second. The clock was ticking, and Rauf knew it, far more than his men on the ground.

The next day, Sarwar got around to answering his boss. He called Pakistan and sent an encoded telephone number, in which the last four digits had to be subtracted by two to generate the "real" mobile number. Sarwar then used that phone number as his private line to Pakistan. Over the next month, he called Rauf—and only Rauf—some thirty times using that number, almost daily.[4]

As the procurement officer, Sarwar emailed Rauf three days later saying he had spoken with a friend about "sorting the price for the phones." "Phones" was code for firearms, and in Britain guns remained difficult to procure. In the same email, Sarwar wrote: "You will need to speak to tall Imi and tell him that you will be passing his two girlfriends to me. Send you some CDs and DVDs over to you soon."[5]

"Tall Imi" was Ali. Sarwar was asking Rauf to make the connections from Pakistan, where he was taking risks every time he spoke on the phone or used a computer, just so Sarwar could avoid driving the hour across town to inform Ali himself—or pick up a phone and do it in person.

Good help was hard to find.

◆

It was a bit after noon on July 13, and Ali ditched his Citroën for another vehicle, a red Vauxhall Vectra, and picked up Tanvir Hussain outside his house on Nottingham Road. Ali wore a blue shirt and pair of beige trousers; despite the still persistent heat, Hussain wore a dark jacket. Their destination was the large Ikea store in Tottenham, North London. Ali and Hussain ignored the particleboard shelving and umlaut-laden labels, as they weren't particularly interested in decorating. CCTV cameras recorded them as they moved through Ikea's maze of furniture to the household items area. The squad tailing them noted they only bought a small glass storage jar.[6]

They hopped back in the Vectra and drove across the parking lot to the Tesco Extra. There, they checked out a number of bulky, unfashionable black fannypacks.[7] Flipping one over and running his hand along the interior, Hussain casually mentioned to Ali, "Yes, I think I could fit a bottle of water in." Making their way around the supermarket, Hussain found a multipurpose tool and a flashlight, talking on the phone in the tool section. Then both men wandered over to the utensils section and examined the large knives on display.

While in the store, Ali and Hussain checked out plastic bottles of water and Diet Coke, carefully examining their caps and seals for several minutes. Their examination of the ordinary consumer products was strange, tantalizing behavior for the authorities tracking them.

They then bought some food and went home. The whole excursion took under three hours, and they went back to their normal lives, with their families, as if the trip had never happened.[8]

◆

"Do you think half Guj can help in getting the products you need?" Rauf emailed Ali the next day. He was trying to prod his operatives along. A distant CEO trying to increase productivity through micromanagement, Rauf demanded status updates from his subordinates. He ended on a hopeful, insistent note. "He can be very helpful. Let me know ASAP."[9]

Ali rolled into the Cheap Calls Internet Café near the busy commercial intersection of Hoe Street and Lea Bridge Road, a little more than a mile and a half from his home. The place advertised "Fast Internet 50p per Hour" as well as fax and photocopying services. He checked his emails daily from internet cafés around greater Walthamstow.

On July 14, he told Rauf, "Guji can't help as he don't look right, but he will if he does the job but not getting products. Is it okay for him to join my band?"[10] Ali figured his school chum Tanvir Hussain, who sported a long beard and sometimes insisted on wearing robes in public, would cause people to notice if he started buying hydrogen peroxide around greater London. But he could serve the group in other ways.

◆

It was now July 15, a little before four in the afternoon. Ali was idling at the north end of Lloyd Park, under the leaves of the trees around its perimeter. Assad Sarwar had come to meet him there. Quite unexpectedly, the two men both lay down on the grass, faced each other, cupped their hands over their mouths, and spoke.

To the surveillance team, this was both confounding and noteworthy. Despite all their audio surveillance capabilities, they couldn't actually hear (or in the case of lip readers, see) what Ali and Sarwar were saying. The two men, recently returned from Pakistan, were discussing something that could not be picked up on a microphone. The police tried to use alternate technical means to listen, but Ali and Sarwar stymied the force by speaking directly into the ground. It was obvious that the men knew what they were doing and that it was so important they were willing to lie face down in an open park to talk.

They spoke for half an hour. They were discussing the feasibility of striking Parliament—specifically the House of Commons. By coincidence, *V for Vendetta*, a film where Britain has become a fascist police state and where Parliament is blown to smithereens at the end, had premiered four months prior. Ali and Sarwar decided against this target. Like the 7/7 bombers discussing and discarding an attack on the G8, Ali and Sarwar felt it was too difficult to subvert the multiple rings of security in the heart of the British government. Striking Parliament was a plan placed back on the shelf.[11]

The authorities had had enough. A police vehicle drove up and stopped near the duo. The cops didn't have much to go on since Ali and Sarwar weren't doing anything illegal, so they didn't speak to the pair about anything in particular.

More importantly, this appeared to have been the first time the police encountered Mr. Assad Sarwar. Despite his numerous connections to Rashid Rauf, his time in a terrorist training camp in Pakistan, his purchases of hydrogen peroxide, and his longtime connections to the IMA, he wasn't on anyone's radar.

They put him on the list.

◆

A telephone at the Thames Valley Police (TVP) headquarters in Oxfordshire soon began ringing. Officer Shaun Greenough picked up the receiver. The voice on the other end of the line, which belonged to someone from MI5, requested "surveillance on these three subjects." The MI5 official then provided the names, all residents of the town of High Wycombe, about a forty-five-minute drive from police headquarters. "Can you please start sorting this out for us?"

"Okay," Greenough responded, carefully. He knew from a briefing the previous Thursday there was an ongoing terrorist investigation with a vague link to his area, but at the time it didn't appear to be significant.

As a senior TVP officer, he helped manage the finite resources and personnel on the force. He asked, "When you say 'you want surveillance on these three subjects,' what do you mean by that? What do you want? Do you want mobile, do you want static? How many hours a day—is it twelve hours, is it twenty-four hours? Most importantly, what exactly are you after?"

The MI5 officer asked Greenough to hold the line. About ten minutes later, he returned. He told Greenough, "We want everything, and we need it by tomorrow."[12]

It was a ceiling-falling-in moment for the TVP, which lacked the personnel required to carry out such a manpower-intensive request. The police had a couple of surveillance teams, grossly inadequate to place multiple subjects under the microscope twenty-four hours a day, indefinitely. They needed more men, and they needed them fast.[13]

Britain at the time lacked a national system of secure conferencing, so Greenough's TVP superior was obliged to take the train into London every day for high-level meetings with his Met, MI5, and MI6 counterparts. This functionally removed him from daily operational planning and placed Greenough, second in command, in charge of the circus now centered upon High Wycombe. The two men called each other three times a day, every day. Greenough then deployed his officers as best as he could before reinforcements arrived.[14]

◆

It was noon the day after the meeting in Lloyd Park. Ali drove to Clapton to deliver an orange-colored package the size of a shoebox to a residence on Alconbury Road. Placing the box under his right arm, Ali walked up the steps, past the mechanical device that allowed wheelchair access to the front door, and knocked. The door opened, and Ali handed over the box to the person inside. Within the box was a book. A bomb manual. And it had Ibrahim Savant's fingerprints on it.

By July 18, Ali reported progress to Rauf. "There are a few lads who want to join up. We have about four lads."[15] Things were moving forward.

◆

That same day, Mohammed Gulzar arrived in Britain. Walking out from the Heathrow arrivals gate, Gulzar and his new wife met the youngster Abdul M. Patel, who took them to his house.[16] This was prearranged—Patel was listed as "KID" in his mobile phone and Gulzar was known as both "ALTAF" and "Car For Sale" in Patel's mobile.[17] Gulzar's wife, Zora, mysteriously parted ways from him soon after touching down in London; she left her new husband to handle his own activities.

At his home on Alconbury Road, Patel handed Gulzar a package the size of a shoebox. He was told that a South African associate of his father's would pick it up one of these days. Within the familiar orange cardboard box were the explosives manual and other items.[18]

Gulzar then shuffled around from flat to flat until he was finally deposited at 7 Priory Road, a vacant terraced house in East London. The person who maintained residency for this property was his new wife's uncle, who in reality lived in Barking, about fifteen minutes away by car. This unit was also a few blocks away from the interchange railway station and the terminus of the Underground's Hammersmith & City line.

The unit was mostly empty save for a gray mattress on the floor. This would be his home for the next several weeks. It was spartan, but Gulzar was not in town for the creature comforts. After picking up a burner mobile, he called another burner number in Pakistan.[19] He would later claim he was reaching out to his sister since she was reportedly getting married, but he didn't call the rest of his family in Alum Rock, the home he hadn't seen in some four years.

◆

But it wasn't just orange boxes arousing suspicion, but also burgundy-bound books with royal coats of arms in gold. On the eighth, Ali filled out a passport application for his infant son, Mohammed S. Ali of 17 Albert Road, Walthamstow. The address was not that of his house but rather of his in-laws. Cossor signed off on the application.[20]

Eleven days later, Ali wandered over to the Walthamstow police station to report a lost passport—this time, for himself. He said he had placed it in his washing machine and left it on his windowsill to dry.[21] Then, "it fell out of the window," he told the officers.[22]

Other friends reported "losing" their passports as well. Tanvir Hussain "lost" his passport on June 28.[23] Ali later commented in an email, "Half Guji has sorted his looks out and no longer looks like a junkie."[24] On July 6 Assad Sarwar put in an application for a new passport, which was issued on the same day. On July 7 Ibrahim Savant also reported to the police that his passport was lost to the winds. He had cleaned himself up for the passport photo.

They were trying to create clean paperwork and hide Pakistani exit and entry stamps. This ploy was taken straight out of the 9/11 attacker playbook. Only five years beforehand, sometime after February 2000, ringleader Mohammed Atta applied for a new passport to hide his travel to Afghanistan and to generate a new, clean-shaven passport photo so that he could attend flight school in the United States.[25]

◆

"Guji is good to join, so are the other guys as long as they are proper," Ali informed Rauf on July 20.[26] Guji—Tanvir Hussain—had a change of heart and was now back in the mix. Ali's team of reliable men was falling into place.

He also had a few other errands to run that day. Ali stopped by the Spy Shop Lorraine Electronics, where he asked about a camera that worked at night. He wanted something with an independent power supply, a battery, or solar power to overcome problems of unstable electrical grids in Karachi.[27] They said they'd look into it.

◆

Meanwhile, in another part of town, a real estate agent wanted to offload a rundown apartment along a busy thoroughfare in East London. The beige, midterraced property with weeds growing from the second-floor ironworking occupied a block with multiple other residences, an auto electrical supply company, and a nondescript Italian restaurant that assured customers the menu was "100% halal."

The bank had initially repossessed the second-story unit that April and farmed out the sale to the Bairstow Eves real estate agency. The prior tenants had trashed and abandoned the property but the bones were still in good condition. The real estate agency, a brightly apportioned business located a stone's throw from the Walthamstow tube stop, spruced up what it could to make it saleable. Two months later, in early June, the unit was listed on the East London Property Mart for £147,500.[28]

Within a few weeks, a man appeared interested in purchasing the unit for the asking price. No mortgage was necessary since the buyer was willing to pay the full price in cash. Everyone won; it was a good deal for the bank, broker, and buyer, and the sale raised no red flags.

The property was thus deeded to a "Samir Ahmed," although the purchase path was more complicated. In April, Dawood Khan had sold a black-doored, two-story unit in another part of Walthamstow. Dawood then instructed his solicitors to gift the proceeds of the sale to his brother, Abdullah Umar Khan.[29] On June 19, Abdullah Umar made an offer for this new property, for £140,000. But Umar then told his solicitors that his brother-in-law, Samir Ahmed, would serve as both the client and purchaser.

The solicitors didn't see a problem with this arrangement. By mid-July, the upstairs flat sandwiched between Brookdale and Pearl Roads was in Samir Ahmed's possession for the sum of £140,191.63. After the paperwork was completed and handshakes exchanged, Umar took the keys from Samir and handed them to his other brother—Abdulla Ahmed Ali—who lived nearby.

That unit—386A Forest Road in Walthamstow, just down the street from Lloyd Park and the Waltham Forest Town Hall—became Ali's new safehouse. The convoluted real estate transactions had allowed him to evade oversight. Samir Ahmed—a British citizen of good standing—and his new property on a busy road weren't on anyone's list.

◆

Sarwar, living across town with his parents in High Wycombe, wrote to Rauf on July 18, two days before the purchase of the Forest Road unit. In his email, he noted gleefully, "Hi ☺ Got some good news that will bring a big smile to your face . . . I have some nice files you will love. It will give you wet dreams after you see it ha ha ha. I have 15 suppliers to give Calvin Klein aftershave. One box of 50 is only £175."[30]

One box of fifty times was code for five 1 L bottles. The "aftershave" was hydrogen peroxide; "£175" was the concentration, or 17.5 percent.

The morning after Ali's extended family completed the purchase of the flat, Rauf emailed Sarwar with an urgent message: "Regarding the aftershave bottles, I need at least 40 100-millilitre bottles. I have the orders for these already so I need these as soon as possible. You need to know when can you get me these. You know the price is always the same, 80 quid, but I need you to get another 30 bottles on top of the 40. The order for those should go through too. I don't want to wait around so it's best for you to get 70 bottles. I need these as soon as possible as I don't want to lose these customers."[31]

Rauf and his men in Britain all knew that they had to be careful—but also had to speed up their actions. Rauf wanted the plot to move forward as soon as possible to avoid attracting additional scrutiny. He didn't know what the police knew, or if they suspected anything. Each day that passed could lead to a slipup and exposure.

Sarwar had good news for Rauf; he had found twenty-eight different suppliers. "They all sell in bulk. Buying them is straightforward. No hassle. Boxes of 50 at a fixed price of only £175."

Sarwar could now source 5 L bottles of hydrogen peroxide concentrated to 17.5 percent from across the British Isles without arousing any attention. The ability to pick up chemicals without notice significantly advanced the plot. Indeed, had Sarwar not met with Ali in Lloyd Park and acted suspiciously, the authorities might have had not known about his involvement at all.

Finally, Rauf sent Sarwar the mobile number that his boyhood friend Mohammed Gulzar was using. He was still in hiding.[32]

◆

Ali's safehouse provided a central location for his cell's activities, and the pace of operations began to quicken. The big push was evident because the members of the cell were constantly calling each other.

In just the afternoon and into the evening the day after the property's purchase, Ali phoned Khatib, Savant, and then Hussain. Ali then called Rauf in Pakistan multiple times. Following that, Ali called Hussain again. Then Arafat Khan. And then Savant again. Then Hussain called Arafat Khan, while Savant called Ali. By eight in the evening. Ali had dialed Savant's number multiple times, as well as rung Hussain and Arafat Khan once more.[33]

In the late evening on the twenty-first, Ali and Hussain, along with three other men, connected in person. They met up by the tennis courts in Lloyd Park in the midafternoon. But these men had little interest in the game. They brought tennis balls to cover their actions, but no one had thought to bring along tennis rackets. The undercover officers observing them didn't recognize anyone except Ali and Hussain.

Later that evening, Ali and Hussain walked over to the unit on Forest Road. The flat, they believed, would be a quiet place to make their explosives, away from their families and the notice of the police. As far as they knew, no one knew what they were up to, as none of them had been called in by the authorities for questioning. Nor had they detected any particular surveillance.

At exactly 11:06 p.m., Ali and Hussain looked out onto the tree-less brick and asphalt roadway from the second-story window. They neglected to notice a member of the surveillance team, a wiry fellow with short-cropped hair and a military upbringing, surreptitiously staring back up at them from across the street.

The authorities now had a brand-new address to watch.

12

Pattern of Life

It was the afternoon of July 22. Ali drove to the Tesco at the Galleons Reach Shopping Park by himself. Wearing a white T-shirt and a pair of shorts, he headed over to the housewares aisle where he carefully examined and placed six glass jars into his shopping basket. While he was waiting in line to pay, he took one out and examined it again. Rauf had emphasized to Ali that he had to perform continuous countersurveillance. He had to watch the angles. Ali was only to start work only when he felt he was in the clear.[1] When he wasn't working, he was to look and act as if nothing was going on.

And so, with his Tesco purchases, he returned to the tennis courts in Lloyd Park, down the street from the safehouse. There, with a few friends, he played tennis for an hour and a half. Ali seemed like just a normal guy taking advantage of the warm weather to hit some balls around with his mates.

◆

By this point MI5 had given the conspiracy a name—Operation Overt—and assigned some of the suspects codenames. Ali was "Lion Roar" and Sarwar was "Rich Food," for example, but there were many others. But this investigation was quickly becoming complicated. Ali, Hussain, Sarwar, and the others were mostly Walthamstow and High Wycombe locals with large, extended families and overlapping circles of friends, coworkers, and acquaintances. The surveillance officers diligently recording their movements had trouble identifying who was part of an international terrorist conspiracy and who was just friendly with the crew. His latest tennis partners joined the list of unknowns.[2] And, even if every one of those individuals was somehow involved, the police didn't have the ability to surveil half of Walthamstow. Thus, in a twenty-floor glass-and-steel high-rise in Victoria, ten miles southwest, a different set of operatives were at work sorting it all out. In one of the Major Incident Rooms over at New Scotland Yard, men and women at a bank of computer screens ran the operation to monitor the ever-expanding cell. Everything was logged: computers, cameras, audio surveillance, and police notes were filed away for analysis and future decisions.

The group's purchases, conversations, and associations were causing great consternation. The metastasizing conspiracy began to require the full attention of the British national security establishment. This case was now far bigger than the Volga embarrassment from the month before. It was an all-encompassing operation. In the back of their minds, the police and Security Service knew that if they were caught flat-footed, as they were on 7/7 and 7/21, it would devastate the country and bring down the government.

◆

Ali knew something, somewhere was wrong. He didn't know what the police, MI5, MI6, and their global partners were doing exactly, but in his bones he knew he was being watched. He was pretty sure it wasn't just his imagination, as he was definitely stopped at Heathrow, and then his family's friends told him the British government asked Pakistani intelligence to tail him. But he hadn't noticed anything amiss once he returned to London, and his batteries never left his luggage.

Now that he was back home, was he on someone's radar screen? Was he being surveilled when he bought the bottles? Played tennis? Went to the gym? What about when he drove to the local Tesco and bought groceries? Little did he realize that the answer to all these questions was "yes."

In the afternoon of July 23, Ali connected again with Sarwar in the northwest section of Lloyd Park. They chitchatted quietly but this time remained upright and off the ground. Sarwar eventually wandered off, and a young man named Nabeel Hussain (seeing an opportunity) approached Ali. Together they walked by the tennis courts and ate sweets. They headed south, joined by a random man with a baby, and started down the alleyway on Bedford Road. A few steps in, the men swiveled and took a hard look behind them, before they continued down the alleyway.[3]

Ali preferred not to take unnecessary chances. After parting ways with Nabeel Hussain, he called Tanvir Hussain and asked to be picked up. Shortly after, Tanvir rolled up in a green Vauxhall Astra, and the two drove south down Hoe street. Ali got out at one of his favorite haunts, the Cheap Calls Internet Café. He walked in, acutely aware of his surroundings and made his way to the furthest terminal from the front entrance. It was 7:49 p.m. when he signed online.[4]

He emailed Rauf: "I don't like Imran. He's a dud. He chats so much shit."[5]

This was code. Ali was dumping his email address. He was out the door at 7:51 p.m. He had only been online for two minutes.

◆

On July 24, toy shop employee Waheed Zaman withdrew the entire balance of his savings account, just over £1,800. He later said he needed the money to buy a new laptop and give *zakat*, or religiously obligatory alms giving.[6] A suspicious excuse; zakat was intended to build the community pot, not drain the pious of their life savings.

At 11:19 in the morning, Ali was behind another computer monitor at another internet café on Lea Bridge Road. After ditching his old email address, he had set up a new one, and now he was in the café with the email open and an agitated look across his face. He sent a text from one of the two phones he had in his possession before he exited the café. He picked up some food and drove his Vectra to a parking lot on the eastern side of Whipps Cross Road, the former boundary line between Walthamstow and the older municipality of Leyton. Tanvir Hussain met him in a green Mercedes.[7]

In an open lot, Ali popped open the back of his car and took out a black package the size of a small videotape. At the same time, Tanvir Hussain removed a brown cardboard box eighteen inches in diameter from his vehicle. Ali held something small in his hand, and he was holding it up closely to his face. He showed Hussain, making a twisting motion with his hand.

◆

Later that day, Sarwar emailed Rauf about procuring more chemical precursors: "When I see your friend, shall I tell him what I supposed to tell Arif [Gulzar]/James?"[8] Unlike the rest of the crew, Sarwar lived far from Walthamstow and he wanted to be prepared with Rauf's instructions before he made a trip into East London that could take an hour by car. "What about dates, does he know about them? What about aftershaves that you brought me over . . . Also, he has a white friend that has many contacts and can be very helpful in getting us quality aftershaves. I think we can get 60 to 90 boxes a month. I will find out about the prices of phones . . . you need to tell me whether the freezer I bought you over there works or not . . . I will be very busy on Wednesday."[9]

Finally, Sarwar wrote, "I spoke with Chatcha [sic] and said that he got a wedding film that he needs to give me. Shall I take it off him?" "Chacha," which means "uncle" in Urdu (or more specifically, one's paternal uncle), was yet another codename for Ali. A "wedding film," in jihadi parlance, was a martyrdom video to be played after a suicide operation. It seemed Ali had one in his possession.

The next day Rauf sent Sarwar a reply a bit after seven in the morning in England, which was after midday in Pakistan. Sarwar was still asleep and he wasn't checking his email at home: "My friend that would like to see you is Arif. He knows about the dates and he knows his aftershaves very well. If you could update him about the ones you were shown by me, it would be helpful. Don't give him all the aftershaves, only give him the amount he requires. He only has two shops to supply so just give him enough for his supply."[10]

It was unclear what the "shops" meant. Did Arif, otherwise known as Gulzar, have other members outside Ali and the rest who were interested in an attack? Was Sarwar servicing other operations within Britain?

Rauf also had a separate bone to pick with Sarwar, stating: "I'm very disappointed about the time it's taking to get a price list for the phones. We need to get a move on, as I have gone through all the hassle of getting the money."[11] Sarwar had failed to procure any firearms. This wasn't America, where the plotters could have outfitted a small army by lunchtime.

After firing off the email, Rauf waited for a reply. But he heard nothing back from Sarwar, and the silence from London irritated him. He wanted results. Being the micromanaging type, Rauf sent another email to Sarwar at 9:49 a.m. asking for a reply to his message. Nothing. He sent a further four messages so hurriedly that he mistyped two email addresses, which bounced back. Still nothing.[12]

What Rauf didn't realize was that Sarwar was out buying chemicals to build bombs. Adopting his Jona Lewis persona once again, Sarwar drove back to Health Leads UK in Wales to purchase more goods. Mixed in with requests for razor blades, honeysuckle, and soap for his fake natural food store, he acquired more hydrogen peroxide.[13] He paid in cash.

Tanvir Hussain was shopping too. On the evening of July 25, he popped down to a nearby Tesco, on the former grounds of a 1930s-era mental hospital, and bought multiple plastic bottles of various energy and soft drinks.

The calls within the Walthamstow network increased. Ali called Hussain and Arafat several times. He texted Umar Islam and also received calls from Hussain and Ibrahim Savant. There were two series of calls where Savant called Zaman, then Ali, then Zaman again. Savant apparently was serving as a go-between for Ali and Zaman; Ali was trying to keep Zaman's number from his phone, lest he be compromised.[14]

On that day, Ali scheduled an appointment to apply in person for a new passport. Prior to his Tesco run, Hussain also telephoned the Identity and Passport Service for similar reasons.[15]

◆

The next day, Arafat Khan rode the Victoria line from the Walthamstow station, a pleasant fifteen-minute walk from the Forest Road safehouse, to the stately two-century-old drugstore John Bell & Croyden in London's West End. Traveling from Walthamstow into the urban core, Khan passed by the exact spot where Yassin Hassan Omar had tried to detonate his backpack a year earlier.

The large windows on the ground floor and the shelves stocked with pharmaceuticals beckoned to him. He located what he needed: 500 ml conical flasks, jugs, several surgical needles, and 10 ml plasti-pack syringes. He put them into his basket, paid, and left.

◆

Easily concealed among downtown shoppers, undercover personnel followed Khan from his home, onto the Underground, and into the cavernous drugstore. Due to his seemingly close relationship with Ali, he was now considered a person of interest worthy of surveillance. They followed the target as he moved through the store's famous displays and loaded his basket with an assortment of medical goods.

◆

Meanwhile, back in Walthamstow, Tanvir Hussain entered the Co-op Pharmacy a mile east of 386A and asked about purchasing surgical needles. The clerk asked what size he wanted. Hussain replied, "The biggest ones." She went into the storeroom and after returning, used her hands to show the size of the four-inch needles in the back.[16]

"No, no," Hussain said. He gestured with his hands, showing he wanted needles twice that length.

The clerk shrugged and suggested inquiring at a nearby joinery shop, farther down on Wood Street, back toward Forest Road. Hussain then walked over to T&T Merchants, housed in a low-slung brick building on the west side of the street. This stop was also a bust; he was inside for only a minute. He left, ducking quickly inside T&I Communications Internet Café, where he bought a phone card. Still inside the café, he called Pakistan. His last stop was a local pharmacy, but he likewise left the premises empty-handed. He returned to his car and drove to his home base: 386A Forest Road.[17]

◆

The text said, "call me." It was July 27, and Tanvir Hussain wanted to chat with Ali.

Ali drove to Hussain's house and then called him. Hussain emerged from his doorway carrying two bags, one white and one dark, and placed them in the trunk of Ali's car. The pair drove to the Ravenside Retail Park shopping mall, along the River Lea. This time, Ali and Hussain stopped by the Wickes home improvement store looking for pipe insulation and drain cleaner. While inside, Ali held up what appeared to be gray plastic pipe about two feet long. Examining a few four-inch coach bolts and some masonry nails, Ali told Hussain, "If we need to attach it, we will nail it, not screw it." The pair left without buying anything.[18]

Ali and Tanvir Hussain then went to a nearby Tesco. The pair's first stop was the disposable camera stand, where they examined the wares on display. Still empty-handed, they walked to the luggage area, where Ali picked up a dark gray toiletry bag with a green zipper. The men inspected it closely, running their hands inside the bag as Ali held it open.

They separated; Ali picked up a glass jar and a pack of blank CDs, while Hussain wandered over to the area selling tennis rackets. Then they both reconvened by the throwaway cameras and asked a Tesco employee a few questions. The pair had an inkling they were being tracked in some capacity; after they paid for the cameras and the jar and exited through the sliding doors, they looked over their shoulders. They saw no one.

They then walked to another DIY store, Hobby-Home on High Street, to look at some hardware and more glass jars. Hussain picked up thirty-eight pieces of felt protector pads—the kind that keep furniture legs from scuffing the floor. Just two men spending their Thursday on a path towards home improvement, nothing outwardly suspicious to the casual observer. They checked out the East Man Army Store on High Street, and then another home and garden store called Peanuts. There, they examined scouring pads and organic plant growing kits. Ali told Hussain, "The white liquid is not thick enough. Insulating foam would be better."[19]

Their final stop was the stalls outside of the local Woolworths. They spent the next half hour meandering outside, looking at various items like an oven lighter with an extended nozzle. Ali picked up a fanny pack, but instead of placing it on top of his T-shirt, he instead lifted the shirt and placed the fanny pack against his stomach. He said, "Can you—?" beckoning to Hussain after he lowered his T-shirt over the bag. The bulge underneath his shirt was large; Hussain shook his head.[20] It wouldn't do. They hopped back into Ali's car and drove over to Ibrahim Savant's house and picked him up. The three men rode together to the safehouse on Forest Road.

They needed to make some videos.[21]

◆

Meanwhile, Arafat Khan took the tube and returned to John Bell & Croydon with a bag full of unwanted items. He carefully placed the conical flasks and measuring cups on the counter. Arafat was returning all the gear that for one reason or another the cell had rejected.[22] The clerk, Mr. Azim, took the items back and gave Arafat his cash refund.

Arafat's behavior echoed that of another penny-pinching terrorist from over a decade before. Mohammed Salameh had rented a Ryder van which he and others used in the 1993 New York City World Trade Center bombing. After detonating the bomb inside the van in the parking lot, Salameh reported the vehicle as stolen. NYPD and ATF bomb technicians working through the wreckage found the vehicle identification number, ran the number, and unraveled the plot. Salameh walked into their hands when he returned to Ryder to collect his $400 deposit.[23]

◆

Multiple squads of undercover cops followed the group around town, making sure to not step on each other's toes. The comings and goings of Ali, Hussain, and others didn't make sense most of the time to the surveillance teams, who were only viewing small pieces of a much larger puzzle. Why did they spend so much time looking at household goods? The police, moreover, could not get close enough in the aisles of the stores to hear what the targets were saying consistently. They were going to have to take a more aggressive stance against the plotters, lest they miss something important.

Because something important was about to occur.

13

Wedding Videos

Dusk was rapidly approaching on July 27 as Ali, Hussain, and Ibrahim Savant sat inside the Forest Road hideout.[1] The men unfurled a large black flag emblazoned with the creed and cornerstone of Islam, the *shahada*—"There is no god but Allah, and Muhammad is his messenger"—and tacked it against a mattress propped against the wall. Ali put on a black ankle-length garment called a *jubbah* and placed a checkered keffiyeh upon his head, obscuring his hairline. His beard and moustache were neatly trimmed. The setup was similar to Sidique Khan's, publicized seven months earlier on Al Jazeera.

Ali looked into the camera and said, "I'm doing this because the rewards, the big rewards that Allah has promised those who step on his path and Inshaallah become martyred and the best of amongst those to me is the guarantee of *Jannah* [paradise] for myself, my family and those that are close to me."

The audio wasn't the best; he was relying on the microphone attached to the video camera. There was a faint buzzing in the background. Aware of the technical limitations, he nonetheless advanced. He pointed his finger at the camera: "On top of this is to punish and to humiliate the *kuffar* [the unbeliever], to teach them a lesson that they will never forget. It's to tell them that we Muslim people have honor, we are people of *issa* [honor], we are brave. We're not cowards. Enough is enough. We've warned you so many times get out of our lands, leave us alone, but you have persisted in trying to humiliate us, kill us, and destroy us."

Scratching his nose, he continued: "Sheikh Osama [bin Laden] warned you many times to leave our lands or you will be destroyed. And now the time has come for you to be destroyed. And you have nothing but to expect that floods of martyr operations, volcanoes of anger and revenge erupting among your capital. So yes, taste that what you have made us taste for a long time, and now you have to bear the fruits that you have sown."[2]

Off camera, someone asked him, "What about the innocent people? Surely just because the kuffar kill our innocent does not mean that we should, that we should kill theirs? What about this so-called 'collateral damage?' What about it?"

Ali answered, "You show more care and concern for animals than you do for the Muslim *Ummah* [the global Islamic community]":

Those who know me, who really know me, will know that I was the happiest person that they could ever have imagined, and those that know me know that I was over the moon that Allah has given me this opportunity to lead this blessed operation. I swear by Allah, I have the desire since the age of fifteen or sixteen to participate in jihad in the path of Allah. I had the desire since then to punish the Kuffar for the evil they are doing.

I had the desire since then for Jannah for the Koran. I want to go to my prophet and his companions. Leave us alone. Stop meddling in our affairs and we will leave you alone. Otherwise expect floods of martyr operations against you and we will take our revenge and anger, ripping amongst your people and scattering the people and your body parts and your people's body parts responsible for these wars and oppression decorating the streets.[3]

Finally, Ali wrapped up his speech. He repeated his profound gratitude to have "the opportunity to do this blessed action."[4]

It was now Ibrahim Savant's turn. He too sat in front of the black flag, put on the checkered keffiyeh, and wore the jubbah. Lacking Ali's surety, he kept looking upward, as if he were trying to remember what he was supposed to say: "I participate within this blessed raid for—upon the enemies of blessed Islam, for several reasons. I have sacrificed my life cheaply, within the sake of Allah, not to save myself from a life of trials and tribulations but to fulfill a covenant and promise with Allah the almighty, and to make it *deen* [roughly: the faith] reign supreme."

The term "blessed raid" was the same one that al Qaeda's Ayman al-Zawahiri used to describe the 7/7 attacks. Ibrahim began to rush through his words.

As for the lovers of life and haters of death, you will class my case as a case of suicide. I say argue your case with the Most High, and as he has said, and never think those who have been killed in the cause of Allah as dead, rather they are alive with their Lord and receiving provision. All Muslims take heed, remove yourself from the grasp of the kuffar before you are counted as one of them. Do not be content with your council houses and businesses and Western lifestyle.

So we also say that if you are among the polytheists while they are attacked, we are free from you whatever may befall you. All Muslims feel the need to dust your feet in the training camps of jihad where men are made.

Cease debate and enter the battlefields seeking paradise. Mujahideen, for years I've desired to meet you, to walk the paths you've walked, to sacrifice what you have sacrificed. Now Allah has honored me with an invitation to his Kingdom. Obviously after this beautiful operation they will accuse us brothers of all sorts of things and most of the things they will accuse us of is killing for the sake of killing, hating freedom, hating the West, being fed up with our lives.

Finally, Tanvir Hussain took center stage. He too put on the costume:

People keep on saying, you know, that we keep on targeting innocent civilians, yeah. We're not targeting innocent civilians. We're targeting economic and military targets. They're the battle grounds of today so whoever steps in these trenches, they, yeah, you haven't got us to blame.

You've got to blame yourself, and collateral damage is going to be inevitable and people are going to die, besides, you know, it's work at a price. You know, I wanted to do this myself. For many years, I dreamt of doing this, but I didn't have no chance of doing this. I didn't have any means. Alhamdulilah, Allah has accepted my *duas* [prayers] yeah, and provided a means to do this.

I only wish I could do this again, come back and do this again, and just do it again and again until people come to their senses and realize, you know, don't mess with the Muslims. Stop supporting the puppets and helping our enemies. If you do this, we're going to leave you alone. If you don't, you're going to feel the wrath of the mujahideen, Inshaallah.

The recordings complete, the men left the property. Filled with adrenaline, they went for a drive before parting ways. Ali then returned home to be with his wife and child.

◆

The police and MI5 didn't know what had just occurred. Despite the number of officers surveilling the cell, the only thing they knew for sure was that Ali and Savant walked into 386A Forest Road at 4:44 p.m. carrying bags containing unknown items. Hussain followed them four minutes later. The shades were then drawn. The suspects then spent over two hours inside the building, exiting at 7:02 p.m. That was the extent of what the police knew.

Even without the full details, they had cause for concern. That evening, Waheed Zaman texted Savant, "Can I get the six movie set tomorrow, please, if you can? JZK."[5] The next day, Zaman texted Savant again: "Tell Amjid I won't be coming swimming today. I'm going to be at Muslim Aid call centre."[6]

Ali picked Zaman up in his Vectra in the afternoon. Despite the heat, the toy store employee was wearing a scarf and a topi—a type of skullcap often worn for religious reasons—and threw them in Ali's backseat. When they arrived at the door of the safehouse, Ali realized he left the housekey in the car and went back to his vehicle to retrieve it. As they walked into 386A Forest Road, he handed Zaman a bag containing the black flag. Entering the foyer, Zaman looked around. It was a dump. *This place looks like it's falling apart*, he thought as he walked through the unit.

Ali had again forgotten something in his car; he again asked Zaman to wait inside while he went back outside. Five, ten, fifteen minutes passed, and Zaman was left in the unit alone. Although he was the newest member of the team, Zaman had inspired enough confidence in Ali that he left him in his safehouse by himself. So Zaman just sat there, alone, in a dingy flat, with his thoughts.

Ali returned, holding his laptop. He took Zaman up a flight of stairs into another room. There was a mattress on the left-hand side; the rays of sunlight shone through a window on the back. Ali gave him the props from the day before—the black jubbah, the black-and-white checkered headdress—and told Zaman to go to the downstairs bathroom to put them all on.

When Zaman returned, there was a folded-up piece of fabric in front of the flag—Ali told him to sit on top of it. He then placed the video camera on top of a box, and the laptop underneath the lens. Ali helpfully made the font on the laptop bigger, so Zaman could read it. "Point your finger," Ali commanded. "Be aggressive!"[7]

Zaman obliged. He said, looking at the camera, "I have been educated to a high standard and had it not been Allah had blessed me with this mission, I could have lived a life of ease. But instead [I] chose to fight for the sake of Allah's deen. All of you so-called moderate Muslims, there's only one way in which to solve this crisis, the problems will not be solved by means of campaigning, big conferences, peaceful negotiations with the disbelievers."

They rehearsed a few more times. Then Ali, getting impatient, told Zaman to ad lib his speech while he scrolled the text on the laptop. "Just improvise when I ask you the questions and if you remember what you read off the screen, just kind of repeat it."[8] Gamely, Zaman tried again: "The only solution to this current situation of the Muslims is by fighting jihad for the sake of Allah, until the enemy is fully subdued and expelled from our lands. America and England have no cause for complaint for they are the ones who invaded and built bases in the land of the Muslims. They are the ones who supply weapons to the enemies of Islam, including the cursed Israelis."

The men had passion in their hearts, but the basic points of filmmaking—such as using a tripod instead of an overturned box to position the video camera—escaped them. The amateur nature of the efforts didn't shake their commitment to the cause, however. "I'm warning these two nations and any other country who seeks a bad end, death and destruction will pass upon you like a tornado," Zaman intoned, "and you will not feel any security or peace in your lands until you stop interfering in the affairs of the Muslim completely."

Zaman remembered Ali's instruction to wave his finger at the camera, but he kept tripping over the words as they tumbled from his mouth:

I'm warning you today, so tomorrow you have no cause for complaints. Remember, as you kill us, you will be killed; as you bomb us, you will be bombed. I will pray that Allah makes us successful in our actions, may he grant us Jannah. May he raise us on the Day of Judgment to be with the prophets, martyrs, and people in the right path. May Allah bless the mujahideen with victory upon victory wherever they may be and may he focus their aim and may he make them of the patient ones.

I have not been brainwashed. I have been educated to a high standard. I am old enough to make my own decisions.

Finally, Ali cut in from off camera. "For the benefit of the brothers, the media brothers—"[9] Ali then provided some general instructions to those who would eventually reedit and disseminate this and the other videos for maximum impact; he was playing his role of propagandist for al Qaeda, just like Mohammad Sidique Khan had done the year before.

Waheed Zaman left 386A Forest Road around 5 p.m. He called Savant and mentioned he had made a video, and Savant replied he had made one the previous day.[10] Ali dropped him off, forgetting Zaman had left his scarf and topi in the car. He never got them back.

During their time in the Forest Road unit, Ali took two phone calls from Arafat Khan. As soon as Zaman wandered into the afternoon sun, Ali called Hussain. Within half an hour, Ali was in the passenger seat of a Kia Pride, with Arafat at the wheel.

Ali and Arafat entered the Forest Road flat at 7:24 p.m. and left about an hour later, at 8:22 p.m. Like his comrades in arms, Arafat was shooting his martyrdom video. He intoned:

We will rain upon you such a terror and destruction that you will never feel peace and security. There will be floods of martyrdom operations and bombs falling through your lands. There will be daily torment in this world and a greater torment awaiting in the hereafter. Now I'd like to address the bootlickers who stand shoulder to shoulder with [the] kuffar in condemning these beautiful operations and the mujahideen.

In particular, I'd like to address the scholars to whom Allah has given knowledge which they concealed and play with to please the kuffar, to save themselves from their disapproval. What a miserable deal. Pleasing the kuffar all while just pleasing Allah. Fearing them instead of fearing Allah. I would like to thank Allah for giving me this opportunity to bless me with this shahada. I ask Allah to forgive me for all my sins, to accept me as a martyr. I ask Allah to help the mujahideen everywhere in every way.

◆

The authorities knew something important was happening within the walls. There was too much going on and too many suspects entering and exiting the facility in short order. They also hadn't known about Ibrahim Savant's involvement until they saw him walk in and out of 386A Forest Road.[11] Many of the men the surveillance teams were tailing kept converging on this one property. But what was occurring was anyone's guess.

MI5 hatched a plan.

14

Probe

"I am with Arif," wrote Sarwar to Rauf on July 29. "Didn't thought it would be him. Top dude."[1] Sarwar was meeting with Gulzar—"Arif" over email and "Atlaf" in person—who had been lying low since his arrival in Great Britain. Just to be on the safe side, Sarwar also established yet another email address that day.[2] The two had lunched at A La Pizza on Upton Lane and went to a mosque to pray. Sarwar then dropped Gulzar off at Barking station.[3]

By now, MI5 was keyed into Gulzar.[4] It appeared he knew quite a bit about bombs and explosives, and MI5 assessed his role was to help the cell complete the mission.

◆

Sarwar then connected with Ali in the Waltham Forest Muslim Cemetery on Folly Lane, the final resting spot for many local residents. Tucked along the southwestern corner of the Banbury Reservoir and underneath a series of power lines, the cemetery was a quiet, tidy place of short white and black headstones spanning a gravel field. Flocks of pigeons fluttered and wandered about, scarfing up bits of rice and bread left over from mourners. For Ali and Sarwar's purposes however, the cemetery had one distinct advantage: it had only one lane in and one lane out. They could see if someone was tailing them in a car.

In the cemetery's carpark, Ali told Sarwar about the creeping sensation that he was being followed. He wasn't quite sure how, but he knew something was afoot. He was certain he was being watched but couldn't provide any concrete examples. Every person who now looked at him sideways could be an undercover cop.

Sarwar chewed on this new piece of information and asked what they should do—abort the mission? Postpone it? He wanted to know if he should cease collecting chemical precursors.

Ali asked if Sarwar felt he was being watched, too. Sarwar responded that High Wycombe was a pretty small town, and he hadn't really noticed anything out of the ordinary. They decided to push forward; the best course of action was to buy the rest of the equipment and chemicals as soon as possible.

Ali thought about all the warnings Rauf had given him over the last several months: dump everything incriminating far from where you live, make sure everything is in code, and make sure you're not followed. Ali also wanted to hand over the martyrdom videos to Sarwar for safekeeping, but he wasn't quite finished shooting them. There were others who hadn't yet completed this task. But Ali knew he couldn't hang onto them for much longer. If the police found that he had them in his possession, who knows what might happen.[5]

◆

The plotters had good reasons to be paranoid. The authorities' understanding of the group and their activities grew with each new datapoint gleaned from all of the investigative resources now deployed against them. Their evasive actions protected them to some degree, as certain surveillance teams were obliged to hold back from specific spaces, but these efforts paradoxically made the forces arrayed against them even more suspicious.

They knew these men were purchasing jars, batteries, and other associated hardware. Some had ordered new passports. Others were trying to generate as much quick cash as possible. There were a dozen different cars in play. The cell was constantly communicating by phone, text, and email both within Britain and with contacts in Pakistan.

By now MI5, MI6, and the police had integrated into one unit to serve the national interest.[6] Each organization and its leaders knew they had to closely coordinate to fight this conspiracy, lest items fall through the cracks. There also needed to be full transparency among the services. Following 7/7, MI5 created provincial outposts throughout Great Britain to handle terrorist challenges from those areas. Those bombers had been mostly from the northern part of the country, a lower priority for the London-centric services. But 7/7 showed the capital wasn't the only game in town, and a terrorist cell from Leeds or Birmingham could reach the city easily to do damage.

The plot was quickly reaching a tipping point, but the authorities were still starved for actionable intelligence. They had already deployed mobile and static surveillance, had access to CCTV footage, used automatic number plate recognition for license plates, and the like. Still, the covert capabilities in place weren't generating the data required to guarantee a successful prosecution. They needed more intrusive measures. They needed to hear what was happening within the walls of 386A Forest Road.

MI5 decided on a risky move to determine what was going on behind that door: they would mount a "creep," or covert entry, of the Forest Road unit to install audio probes and a camera directly within the flat itself.[7] SO15 commander Peter Clarke noted, "It was the only way we could find out what was going on."[8]

There were challenges to be surmounted. The house sat on a part of the road that forbade on-street parking; a parked van would immediately draw attention to the men breaking into the building. The house might already be wired with surveillance devices. After all, the officers trailing Ali had seen him enter a store that specialized in covert cameras; perhaps that was for this property. For all they knew, the place also could be booby-trapped with explosives. And a final, more mundane concern: while it didn't appear as if anyone was sleeping there during the night, one of the plotters might return to the unit while the team was installing its devices.

The plan was simple enough—wait until Ali and Hussain had cleared out of the building, then deploy the team to install the probes. Everyone held their breath for this opportunity, and when the time was right, they went in.

The small team broke in through the unit's front door late at night and ascended the stairs to the second floor. Once inside the rooms, they placed recording devices where they thought they would generate the most information. They were professionals and knew what they were doing, but they were nevertheless nervous about exposure. They placed the probes in the light fixtures and one video camera in a vent by the floor, providing a worm's eye view of the unit. The team had also placed a static camera feed across the street from the safehouse to capture the entrances and exits of people in the flat.[9] "Once I knew the deployment was successful," one MI5 officer named Jon said, "then the pressure was off."[10]

The audio and video sprang to life, and the sound and images they picked up were piped into the ops room. The authorities now had eyes and ears within the unit. Now they waited for the suspects to reenter the flat the next evening. One of the first things they heard was Tanvir Hussain telling Ali, "You know what, it's quite a big kitchen, innit?" To which Ali replied, "Bring all the bottles and all the batteries and everything and the pan. Bring everything. Let me go to the toilet and then I will help you."[11]

15

"Today's Date Is September 12, 2001"

On the other side of the Atlantic Ocean, U.S. intelligence agencies knew something terrible was afoot in Britain since the springtime. But this wasn't the only issue the Americans had on the front burner. During the spring and summer of 2006, U.S. policymakers were juggling multiple crises. Iraq was boiling over into an all-out sectarian civil war. The Taliban had finally regrouped in Afghanistan and were killing American and Afghan troops, precipitating the largest ever NATO-led attack in the south of the country that August. The FBI arrested several men in June for a half-cocked plot to blow up the Sears Tower in Chicago. North Korea was testing new missiles again. The Israeli military entered Lebanon after Hezbollah launched multiple cross-border raids that July. And, though few in the national security community comprehended it at the time, the enormous American housing bubble began to soften, causing prices to fall by 40 percent, foreshadowing the mortgage melt-down the next year and the subsequent Great Recession.

On the seventh floor of CIA headquarters, senior staff discussed counterterrorism issues with the director and his CTC chief inside a wood-paneled conference room every Monday and Wednesday afternoon.[1] Meetings were mostly focused upon Iraq, Afghanistan, Pakistan, and other "hot spots." But intelligence from Britain kept bubbling up on the agenda. Across the Potomac River, the White House staff also discussed the intelligence at their "Terror Tuesday" meetings. These meetings were often the most important ones of the week: officials in usual attendance included President Bush, Vice President Dick Cheney, National Security Advisor Stephen Hadley, Attorney General Alberto Gonzales, and the heads of the FBI, Department of Homeland Security (DHS), and National Counterterrorism Center (NCTC), as well as advisers Fran Townsend, Juan Zarate, and the president's longtime President's Daily Brief (PDB) briefer, Morgan Muir.[2]

From the president on down, the end goal in these meetings was always the same: to destroy al Qaeda. As such, the CIA's Office of Terrorism Analysis consistently fed the insatiable appetite for the latest counterterrorism intelligence. The White House knew the terror groups in the FATA and elsewhere were regenerating faster than the United States could crush them. As deputy national security adviser for combating terrorism, Juan Zarate quickly realized the United States had to think aggressively not just about intelligence acquisition around particular threats but also about how to "pressure the environment more aggressively and consistently" to constrain al Qaeda's expansion regionally.[3] Bush's senior national security officials held constant meetings about this, in addition to the daily Secure Video Teleconferences (SVTCs) attended by lower-level officials.

Although there had been bits and scraps of threatening intelligence floating about, the contours of the British plot remained fuzzy. Pakistan connected various persons of interest, but the final targets and the actual method of attack remained hidden from view. Intelligence analysts tried to turn the dial to sharpen the picture, pulling together information from different sources. In the first half of the year, the CIA authored multiple products that made their way up the chain, but the analysts couldn't come to any clear conclusion because their terrorist adversaries hadn't themselves figured out what they wanted to do.

Given the sheer size of the U.S. collection effort of both SIGINT (signals intelligence) and HUMINT (human intelligence), the Americans held a few critical pieces of the puzzle. Around this time, MI6 came to the CIA for assistance. As MI5's director-general Eliza Manningham-Buller told one official inquiry, the United States was just as invested as the

British in thwarting this conspiracy because America's security was "absolutely bound up with ours."[4]

One of the CIA's top men at the time was Jose Rodriguez Jr., a compact, longtime Latin American case officer with flecks of silver in his goatee. Over the course of his thirty-plus-year career, he had risen through the ranks to become the director of the National Clandestine Service, formerly and later known as the Directorate of Operations. Rodriguez had a reputation as cocksure operator—a status he didn't deny. Following the 7/7 attack and its aftermath, the British complained during a high-level meeting about how aggressive the agency was with certain counterterrorism operations. Rodriguez turned to MI6 chief Sir John Scarlett and replied in his usual understated way, "You look here, you haven't been whacked by the grace of God and the Central Intelligence Agency."[5]

The transatlantic relationship somehow survived. Scarlett had lots of other friendly contacts among his American counterparts, including the CIA's deputy director, Stephen Kappes. Kappes had known Scarlett for years, as he had run MI6's equivalent of the agency's Central Eurasia (CE) Division.[6] "Can you help us?" the British asked. The answer was almost always "yes."

By the middle of the decade, the CIA had already built independent lines within Pakistan, autonomous of the ISI liaison relationship; these consisted of HUMINT and walk-ins, as well as SIGINT collection capabilities via phones and emails.[7] As one senior CIA official said, "The Pakistanis were only going to help you so much. But we were developing a lot of unilateral access."[8] Accordingly, Uncle Sam was developing additional human sources in Kabul, Islamabad, Peshawar, and various forward operating bases in Afghanistan.[9] The U.S. government became quite adept at finding new sources; it also deployed a robust network of "spotters"—people on the ground who didn't know all the details of any given operation but were motivated to keep an eye out for nefarious foreigners causing distress in the local community.[10]

From its black-cube headquarters at Fort Meade, Maryland, the NSA's cryptologists worked with Britain's signals intelligence agency, GCHQ, to infiltrate the various throwaway email accounts and messenger chat functions that Ali, Sarwar, Rauf, and the others were using to communicate.[11] The two organizations sat cheek-to-jowl, especially on counterterrorism issues. In some ways, the transatlantic relationship was so close that it was not entirely clear where one ended and the other began.[12] In spite of these efforts, communications between all the operatives remained frustratingly opaque enough to obscure their true meaning.

The British services were concerned not only with catching the terrorists but also with making sure all evidence could be presented in open court. The suspects were British nationals on British soil, and it was critical the intelligence could be used in front of a judge and jury. Future prosecutors weren't allowed to use SIGINT traffic. Thus, the email traffic from Rauf to all his operatives could not be introduced in court.

◆

By the middle of the summer of 2006, the Americans—still on high alert following 9/11—generally thought the British were not taking the threat of global terrorism seriously enough. While the intelligence relationship between the two countries was among the closest anywhere in the world, there were some fundamental differences in the mindset and approach to counterterrorism. These were differences that were in part shaped by their experience of terrorist attacks against the homeland.

As a result of its recent experience with global terrorism, the U.S. national security community felt compelled to pursue a far more forceful response against al Qaeda threats. As Charlie Allen, the workaholic grand old man of U.S. intelligence, recounted, "The White House had suffered deeply because of the 9/11 attack; intelligence had suffered deeply, that was very much in my mind, in fact, never again can we allow this country be attacked."[13] The directive from the White House on down was that a 9/11-like strike would not ever happen again. This mentality completely permeated the national security infrastructure; as CIA director Michael Hayden once told his employees at the CTC, "Today's date is September 12, 2001."[14] And every day afterward would also be September 12.

◆

By contrast, the British had been dealing with the pressures of terrorism on the British mainland for over a century. That knowledge and experience factored into the day-to-day workings of the UK security establishment.

As far back as 1883, Irish republicans set off two bombs inside the Paddington and Westminster Bridge stations, which had only opened to the public a decade and a half before.[15] Victoria, Charing Cross, and Ludgate Hill were targeted the next year, and these subterranean spaces quickly became dens of intrigue and terror in the public's imagination.[16]

Over fifty years later, from 1939 to 1940, the Irish Republican Army ran a "Sabotage Campaign" in London and elsewhere, striking King's Cross, Victoria, Tottenham Court Road, Leicester Square, and Euston stations, among many other places. But the city held fast.

During the Troubles, bombs again detonated across London's extensive transport system, inside King's Cross, Victoria, and Euston stations in 1973, while others were discovered and defused by the police. A few years later, in 1976, the IRA hit trains at Cannon Street, West Ham, and Wood Green stations. Paddington and Victoria stations were struck in 1991; London Bridge was bombed in 1992. So was the Imperial War Museum. The day after Prime Minister John Major won a general election in April of that year, a fertilizer bomb wrapped with a hundred pounds of Semtex plastic explosive inside a van exploded in the heart of London's financial district, blowing the Baltic Exchange to smithereens and murdering three bystanders.[17] One was a fifteen-year-old girl. But the city held fast.

Another IRA truck bomb loaded with a thousand pounds of fertilizer destroyed Bishopsgate, a major financial thoroughfare in the City of London, on April 24, 1993. That terror operation murdered a photographer, put a fifteen-foot crater in the street, ruined the NatWest Tower, and wrecked the nearby Liverpool Street station. It also collapsed St. Ethelburga, one of the last medieval churches in the City, a structure which had survived the Great Fire of 1666 and the Blitz. And yet London held on.

Even after the 1998 Good Friday Agreement, the threat to the UK mainland from dissident Irish Republicans would remain. Even as late as 2000, the green-glass and cement MI6 headquarters on the banks of the River Thames were hit by a rocket-propelled grenade fired by an IRA splinter group. And there were the other, post-9/11 Islamist terror plots. But London held on.

Great Britain could certainly use ruthless force in many circumstances; since at least the 1970s, British government officers had co-opted senior IRA interrogators and bombmakers and, over a period of time, hollowed out much of the organization from within.[18] It was an ugly, drawn-out effort that left many innocent (and many not-so-innocent) people dead and mangled upon a shadowy battlefield. It was perhaps a result of this long and troubled history that the British security apparatus had already confronted many challenges that their U.S. counterparts were grappling with in the post-9/11 era.

◆

As the Overt investigation continued to play out, the White House and CIA were pressing their UK counterparts for more concrete action. Admiral Scott Redd, who led the NCTC, viewed the emerging conspiracy as "a loaded gun."[19] The Americans wanted this thing shut down immediately and were pushing the Brits hard to squash it. Saving lives—Americans, British, Canadians, and anyone else—was the most important priority; the messy legal cases would come later. But it was ultimately up to the British to make the arrests. "We need time," the British informed the Americans, including Jose Rodriguez, Fran Townsend, Stephen Hadley, and, of course, President Bush.

"Don't rush to judgment," MI6 officials told Rodriguez, "trust us."

To which he replied, "Famous last words."[20]

Rodriguez and the others knew that despite all the technological advances of the previous decade, there remained places intelligence services simply couldn't go and secrets they couldn't access. They couldn't resurrect phone calls they weren't listening to and recording in the first place; the system didn't work that way. There could've been emails that went unread. There could be plotters whose identities remained unknown. There was never 100 percent certainty about anything, ever, especially when the plotters were trying very hard to cover their tracks.

As Charlie Allen diplomatically put it, "We had great confidence in British security and security services, but we were nervous there were other things that could occur, untold, that someone had been missed, or an element of the plot had been missed by the British."[21] And there was always a possibility that the ever-expanding investigation would leak to the press.

◆

At the CIA's afternoon meetings, there was certainly sympathy for the British perspective. Had the roles been reversed, and the FBI were trying to craft a case against a large terrorist cell within the United States, the Americans would absolutely expect another country's security services to hold their fire.[22] These senior staff, with decades of government experience among them, could also appreciate that the longer the British held off, the more intelligence and connections to nefarious individuals could be developed for follow-on strikes. But, as the CIA's Kappes argued, "Presidents and prime ministers' sacred duty is to protect their citizens."[23] In any case, the agency figured it could gain enough intelligence on those threats by nabbing the suspects now. Kappes shared the sentiment that the Brits were taking their merry time to crush the cell.[24]

The CIA was independently searching for clues as well. The term Overt had by now been adopted on both sides of the Atlantic, and there was a concern the plotters were connected to larger jihadist networks wreaking havoc in Iraq. One counterterrorism analyst who worked in the CTC's Iraq Jihad Analysis group was tasked with checking the classified databases for possible connections. He was quickly pulled off the case when he couldn't find any links to the conflict in the Middle East and replaced by another analyst more willing to make connections. She produced some half-baked analysis that initially generated a lot of attention but eventually went nowhere.

But even without a direct link to the battlefields of Iraq and the Levant, everyone knew the clock was ticking. Someone would blink, or one of the hundreds of surveillance officers would mess up. Then either the bombs would go off or all the plotters would destroy the evidence and go underground.

Fig. 1. Rashid Rauf. Photograph by Farooq Naeem. Courtesy of Getty Images.

Fig. 2. The Mangla
Dam. Photograph
by Yasir Shahzad,
Shutterstock.

Fig. 3. British prime
minister Tony Blair in
2005. Photograph by
360b, Shutterstock.

Fig. 4. Waltham Forest Town Hall. Photograph by AC Manley, Shutterstock.

Fig. 5. Headlines in London following the 7/7 attack. Photograph by Ellywa, Wikimedia Commons.

Fig. 6. 386A Forest Road, Walthamstow. Photograph by the author.

Fig. 7. Exterior of Thames House, headquarters of MI5. Photograph by Cnbrb, Wikimedia Commons.

Fig. 8. Exterior of New Scotland Yard. Photograph by Man vyi, Wikimedia Commons.

Fig. 9. Screenshot from Abdulla Ahmed Ali's martyrdom video. Courtesy of the Metropolitan Police.

Fig. 10. Pakistani chief of army staff Gen. Ashfaq Pervez Kayani on December 28, 2010, in Karachi. Photograph by Asianet-Pakistan, Shutterstock.

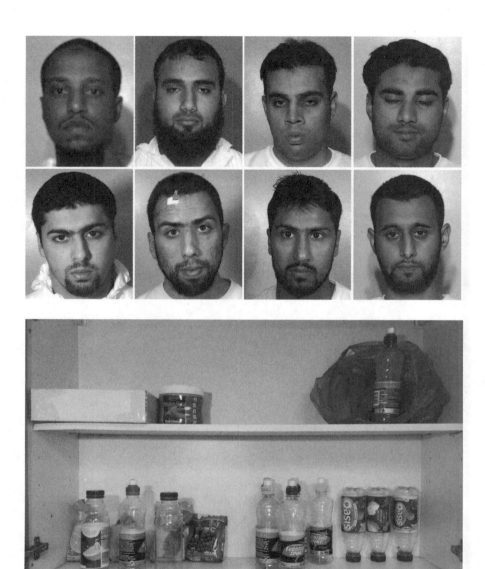

Fig. 11. The Overt main suspects. Top row (*left to right*): Umar Islam, Waheed Zaman, Assad Sarwar, and Mohammed Gulzar. Bottom row (*left to right*): Arafat Khan, Ibrahim Savant, Abdulla Ahmed Ali, and Tanvir Hussain. Courtesy of Getty Images.

Fig. 12. Bottles found at 386A Forest Road. Courtesy of the Metropolitan Police.

Fig. 13. Hollowed-out batteries to be used to hide the detonators. Courtesy of the Metropolitan Police.

Fig. 14. Jars containing batteries, syringes, and food coloring found at 386A Forest Road. Courtesy of the Metropolitan Police.

Fig. 15. This bottle contained hydrogen peroxide and was found in King's Wood, High Wycombe. Courtesy of the Metropolitan Police.

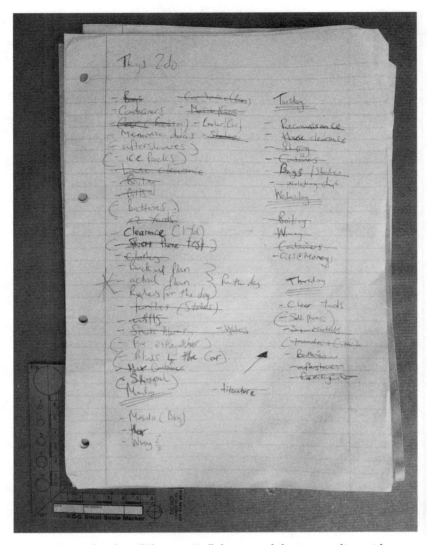

Fig. 16. Notes detailing "Things 2 Do" discovered during a police raid.
Courtesy of the Metropolitan Police.

Fig. 17. The exterior of ʜᴍᴘ Belmarsh in London. Photograph by Katherine Da Silva, Shutterstock.

(Rev. 01-31-2003)

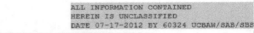

FEDERAL BUREAU OF INVESTIGATION

Precedence: ROUTINE   Date: 08/27/2007

To: Director's Office   Attn: ☐   b6
                                         DD John S. Pistole   b7C
                                         EAD Willie Hulon
                                         AD Thomas V. Fuentes

       Counterterrorism   DAD Arthur M. Cummings, II

From: Counterterrorism
          Contact: Joseph Billy, Jr.

Approved By: Billy Joseph Jr

Drafted By: Billy Joseph Jr:jb

Case ID #: 315N-WF-234463 — *160*

Title: DIRECTOR MUELLER TELEPHONE CALL   b6
        ☐   b7C
                        and RASHID RAUF   b7E

Synopsis: To document Director Mueller's telcall ☐   8/26/0.
and request for FBI access to detained individuals ☐   and
Rashid Rauf

Details: On 8/26/07, Director Mueller placed a telephone call ☐
          ☐ who advised the Director that he was ☐
          ☐ Director Mueller thanked ☐
          ☐ for taking his call and went on to request ☐ support
in allowing FBI/USG access to ☐   and Rashid Rauf,
          ☐   In response, ☐   said he
would take the Director's request under consideration. Director Mueller
also requested ☐   allow FBI personnel to review the evidenc
seized at the time of Rauf's arrest. Director Mueller also noted the b6
possible release from custody of both subjects in the coming days and t b7C
urgency for FBI personnel to interview them.   b7E

          ☐   advised he would look into the Director's request
to review the Rauf evidence. ☐   also advised ☐
          ☐

          In addition, Director Mueller thanked ☐   for
considering his request for access, and said he personally looked forwarc
to seeing ☐   upon his next visit to Washington.

Fig. 18. FBI readout of a telephone call between Director Robert Mueller and a high-ranking Pakistani official in which Mueller requested permission for FBI debriefers to interview Rashid Rauf. This request was rebuffed. Federal Bureau of Investigation.

Fig. 19. Fran Townsend. Photograph by Aude, Wikimedia Commons.

Fig. 20. Fran Townsend and Juan Zarate. Courtesy of the Center for Strategic and International Studies.

16

Sarwar's Hole

Sarwar needed to hide his expanding cache of hydrogen peroxide. He couldn't risk having all his chemicals and gear inside his home, because he still lived in his family's semidetached house on Walton Drive in High Wycombe. He had been buying hydrogen peroxide at a steady clip, but he now had to store it somewhere off-site.

So on the last day of July, he drove into town and picked up a thermometer, which was necessary to monitor the temperature of explosives like TATP and hexamethylene triperoxide diamine (HMTD), as well as three miniature light bulbs. He then stopped by a local Asda supermarket to pick up a shovel and some biscuits. He also headed to the local Woolworths, where he purchased a large silver case with a solid retractable back and a black seal around the middle. He placed his gear in the boot of his car.

That same day, he placed an order for four glass containers, conical flasks, beakers, and a measuring cylinder from the Hop Shop store in Plymouth. He needed this to manufacture the HMTD that would serve as the spark for a larger explosion.[1] Rauf had been adamant the last time they met in Pakistan that he needed concentrated hydrogen peroxide at 80 percent mixed with some aluminum powder, along with an HMTD detonator.[2]

Sarwar kept a notebook in his bedroom, where he'd scribble down items like "get more HP" and "80 HP" and "get black HP." After his meeting with Ali on the fifteenth, he wrote, "Investigate in Bact, TH, Coryton, Fawley, Kingsbury and Haven."

This was not in code, since it was just for himself, translating to "Bacton, Theddlethorpe, Coryton, Fawley, Kingsbury, and Haven."[3] These were all energy terminals around Great Britain: Bacton, Theddlethorpe, and Kingsbury were gas terminals, while Coryton, Fawley, and Haven were oil refineries.[4] He had been researching Britain's gas and electricity grid on his home computer as well.

On that day, Sarwar checked out a wooded area near his home called Booker Common Woods, as well as an enclosed area called King's Wood—almost two hundred acres of ancient beech woodland and flowering plants, encroached by suburban sprawl.[5] Sarwar drove to the edge of a spur, where a tract of houses dead-ended into the Wood. He jumped out a hundred feet from the entrance with a large green bag in his left hand and walked along the main path. He walked another six hundred feet into the Wood, near freshly cut grass in the shape of a semicircle, and continued along the path to the right. Then he abruptly turned around and started back toward his car, tightly clutching his bag.

Sarwar returned to his car and drove to a triangular parking area by the entryway to the Wood closest to his home. Again holding his green bag, he entered through a gate and then walked straight on into the wooded area, approaching a three-way fork. He followed the center path, which then dipped into a shallow gulley, and disappeared into the forest.

◆

It was still daylight outside, but the TVP officers tailing Sarwar had to be careful to remain out of sight since there were few people wandering around the Wood at that time. Luckily, the officers were far enough back to remain unnoticed after his first stop but now, at the second, they were stuck as he disappeared from their view. Victims of unfavorable topography, they would have walked in from a rise in the ground. Had Sarwar turned around, he would have seen them. TVP didn't have any aerial support to watch him from above, which wouldn't have helped much anyway because of the dense tree cover. Frustrated, the officers decided that their best course of action was to hold their ground, even if they didn't have eyes on the target.

Half an hour later, Sarwar reemerged from the densely wooded area without his green bag.[6] What his tail didn't realize was that he used it to mark a tree deep in the Wood as a suitable place to dig a hole.[7] All the TVP knew was that he went into the Wood with a green bag, and then returned without it.

Early the next morning, Sarwar returned to the Wood, this time with the shovel and silver suitcase he had purchased the day before. Within the suitcase, Sarwar had packed his probe thermometer, syringes, Pyrex flasks, food coloring, plastic bottles, citric acid, and a Saxa salt container that contained a bag of hexamine—the science kit required to build HMTD detonators.[8] He found his plastic bag in the dense forest under a tree. It was maybe four or five in the morning, before the dogwalkers and other joggers would pass through the area. Quite a plan, Sarwar thought to himself. He started to dig.

Unfortunately, Sarwar hadn't realized how much earth he'd have to displace to bury a well-sized suitcase into the ground. He also hadn't reckoned how hard the ground would be in the Wood. He grunted and sweated and struggled to dig for the better part of half an hour. The English soil refused to yield, and so he gave up, abandoning his new shovel in the dense underbrush.

Maybe he didn't have the right technique, Sarwar thought. Perhaps digging a hole in the ground required some sort of expertise; a proficiency in the manual arts he lacked. He returned home and googled "how to dig a hole." He took notes. And then he went back the next day, again around four or five in the morning, to keep digging. Again, he exerted great energy before eventually giving up.[9] Hiding the chemicals was proving to be more difficult than he thought.

He went back to the Wood a third day in a row. Sarwar's Google research indicated the earth could be clay and that by moistening the soil it may become easier to dig. He brought a bucket of water from his house—again, in the dark hours of the early morning—and dumped it onto the area where he had started to dig a small, nonsuitcase-shaped hole. He peered inside, hoping to see the earth below it melt to reveal a hiding spot. It didn't. Feeling disheartened and somewhat tired, Sarwar gave up, drove home, and crawled back into bed.[10]

Later that afternoon Sarwar returned, now for the fourth time. The land refused to yield to the quartermaster. He wandered around some more, and, after a few minutes, saw a downed tree. At the foot was a large cavity, perfect for his suitcase-related requirements. He returned early the next morning, again in the morning hours, and dumped his suitcase there.

But the hole at the base of the fallen tree was too small for the suitcase, so its top part stuck up from the ground. Luckily, there were fallen leaves nearby, so Sarwar drove to Homebase on August 7 and purchased a garden rake.[11]

◆

The police didn't know what was happening. During the middle of the night, the TVP inserted units into the Wood to try to find the stash, using rudimentary and ultimately ineffective technical means to track Sarwar.[12] What the authorities had also completely missed were the other locations Sarwar had used to hide his stockpiles throughout the area. That's because he had been squirreling away bags of hydrogen peroxide and HMTD precursors for months, in another ancient beech forest called Fennels Wood—originally the property of the Knights Templar of Bisham Abbey, just across the River Thames in Buckinghamshire—and also within his garage.

◆

Rauf sent Ali in an email midday on the thirty-first: "By the way, how is the skin infection you told me about? Is it getting worse or is the cream working?"[13] Ali told him he remained concerned about surveillance, or the possibility of surveillance, following him. Both Rauf and Ali were aware that the police might be catching on, but both wanted to press on with the operation.

Back in the Forest Road unit, the hidden microphones and cameras began to capture the comings and goings of the men, as well as some of their conversations. Far from Hollywood's high-tech version of twenty-first-century counterterrorism efforts, surveillance technology was not as crisp or as sharp as one would hope. There was a lot of muffled, disjointed, distracting crosstalk on the audio. Furthermore, external noise from outside of the flat, like the honking of car horns, made the experience of this programming tiresome.

Nevertheless, the officers with the large headphones in their secure rooms could hear other distinct noises. A rattling kitchen boiler. The sound of drilling.

Much of the verbiage was garbled and indistinct, which made this process difficult. The listeners weren't quite sure what was being said. Was Ali saying "so burned" or "so bad"? Did he say "mission" or "the machine?" There was also a lot of muffled talk that just didn't make much sense. For example, Ali once said, "They knew when Bobby's going kitchen, innit? Yeah, yeah, obviously, but bring all the balls and all the batteries and everything and the pan, just bring everything. I've got them good quality at . . . They're not going to, you know, and stick, how come you laid it up, yeah, like that, you know what all that happens is, everything gone down the —"[14]

Ali and his crew knew they had to hide the detonators; batteries were chosen as innocuous casings for the HMTD. They had discovered the Energizer batteries bought from local stores were difficult to slice open and then reassemble; however, the cheap batteries made for the domestic Pakistani market were flimsier and could be taken apart easily. Those batteries were the ones that had flummoxed authorities at Heathrow; this answered the question why Ali brought back several packs of shoddy batteries from his recent trip abroad.[15]

In the middle of this, Hussain told Ali, "Should've got bleach, you know."

"For what?"

"For your batteries."

"Why?"

"You put bleach in all of them, yeah, leave them overnight, yeah, empty them then, much easier then."

The two men experimented with plastic bottles, attempting to replicate the Lucozade drink by dropping Tang powder into the water. Despite what the authorities originally surmised, the Tang was not an explosive accelerant at all but was meant to be used as a coloring agent. They had extracted the sports drink and filled the bottle with other fluids. What they discovered was that at first, the liquid became opaque, taking on the appearance of the original sports drink. However, if left out for a day or so, the powder separated from the water.

Ali told Hussain, "You know the Tang, no, it's not that. You know the Tang, yeah, mmm, it's probably neither of those into it, so I thought dissolved so if I make the misty no it's all clear, can you . . . can see the real rings in the rough stuff it's not, yeah."[16]

Ali then said, "Perfect from the top do you think I'm dry? No. This one's holding out. That must be the difference. Mmm, it's not so burned that you can't tell. I can see through it. That's no fucking good, yeah, so long. The Tang is going to dissolve properly as I'm making this table. You hear from me now . . . get it done, okay. Yeah, that's good. Are you sure? Yeah, yeah. That's boom, that's boom, mate."

What did "That's boom, mate" mean, the surveillance team wondered. Were they referring to bombs, or was it just slang for "that's good?" The authorities listening in weren't sure.

There was more drilling over the audio, obscuring the conversation. Finally, it stopped, and they could hear Ali more clearly, "It's over there. Should have gone and checked out all of these, yeah. Yeah, all of them foreign birds do you think, orange, or our own, yeah, we've got our virgins so very good, perfect."

Foreign birds. Virgins. The usual patter of men talking about women. While they chatted, Ali and Hussain continued to experiment with injected liquid in the bottom of the soda bottles. They then closed the holes made by their needles with a plasticine material that appeared to be part of the bottle's fabrication process. It now looked like a perfectly sealed bottle.

◆

To detonate the bombs, the men planned to connect the bottles to small light bulbs via metal wires. When each bulb turned on, so too would the detonator, and then the larger explosive itself. It was a simple, elegant solution. It was similar to what Muktar Ibrahim tried to do the previous year. But this was a far better idea: what security guard would bother to examine an unopened soda bottle?

Ali exclaimed, "Oh shit, that will come off. Look at that completely, the head off. There's two of them—No, don't joke—You can use these for the attack then, hey, yeah."

The duo found that if they weren't careful when piercing tiny holes in the lightbulbs, the glass head would come apart in their hands. Sometimes it would break, but the filament would remain intact. They used their multimeter to see if the filament stayed whole; the meter would make a bleeping noise if so. If the filament within the bulb remained unviolated, it would still light up when charged. That would mean it worked.

♦

Ali told Hussain about his run-in with the ISI in Pakistan, and how local forces and his family helped him wriggle from the net: "Mmm, I never hoped that we can at least do a decent job. My great suspicions are that we're under surveillance. Well, a number of us are just waiting to pick out the two or three that have gone down. A number wait on one hand though. Whenever you get the terminal there, there are four terminals."[17]

The authorities missed a crucial clue here. They heard "My very position, bruv" crackle over the audio, instead of what Ali actually said, which was along the lines of "My great suspicions are that we're under surveillance."[18] But for one reason or another, the authorities missed that completely.

As they tested the electrical circuits, Ali took the time to trash Arafat Khan's martyrdom video, which they had shot several days beforehand. "I mean, when we first practiced it, he did a really bad job," he told Hussain. Arafat was "stuttering all over the place. He just did a quick rush job."

Hussain replied, "He doesn't take it seriously."

Ali agreed. In his view, Arafat simply didn't take anything seriously. The script was completely written out for him, and all he had to do was read it for the camera, but Arafat wasn't the brightest. He kept getting confused and couldn't focus on the task at hand.[19]

They then drifted off and talked about other things, like George Galloway getting fired from *Talk Sport*, about political gadfly and Islam convert Yvonne Ridley, and about a couple being caught having sex on an airplane.

Ali mentioned to Hussain, "We've got six people, innit? Me, Omar B., Adnan, Ibo, Aro, Waheed."

"I thought you had six?"

Ali responded, "That's seven."

They then listed everyone on the team: Ali, Tanvir Hussain, Adnan (Adam) Khatib, Ibrahim Savant, Arafat Khan, Umar Islam (a.k.a. Omar B), and Waheed Zaman.

"So seven?"

"There's another three units."

"There's another three units, three groups. Uh . . . ?" Ali was getting a bit confused.

Hussain then counted: "Seven, eight, nine, ten, eleven, twelve, thirteen, that's fifteen, eighteen. Phew, think of it. Yeah, all right. One man more."[20]

◆

Imagine the shock of the officers listening with the large headphones to their conversation. Ali and Hussain had just revealed there could be up to eighteen suicide bombers somewhere in London. At that point, only this cell—perhaps several people, along with a number of other peripheral individuals—were under twenty four-hour surveillance.

Other audio crackled from the feed, "One man more . . . so what do you want to do . . . is there any more batteries in there?" A boiler rattled in the background.

As for the precise nature of the attack, Ali hadn't quite decided, even though Rauf was increasingly insistent on setting a date. So he told Hussain, "Still moving, something closer at the end of the year."[21] It all depended on how quickly they could build their weapons and secure their passports.

And then: "Texas, thinking I've got Dallas or Chicago or North Carolina, South Carolina . . . that California anyway?"[22] And then, "California, beaches, innit, Los Angeles, yeah, I'm going."

And: "This mission is a great mission, you know that. It's not easy man, you know what it is."

◆

Nearly everyone in the security establishment who had experienced 7/7 and 7/21 felt with a sinking feeling that they were always playing catch-up. They needed more personnel to grapple with this metastasizing crisis. The clarion call thus went out across the land: officers with surveillance experience were needed—immediately. As a back-of-the-envelope calculation, if a team of ten officers worked an eight-hour shift, then each suspect required about thirty cops watching him for a twenty-four-hour cycle, making the total need a force of 240 officers for eight suspects. By the beginning of August, hundreds of officers from all over England, Wales, Scotland, and Northern Ireland converged on the capital.

And it couldn't just be any cop on the force. The individuals most successful at this sort of work have two general traits: they are ordinary, forgettable-looking people, and they are willing to let their job take over their life. They have to be willing to be out at all hours of the night, on the weekends and holidays. They miss birthdays and anniversaries. Funerals too. It is a hard job in which to maintain stable relationships, because one is always on the move.[23]

Overt became a 24/7 operation. Officers stopped going home to their wives, husbands, and children. Some were living in hotels and only seeing colleagues on the force. They bought clothing and toiletries as needed. Many had little idea of the plot's full scope, or what was happening, or what the Americans were up to in Washington DC or in Pakistan. Many who worked for SO15 were staying in accommodations near the Paddington Green Police Station, an unpleasant-but-centrally located 1960s-era cement edifice for high-security terror threats. The TVP remained responsible for monitoring Sarwar and a few others out in High Wycombe.

These highly trained individuals had to ensure they weren't spotted by the suspects or their friends—a complex task made more challenging by the increasingly paranoid group of targets. Their work was grinding and boring, punctuated by short bursts of activity. In East London, surveillance vans, static and mobile teams contended with crowded streets and thoroughfares in places tightly bound by kith, kin, and faith. But in recent years, the police tried to hire different types of people to be more representative of the communities they served, which helped them to fit in and remain out of sight. By 2006 the authorities had a lot of practice tailing suspects in these areas.

Over eight hundred officers eventually worked the case, pulled from just about every surveillance team in the country.[24] The British government even pulled teams from Northern Ireland from monitoring splinter IRA groups, as well as from the uniformed military. "If the Boy Scouts had a surveillance team," the Met's Steve Dryden dryly noted, "we'd have used them as well."[25] But Great Britain was running out of teams.[26] Nigel Inkster, the former deputy chief of MI6, noted that by this time MI5 was, like the Met, being stretched to the limit.[27]

At the TVP headquarters in Oxfordshire, the force was running on all cylinders. Officers were working continuously, sometimes twenty-four-plus hours straight. Some tried to catch a nap on the floors and the various couches inside the station, often with little success. The officers were also beginning to grow weary from the never-ending pace of operations, for there was no real end in sight. Burnout, and the sloppiness that would accompany it, was a very real challenge. TVP tried to stave off the inevitable slipup by giving officers a day off every so often to catch up on sleep, say hi to the missus, and play with their kids. But that was more the exception than the rule.[28]

Tens of thousands of bits of data flowed in, from multiple surveillance teams working across many venues and targets. Top secret data was streaming in from the Americans, much of which most cops weren't allowed to see. The threat data was voluminous: they had to systematize, validate, cross-check, and then organize the information as it came in, in almost real time. There were senior working-level meetings at least three times daily just to deconflict all the bits and bobs from the case.

Some officers would work double or triple shifts to keep it going, both for mobile surveillance and static teams.[29] The strain was compounded by senior policymakers, including the home secretary and the prime minister, as well as the heads of MI5 and MI6, who needed to be updated and informed on a continual basis.

Overt had become a national emergency—but one where the public was completely in the dark.

17

Transatlantic Tensions

When the audio probe intelligence indicated the terrorist cell was bandying about place names like "California" and "Dallas" and "Chicago," the results were exactly what the British expected and feared.

The Americans lost their minds.

The contours of the plan were now coming into view. The bombers were going to evade security and somehow get to the States. It was obvious they were going to take a flight, or multiple flights, to do so. For the Americans, 9/11 remained fresh in everyone's mind; everyone knew exactly where they were when the planes hit the World Trade Center, the Pentagon, and a field in Pennsylvania. The destinies of almost all in Washington who had to make life-and-death decisions were forged on that Tuesday morning. Everyone knew the consequences of inaction. Everyone knew someone who had perished that day. Al Qaeda was resurrecting an audacious plan, and the target was, once again, the United States of America.

Unlike the last time however, America might be able to get the drop on the enemy.

◆

Yet as Overt reaching a boiling point, MI5 and MI6 were annoyed with their American counterparts over a completely different problem. The American investigative journalist Ron Suskind had inadvertently blown the cover of one of their most important counterterrorism assets for his book *The One Percent Doctrine*. This asset, Aimen Dean, had reported on Sidique Khan and his crew attending Anwar Awlaqi's sermon in Dudley a few years beforehand. This book went to press in June 2006 and became an instant bestseller. Within it, Suskind revealed an asset named "Ali"—Dean's birth name—and his intelligence on a plot to strike the New York City subway system with a chemical gas–producing device called *mubtakkar*, or "invention."[1] At the time, the CIA took this plot so seriously it even built a mockup of the device—a cylindrical device that could be placed in a backpack—and placed it on one of the tables in the Oval Office for the president.[2]

Al Qaeda operatives quickly put two and two together. As word got out that the tight-knit organization had a mole, the British had to scramble to protect Dean from overlapping networks of jihadists and jihadist wannabes throughout Europe. Dean later noted one of al Qaeda's military commanders eventually issued a fatwa to have him killed.[3] This death threat eventually made its way back to the jihadist networks in Great Britain.

The British surmised the leak came from the Office of the Vice President. The U.S. national security establishment was a notoriously leaky ship, as different people and offices jockeyed for praise, credentials, and bragging rights. The more the Americans knew, the more might get into the press. This also meant word of Overt might spill at any moment.

The British also had another longtime axe to grind with the Americans. Following the 7/7 plot, they had naturally shared a great deal of intelligence with their U.S. counterparts. Soon after this information was provided, a fair amount of sensitive material found its way into the American press.[4] For example, the NYPD revealed in what one press article termed "an unusually wide-ranging briefing" to business leaders that those bombers used TATP—much to the annoyance of British authorities, who hadn't given authorization to share this information publicly.[5] The secret keepers at Vauxhall Cross, Thames House, and New Scotland Yard were quite displeased.[6]

But what could London really do but continue to work with Washington and send them its most sensitive intelligence? Britain had far greater incentive to work with America than vice versa. Yes, the British punched far above their weight when it came to intelligence collection, but the second oldest of human professions has always been a team sport. This held especially true when fighting global terrorism.

Britain's intelligence community also could not compete with the resources and personnel the United States could throw at a problem. MI5 had about fifteen hundred employees in 2001, but with the waves of jihadist plots threatening Britain's shores, that number rose to some four thousand by the end of the decade, its budget doubled.[7] MI5 would eventually have more resources than it did during the Cold War—with the bulk reoriented toward fighting terrorism.[8]

Even so, it wasn't enough. As its chief noted in 2011, "The American relationship is special to the degree that the Americans have much more intelligence and substance than anybody else."[9] After all, the CIA's CTC expanded from three hundred employees on 9/11 to about two thousand, with all the financial resources that came with a new war.[10] Meanwhile, the FBI surged almost two thousand personnel to its national security programs within a single year.[11]

The British believed the United States had generally two main strategic advantages in this fight in the shadows. One was, as MI6's Nigel Inkster noted, that it was "clearly the de facto global counterterrorism czar." The other was that the Americans were the "collector of first resort."[12] Most of the internet was routed through the United States, so email traveling to and from Pakistan that passed through American companies and American fiber-optic cables could be examined with a court warrant. Also, America had better relations with Pakistan than Britain did, for cultural, historic, and legal reasons. Washington's billions in aid to Islamabad helped too.[13]

But there were spidery cracks forming in the relationship. America viewed the fight against al Qaeda as a war against an implacable enemy, while the British generally viewed the group more as a criminal organization. This difference in perspective meant the Americans were more aggressive worldwide in confronting the threat than the British, who were attempting to build a case that could hold up in open court.

◆

From America's perspective, Britain, its closest ally and member of the FIVE EYES intelligence-sharing alliance, was competent, professional, sharp, and imperfect. The 7/7 and 7/21 bombers had made significant contacts inside the country, traveled to Pakistan for training, returned, and built and deployed sophisticated bombs—without anyone making the connection. Thus, it was unsatisfactory to the White House, to the president, to Fran Townsend, to the CIA director, and to the grim, chain-smoking éminence grise at the CTC that questions remained about the Overt plot.

On behalf of the president, Townsend took charge of White House communications with her British counterparts. Her ground-floor office felt like she and her staff worked on a submarine, as the office ceilings felt unnaturally low. This was no particular problem for the petite Townsend, but it seemingly obliged taller individuals like the CIA's Steve Kappes to bend slightly on walking into her office.[14] At this point, Townsend had more or less begun to sleep on her office couch at the White House, just in case events broke and she needed to be at her battle station.

Townsend peppered the British with questions like: How many people were actually in this cell anyway? Who did they speak with? Did any one of these two dozen or so suspects have friends in the airline or transportation industry?[15]

The Americans had other, more specific issues. Since the plotters appeared to want to travel to the United States, did any of them have airport Secure Identification Display Area badges, or could they get access to one? Perhaps at Heathrow? The largest airport in the country employed some seven thousand people, and Gatwick, Luton, and London City airports employed many thousands more. Were any of the baggage handlers, aircraft mechanics, ground crew, janitors, or food and beverage service personnel related to or friends with any of the suspects? How many airport workers prayed at the same mosque as the suspects? Did any of them hang around the same boxing clubs, pizza joints, or internet cafés?

And what, specifically, were the targets?

Townsend was also concerned the British had not informed baggage screeners and security personnel across the transportation sector about this new threat. The bombs were shaping up to be new types of explosives, and the tens of thousands of screeners had little idea what hydrogen peroxide might look or smell like. Concentrated HP itself is a thick, viscous material, like syrup. The only way to make an accurate determination was to take the bottle and shake it to see if the liquids behaved the way soda normally would. The security screeners at Heathrow, JFK, O'Hare, LAX, or any other airport wouldn't particularly know what to look for, and the powerful detection machines purchased and operating following 9/11 wouldn't pick it up.

Very quickly, Townsend ran into turbulence with the British and their desire to keep the investigation open-ended for the purposes of making a court case. The senior MI5 representative in Washington, an agreeable fellow with a prime perch from the UK embassy on Massachusetts Avenue, told Townsend that they had it under control. Everyone of any consequence was under surveillance. But when asked the very basic questions about airport security, he replied with a polite "We'll have to get back to you on that."[16]

But the state never controls everything all the time. And even if the British did, which they likely didn't, the American services and the White House hardly had perfect visibility into the plot. Yes, MI5 had gotten into the safehouse on Forest Road, but what about Ali's flat? What about Sarwar's family home? And Tanvir Hussain? What were peripheral suspects like Waheed Zaman doing all the time? The British obviously didn't know what Ali and Sarwar spoke about on their bellies in Lloyd Park, so what else would they be missing? Why didn't Ali's Vauxhall—which ferried around multiple members of the plot—have an audio bug placed in it, like the suspects in the Crevice had a few years beforehand?

CIA director Hayden and the rest of the agency brass were clear-eyed about the plot and the potential ramifications of inaction. "We knew what al Qaeda was trying to do," he said. "That's good enough! Let's arrest them." As for the follow-on legal consequences, "You [British] figure it out."[17] Of course, MI6 pushed back on this, saying law enforcement still needed to build the case. To which Hayden replied, "No. Just arrest them. Because we were thinking sometimes on a Monday or Tuesday, if we didn't think of this or this, three planes would go down. C'mon. Bring 'em in. Just bring them in."[18]

At the center of the spider web, hundreds of British officers were working a high-wire act. They knew the Americans were now hot, bothered, and demanding immediate action. "There was disquiet between our approach and the approach by the Americans in Pakistan," recalled Steve Dryden, diplomatically. "The Americans took, and always do take, a different view. And they will spoil the plot, disrupt it, and deal with what they've got there and then."[19] In other words, the Yanks would blow the Met's case to smithereens at the earliest possible moment.

Laughing about it later, Fran Townsend understood the British were "aggravated in the extreme from getting a lot of rudder from some lady in the White House when it was their case."[20] But the planes were going to fly to America, and no one quite knew when or where an attack might happen, or how many plotters were in circulation.

She noted, "It felt like August 2001 on steroids."[21]

♦

What America and Britain didn't know was that al Qaeda had already successfully conducted a dry run of an operation. The group placed all the people and the components minus the explosives on a passenger flight somewhere in the world. "The purpose of the exercise," Rauf later recalled, "was to test that none of the components would be checked manually."[22]

They weren't.

18

Skin Infection

It was a bit after half past ten in the morning on the first of August, and Sarwar had a packed day full of excitement. He made his first stop at the post office, where he mailed a folded A4 size brown envelope. Next he stopped at a neighborhood pharmacy and purchased two bottles of citric acid, one of the ingredients needed to manufacture HMTD. He then filled up his car's tank and headed to two other pharmacies to buy additional bottles of citric acid.[1]

By early afternoon, Sarwar left High Wycombe and headed east. After a quick solo lunch at the Medina Restaurant in Slough, he hit up the One World Café to check his email. Sitting at terminal number 17, Sarwar had to sign into a new account, so he entered a username. He couldn't quite remember the password, so he felt inside his pockets and produced a piece of paper with some handwritten scribbles. After typing in the relevant information, he ripped the paper into tiny pieces and placed the litter back in his pocket. He opened the account and noticed it had only one message. He replied to it and left. It was from Rauf.

Sarwar then called Ali and then Gulzar from two separate telephone boxes to inform them about the latest commands from Pakistan. After connecting, Sarwar picked up some latex gloves and superglue. He figured that after extracting the contents of the sport drinks' bottles with a needle, they would need to stop up the resulting hole. A healthy glob of glue would do the trick.[2]

The next day he called both Ali and Gulzar multiple times, both directly and via calling card, followed with yet another call to Rauf in Pakistan. At this point he either didn't believe or didn't realize these calls were being monitored.

◆

The rest of the crew was likewise busy. Tanvir Hussain applied over the phone for a personal loan for £8,000 from Halifax plc to complement the career development loan he had already received from Barclays Bank. Ibrahim Savant the next day also received good news: Barclays had confirmed his application for £10,000, supposedly to purchase a car.[3]

Meanwhile, Ali was engaged in planning for the next month. In between playing the doting father and husband, taking Cossor and his little boy shopping at the local department stores, he ran a more important errand on August 2. That afternoon, he purchased a ticket at Walthamstow Central, walked to the platform, and connected with Tanvir Hussain. The pair headed to the end car and chitchatted about nothing in particular during their journey. They exited the train at Victoria station, two souls among a quarter of a million who passed through its doors that day. They left and headed south on the busy Buckingham Palace Road, past the hordes of tourists and the taxis.[4] Ali was adamant that he was being followed, a gnawing feeling that he experienced daily, and so he kept turning back to look around him. But there were too many people on the street for him to spot anyone tracking him.

Ali and Hussain headed to the nearby HM Passport office. As Ali stepped into the sliding doors, he repeatedly gazed along Eccleston Bridge, the roadway over the railway tracks. He didn't see anything that piqued his interest, and so the two men joined the long line inside. Ali and Hussain had both made appointments for new passports, but Ali suddenly left the line and headed out to the café across the street, phone in his ear. He was acting unpredictably and furtively looked around—down the street, at a nearby telephone box, watching, looking for someone to be watching back. Ali remained on his call, looked around again, and sat down on the bench. Hussain soon joined him.

Ali went back inside the passport office, but Hussain remained on the bench with his phone in his ear, scouring up and down the streets for surveillance. It was a breezy day in London and there were hundreds of people milling about. He scrutinized the folks waiting by the bus stand, the bikers, the tourists exiting the nearby hotel, the gentlemen enjoying a midafternoon pint at St. George's Tavern on the corner. The officers, if there were any, could have been hiding in plain sight. But they couldn't tell.

Finally, Ali came out and they returned the same way they came, across Eccleston Bridge and into the packed Victoria station. They didn't say much on the forty-minute ride home to Walthamstow. But they knew they were being watched, somehow, and their body language telegraphed their nervousness. When they arrived at Walthamstow station and took the neon-lit escalators from the subway to the outside, they stood back-to-back; Ali faced forward and Hussain looked back down, scanning for anyone who may be behind them.[5]

They didn't see anything. The men shrugged to each other, then walked over to play tennis in Lloyd Park.

◆

The surveillance officers tailing Ali and Hussain were experts at their profession. They had indeed spent the afternoon following Ali and Hussain from Walthamstow Central to Victoria station, south on Buckingham Palace Road, across the Eccleston Bridge, and to the passport office. They noted that both men were giving off unmissable signs of agitation, since they kept looking around for signs of surveillance. The officers did an admirable job of blending in with the hundreds of other people on the street and on public transport. They also followed them back on the same route, all without being seen. In fact, the people who Ali most likely suspected were tailing him had nothing to do with anything; they were just regular folks going about their lives. The actual surveillance team remained completely undetected.[6]

◆

Around that same time that Ali and Hussain were waiting at the passport office, Sarwar was making his way back to the large, wooded area in High

Wycombe where he had vanished several days prior. This time, he held a white bag in his hand. He disappeared into the green, dense forest, alone. An hour later, he reemerged from the Wood, empty-handed.

The TVP surveillance squad again did not want to follow him into the dense underbrush since that would have alerted him to their presence. The police had little idea what was in that bag, or where it went.

◆

Ali was feeling the heat. The next day, a Wednesday, he went to Magan Communications Internet Café on Chingford Avenue and shot a note to Rauf: "The cameraman has a couple of Polish birds he wants to pick up his dirty laundry . . . Listen, it's confirmed, I have fever. Sometimes when I go out in the sun to meet people, I feel hot. I check with doc and he confirmed . . . by the way I set up my music shop now. I only need to sort out the opening time. I need stock . . ."[7]

The "fever" referred to his growing and justified paranoia. He just knew something was wrong, really wrong, and that he was being followed. He thought he spotted a couple of people around Walthamstow that looked out of place and assumed they were watching him.

He then wrote, "By the way, I've set up my mobile shop now. I only need to sort out an opening time and I need stock from Nabsy."[8] Nabsy was a nickname for Sarwar (not Nabeel Hussain).

After sending that email, he took off, and then spent the better part of the day in 386A Forest Road. Had Ali waited around a bit longer, he would have seen Rauf's reply: "Your skin infection is contagious. Don't want it spreading. By the way, how bad is it? Do you always get it when you go out or is it only sometimes? I need as much details as possible so my friend the skin specialist, Paps, can help."

"Paps" was probably an al Qaeda operative who knew more about thwarting surveillance. But Rauf knew the men were getting jumpy. They had come so far; Rauf knew they were almost there. They just needed to fulfill the mission before the authorities put all the puzzle pieces together.

True to form, he nagged Ali, "Do you think you can still open the shop with this skin problem? Is it only minor or do you think you can still sort an opening time without the skin problem worsening?" Then further down: "Has Kala done his rap show?" This was Umar Islam, who had not yet recorded a martyrdom video for the cell. He was slated to shoot it in about a week.

Finally, at the end of the email, Rauf reiterated his extreme concern with police exposure: "PS: have any of the shop assistants also got this infection?"[9]

◆

The surveillance specialists finally got the video system, which had a few initial hiccups, to work properly. They had installed a wide-angle lens, but the one in the kitchen was nestled on the far end from the door. The drawback to this worm-level vantage point was that the officers basically only saw the linoleum floor, shoes and trousers of Ali and Hussain, and the bottom of a large bin in the center of the room.

The men had turned on a radio in the kitchen. The radio station went to a commercial break, and the first advertisement featured Cliff Richard and the Shadows' 1963 hit, *Summer Holiday*.[10] Tanvir used his hand-held drill and popped out the bottom of a bottle, and then two men stood over it to examine their work. Tanvir drilled some more bottles.

◆

Sarwar was also on the move. He left High Wycombe and drove southeast for an hour, past Walthamstow to Barking, parking near the station. Heading out on foot, he made a call from a telephone box and then very shortly met a man wearing a gray jacket and a cap—Mohammed Gulzar, now codenamed as "Pie Chart." They met at an otherwise uninspiring intersection and roundabout of Longbridge and Cecil Roads, and said hello. Sarwar handed Gulzar an Asda shopping bag that he had been carrying; inside it had Tupperware containers filled with curry and rice.[11]

Gulzar had been staying off the grid and craved some decent home-made food. Sarwar was also carrying an additional shopping bag from Tesco; inside it sat a plastic orange bottle similar to a sports bottle.[12] The duo ambled down a residential throughway that intersected with

Priory Road, where Gulzar had been bedding down since returning. The two men, not saying much, entered Gulzar's hideout.[13] They stayed inside for two hours and talked about a great many things over the curry and rice. Sarwar told Gulzar that Mohammed Patel was sick, while Gulzar informed Sarwar that he was running low on funds.[14] They spoke about other issues too.

Eventually Sarwar left the flat, carrying a plastic bag. He made his way to a telephone box and called Ali three times, all using calling cards. In spite of the prevalence of mobile phones, this was the cell's preferred way to mask who was calling whom in an attempt to confuse anyone monitoring their phones. Sarwar then walked to his car and took off.[15]

◆

A surveillance team followed Sarwar and Gulzar from a distance, surreptitiously taking video. When the two men turned into the Priory Road unit, they vanished from line of sight of the observing officers. Given that the small road had almost no foot traffic, the team had to stay toward the end of the block, unable to observe the plot's quartermaster's and an explosives expert's activities. Frustratingly, the officers could only note the upstairs window was open, which meant they might have been able to listen in if they could get closer.[16] But the risk of exposure was too great.

After Sarwar left, Gulzar left the flat ten minutes later. One set of officers had already left with Sarwar; the other set kept monitoring Gulzar. They observed he was acting quite unnaturally, unlike when he first met Sarwar. While he walked down Priory Road, he turned his head around twice. He, too, thought he was being watched.[17]

◆

Sometimes in an investigation there are things that occur that make no sense, or appear hair-on-fire important at the time but actually turn out to be nothing. Here was one of them. The surveillance team noted Sarwar went to the One World Internet Café in Slough again on August 4. While sitting at the terminal, he procured a small piece of paper from his wallet and carefully typed in the user ID and password.

After checking his email, he left, but took care to put the piece of paper in his mouth and literally eat the evidence.

Afterward, they followed him to the local post office, carrying a brownish cardboard box and several A4 sized envelopes with internal bubble wrapping. He walked in and waited in the queue. Then, the officers watching him thought he mailed a box to an address in Los Angeles.[18]

It turned out Sarwar was actually mailing a request by special delivery to the Hop Shop, a company that sold conical flasks and other lab equipment.[19] But the authorities at the time thought he was sending a package of unknown contents to California, raising the possibility of further, as-yet-unknown connections in the United States. This was quickly ironed out on the backend, but it was not clear if this information was immediately relayed to the Americans, who would have no doubt taken this opportunity to pressure the Brits to crush the cell immediately, no matter the cost to the future prosecution.

◆

Ali was agitated. He drove out to Slough alone and sat down at the One World Internet Café. He checked his email and saw a note from Rauf in his burner account. In it, the boss in Pakistan nagged him to move forward, and Ali read his commentary about the "skin infection."[20] He stood up and then sat back down. From behind his computer terminal, he looked around, waiting for someone.

Finally, that someone arrived—Sarwar. The man from High Wycombe was a creature of habit; they went back to the Medina Restaurant on Farnham Road, next to the internet café.

In hushed tones, the two men caught each other up on their work over the last few days. Ali told him about the videos and the work he was carrying out at the Forest Road safehouse. He had finally figured out how to hollow out the batteries correctly, as well as how to modify the light bulbs and the bottles. Sarwar had been less successful; he had been fumbling around with his batteries at home but couldn't insert the detonators correctly. Ali was working on how to color the hydrogen peroxide in such a way that it would look like an untampered sport drink. Sarwar told Ali about Gulzar being in town and how he had money problems. Ali said he'd try to get some cash together, but wasn't sure how much he'd really need to float. Ali also revealed that Heathrow was a target, or part of the target, while passing along a cylindrical glass jar and some propaganda videos on a Sony videotape.[21]

The next day, August 5, Sarwar expressed his annoyance to Ali about their mutual boss in Pakistan. As a distant CEO, Rauf was pushing both men to move forward quickly with the operation. So Sarwar emailed Ali, "My friend's uncle will be going abroad on Monday morning so I will need the film by Sunday afternoon at the latest. You still haven't got back to me about the yard that I need ASAP. Joseph had a go at me because I haven't sorted my things out."[22]

Ali grumbled later, "Okay, I'm on the case."[23]

19

Our Citizens, Our Planes

"I will still open the shop," Ali wrote to Rauf on August 6, a bit before noon from T&I Telecom Internet Café on Wood Street in Walthamstow. "I don't think it's so bad that I can't work. But if I feel really ill, I'll let you know."

Instead of hanging back on the street, the pavement, or the van, the surveillance team decided to take a bold move. A female police surveillance officer in her twenties was chosen to follow Ali through the doorway of the tiny internet café.[1] She was close enough to Ali that she could've run her hand along his shoulders as he stared at the computer.

Still paranoid the cops were tailing him, Ali was on guard for people who fit a certain profile: a white male who looked like a cop. So he didn't think much of the brunette behind him and continued his work. Ali received a call on his mobile and spoke in hushed tones. After hanging up, he clicked to the British Airports Authority (BAA-Heathrow) website and checked out the timetables.

Ali dashed off a quick text to Rauf about his "sickness"—that is, being watched by the police or MI5. "It's not all the time." he wrote. "It's here and there, usually when I link someone by myself."[2] Little did he know that he could've stood up, turned around, thrown a wild haymaker, and likely connected with the nose of an undercover officer.

He then received another call, and he answered in English. The undercover officer caught snatches of the conversation—"take them out of the box . . . let me know about the weight . . ."—but couldn't put them into context.

After the BAA-Heathrow site, Ali opened a new tab with the American Airlines website. On the side of his monitor, he had another window open titled "timetable notepad" where he typed some commentary.[3] He checked on a series of flights, seven in all, from London to points in the United States and Canada, all within a three-hour window. All seven were direct flights, and each departed Heathrow daily, carrying two hundred-plus passengers and crewmembers. One could imagine all of these aircraft on the runway at Heathrow, in formation, taxiing and waiting to take off, bound for North America.[4] If they left on schedule, all seven wide-body aircraft would be somewhere over the Atlantic Ocean or the vast urban areas of the North American continent at more or less the same time.

Ali checked out further information about security information, baggage, and restricted items at Heathrow. Recording what he learned, Ali typed, "some time after 16.50, on any day, all seven aircraft would be in mid-air over land or sea." He then put all of the information into his open notepad, popped a memory stick into the computer, and downloaded the information. It read:

1. 1415—UA931 LHR-SAN FRANCISCO (United Airlines)
2. 1500—AC849 LHR-TORONTO (Air Canada)
3. 1515—AC865 LHR-MONTREAL (Air Canada)
4. 1540—UA959 LHR-CHICAGO (United Airlines)
5. 1620—UA925 LHR-WASHINGTON (United Airlines)
6. 1635—AA131 LHR-NEW YORK (American Airlines)
7. 1650—AA91 LHR-CHICAGO (American Airlines)

There were no return flights from any of these locations added to the list.

He put the stick in his pocket and finished up his missive to Rauf. "I also have to arrange for the printers to be picked up and stored . . . I have done all my prep, all I have to do is sort out opening timetable and bookings."[5]

◆

It was now nighttime. At the top of the eight o'clock hour, Sarwar parked his Nissan at a telephone booth in Wembley. Once inside, he fumbled around with a calling card, punching in the thirty or so numbers, and made a call to Gulzar's mobile phone. Following that, he made another to Ali.[6]

An hour later, Gulzar was enjoying an ice cream on Upton Lane, three miles west of his hideout in Barking. At a predetermined time, he entered a telephone booth between 55 and 59 Upton Lane and made a call to Sarwar, who was standing at a completely different box on the A112 road. The call was nineteen seconds long, and it seems as if the message had some problem since they had trouble connecting, or the line was fuzzy; Gulzar then phoned Sarwar again thirty minutes later directly to his mobile.

By 9:44 p.m., East London was dark, and Gulzar was still wandering around Upton Lane. He idled for a bit outside the large, street-facing windows of A La Pizza. Several minutes later, a man wearing a dark baseball cap approached him. They chatted for a second, and then Gulzar and the man walked a block south to Glenparke Road and entered a waiting red car.

The man with the dark baseball cap was Sarwar, and they entered Ali's red Vauxhall Vectra. Ali was sitting in the driver's seat.

For the first time, the three top men in the conspiracy were sitting a foot away from each other. This was the first time Ali and Gulzar had met, and Gulzar had only connected with Sarwar a few days beforehand. They spoke quickly; fifteen minutes at most. About Mohammed Patel's illness. About false documents. About Ali's desire to carry out a "blessed operation." He had told Rauf about the prep and now he was telling Rauf's best friend about the next steps.[7]

◆

It was dark and the surveillance team couldn't immediately figure out who Gulzar was in this meeting. But it was quickly apparent something big was happening, once they saw the other teams skulking around the same sidewalk. Things were coming very obviously to a head. But it was dark along the residential side street; they couldn't risk walking toward them without being seen by the three hyper-paranoid men. The car was parked facing away from the squads; the surveillance team could make out Ali in the driver's seat, Sarwar and Gulzar sitting in the back—Sarwar was sitting in the middle, while Gulzar was on the right.

The only light on Glenparke Road filtered out from the front rooms and doorways of the nearby homes. The neighborhood was wise to outsiders, especially cops; only eight weeks beforehand, the Met had sent over two hundred cops to seal off and smash in nearby doors during the Volga debacle. The squads did the best they could. One officer shot a grainy video of the encounter, but the resolution was poor; they couldn't even make out the targets' lips for the lipreaders back at the office.

Unlike the Crevice conspiracy from 2004, the authorities hadn't placed a microphone in Ali's Vauxhall, despite it being left unattended on the street for long periods of time. The Americans would eventually ask about this issue, perhaps call it "an oversight."

A quarter of an hour later, the men exited the vehicle and started walking back toward Upton Lane. Gulzar disappeared into the night, Ali and Sarwar headed back to the pizza joint. Over cheese slices, Ali mentioned he still needed his camera because he had one video left to produce. Once he was done, he'd give Sarwar both the camera and the videotapes.[8]

One more wedding tape to shoot.

◆

In both the United States and in the United Kingdom, there was a strange duality at work. The fearsome counterterrorism apparatuses of both nations were whirring at full tilt, but their leaders continued to project placid calm. They had all headed out on their August vacations.

President Bush was summering at his sixteen hundred acres of ranchland in Crawford, Texas, the so-called "Western White House," clearing brush. Prime Minister Tony Blair and his family took their holiday in Barbados, guests of Cliff Richard in his six-bedroom villa "Coral Sundown," inside the Sugar Hill tennis resort in West Moreland St. James. Vice President Dick Cheney was at home in Wyoming.

Blair and Bush spoke daily. The Americans knew the British were expending so much of their finite resources to watch this ever-expanding cell that they were starving other operations. Washington also fundamentally understood the cell now wanted to smuggle liquid explosives onto North America–bound passenger aircraft. The intercepted emails back and forth from Pakistan suggested this, even though Ali, Sarwar, and Rauf used codewords. The surveillance officer who followed Ali into the internet café and saw him downloading one-way flights to the United States and Canada cemented this notion. The pieces were coming together, but the specific plans remained hazy. Analysts hustled to devise potential scenarios. Would they try to detonate the planes in the air? Or over some city in America, killing not just the 250 or so people in the plane, but hundreds more on the ground? Maybe they would try to explode over a nuclear power plant or an industrial chemical facility? The possibilities for mayhem seemed endless.

Based on the intelligence, the White House tasked the U.S. intelligence community to determine if this homemade weapon could be reasonably smuggled onto an aircraft. "Leave the explosive out," Fran Townsend commanded, "but make it look like it was the bomb."[9] Officials at Homeland Security thought that maybe technical means or TSA officials at the airport could detect the liquids. Meanwhile, the Agency built a mockup in an orange bottle of the Gatorade sports drink—Lucozade wasn't sold in the United States—along with a real, unadulterated bottle.[10] Under scanners used at American airports, the two bottles physically looked the same. Moreover, the disguised hydrogen peroxide explosive and the sports drink within the bottles were indistinguishable to the naked eye and to the machines.[11]

Furthermore, the CIA conducted a chemical analysis to determine whether the Overt plotters could produce a viable explosive that could bring down a plane. They learned that, yes, they could do so, and the chances for success rose if the bomb were placed in one of a number of critical spots within the aircraft itself.

There were also no technical countermeasures available. The explosives just looked like an unopened plastic sports drink. And unless a TSA employee physically picked up every single sports drink bottle and shook it, they wouldn't see any difference at all.

They knew had a five-alarm problem on their hands.

◆

On the day Ali, Sarwar, and Gulzar crammed into the Vauxhall Vectra to discuss next steps, President Bush and Prime Minister Blair spoke at length about the best time to take down the cell.[12]

Despite their different political orientation, the two leaders were personally fond of each other.[13] They talked all the time; Blair had been the first head of state Bush called on September 12, 2001, and Bush viewed theirs as the closest friendship he had formed with any foreign leader.[14] Blair felt similarly close to Bush. Still, the fundamental impasse between the two allies remained: America wanted to shut down the conspiracy, while the British wanted to collect more information for the trial.

Bush was laser-focused on counterterrorism and was an enthusiastic and intelligent customer of intelligence. His administration had been defined by 9/11, and he was determined to crush al Qaeda. Oftentimes, according to the White House's Juan Zarate, he knew the details better than the people briefing him, especially staffers who were new to the issues.[15] He could also spot when a staffer didn't know something. "If you were bullshitting," the NCTC's Admiral Scott Redd recalled, "he'd take you down."[16]

Twice a day, the president would contact Townsend, asking, "Are you comfortable letting the planes fly?"[17] Bush wasn't micromanaging the process or running a war room; he just wanted to be kept informed if any news broke.[18] And, twice a day, after studying the situation and consulting with multiple officials across the U.S. national security community, she and the other principals in Washington told the president that, yes, they should let the carriers fly for another twenty-four hours. She was key to the smooth running of the American system since the president of the United States listened to her and took her counsel.

But what also weighed on Bush's mind was that he knew that he'd be blamed if another devastating attack occurred on American soil or against American interests on his watch.

"It's not the easy thing," Townsend later recalled, "but we're going to try to do the hard thing and make the hard decision." Then again, she said, "If you make the wrong one, then thousands might die."[19]

And if that happened, "At best we're going to get fired; at worst we're going to get indicted."[20]

◆

In the first week of August, the latest bits of white-hot intelligence were coming in faster than the CIA could properly process, analyze, draft, and publish in the PDB. Physically putting together the "book" that became the PDB was a process that started the day before, continuing through the middle of the night, to be disseminated to the president and others in the early morning. But by the time the book was published, the president had already been briefed two or three times from the American side, and by Prime Minister Blair himself, the day before. Unless new information came in at 4 a.m. Washington time, it was already stale. Thus, Townsend and the CIA's Morgan Muir devised a solution: Townsend would take the lead in briefing the president in the morning, but the two would have already interacted with all the relevant that previous day.[21] This would also be backed up by lower-level SVTCs among intelligence personnel from across the community.

In a still half-built McLean, Virginia, office structure called "Liberty Crossing," deliberately obscured from the road by rising hills and clumps of trees, resided the NCTC. According to its director, Scott Redd, a silver-haired vice admiral with the U.S. Navy, this conspiracy was the organization's "graduation exercise"—a "drop-everything" kind of situation.[22]

Andy Liepman, a well-liked fiftysomething analyst with a boxer's physique, had just rotated to the NCTC to become its director of intelligence. He had come from the CIA, where he served as the CTC's second-in-command to the chain-smoking "Roger." Luckily (or unluckily) for him, his new assignment coincided with Overt coming to a head. He began working daily with Redd and struggled mightily to decipher and correctly interpret the admiral's naval metaphors and nautical terminology.

By the first week of August, Liepman explained, "We got word there was a plot underway. It was in Britain. It involved airplanes. They were trying to make liquid explosives." And, "It happened really fast."[23] Despite all the variables, he and his band of NCTC analysts remained skeptical the operatives could competently build a liquid explosive to subvert British aviation security. At the same time, Liepman didn't have full visibility into all the moving parts of the conspiracy, and he knew it. He recalled, "I remember the uncertainty was what killed us. The worst of all outcomes was obviously that the plot was more advanced than we thought."[24]

Redd and Liepman felt enormous pressure from the White House bearing down upon the intelligence community. "Every day Bush wanted to shut it down," Liepman recalled. "'Arrest all these guys' he'd say."[25] As Ali glanced over his shoulder, searching for the security team, the national security professionals on both sides of the Atlantic were in turn paranoid the operation—which now occupied a sizeable portion of attention of intelligence and law enforcement establishments in both America and Britain—would leak to the media.

Knowledge of the operation remained a closely guarded secret, even within the leak-prone U.S. government. For some, there was an intensely personal stake in the game. National Security Advisor Stephen Hadley had a daughter traveling in the UK at the time. White House spokeswoman Dana Perino was also in Britain with her husband.[26] Despite the danger they might have been in had they boarded a plane with an al Qaeda operative onboard, neither Hadley's daughter nor Dana Perino were briefed on the plot.

♦

Another person kept out of the loop until then was the TSA's chief, Kip Hawley. On August 4, he was home with his wife in California celebrating their wedding anniversary.[27] That afternoon, he received a mysterious call to immediately return to Washington DC, but the person on the other end of the line couldn't quite tell him why. Hawley was about to dine with a powerful member of Congress who sat on the committee that approved his budget, and he couldn't miss that dinner. The desperate entreaties from Washington, whatever they were, would have to wait until the day after.

When he arrived in DC the next day, he was only the fifth person at DHS informed about Overt and the global efforts to crush it.[28] And he was only brought into the circle of trust because his British counterpart, Director of Transport Security Niki Tompkinson, "applied some torque" to her higher-ups. The president personally had to greenlight anyone in the U.S. government to be informed about the conspiracy. Anyone, that is, besides the hundreds of analysts, case officers, special agents, and other lower-level national security types who had partial access to the classified system.

On August 7, after a video teleconference with the president, Hawley spoke to Tompkinson via secure phone at the British embassy. They agreed that when the hammer came down, they had to secure the airspace in both countries. The two also wrestled whether to impose a complete liquid ban on flights; Tompkinson wanted to ban all carry-on luggage as well, but ultimately backed down.[29] It also occurred to them that the European Union transportation officials didn't know about the conspiracy and about the draconian bans that were coming down the pike; the EU would be alerted, eventually. But not quite yet.

When Hawley returned to TSA headquarters, he began putting together guidelines and new protocols for whatever security measures would be needed when the police action went live. He also quietly authorized a few hundred federal air marshals to fly to western Europe, to man every flight departing London for the United States, although they weren't told why.[30]

◆

Some within the intelligence community saw distinct echoes of the 1990s-era mega terror plot by Khalid Sheik Mohammed and his nephew

Ramzi Yousef. The year after the 1993 attack on the World Trade Center, KSM and Yousef cooked up a plot to use chemical bombs and place them on twelve aircraft headed for the United States. The goal was to destroy these aircraft over the Pacific Ocean over the course of two days in January 1995, in a plot known as "Bojinka."[31]

KSM had a flair for the dramatic. Al Qaeda's subsequent 9/11 operation was a scaled-down version of what KSM once had in mind. The original plan was to crash planes into CIA and FBI headquarters, the tallest buildings in California and Washington State, and a few nuclear power plants. He would then personally land the last plane, murder all the male passengers, and then surrender. Unlike all his confederates, he wasn't going to die. Rather, he was going to live forever as a terrorist superstar, a household name for a century.[32]

From a hideout in Manila, the duo, along with other conspirators, cased flights in Seoul and Hong Kong. Ramzi Yousef smuggled a bomb armed with a timer as a prototype onto a Philippine Airlines flight that made multiple stops. Before getting off at the first stop, Yousef made sure to rig the explosive to detonate during the second leg of the flight. The bomb killed a young Japanese businessman, and had it not been for the pilot's valiant efforts to keep his bird in flight despite a gash in the fuselage, the plane might have crashed. Had Ali and Rauf operated in the pre-9/11 era or immediately afterward, it would've been easier to smuggle their liquid bombs onto flights leaving from Heathrow, Manila, or any other international airport. The conspiracy eventually unraveled after Philippines police raided the plotters' hideout, causing them to flee. But the ambitious Bojinka megaplot coincided with bin Laden's evolution from terror financier to full-blown terrorist ringleader—at least, that's what the CIA's analysts believed at the time.[33]

And yet, there was no particular scrap of evidence, no captured conversation, no datapoint that suggested Rauf, Ali, Sarwar, Hussain, Gulzar, or anyone else had decided to rerun the Bojinka operation from twelve years beforehand. Certainly, Bojinka was well-known throughout the national security world, and even among the public: the *9/11 Commission Report* had been published in June 2004, and it detailed that thwarted terror operation. But KSM, Ramzi Yousef, and the others were now permanent prisoners of the U.S. government, and so could not have communicated the particulars to the Overt plotters.

It might have just been a coincidence.

◆

What continued to unnerve the Americans was how the British continued to run the op. SO15's Peter Clarke and the other senior police officers wanted to play to the very edge, to allow the plotters to continue developing the conspiracy until they had absolutely everything. They wanted to make sure the bombers built their explosives, bought their plane tickets, and were headed to the airport—and only then would the police swoop in for the capture. They wanted an airtight case to put them in prison, forever.[34]

More alarming to the United States was that this was London's somewhat more conservative plan to bring the conspiracy to its conclusion. At one point, the British floated an edgy proposal to catch the plotters red-handed: They would permit the five, six, seven, ten, eighteen-strong crew to pass through Heathrow airport security with their explosives, board the North America-bound planes in Terminal Three, and let them settle onto their flights. At a predetermined time, the pilots would then announce on the intercom that the planes regretfully had some sort of mechanical problem, union issue, or some other excuse. All the passengers, including the bombers, would then be asked to get off the plane to fix the problem. British authorities would be waiting at the entryways, beyond the jet bridge, where they would arrest the suspects.[35]

When briefed on this scenario, the United States gently responded, yes, the plan might work, and they might be able to catch the terrorists with their weapons intact. Then again, Ali or Hussain or Savant or anyone else might see each other inside the terminal and realize what was about to happen. One of the plotters might then decide to blow up right then and there—within the confines of a crowded airport or a fully fueled U.S. carrier with 250-plus people strapped inside. A widebody jumbo jet on the ground is still a fat target, and the explosives would be powerful enough to wreak havoc even on the tarmac. Once one detonated, the others might hear the distant explosion, guess their cover was blown, and likewise detonate.

The Americans couldn't believe this was a serious plan to catch the Overt conspirators. So, it was, as they say, shot down immediately.[36]

At the CIA director's late afternoon meeting, there was "lots of angst and concern" that Great Britain was moving at the speed of molasses. The CIA thought 7/7 was a clear signal to London that it had to ruthlessly excise the malignant Islamist elements in British society, before an even more successful plot occurred. "People thought that was the wake-up call for them," the director's chief of staff Larry Pfeiffer recalled, "but here it was, a year later, and they still were struggling."[37] London was a hotbed for all manner of nefarious jihadist activity, and even the most competent force in a democracy would struggle to keep a handle on dozens of suspects. The prevailing opinion at Langley and elsewhere in the U.S. government was the British weren't adequately resourced. The agency simply believed Great Britain "didn't have the capacity to handle a major case like this and also keep their eyes on other stuff."[38]

This plot had already pretty much dominated a few months of the lives of many senior officers, recalled Pfeiffer.[39] They wanted it to conclude sooner rather than later. Still, the CIA also knew if British forces moved in too quickly without prosecutable evidence, the whole effort would have been for naught, and those al Qaeda operatives would remain free men.[40]

What drove the Americans' desire to act was that a terror organization was again threatening to kill thousands of civilians. Homeland Security Secretary Michael Chertoff said, "Once we knew they were focused on aircraft going to the US, it became our problem. I mean, until then, we thought it was a serious issue for the UK government, but then it became our jurisdiction when we became the target."[41] CIA director Hayden, alarmed by the British reticence, put it more directly to his UK counterpart. He said, "Let's just do it!"[42]

London kept Washington pacified as best as it could. British police and intelligence had been dealing with the IRA bombers for decades with a fraction of the resources currently at their disposal and they felt they could handle the challenge. But Britain also wanted to keep things quiet in South Asia just in case Rashid Rauf got spooked and called the whole operation off. London's overarching perspective was to keep this plot simmering for as long as possible without the pot bubbling over.

The United States also couldn't figure out how Ali had slipped the net in Islamabad the last time. He had walked through the most secure airport in the country and then mysteriously disappeared into the tribal areas for training with al Qaeda. He then was able to return to London unmolested, despite MI6 alerting ISI to his whereabouts and his importance. Ali was just the man on the ground, but he certainly wasn't the only one in play. Moreover, Rauf's connections continued to confound local authorities. He had excellent connections to the jihadist underworld. The parts of the ISI that cooperated with the Americans hadn't yet been able to pinpoint his exact whereabouts, despite his being on email and phone calls with his men in London almost daily.

It was obvious to Washington that someone was falling down on the job. Thus, on the American side, the direction forward became quite clear. Washington was going to crush this conspiracy one way or another, and as soon as possible. They knew who the principals in Pakistan were, as well as some large percentage of the suicide bombers in London. They also generally knew how they were going to carry out the attack, and more or less which aircrafts were going to be targeted. There was little appetite for waiting much longer.[43] Every single person who could make a difference, from the president on down, had gone through the crucible of 9/11 and failed to connect the dots in time. They weren't going to let this happen again.

Every day was September 12.

The United States could not arrest or kill anyone in Britain itself. However, the Americans could lean very hard upon Pakistan to find Rauf and take him down in one way or another. The CIA's Steve Kappes noted, "In the post 9/11 environment, if Rashid Rauf was a threat, then we'd take action against him."[44] The minute they found Rauf, they were going to grab him.

The American view was "Our citizens. Our planes."[45] This was also the hard line from the White House. Fran Townsend was adamant that stopping the plot was far more important than collecting further evidence for a trial, remarking, "I don't give a shit if it blows the case."[46]

The Brits were furious with this response and pushed back every chance they could get. Sometimes they were diplomatic, other times less so. "This is not your case," they told their CIA and FBI counterparts up and down the line, as well as their counterparts at the White House.[47] "This is just another case."[48] And most galling to them was that the American national security people didn't seem to be in charge: the political people were. But what British intelligence didn't fully appreciate was that both the civil service and the political appointees in America were marching in lockstep.

20

It Fell out of My Pocket

It's possible that around this time Sarwar had a change of heart after chatting with Ali and Gulzar in the back of the car. This was because Rauf sent Sarwar a cryptic note: "I hope you're in the best of health. I hope business is good too. I heard you're getting married. I hope it works out for the best."[1] Sarwar had no plans to get married in real life. Perhaps over the course of the last several weeks, Sarwar wished to join his comrades in their final flights.

Ali also received the go-ahead about carrying on from Rauf, who was itching to move forward. Referring to the surveillance, he wrote, "Good news that it's just here and there [that is of course the skin infection]." Rauf needed to keep everyone together, and motivated. "Give your girlies a big up from me, Guj, kid and rest."[2]

◆

Ali drove around Walthamstow on the afternoon of August 9. He was in a new car: a silver-toned Kia Pride owned by Arafat's sister, Nameera. He wasn't sure, but he figured it was unlikely the cops had placed an audio probe in this "clean" car.

At 5:09 p.m., he texted Umar Islam, "I'm on my way. Ten minutes." Forty-eight minutes later, Islam, who had been patiently waiting at the Chick Inn London takeaway on Hoe Street, entered the car carrying a black duffel bag. They drove north and parked on Diana Road, which ran perpendicular to Forest Road. They then got out and made their way to the safehouse.[3]

Once inside, the director needed to know if Islam had actually put pen to paper to develop a script. "Listen," Ali told Islam, "I need to see your thing." Handing over the paper, Islam replied, "It's very short, man, but I . . . are all the brothers are going to have one then?"

Ali didn't look up. He was scanning Umar's script. Finally, he half answered, "Mine is the longest one."

Islam then asked, "Did you hear anything about getting my missus out of here?"[4] Ali told Islam about the plans after the operation had been executed; he thought it would be better for Islam's wife, Rizwana Khan, to leave Britain. Ali replied, "After a couple, few months, just as soon after the whole shock of this, that and the other . . ." They had thought she could transit to Pakistan, and then on to wherever she wanted afterward.

"But how's she going to—how they going to get to [Pakistan] and tell her where to go?"

Islam had already been thinking about it, telling Ali, "there's another brother I could send my wife to in Sri Lanka." It was impermissible in his restrictive view on Islam to allow his wife to travel without a male relative chaperone, but maybe she could convince a nephew to take her away from Britain.

Ali concurred. "They want her to come."

"Yeah."

Speaking of Rauf and the other brothers in Pakistan, Ali reiterated, "But I think they want her to come out. They don't want her to know anything, definitely."

"Afterwards, is going to be hard for her, man, because they're going to be watching."

"She's better off if she goes now, bro, then she looks like she was in on it, she was in on it, the planning." Islam understood and was resigned to the fact that his soon-to-be-widowed wife and his young son's lives were going to become very difficult in the months ahead.

He also needed to get something off his chest. Ali had provided him with handwritten notes to prepare his speech some time beforehand. It was a single sheet of paper with some bullets: threaten imminent attacks on European soil unless Western troops left Iraq and Afghanistan. In the time that had passed, Islam returned from work one evening and saw this note on his desk among the piles of other junk. His wife had discovered it while tidying up the flat.

"How did your wife find it at home?" Ali demanded. He was incredulous that his "blessed operation" might come completely undone by this stupidest of slipups.

Islam said, defensively, "It fell out of my pocket. I didn't realize, stupid thing."

"What did she say?"

Sheepishly, he replied, "She just said, 'Ah, I saw that thing.' I goes . . . because I came in and I saw it on the table, innit? I was hoping she didn't read it and then she goes, 'I read that thing.'"

Ali was nonplussed. "Mm-hmm."

Islam then quietly said, "She goes, 'Is that what I think it is?' And I goes, I just said, 'Don't ask no questions,' and then, um, she just left it . . ."

Ali could not believe the idiocy of what he was hearing. "That's a serious lapse, man. I told you to do it on the laptop, didn't I?"

"Mm-hmmm."

He pressed on. "Why'd you do it on paper? I told you the security of you doing your laptop as well, put it in a hidden folder." And, "I thought you were going to get rid of that." He returned to this truly silly thing that Islam had committed with his wife. "I thought you had it on a computer."

Islam responded: "It's the same thing. It's still there."

Ali retorted, "It's not, mate. On a computer it's hidden. She would never know it's there. You put it into a hidden file. I told you how to do that, you put it in folder no one go into. Paths are protected. No one can get into it."[5] It seemed Ali was more concerned about the prying eyes of family than he was about the NSA or GCHQ.

"But I needed it so, you know, like you structure it."[6]

Islam switched gears because arguing with Ali was exhausting, and he also knew he was going to lose. He also wanted to know the time frame for the mission. "How long we got to go?"

Ali didn't quite understand: "Ten, fifteen minutes."

Islam shook his head. "No, not this," meaning the video.

"A couple of weeks."

"A couple of weeks?" Islam stopped. This was the second flub. He felt his heart sink. "I still gotta—I ain't even been."

"Where?" Then it dawned on Ali. Islam's passport had an error; for some reason, his date of birth on his official document was listed as April 23, 1948, instead of April 23, 1978.

"You'd better go, man," Ali implored, telling his man to get his travel documents sorted out, and fast. "This mission is a great mission, you know. It's not easy, man."

Apologetically, Islam said, "I'm going to go there in a day to the Passport Office and get a passport one time and then just book . . . book a trip . . ."[7] Then he told Ali, in order to reassure him, "She understands this proper. I think probably if I were to say to her to do this, one of these operations, she might even find it in herself to do that."

"What about the baby?" Ali asked. He was talking about Islam's sixteen-month boy. Ali also knew Islam's wife was pregnant.

Islam replied, "Obviously she's got babies and if she knew someone was going to be there to look after them, maybe, I don't know. Maybe she would take them with her."[8]

"Maybe, she'd take them with her."

Islam was warming to the idea. "Maybe, you know what I mean. She'd like to do it though."

Ali said, "Not sure. I know a brother wanted to do that." A fellow who wanted to take his child on a doomed airplane.[9]

Ali finally got around to asking him the question Islam had been dreading: did he actually compose the rest of the script? Islam had been tied up at work as a bus ticket inspector and forgot to write it down until Ali badgered him about it the previous day. When Ali called, Islam lied and said yes, the script was done and he was ready to shoot the video. In reality, he hadn't done much beyond put a few bits and pieces together. Just before go-time, Islam scribbled some last-minute words for his part of the project.

Time was up. They had to shoot the video. To get the juices flowing, the two men watched a bit of Adam Khatib's effort. Islam put on the black outfit and checkered headdress. He made himself comfortable in front of the black flag.

After he turned on the camera, Ali emphasized the conversational nature of these speeches. He had patterned them on the Sidique Khan video from several months prior. "All right, you know what to say, innit? Don't try and speak posh English. Speak normal English that you normally speak." He wanted to make sure these speeches were by regular men of Britain—for once they were gone from this earth, others would take up the banner of jihad.

The bus ticket inspector still needed some coaching. Ali continued to advise, "When you mention Allah, do that. When you're making a point, point, away the hand movement, you're warning the Kuffar, give a bit of aggression, yeah, a bit loudly if you want leave more, they're very good, we're higher than everyone else. No one there. There's no threatening rules."[10]

So Islam began: "To Mullah Omar and Osama and all brothers, keep on going and keep on remaining firm. But truly you have inspired many of the Muslims and you have inspired me personally. This is from Umar Islam, the son of Islam, to the people of the world. To let you know the reasons for this action which Inshallah I am going to undertake. Firstly, this is an obligation on me as a Muslim to wage jihad against the kuffar."

He began to gain confidence. Like his compatriots, he followed a similar line of grievances and threats about Iraq and Afghanistan, as well as a litany of insults for his fellow citizens. Pointing his finger at the camera, he said,

We are doing this in order to gain the pleasure of our Lord, and Allah loves us to die and kill in his path. And anyone who tries to deny this, then read the Koran and he will not be able to deny this.

We will not leave this path until you leave our lands, until you feel what we are feeling. This is revenge for the actions of the USA in the Muslim lands and their accomplices, such as the British and the Jews. Now without doubt your dead are in hellfire, while the Muslims that die due to your acts will be in paradise. Martyrdom operations upon martyrdom operations will keep on raining on these kuffars until they release us and leave our lands.[11]

Islam hadn't bothered to change much from Ali's suggested bullets. He spoke almost word-for-word the text Waheed Zaman had uttered earlier: "I say to you disbelievers that as you bomb, you will be bombed. As you kill, you will be killed. And if you want to kill our women and children then the same thing will happen to you. This is not a joke."

Addressing the supposed complicity of his fellow British citizens in international conflicts, he said, "You're just sitting there, you're still funding the Army, you have not put down your leader, you have not pressured them enough. You are too busy watching *Home and Away* and *EastEnders*, complaining about the World Cup and drinking your alcohol, to care about anything. That is all you seem to care about and I know because I have come from that."[12]

He stopped halfway through his prepared remarks and his finger-jabbing, and asked Ali, "How did I do?"

Ali had some notes. "Puff it up a bit. You know, this bit you give it some." He hoped Rauf would be pleased because he had coached the others in the same way. "The brothers, they're coming," he told Islam. The verbiage of jihad was getting shopworn, even to the jihadis themselves. Ali coached, "Martyrdom operation after martyrdom operation gonna erupt in your lands. Dadadada, dadadada. Some rhetoric. Some go power, yeah?"[13]

Islam gamely carried on with the rest of the speech. Toward the end, Ali asked Islam off camera if he was brainwashed. His answer: "Yes, my brain has been washed, and it has been washed by the clean and cleansing water of Islam."[14]

It was like they were playing jihadi mad libs.

The video mercifully terminated at the 18 minute 45 second mark. Apparently satisfied, Islam changed back into his street clothes.

◆

The watchers noticed the two leave the safehouse at 7:06 p.m. The shimmering last rays of late afternoon warmed their faces. Ali looked around, searching for the surveillance he could feel was there, but saw nothing.

◆

Around the time Ali and Islam were shooting their martyrdom video on the afternoon of August 9, a passenger flight was in the air over the Atlantic Ocean. The plane had departed from a sunny island in the Mediterranean some hours beforehand, bound for America. On board was an extroverted, hypercompetent woman in her midtwenties returning to the Washington DC area after visiting her European cousins. It was peak travel season, and the only ticket home was an expensive one in economy class, wedged between two fiftysomething women. The trio immediately hit it off; someone came up with the bright idea of a round of drinks. Ice swirling around their plastic cups, each woman shared a bit of her life with the others. Sometime past the third round, one of the women asked the young woman what she did for a living.

She lowered her voice, "I'm an intelligence officer." This was not a state secret; she was an overt counterterrorism analyst with the NCTC, heading back to a gray, anonymous cubicle in suburban Virginia.

The women smiled, impressed by their traveling companion's career. Then, in a nervous voice, one asked, "Is it safe to fly?"

"Pffft," the young woman waved her hand. "It's never been safer."[15]

21

The Railway Crossing

Rauf took public transportation to get around Pakistan. Since arriving in the country of his birth four years earlier, he had found Pakistan welcoming. Rauf didn't stay exclusively in the tribal areas; he had a wife and children living in seclusion elsewhere. The local authorities didn't hassle him at all, despite his guiding hand in the 7/7 and 7/21 bombings, which led him to believe that he remained both anonymous and in the clear. At some point during the late spring or early summer of 2006, Rauf went home to his family's village of Haveli Beghal, in the Mirpur district of Kashmir, where he freely interacted within the community.[1] While he was certainly concerned with his personal and operational security, he didn't feel the need to stay on alert all the time. In any case, al Qaeda's operatives had to live within their means. So, after emailing Ali about hand creams, store openings, skin infections, and the like, Rauf boarded a multicolored, well-festooned jingle bus. He found a seat toward the rear of the vehicle, carrying his bag and four mobile phones. As the jingle bus slowly lumbered onto the highway, he quickly fell asleep.

◆

Little did Rauf know what was waiting for him as headed down the road. The White House and CIA had finally identified him as a priority for capture and were leaning hard on the Pakistanis to round him up, no matter where the British were in the investigation.

In a bit of coincidental timing, CIA director Michael Hayden, his chief of staff Larry Pfeiffer, and his operations chief Jose Rodriguez were in Islamabad that second week of August. They had been traveling together on Hayden's first major trip abroad as the head of the agency—they had just flown in from Iraq, where they met with their counterparts as the country spiraled into civil war.

The CIA leaders were well briefed on Overt. This was to be expected: Tony Blair and George Bush were in near daily contact to discuss the conspiracy. And leaders like Steve Kappes, the number two at the agency, the White House's Fran Townsend, Stephen Hadley, and Juan Zarate were each in regular contact with their counterparts in Britain. Despite repeated assurances the allies would move in lockstep, one thing was clear: if Pakistan detained Rauf, British authorities would have little choice but to arrest the suspects immediately.

It was the height of monsoon season in Pakistan; rolling storms buffeted Islamabad when the military plane carrying Hayden and his team touched down on the tarmac. The men and their security detail were picked up as guests of honor and whisked to a military compound on the edge of the city. Behind guns, gates, guards, dogs, and other rings of security and surveillance, they met Ashfaq Parvez Kayani, the head of the ISI, for a chat in a large conference room that was designed to appear to have a seamless wooden interior.[2]

This was an introductory meeting between intelligence heads, and both Kayani and Hayden were quite genial. Hayden had never met Kayani before this trip to Pakistan. Often described by contemporaries as a "soldier's soldier," the Pakistani spy chief sat in a haze of blue cigarette smoke and reminisced about his time as a young officer at the U.S. Army's Command and General Staff College in Leavenworth, Kansas, on an international military exchange.[3] Pleasantries aside, the intelligence officers indicated capturing Rashid Rauf and stopping the plot in London was important to them, but there were broader security issues the Americans wanted to hammer out with the Pakistanis, mostly to do with fighting al Qaeda in the border regions.

At one point, Kayani muttered, "I'm tired of you Americans saying we are not doing enough to fight the terrorists."[4] The Pakistanis were quite irritated for being blamed for every slipup that occurred. The CIA and ISI carried out multiple joint operations, and the successful ones often stayed hidden from view. On the other hand, the failures always seemed to emerge in the press, making the ISI look incompetent. They also didn't want to be left hanging if an operation went sideways. So in the meeting, Kayani asked Rodriguez, "Are you with me?," meaning would the CIA support the ISI in their counterterrorism operations? Rodriguez knew what the answer was to keep the relationship on track.

"Of course."

No trip to Pakistan was ever a lovefest for the United States, as the Americans' primary goal in town was to gently, or not so gently, convince the Pakistanis to spend less time worrying about India and more time worrying about the terrorists in the tribal areas.[5] Perhaps they should have been looking closer to where they were sipping their tea; Public Enemy Number One Osama bin Laden was lounging at his Abbottabad compound a little over two hours by car on the E35 Expressway.

The meeting went on for so long that at one point, Pfeiffer felt the call of nature, stood up, and began surveying the wooden walls for a door. Failing to visually locate an exit, he felt along the walls to identify the panel that would free him from the conference room. No luck. Eventually, Kayani himself sensed the American's desperation and mercifully pointed him in the direction of the correct panel.[6]

After the initial conversation, Hayden and Rodriguez reconnected with the ISI chief in his home, which resembled a tidy admiral's quarters on a U.S. naval base. Kayani came down to meet his guests dressed in a pair of slacks and a polo shirt, instead of his regular crisp military uniform, and served his guests juice and tea.[7] As he sipped his orange-flavored drink, Rodriguez leaned in to hear the soft-spoken commander; he thought Kayani sounded like he had marbles in his mouth. The Americans politely kept the fact that they couldn't understand what he was saying half the time to themselves.

Shortly thereafter, Director Hayden and Pfeiffer departed Pakistan and flew on to Afghanistan, leaving Rodriguez behind. He wanted to meet his subordinates scattered throughout the country and see the counterterrorism battlespace with his own eyes. The ISI deputy director-general, Brigadier Azmat Hayat Khan,[8] was quite obliging in this regard. As soon as there was a break in the rainy weather, he said he would take Rodriguez and the agency's chief of station, referred to here under the pseudonym "Cox," in a helicopter of unknown vintage westward for a tour over the tribal areas. At first, Hayden wanted to make the journey too, but his security detail felt placing the CIA director over these volatile areas was not worth the risk.[9]

The blustery, uncooperative weather finally opened up, providing the men a window to see the country from the skies. They drove out to an ISI landing zone, where a creaky Soviet-era MI-17 transport helicopter awaited them. This was quite a treat; Pakistan's military only had a handful of operational MI-17s, and helicopters were desperately needed for counterinsurgency operations. As they boarded, Rodriguez mused how the fuel tanks, containing hundreds of gallons of gasoline, were right underneath their seats. If the chopper went down, everyone on board would come to a flaming end.[10]

Brigadier Khan had the Americans' genuine respect. He was a thoughtful, cultured officer and seemed to enjoy the company of his counterparts from the States. He was certainly loyal to Pakistan and kept his cards close to his chest. Nevertheless, the Americans who got to know Khan over the years thought he possessed genuine insights into the counterterrorism fight and did his best to keep the rocky U.S.-Pakistan relationship from foundering.[11] General Hayden noted, "We got more cooperation out of him than the other ones . . . Khan was very good on counterterrorism."[12]

When the CIA officers returned to the U.S. embassy in Islamabad some time later, Cox's deputy briefed them on the latest intelligence from the Overt case. Between his official meetings in Iraq and Pakistan, fighting the effects of travel and juggling other crises, Rodriguez had missed the latest developments in the London plot. The deputy chief told him about how the undercover policewoman had observed Ali jotting down flight timetables to North America. After the briefing, Rodriguez realized, "Holy shit, this is really serious."[13]

Unbeknownst to Rodriguez, Kappes and Michael Chertoff had separately assured their UK counterparts that America would continue to provide the British more time to collect information. Both senior U.S. officials were echoing a position that Bush had also stated with Blair multiple times.

Had Rodriguez been briefed on these high-level discussions occurring half a world away, the decision he was about to make would have been far more complicated.

♦

Intelligence derived from one of Rauf's cellphones indicated he was on the move. His phone was pinging off of a series of cell towers and was moving fast in a specific direction. He was probably inside a vehicle.

Maybe inside a bus.

That evening, Rodriguez and Cox were scheduled to meet their Pakistani counterparts again for dinner. Brig. Azmat Khan picked them up in his official vehicle around six thirty or seven in the evening. The four men—Rodriguez, Cox, Azmat Khan, and the ISI driver—sped through Islamabad toward Kayani's compound. On their way, Cox received an urgent call. It was from one of his officers, embedded with an ISI team. They were at a mobile checkpoint on a patch of earth of little consequence, but it happened to be where the highway intersected with some railway tracks.[14] The officer, who was providing technical assistance to the ISI, rattled off the fast fact that Rashid Rauf was in a bus headed toward them.[15] The mastermind's cellphone had been positively identified.

The officer then asked for permission to give his Pakistani counterparts America's go-ahead to stop the bus and arrest Rauf. At the same time, Brigadier Khan received a call from his men on the ground, with the same information. Rauf was approaching.

Khan turned to Cox and asked, "Do we go?"

In turn, Cox turned to Rodriguez, "What do we do, boss?"[16]

A thousand different considerations fired instantly in Rodriguez's brain. There was no way he was going to call back to Washington DC to figure out a game plan. He was a senior decisionmaker for U.S. intelligence, and he already knew what the White House wanted done. Asking for permission could create a situation where someone, somewhere, might tell him to slow down. He also likely surmised America's close allies were going to be unbelievably annoyed if Rauf was captured or killed in the next half hour.

Then again, this was a golden opportunity to take down a serious al Qaeda operative. He was directly targeting American citizens, potentially thousands of them. To let Rauf pass through the checkpoint unmolested may mean he could escape into the tribal areas, where it was far more difficult, if not impossible, to capture him. If he didn't act, he would be violating his assurance to his Pakistani counterparts that they were in the fight together. It also crossed Rodriguez's mind that if planes started exploding over the Atlantic, he'd be eventually hauled in front of a hostile congressional committee and asked, "You had him within your grasp, and you couldn't make a decision?" He would become the world's fall guy.[17]

The White House wanted him taken down. CIA wanted him taken down. Rodriguez was the senior man in the agency on the ground. Every day was September 12.

His decision was obvious.

◆

Rashid Rauf was still snoozing as the bus approached the checkpoint. When it suddenly came to a halt by the railway tracks, Rauf opened his eyes and glanced out the window. It wasn't the usual bored policeman or train operator idling along the side of the road, but a unit of elite police officers armed with gleaming Kalashnikov rifles. In the group were several plainclothes men; one motioned to the driver to open the front door. The driver obeyed and the officers told him to pull the bus over to the side of the road and then cut the motor. The bus driver quickly complied.

As the fog of sleep lifted, Rauf quickly put two and two together. He felt a terrible sinking feeling because he suddenly realized he had forgotten to switch off one of his cellphones. This simple oversight was his fatal mistake. He constantly berated Ali and the others to always be aware and be careful with their electronics. But this time, he hadn't taken his own advice. He had become too complacent about his own operational security. His adversaries had been able to track him down. In a desperate, pointless effort, he turned off a few phones before the authorities made their way to the back of the bus. They visually identified him. Then the officers grabbed, cuffed, hooded, and bundled him into the back of a waiting van. He didn't put up a fight. It was over in a few minutes.

Rashid Rauf was in custody.[18]

♦

Rodriguez was informed as soon as Rauf was in the van with a black hood over his head. It was now past seven or eight in the evening in Pakistan, after nine or ten in the morning in Washington DC, and two or three in the afternoon in London. He knew, despite having tacit authorization from the White House, that he had just kicked over a diplomatic hornet's nest. Everyone was going to be mad as hell—at him.

The CIA's primary means of communication from the field is its extensive, decades-old cable system; if it's not written down and inserted into the system, it's as if it never happened, bureaucratically. But there wasn't time to draft, edit, and send a cable, typed in all capital letters, informing headquarters what just happened. So Rodriguez instead picked up the phone. His first call was to the CIA front office to inform headquarters. His chief of staff, Gina Haspel, picked up the phone. He instructed Haspel—who, a dozen years later, would rise to become director—to tell Kappes, who was running the day-to-day of the CIA while the director was away, what had just transpired.[19]

When he called Rodriguez back, Kappes kindly informed Rodriguez he had just assured the head of MI6 the United States would not move without first warning the British.[20] President Bush had issued the same guarantee to Prime Minister Blair. Now everyone had to go back and eat their words.

Sheepishly, Rodriguez and Cox drafted the official cable detailing Rashid Rauf's arrest. After finalizing it and sending it out, they stayed up until till three in the morning Islamabad time monitoring events before going to sleep. Neither Rodriguez nor Cox had laid eyes on Rauf, now locked in a cell within a Pakistani military compound.[21] They didn't feel like this was a problem, however, since they figured the Pakistanis would soon provide the Americans full access to their new detainee. The Pakistanis knew how much the CIA wanted to get in the interrogation room with this high-value capture, just as they had with other senior terrorists. There would be more than enough time to debrief Rauf on his ties to senior al Qaeda leadership, the whereabouts of the explosive training camps in the tribal areas, his knowledge of terror operations in Great Britain and elsewhere, as well as his role in 7/7, 7/21, and Overt.

Rodriguez would be proven quite wrong.

◆

Information about Rauf's capture was quickly transmitted from the field to CIA headquarters and then on to the White House, which had been on tenterhooks for days. Fran Townsend was in her sunken, ground-floor office and immediately called President Bush at his ranch in Texas. Bush responded that he was going to call Tony Blair in his Caribbean hideaway right away to give him the news. Townsend asked the president for a breather to give her counterparts on the other side of the Atlantic a heads-up.

The president said, "Sure."[22]

London didn't want to hear from Townsend, who was seen as leading the more aggressive side of the White House; rather, they preferred to hear from the courtly Stephen Hadley. But the timer was now ticking, and Townsend had to ensure her British counterparts found out quickly. After they got over the momentary shock of what Pakistan (with America's blessing) had just done, they asked for a favor: "Can you please ask President Bush to not call the prime minister so he doesn't hear it from you."[23] It would be embarrassing for the British national security system if the prime minister first heard about a decisive break in the largest investigation in recent UK history from his American counterpart. Moreover, explaining why the prime minister was on holiday in the Caribbean during this time of crisis was also going to have be deftly messaged. This had the possibility of becoming a public relations nightmare.

The British authorities were quite displeased about this recent turn of events. so15's Peter Clarke was "well and truly miffed;" surveillance chief Steve Dryden was "angry," and they were not alone: "There was consternation on the fifteenth floor of Scotland Yard."[24] "Livid," was how Margaret Gilmore, the BBC's senior home affairs correspondent, described how the cops felt. "Until then, they'd been ahead of the game. Now they were being put on the back foot."[25]

This was an enormously complicated, intricately calibrated operation involving hundreds, perhaps thousands, of officers across Great Britain. The surveillance squads were working at full tilt; few had any semblance of a normal home life. The Met had been also putting into place a plan readying twenty-three different vehicles and arrest teams to take the suspects into custody almost simultaneously. But now the American bull had barged into their china shop.

Peter Clarke called Dame Manningham-Buller at MI5 to inform her about the rapidly unfolding events, just in case she hadn't heard already.[26] In a bit of further bad timing, the Met's assistant commissioner Andy Hayman was on holiday in Spain and was just sitting down to a plate of paella when he received the call. It was a bit before eight in the evening. "It's fine in America," sneered Hayman in exasperation when he heard about the arrest, "where everything is fine and dandy."[27] The Met immediately booked him on a commercial flight back to London, leaving at midnight. He rushed to the place where he was staying, grabbed his travel gear, and took off for the airport in a cab. In another twist of bad luck, Hayman in his haste had accidentally taken his daughter's passport instead of his, necessitating a frenzied return to his rented room and then a mad dash back to the airport. He barely made his flight.[28]

Earlier that afternoon, John Reid had finished a muscular national security speech at Demos, a London-based think tank. He had taken over as home secretary from Charles Clarke three months prior in a large cabinet shakeup following Labour's poor showing in that May's local council elections. In his talk, knowing full well the Overt investigation was cranking away in the background, he had warned, "We are probably in the most sustained period of severe threat since the end of World War II. While I am confident that the Security Services and Police will deliver one hundred percent effort and one hundred percent dedication, they can never guarantee one hundred percent success . . . It is up to each and all of us to ask the questions: What price security? At what cost preservation of freedom? What values are at stake? And what is the cost of making the wrong choices?"[29]

The speech concluded, he stole away and was enjoying a relaxing evening, watching a friendly preseason match between his beloved Celtic football club and Chelsea. He was lounging at an executive suite at Stamford Bridge stadium when the urgent call came in.[30] At halftime, he abruptly rose from his chair, said a couple of quick goodbyes, and took off for Whitehall where Manningham-Buller briefed him about the situation. It was time to arrest everyone and bring the curtain down on the plot.

At the same time, senior Home Office personnel were summoned from their dinners and evening commutes to return to their Marsham Street headquarters; no reason was given since they were on unsecured, unencrypted mobile phones. It also happened that the police had, on that night of all nights, sent the Home Office documents that indicated the tabloid *News of the World* was targeting the voicemails of cabinet ministers, royals, 7/7 victims, and others, touching off a scandal that would eventually bring down the publication.[31]

The UK secretary of state for transport Douglas Alexander was on the Isle of Mull in Scotland on holiday unsuccessfully catching lobsters with his family. When he received the call from the permanent secretary in the Department of Transport on an open, unsecured mobile phone, he left his wife in a muddy field. A Royal Air Force helicopter picked him up, delighting his young son.[32] Chancellor Gordon Brown, who would later become prime minister, was also in Scotland on paternity leave after the birth of his son; he was told the news as well but had not been given a chopper to bring him back to the capital.[33]

At the Home Office, Reid, Manningham-Buller, Alexander, and other senior police and staff had to figure out a plan of action, and quickly.[34] Multiple people were in daily contact with Rauf via email, text, and phone; for him to suddenly fall silent or disappear would arouse great fears. The plotters needed to be rounded up at once, lest one of them figured out Rauf had been detained. Ali had long been suspicious and jumpy of his surroundings, seeing surveillance under every rock and up every tree. If he heard about Rauf's arrest, logic dictated he might start destroying evidence, or even try to carry out an attack then and there.

An absolute logistical nightmare began spreading across East London and the Thames Valley. When the phone call came in on August 9, senior officers of the TVP were in a 9 p.m. meeting in their Oxfordshire headquarters to sort out their overall strategy regarding Overt for the next few weeks. But now they were told they had to arrest all the suspects. This minute. Now.

The officers grabbed everyone in the office and jumped in their cars for the journey down to High Wycombe.

Reid chaired the first of three intergovernmental meetings that night at 9:30 p.m. Hundreds of cops fanned out across London and elsewhere; many didn't know who Rashid Rauf was or the ins-and-outs of what had happened in Pakistan.

MI5 provided the TVP lists of suspects to arrest; not just the obvious suspects but also a number of peripheral individuals of interest. Problematically, there were names entering the arrest list while others were coming off, even as the police were driving toward High Wycombe. The police didn't definitively know who was or was not involved, or what sort of evidence could be used against them in a court of law. The lists were being updated as the force sped down the darkened motorway on a warm summer night.[35]

The trip from the TVP headquarters in the village of Kidlington to High Wycombe normally took about forty-five minutes, door-to-door, but the cops made excellent time in the mad rush on the M40 motorway. A number of TVP personnel, including many of the senior officers on call that evening, arrived in High Wycombe well before armed support. They didn't know if the suspects had hidden weapons or working explosives ready to be used at a moment's notice.

So, the senior officers of the TVP sat in the darkness, keeping watch over the targets. They hoped no one would emerge whom they would have to tackle without weapons. After an age, the armed support finally, mercifully arrived.[36]

And they did their duty.

22

Fellowship Is Life

Darkness enveloped Walthamstow. Ali was again hanging around Lloyd Park. He entered a phone booth on Forest Road and gave Sarwar a ring at 8:49 p.m. They chatted for a few minutes, and then Ali returned to his borrowed Kia Pride. He drove the car into the carpark within the Waltham Forest Town Hall complex, making a U-turn on Forest Road. Exiting the car, he entered another telephone booth across the street by the YMCA and again called Sarwar using a prepaid card. Somehow they had again missed each other, but now they knew where to meet.

By 9:30 p.m., as Home Secretary Reid, Manningham-Buller, Peter Clarke, and others were meeting twelve miles southwest, Sarwar's Nissan was following Ali's Kia into the Town Hall carpark.[1]

Both vehicles stopped just east of the Walthamstow War Memorial, in front of the Town Hall facing the green. The men emerged from their cars and together went to the back of the Nissan and rummaged around in the boot. Ali held a plastic bag with his right hand. They didn't find what they were searching for, because Sarwar forgot to bring it. Defeated, they walked away chatting, idling by a wall next to the Walthamstow War Memorial.[2]

They continued to wander aimlessly around the Town Hall grounds. Twenty minutes to ten, the two sat next to each other by the gray Walthamstow Assembly Hall, facing the giant robin's egg-blue fountain.

Above them were carved the words "Fellowship Is Life and the Lack of Fellowship Is Death."[3]

◆

The command crackled over the comms: the surveillance team was ordered to move in and arrest Ali and Sarwar. The quartermaster and the ringleader were in one place. But the team didn't have any firearms. They were the watchers, not the armed responders.

These men and women were suddenly tasked to bring down the two top suspects in the largest plot in British history without a single weapon among them. All they had were handcuffs.[4] They hoped the two men wouldn't have a gun or a blade on them. Or a bomb.

◆

Shockingly, Ali and Sarwar gave themselves up immediately. For all of their paranoia, they simply hadn't seen the unarmed members of the surveillance team lurking in the shadows. As if in a dream, the team slapped cuffs on the two men. It was 9:43 p.m. Ali's jacket, which he had been holding, fell to the ground.

Detective Sergeant Patrick Holt, attached to SO15, was one of the first officers on the scene. He wasn't in uniform, but he was wearing surgical gloves and produced a warrant card, which he showed to Ali. The suspect was kneeling on the concrete and had already been told he was under arrest for "the commission, preparation, or instigation of acts of terrorism."[5]

Still in shock, Ali stared straight ahead and took deep breaths. After advising Ali of his rights, Holt helped him stand up and placed his feet wide apart.

Holt told Ali, "Listen very carefully to what I am about to say, because it's very important."

Ali turned to the detective. Holt said, "Is there anything on your person that will cause harm to me, you or other persons in this area?"

"No."

"Is there anything in this area that will cause injury to persons?"

"No."

"What about in the car park area?" He gestured to the Kia and Nissan.
Ali said, "No, there is nothing."

"What's your name?"

Ali replied his name was Abdulla, and he sometimes went by Abdulla
Ali.

"Address?"

"68 Banbury—no, sorry, 18 Nash House." 68 Banbury Road was
where his parents lived.

"Which one?"

"I live at 18 Nash House."

The police searched Ali thoroughly and then placed him into a
white forensic suit. Holt fished out the key to the Kia from Ali's pocket,
which he passed along to Detective Constable Clark, who placed it in
an exhibit bag.

"That car. It belongs to Arafat Khan," Ali volunteered.

"Is this your jacket?" asked Holt, picking up the jacket. He could
feel a bulge inside one of the pockets through the fabric.

"Yes."

Holt produced something from the right-hand pocket and asked
Ali what it was.

"A usb stick."

"Whose is it?"

"Mine."

Did it contain a password or some sort of encryption, the detective
asked, holding the drive in his palm. Some sort of self-destruction
mechanism if it was improperly accessed?

"No."

"What's on it?"

"Holiday destinations in America." It was the stick with the flight
schedules to North America that he had looked up a few days before.
And now the cops had caught him, red-handed, with the information
on his person.

In his left pocket, the police found a piece of paper with an address
in Belfast. Ali claimed he picked it up in the street the day before. Holt
then pulled out a black diary, with diagrams and notations. He quickly

flipped through it. It was a to-do list: "Clean batteries. Perfect disguise. Drink bottles, Lucozade orange, red. Oasis, orange, red. Mouthwash, blue, red. Calculate exact drops of Tang, plus colour. Make in HP." There was a travel-ready shopping list: "Check time to fill each bottle. Check time taken to dilute in HP. Decide on which battery to use for D. Small is best. Get bags, key rings, electrics for batteries, toothbrush, toothpaste, aftershave."

The following page included other advice about smuggling in the explosives: "Select date. Five days B4. All link up. Prepare. Dirty mag to distract. Condoms. One drink used, other keep in pocket maybe will not get through machine, plus keys and chewing gum on the D in the elec device. Keep ciggies. Cameras take. The drinks that you should drink should be dif flava."

On the next page, an answer to the outstanding question regarding the optimal number of Tang and color drops: "Lucozade, red, 1.5 drops, one teaspoon Tang, one teaspoon orange, 12 drops. Oasis, red. On, red dye. Orange, two times mango."[6]

Holt showed Ali some of the diagrams in the diary and asked, "What's written on it?" showing him one of the diagrams. Ali replied, "Just garbage."

"What are the diagrams in the diary?"

Ali said, "Just plots of land—" Holt cut him off. "And the lists of batteries, Lucozade, and orange, et cetera?"

"I can't remember what that is."

◆

At the same time, Detective Sergeant Jonathan Mearns from SO15 was interrogating Sarwar. He was fully compliant and was kneeling quietly on the grass. He later claimed he had been praying when the police came up from behind him and tackled him.[7] After cautioning him, Mearns asked Sarwar for his home address and telephone number. He gave it up easily and then asked why he was being put into a paper suit. "To preserve evidence," tersely replied Detective Constable Partridge, who was taking notes. Sarwar was asked about his Nissan.

"Everything in the red car is mine," he replied.

The detective sergeant asked, "Is there anything dangerous in your car that could cause a risk to the public?"

Perhaps in an attempt to be witty, Sarwar replied, "No, only the handbrake."

◆

After searching Ali, they retrieved the Kia key from within the evidence bag. Ali had said it wasn't his, it was Arafat's.

"Who's he?" asked Holt.

"An old friend from school."

"When did you get it?"

For the first time, Ali looked nervous and uneasy. He glanced up at the darkened sky and lied, "A couple of hours ago." The cops knew he had actually been driving it around for days. But they weren't sure what was actually inside, or if the car had been rigged to explode.

Holt and another colleague, Detective Sergeant Mullan, called in the bomb disposal to search the car. With the Explosive Ordnance Disposal unit not yet on the scene, Holt walked over to Sarwar, already inside a police vehicle, to ask about the car. Anything the Met should know about in the vehicle, he asked.

He said, "A camcorder in the boot."

Holt replied, "Whose is it?"

"Mine."

What was on it, Holt asked.

Sarwar replied unenthusiastically, "I don't know." Of course he knew what was on the camcorder. On it were speeches made by Arafat Khan and Umar Islam.[8] Sarwar further failed to call attention to the black flag behind everyone from the videos, which the cops later found inside his vehicle.

Had he used the camcorder, asked Holt.

"No."

"Who had?"

"He has," nodding over to where Ali was standing.

"Who?"

"Ahmed."

Ali had now decided to shut up lest he said anything incriminating. "I don't want to say anything," he said to Holt, after which he was put in a police car and brought to the station.[9]

◆

Hundreds of other police fanned out across East London and High Wycombe to bring down the conspiracy, all at once.

They picked up Tanvir Hussain at 10:15 p.m. as he was walking down Canterbury Road in Leyton, two miles south of where Ali and Sarwar had been arrested a half hour beforehand. "Are you sure you have the right man?" he cried as they confronted him and read him his rights. At his house, police found three mini lightbulbs attached to black and yellow wires in a bedroom drawer.[10]

Umar Islam—his martyrdom video recorded mere hours before—was taken down at 10:30 p.m., west of the Town Hall on Bushey Road. Police approached him from behind and tackled him to the ground. At first, he thought he was about to be beaten up and robbed, before realizing his fate was actually going to be far worse. He had just told his pregnant wife that he was going to pray at the mosque around the corner, and now he was lying face down on the pavement, surrounded by police.[11]

Five minutes later, at 10:35 p.m., Arafat Waheed Khan was cuffed at his family's home at 71 Farnan Avenue. He, his mother, and his three sisters lived just around the block from the Town Hall but hadn't heard the commotion when Ali and Sarwar were arrested. The police confiscated all of the family's computers. Ali's red Vauxhall Vectra was parked nearby.

Six minutes before midnight, officers arrived at 7 Priory Road to collect Rauf's boyhood friend, Mohammed Gulzar.[12] They came to the front door and ordered Gulzar to come out. He came to the door but refused to open it, opting to retreat into the premises. As Gulzar made his way back, he turned off the lights, retracing his steps through the house.

It was going to be the hard way, then. Out came the battering ram. The police bashed the door in and tackled Gulzar, clad in a white T-shirt and tracksuit bottoms, in the hallway. In the takedown, he sliced his leg on some glass as he fell. When the police asked whose house it was, he said he wasn't going to answer any questions without a solicitor present. After treating his cut in the front room, they drove him to the station. Sticking to his silence, he refused to give any information about his identity or about the forty Toshiba batteries found in his room. The documents taken from the sparse living quarters bore the name "Altaf Ravat"; that was the name used when the police booked him. It actually took authorities two days and a fingerprint match to determine he was indeed the long-lost Mohammed Y. Gulzar of Birmingham.[13]

Ibrahim Savant was arrested at his home on Denver Road, less than a mile away from Umar Islam. The cops took down the front door. When the police came rushing in, he had just awoken to use the bathroom. The cops threw him against a window, smashing it with his head. Savant started bleeding on the carpet, and one of the officers reportedly said, "Look, you're getting blood on the floor."[14] The police hauled him to Paddington Green wearing only his boxer shorts and a T-shirt. In the initial search, they found messages that closely resembled the text from his martyrdom video signed, "Ibrahim Savant al Britani."[15]

At Savant's house, there was also a note from "Waheed Zaman al Kashmiri," who was arrested at 12:50 a.m. after leaving his home on Queen's Road in Walthamstow. Instead of hauling him to Paddington Green like the rest, the police brought him to the Belgravia Police Station.

The final players were rounded up over the course of the night. Adam Khatib was arrested at his home on Wellington Road in Walthamstow. Inside, the cops discovered a recipe for HMTD, along with a list of chemical ingredients. Police detained Mohammed Shamin Uddin; Ali and Arafat Khan had at one point visited at his home on Cazenove Road and used his computer.[16] Muhammed Usman Saddique, another IMA associate, was also arrested. The teenager Abdul M. Patel was detained as well. Ali's wife Cossor was picked up, as was Nabeel Hussain, viewed as a link between Ali and Khatib. But Cossor, Uddin, and Nabeel Hussain were allowed to post bail and leave police custody. Another High Wycombe resident, Donald Stewart-Whyte, was also arrested and given bail; his father was a Tory party activist and his half sister Heather Stewart-Whyte was a former Gucci model.[17]

The police also detained several others but released them without charge, including Ali's brother, Assan Abdullah Khan; Nabeel's brother, Umair Hussain; Amin Asmin Tariq, an employee of the private Indian carrier Jet Airways; Waseem Kayani; and Shazad Khuram Ali. Rashid Rauf's brother, Tayib, who was still helping run the family bakery in Birmingham, was also arrested but released without charge.

In the days and weeks following the arrests, several British newspapers—the *Birmingham Mail*, *Birmingham Post*, *Sunday Mercury*, *Guardian*, *Daily Mail*, and the *Times*—accused Rashid and Tayib Rauf's father, Abdul, of involvement in this plot. Abdul Rauf subsequently sued these organizations for libel. The newspapers eventually agreed to pay the Rauf patriarch "significant libel damages" and offered a public apology in May 2007.[18]

◆

The raids went on through the night and into the next day. 386A Forest Road was hit. So were the homes of the plotters.

The TVP came calling a bit after midnight to Sarwar's family house in High Wycombe. They had already received word that Sarwar had been arrested in London, so there was no need to bash his family's front door down. Detective Sergeant Ian Elgeti, a forensic scene examiner and exhibits officer attached to SO15, led one team to fully examine the premises. Sarwar's family vacated the property so the police could take apart the house bit by bit.

When the cops opened the garage door, they found four 5 L plastic bottles inside, as well as eighteen liters of hydrogen peroxide at 20 percent strength. They identified a thermometer and latex gloves, as well as other items for measuring chemicals. The officers also uncovered a glass Ragu tomato sauce jar that contained twenty small bulbs and wires taped together, with traces of Tanvir Hussain's DNA on it.[19] But what most interested authorities was an 8 mm videotape, hidden above the neon light over the door between the eave and the roof. The label had Ali's right middle fingerprint on it. On the tape, the cops watched Ali, Savant, Zaman, Hussain, and Arafat Khan give their angry goodbyes to the world.[20] DS Elgeti and his pair of search officers also found USB drives containing information about the gas pipeline that ran between Great Britain and Belgium, Canary Wharf, London's electricity grid, and firms where hydrogen peroxide could be bought. There was also a file with a curious document entitled "The Islamic Ruling on the Permissibility of Self-Sacrificial Operations," which offered the piece of advice, "Slay the infidels wherever you find them."[21]

They busted into Sarwar's bedroom, a first-floor room in the rear that he shared with his brother, who was away at university. There they found his used boarding pass—seat 30H from July 8 for an Islamabad-to-London flight. They also found SIM cards, a Panasonic Toughbook, mobile phones, flashlights, batteries, funnels, squat beakers, and a number of other items, which all went into the evidence bags.

On the bookshelf and scattered about the room was a selection of books related to the pursuit of jihad, including *Army of Madinah in Kashmir* by Dhiren Barot of the Rhyme conspiracy; *Jihad: Definition of the Most Important of the Obligations of Islam Jihad*; *Race with Death: 22 True Stories from the Bosnian War*; and *Jihad in Afghanistan against Communism*.[22] They also found the diary Sarwar had used to jot down notes over the last several weeks about oil refineries, moisturizing cream, and a series of email addresses he had used to communicate with Rauf, like "TANVMSD/LOVERBOY123" and "RAHAN_KHN/PAKISTAN1."

Complicating matters was that there might have been others. Rauf had been in contact with at least two individuals who wanted to be suicide bombers who had until that point been completely unknown to the police.[23] One individual, then a minor, lived in the northwest of the country and appeared to have been tangentially involved. He hadn't been in contact with the London cell but had come to the attention of MI5 following the roundup. Known in subsequent legal documents as "AM," he was a single man with several sisters who was believed to have trained at a terrorist camp in Pakistan as a teenager. MI5 assessed AM "was in contact with Rauf and possibly [Abu] Ubaydah." Furthermore, the Security Service assessed that AM may have met both of them during his trips to Pakistan in 2004 and 2005.[24] He also had links to

Mohammed al-Ghabra, the Forrest Gump of just about every British terrorist plot during this period. AM's real identity was never publicly revealed, and it is unknown where he is today.

◆

In the prime minister's absence—he was still in the Caribbean—John Reid held another COBR meeting in the middle of the night. At two in the morning, JTAC raised the security threat level to "critical," signaling that a terrorist attack was imminent, the first time this new warning system had been upgraded to its highest level. Prime Minister Blair spoke to President Bush to keep him updated. Around four in the morning, Reid called Gordon Brown, likely awake with his newborn, who then set into motion freezing the financial assets of all the suspects. By five in the morning, Reid held his final COBR meeting; it was decided he would brief the opposition Tories and the Liberal Democrats, while Deputy Prime Minister John Prescott spoke to Labour MPs.

Dawn spread her rose-tipped fingers over London at 5:38 a.m. on Thursday, August 10, 2006. One of the most tightly held secrets in the Western world was about to break wide open and throw the worldwide transportation system on its axis.

The scramble to fix a massive vulnerability in global aviation was on.

23

Scramble

It was deep in the evening of August 9 on the East Coast of the United States when the TSA's top brass began phoning the airlines' CEOs and their security personnel about what had just transpired in Britain. TSA chief Kip Hawley personally called the CEOs of the targeted companies. They also alerted the rest of America's transportation bureaucracy: the FAA, the rest of the TSA (whose employees had little idea what was happening), and other senior leaders across critical aviation nodes. Hawley and his colleagues were dialing from an unfamiliar office at DHS headquarters; while they were making calls, it was never quite clear if the handwritten and typed numbers physically written on the phones they were using were actually accurate. They also had no access to the voicemail on those devices if someone tried calling back and left a message.[1]

As it happened, the security coordinators for the airlines were all in Reno, Nevada, for an "Airlines for America" quarterly meeting. The group usually met in the Washington DC area, but had decided to meet this time around in the Biggest Little City in the World instead of the sweaty swamp of the capital. Mostly middle-aged aviation security experts, the group had known each other for years and were looking forward to tucking in to a good meal after a long day of speeches and hotel coffee. United Airlines' managing director of global security Rich Davis recalled, "We were all sitting down, glass of wine in our hands, for dinner."[2] Like in a movie, all at once, everyone started receiving frantic calls. Their bosses, the CEOs, needed them immediately. Dinner had to wait.

The United States was going to ban all liquids on airplanes, effective 4 a.m. Eastern Standard Time, before the first wave of morning flights took off. Davis and his deputy decided to return on the first flight the next morning to United's headquarters in Chicago because they knew it would be chaos at the airport. When they arrived at the Reno airport early the next morning, they experienced first-hand the effects of an unannounced ban on liquids. Passenger lines snaked around the airport. Haggard federal security directors had only been briefed on the aggressive procedures a short time beforehand, and now their blue-shirted security personnel were obliged to explain them to tens of thousands of bleary-eyed passengers as they arrived for their Thursday morning flights.[3]

Despite a multibillion-dollar budget, most TSA offices at the nearly 440 airports across America didn't own large office printers. These offices now needed to print hundreds of signs to indicate to passengers what was, and what wasn't, allowed on aircraft. Some officials went to twenty-four-hour printshops to copy their new security directives. At other locations, like JFK Airport in New York City, TSA officials just scribbled handmade signs and distributed them across the massive international air gateway.[4]

Across the nation's airports, there was not 100 percent understanding or compliance with the new rules. Some screeners allowed baby formula through the checkpoints while others did not. Some waved through medicine for passengers who provided prescriptions, although screeners lacked a way to verify the paperwork. Once they passed though the security area, passengers could buy drinks in the sanitized area, but then had to throw them away before entering an aircraft.[5]

In an effort to stem the rising tide of forbidden products, the TSA placed the largest plastic bins they could find on short notice in front of the security line. People were obliged to throw away their morning coffee, water, toothpaste, shampoo, conditioner, cough syrup, lotion, perfume, fine Kentucky bourbon, or any other liquid they had on them as they passed into the secure parts of the terminal. It didn't matter if the liquids were sealed or not. TSA officials frequently hauled these bins outside to the airports' dumpsters, which quickly overflowed with trash.

◆

By six in the morning of August 10, London Heathrow was a hot mess. The summer travel season heightened havoc at the airport, a situation now compounded by the decision to close Great Britain to flights from continental Europe.[6] British Airways suddenly cancelled eleven hundred flights, stranding tens of thousands of people across the globe.[7] Massive queues snaked through all the buildings and out into the loading zones. Large crowds of annoyed passengers clumped around the airport with their baggage. Armed police, a strange and disconcerting sight in Britain, roamed the terminals. Twenty thousand bags mysteriously went missing.[8] The spur road leading to Heathrow was bumper-to-bumper gridlock; the road to Stansted Airport became a parking lot for miles. The British papers roared "Mayhem" and "Chaos" in their headlines. Even VIPs were affected: U.S. senator Charles Schumer had landed in Heathrow that day on a family trip and spent hours sitting on the tarmac, not knowing what had happened until a fellow passenger showed the famously technology-averse senator the news on his Blackberry. Despite his high political status, Senator Schumer and his family then spent the rest of the day among the crowds trying to find their lost luggage and waiting in never-ending lines.[9]

No item could be held in a pocket. All hand luggage had to be stowed away in the hold with the exception of critical items like baby milk, which had to be tasted in front of security. Sunglasses cases had to be placed in stowaway or discarded.[10] Electrical items like mobile phones, computers, key fobs, and the like were banned from the cabin, for fear they could be used as detonators.

One traveler, Syl Tang, then a *Financial Times* journalist, was scheduled to fly from London for New York late that day. Flying a now-defunct airline that offered only business class tickets, she received a notification that indicated, for somewhat vague reasons, that she wasn't going to be able to bring "anything" on board the plane. So she left her clothing, wallet, housekeys, and cellphone with a friend in London and left for the airport six hours before her flight. When she arrived on the other side of the security check, holding only her U.S. passport, she saw the other passengers in the lounge. Nobody had laptops or reading material. All well-heeled business-class strangers, they just stared at each other, in a daze. Like Tang, they were also all holding their passports in their hands, shorn of everything else.

Tang was worried the flight might not actually take off. She secretly hoped her flight to America would be allowed to leave before all planes were grounded indefinitely. With the demeanor of doctors prepping for major surgery, the airline staff came around every so often with small snacks, reassuring the passengers they were doing all they could. One well-dressed man had a small meltdown. But most were silent.

They finally took off hours later. Once airborne, most of the passengers fell asleep from stress and exhaustion.[11]

◆

By ten in the morning in London, from a sparse desk in front of a purplish television backdrop emblazoned with the Home Office seal, John Reid and Douglas Alexander addressed the nation:

> The police, acting with the Security Service (MI5), are investigating an alleged plot to bring down a number of aircraft through mid-flight explosions, causing a considerable loss of life. The police believe the alleged plot was a very significant one indeed. At two a.m. this morning, the Joint Terrorism Analysis Centre raised the UK threat state to its highest level: critical. This is now being publicly announced as I promised to Parliament last month. This is a precautionary measure. We are doing everything possible to disrupt any further terrorist activity. This will mean major disruption at all UK airports from today.

Later that morning, the Met's bald, bespectacled deputy commissioner, Paul Stephenson, was in front of the television cameras as well. Peppering his speech with appreciation for the police services, he said:

We are confident that we have disrupted a plan by terrorists to cause untold death and destruction, and to commit, quite frankly, mass murder . . . We believe that the terrorists' aim was to smuggle explosives onto airplanes in hand luggage and to detonate these in-flight. We also believe that the intended targets were flights from the United Kingdom to the United States of America. I can confirm that a significant number of people are currently in custody, and the operation is ongoing . . . The United Kingdom is now at the highest possible level of alert . . . We cannot stress too highly the severity that this plot represented. Put simply, this was intended to be mass murder on an unimaginable scale.[12]

No one outside of the United States and Great Britain knew what had just occurred. Early morning flights had already taken off throughout Europe from points outside of London. The TSA's Hawley called his counterpart, Marjeta Jager, the EU's aviation security chief, who, like millions of others in August, was on holiday. She was on her yacht in the Adriatic, sipping coffee, generally cut off from the news cycle. Hawley quickly explained the Overt conspiracy, what the bombs were designed to do, and the necessity to ban liquids immediately across European airports.

Jager was caught completely unaware; the Americans were now pleading for her to take an uncompromising stance on security impacting everyone in the air across Europe. She knew her decision would cause serious transportation disruption across the Continent. A seasoned professional who immediately grasped the severity of the threat, she told Hawley, "I believe all our member states will give you total support." And then added, "This is an emergency, but I just ask one thing. When it comes time to adjust these rules, Kip, please consult with us."[13]

◆

The British and the American transportation bureaucracies faced a difficult challenge. On the one hand, banning liquids indefinitely was a nonstarter: the traveling public wanted their lotions and potions and would invariably find ways to sneak them onto planes, defeating the purpose of the ban. On the other hand, allowing everything on board was likewise unacceptable, as it would merely take a group of likeminded individuals to pull off an Overt-style attack, easier now with many of the details publicly available. So after much wrangling inside a London conference room, the United States and the EU compromised on September 26 to allow liquids in small containers onto passenger planes.

Rolled out as the "3-1-1" rule, it allowed each traveler 3 ounces of gels, liquids, and aerosols containers in one quart-sized, resealable bag. Often shorthanded as the "3-ounce rule" in the U.S., it's actually the "100 ml" rule—America's hoary system of weights and measures meant that Americans were allowed an extra 0.4 ounces in order to harmonize with the metric system used by the rest of the world. By the end of the year, "3-1-1" became the global standard.

For leaders, "3-1-1" seemed like an acceptable level of risk. Still, could a team theoretically assemble explosive liquids under 100 ml to clear security, pass through the secure area of an airport, and then mix them together? It would be somewhat difficult, but according to the TSA's Kip Hawley, the answer would always be "maybe."[14]

The next year, investigators from the U.S. Government Accountability Office decided to test whether it could actually smuggle liquids onto planes. In March, May, and June 2007, their teams successfully penetrated security at nineteen different American airports with components for explosive and incendiary devices hidden inside their carry-ons and on their person.[15] A leaked report in 2015 further suggested undercover investigators tried to smuggle weapons or explosives onto aircraft and succeeded sixty-seven out of seventy times.[16] Compounding this challenge was that the DHS inspector general in May 2020 reported the TSA doesn't monitor over time its Advanced Imaging Technology system to make sure it is capable to detect threatening nonmetal items hidden on airplane passengers.[17]

◆

Immediately following the takedown, President Bush made a few comments on a tarmac after arriving in Green Bay, Wisconsin. "The recent arrests that our fellow citizens are now learning about," the president remarked, "are a stark reminder that this nation is at war with Islamic fascists who will use any means to destroy those of us who love freedom, to hurt our nation."[18]

Five days later, wearing a clashing brown suit and red necktie, the president made his way to the NCTC Operations Center in McLean, Virginia, where the press was waiting. Inside the photography-friendly center, in front of a large, modern structure with multiple computer stations atop custom-built desks and large overhead screens, and flanked by his senior national security team, the president said:

> The enemy has got an advantage when it comes to attacking our homeland—they've got to be right one time, and we've got to be right a hundred percent of the time to protect the American people . . . Because of the good work in Great Britain and because of the help of the people there at NCTC, we disrupted a terror plot, a plot where people were willing to kill innocent life to achieve political objectives . . . Our most solemn duty in the federal government is to protect the American people, and I will assure the American people that we're doing everything in our power to protect you. And we've got some good assets, and the best asset we have is the people, people represented right here in this building.[19]

After his speech, Bush spent a few minutes chatting with some of the analysts sitting around the Ops Center. One, a young Coptic woman, had some Arabic script on her computer monitor. The president remarked, "You read Arabic?"

The analyst, star-struck by the U.S. president trying to make awkward small talk, could only muster a "Yes, sir."

The president continued, "Thank you for being here. I know you can do many other things with that."

She quickly found her footing and added, "It's an honor to serve in your administration."

The president replied, "It's not you serving me, or me serving you. It's us serving together."[20]

The analyst then watched the president try to leave the Ops Center. The public affairs folks had marked the floor with tape and arrows to indicate where he was supposed to walk after the press conference. But Bush, not one to follow directions or to be handled, set his own course and went off in a different direction instead.

◆

The Bank of England soon froze the financial assets of nineteen of the twenty-four individuals arrested on August 9 and 10. This meant they couldn't use any of their funds unless they petitioned the government for a license. Oddly, Mohammed Gulzar wasn't one of the nineteen, even though he remained in detention.[21] This executive action didn't require a level of proof beyond a reasonable doubt, according to HM Treasury senior counterterrorism advisor Andrew Cummings.[22] Following the 7/7 attacks, Britain passed sweeping new antiterrorism laws, allowing the government to unilaterally designate someone and freeze their assets as long as a minister—and not a judge—approved. After 2006 this tool was increasingly used to disrupt domestic terrorist plots. The knock-on effect was that it disrupted the daily lives of suspects, theoretically reducing the time they could devote to planning and facilitating terrorist activity. It was also a way, according to Cummings, for the authorities to signal to certain individuals that "we know what you're doing and we are watching."[23]

Still, only four days after the great roundup, Home Secretary John Reid announced on August 14 that Great Britain was lowering its threat level from "critical" to "severe." Airports around the country relaxed the almost-complete ban on hand luggage and liquids. Laptops were again allowed in the passenger cabins, as were books and magazines. Liquids purchased after passing through security were allowed, except on U.S.-bound flights. "There is still a very serious threat of an attack," Reid warned. "The threat level is [still] at 'severe' indicating the high likelihood of an attempted terrorist attack at some stage."[24] Within a week, airport service had almost returned to normal, with British Airways well on its way to clearing a backlog of five thousand pieces of luggage still lost amid the chaos.[25]

The British were also concerned with tainting the potential jury pool for the future trials, especially given the wall-to-wall media coverage. On August 28 the *New York Times* took the extraordinary step of blocking IP addresses from Great Britain after publishing an article entitled "Details Emerge in British Terror Case." The newspaper's readers in Great Britain received a note stating, "On advice of legal counsel, this article is unavailable to readers of nytimes.com in Britain. This arose from the requirement in British law that prohibits publication of prejudicial information about the defendants prior to trial."[26]

In New York City, the liaison officer NYPD had posted with the Met Police provided America's largest city police force the details of Overt a few days before it was all brought to a head. After learning about the extensive surveillance operation needed to monitor all of the suspects, NYPD commissioner Raymond Kelly quickly realized that a massive conspiracy like this would completely overwhelm his surveillance capacities. The force certainly had capacity and the skills to monitor a few suspects, but the NYPD simply did not have the resources or the trained officers required to watch twenty-plus individuals twenty-four hours a day, seven days a week. Commissioner Kelly and Deputy Commissioner of Intelligence David Cohen thus embarked on an ambitious effort to retrain hundreds of detectives in surveillance operations. Overt was the wake-up call the Big Apple needed to stay on its toes; this would later pay dividends in another al Qaeda plot targeting New York's subways only a few years later, codenamed High-Rise.[27]

◆

The searches across Britain continued. The police and the forensic units eventually descended upon forty-nine residences and businesses across London, Birmingham, and High Wycombe.

The police went back into the deep forest looking for clues. The TVP divided up King's Wood into zones and meticulously searched it by hand. They asked for assistance from the public, posting blue and white signs at the Wood's entrance, asking, "Have you seen any suspicious activity within this woodland area? Please contact ANTI-TERRORIST hotline."[28] It took authorities a full week to find Sarwar's suitcase and stash of chemicals in the hollow of the fallen tree trunk.

And yet, something was definitely missed in the investigation. Around this time, TVP officers discovered bottles with hydrogen peroxide residue in a recycling bin in the High Wycombe area. Police also discovered smashed bottles with the same residue in a bag alongside the M40 motorway leading out of town.[29] Someone was destroying evidence at an undiscovered crime scene.

But who was doing it? Sarwar was sitting in a lockup in London. The others who had made suicide tapes were in custody as well. There were a few other individuals who were connected to High Wycombe, but they were released either on bail or without charge. It would have been foolish for those individuals to take deliberate action. But it was obvious somebody was destroying incriminating evidence.

That person was never identified.

◆

Ali, Sarwar, Tanvir Hussain, and most of the rest were held in the bowels of the Paddington Green police station for the first few weeks of the investigation. The police were allowed to hold suspects for a maximum of twenty-eight days without charge. A grim facility, Paddington Green's vinyl-tiled walls were painted an unpleasant hue of dirty brown; the cells' interiors were covered in brown paper in order to capture any explosive residue.[30] The secure "custody suites" purpose-built for terror suspects were small rooms, with a toilet and a raised metal platform for a bed, provided with a mattress and blankets.

The lawyer Gareth Peirce, who represented Patel, likened the Paddington Green cells to "old Victorian lavatories, airless with tiled walls and are either too hot or too cold, depending on the season. It's like being in a dentist's waiting room, locked in and not able to get out— just endless waiting and a sense of fear and isolation."[31] In 2006 the European Committee for the Prevention of Torture and Inhuman or Degrading Treatment or Punishment published a report indicating that "the present conditions at Paddington Green High Security Police Station are not adequate for such prolonged periods of detention."[32]

Ironically, this report was sent to the British Government the day the Overt plotters were hauled to the holding cells. In 2010 the cells were refurbished to make them seem friendlier; the police station itself was shuttered several years later.

Ali was searched again after he was brought to Paddington Green. Police took his belongings and placed them in an exhibit bag, then took his fingerprints and a DNA swab. He was issued a prison uniform and placed in a windowless cell. He didn't have his phone or a watch, so it was impossible to determine what time it was. Through his disorientation and fear, he thought about his wife and child.[33] He eventually passed out on the mattress.

For the next ten days, police interrogated Ali about his role in the plot, with legal counsel present.[34] His lawyer advised him to say nothing, especially now that a media circus was occurring outside the station walls. He remained mum, stymying the police. He spent twenty-five days at Paddington Green, after which he was sent to the maximum-security Belmarsh prison to await trial.

Sarwar was likewise interviewed between August 11 and 21. Police played the martyrdom videos for him, which he later claimed was the first time he had seen them.[35] After the twenty-first, police charged him with "conspiracy to murder" and "committing acts preparatory to acts of terrorism."[36] He did not reply to those charges.

Tanvir Hussain was brought to Paddington Green and then held at Belmarsh for about a year. He didn't talk to anyone; he believed he was under twenty-four-hour surveillance and didn't trust his legal counsel in prison. He only relented and provided instructions once a judge assured him the police weren't listening to his conversations with his legal team.[37]

When he arrived at Paddington Green, Ibrahim Savant was so nervous he couldn't sleep; the authorities had to provide him sleeping pills. His interrogations began on August 12, forty-eight hours after his initial arrest. They were short, perhaps twenty minutes long, during which the police asked him about explosives and the conspiracy to blow up airplanes in flight. On the advice of his solicitor, he refused to answer any questions.[38]

Umar Islam was similarly shackled in the maximum-security facility. Eventually, he was allowed to call his wife, Rizwana Khan. She informed him the police had raided his mother-in-law's house around five in the morning and put her and her mother in handcuffs. Hearing the story, he replied, "Sorry, sorry, tell her sorry for everything. I can't speak. Things could be worse. Don't be negative. Look on the positive."[39]

It's unclear how the heavily pregnant wife of a man locked up on terrorism charges could "look on the positive." Perhaps her mind drifted back to the suspicious document she had found on her husband's table not even a week beforehand. Stranger still, it seemed at the time her brother might have been an MI5 informant.[40] While searching their home, the police found a book on a bookshelf in the living room with a series of codewords and their meanings. Among other codes were the following:

Stationery shop:	American Embassy
Sweet shop:	British Embassy
Simon:	The brother in California
Andrew:	Police
Samantha:	Intelligence service
Your manager:	Sheikh Osama [bin Laden]
Argentina:	Great Britain
UK:	Pakistan
Italy:	New York
France:	Washington DC
Germany:	Orlando, Florida[41]

It was never made clear who "the brother in California" was, as there were no follow-on arrests in the U.S. Like his compatriots, and on the advice of his solicitor, Islam replied "No comment" to the interrogators' questions. This went on for twenty-two months, even after he was sent on to Belmarsh.

Each of the men had access to competent legal counsel, and they mostly chose to remain silent. For almost two years, the conspirators were held at Belmarsh, a Class A prison in Thamesmead in southeast

London. They were in likeminded company at the facility, where Britain detains and often houses individuals convicted of terrorism offenses and other serious crimes. By November 2006, according to the Home Office, there were fifty-two prisoners at the Belmarsh prison held on terrorism-related offenses.[42]

◆

Meanwhile in Pakistan, authorities celebrated the ISI's arrest of Rashid Rauf. Islamabad had played a pivotal role in halting a terror act that would have killed thousands and was going to milk the story for all it was worth. A British diplomatic cable from Islamabad a few days after the takedown dryly noted, "It is clear that the Pakistani authorities and agencies are seeking to extract maximum domestic and international credit from Thursday's events through statements and leaks to the media."[43] Officially, Pakistan took pains to distance itself from the plot. On August 15 a foreign ministry spokeswoman declared to assembled reporters, "This was an al Qaeda operation, and al Qaeda based in Afghanistan." She also noted, "Rashid Rauf is a British national. We do not have any extradition treaty at the moment but yes, because he is a British national, the possibility of his extradition remains there. We have not received any request for extradition so it would be hypothetical at this stage."

The ISI brass was initially pleased as well. Rauf's jailers even showed him BBC's coverage of the police raid and arrest of Ali, Sarwar, and all the rest. The Pakistanis crowed how they had details about what the conspiracy was trying to achieve—namely, smuggle hydrogen peroxide explosives on to multiple aircraft disguised as soft drinks.[44] Reportedly, the Pakistanis even drove Rauf to both the borders with Afghanistan and Iran to compel him to divulge the locations of al Qaeda training camps.[45]

But when Rauf really started talking, it was not the narrative Pakistani intelligence wanted to hear. He told them he was first and foremost a "Kashmiri freedom fighter," fighting to liberate Jammu and Kashmir and attach it to Pakistan proper. Moreover, he claimed he had trained in Kashmir.[46] It became apparent to his interrogators that he was too close to the ISI and their machinations aimed at keeping Kashmir at a slow burn. Rashid Rauf was the inevitable fruit of the poisonous tree, the decades-long Pakistani effort to subvert Indian rule in the disputed region. His militancy had bled into working with al Qaeda and other noxious groups and had evolved into blowing up targets and killing civilians in the West. That was too much. If this information ever became public, it'd be embarrassing for both the Pakistani state and for the ISI.

The Pakistanis needed to keep this information under wraps, but the Americans were already asking to interrogate him. So the ISI devised a simple solution: their prize prisoner would simply become permanently unavailable to chat.

24

The System Worked?

Following a spectacular counterterrorism success like this, few remember the subsequent trials held long after the event. The system worked, after all. Thousands of people who might have perished lived to see another day, completely unaware of their possible brush with death. Many more were inconvenienced, but generally things worked out for the best.

Justice would eventually prevail . . . right?

◆

Almost two years had passed since the Overt conspirators were arrested. On April 2, 2008, a drizzly Wednesday morning, the men shuffled into a courtroom in Woolwich Crown Court, a modern, functional structure at the southeastern reaches of London. They sat in two rows on wooden chairs. They had been brought under tight security from the adjacent Belmarsh prison complex via a specially designed tunnel from the jail to the courtroom.[1]

Eight defendants—Abdulla Ahmed Ali, Assad Sarwar, Tanvir Hussain, Mohammed Gulzar, Ibrahim Savant, Arafat Khan, Waheed Zaman, and Umar Islam—and their legal counsel faced the judge and the jury for the biggest terrorism trial since the failed 7/21 bombers' trial in mid-2007. This particular indictment was severed for Adam Khatib, Nabeel Hussain, and Mohammed Uddin; they would have to wait till October 2009 to face trial.

All the defendants were charged with conspiracy to murder (Count 1) and conspiracy to endanger the safety of an aircraft (Count 2).

For the most part, they dressed in somber, serious outfits for their first day in court. Ali wore a blue suit with a black necktie; Sarwar had a light blue outfit with a dark blue tie; Tanvir Hussain went tieless in a blue suit; and Ibrahim Savant wore a puckish black and silver ensemble. Only Arafat Waheed Khan wore a T-shirt and sweater.

A 1925 Act of Parliament banned court artists from capturing the likenesses of the defendants while they were physically in court. All courtroom drawings of the Overt trial floating around the internet since then were drawn by an artist who committed the scene to memory and rendered it outside of the courtroom doors.

Peter Wright QC, a stately, experienced prosecutor, was tasked to lead the case for the Crown Prosecution Service (CPS). He began his opening speech:

> On the evening of ninth August 2006, two men met in the vicinity of the town hall, Forest Road, Walthamstow. One was the defendant Abdulla Ali, the gentleman who sits furthest away from you in the dock. The other was the defendant Assad Sarwar, the gentleman who sits closest to him . . . Although these men lived some distance apart, they were known to each other. They shared a common interest. It was an interest in which they were actively engaged at the time of their arrest, an interest that involved inflicting heavy casualties upon an unwitting civilian population, all in the name of Islam . . . It is the prosecution's case that they intended to cause a series of explosions on board a selected number of trans-Atlantic passenger aircraft. The explosions were to be caused by the detonation, in flight, of home-made bombs, commonly referred to as improvised explosive devices . . . The component parts of these devices would be designed to resemble soft drinks bottles and their liquid contents, batteries and other innocuous items of hand luggage. Once assembled, these items would have the capability of being detonated, we say, with devastating consequences. The devices were to be smuggled onto the aircraft and detonated in flight by a suicide bomber, a bomber

prepared to lose his or her life in this way . . . They are men with the cold-eyed certainty of the fanatic, prepared to board an aircraft with the necessary ingredients and equipment to construct and detonate a device that would bring about not only the loss of their own life but also all of those who happened by chance to be taking the same journey.

Naturally, the defendants argued this characterization was most definitely not the case. Instead the defense argued that, while the men were planning to cause a disturbance, it was merely to call attention to Britain's actions abroad. When Ali took the witness stand on June 3, he explained: "Basically, we wanted a change in the foreign policy because we recognized that it was the foreign policy that was the root of the problems we're seeing in the world today, both in places like Iraq and Afghanistan and also now in Britain as well, and I told [Tanvir Hussain] that the key to the whole issue was the public and the public opinion."[2]

They claimed they had planned to influence public opinion through a series of disturbances and scary videos. To execute this plan, they were going to create small incendiary devices. That's why they researched hydrogen peroxide and purchased glass bottles. Ali also claimed he and Hussain had tried to build a firecracker-like device in the late spring of 2006 before aggressive police surveillance had begun. He said they went to Hollow Pond, a secluded area on the edge of Walthamstow, and tried to detonate a small device by throwing a mixture of hydrogen peroxide and powder against a tree. He said it didn't work.[3]

Ali also tried to explain away the continued engineering of superior hydrogen peroxide bombs by saying their political demonstration would be more effective because "there was already a fear and threat from al Qaeda so they think anything involving; it's like a signature. If they see that, they think, 'This must be serious. This is these guys.'"[4] In other words, Ali claimed he and the others wanted to mimic other al Qaeda bombings and their videos but didn't want to actually harm anyone.

Ali and Hussain insisted the Houses of Parliament, not airplanes, were their primary targets for quite a while. They explained that security stationed at Parliament's public galleries was such that they could have smuggled in their explosives.

Soon after the trial began, the prosecution played the martyrdom videos on several large monitors arranged around the high-security courtroom. There, the jury watched Ali give his taped confession: "We've warned you so many times get out of our lands, leave us alone, but you have persisted in trying to humiliate us, kill us, and destroy us. Sheikh Osama warned you many times to leave our lands or you will be destroyed and now the time has come for you to be destroyed."

This went on for an hour. "We love to die like you love life, so you can't win. As you bomb, you will be bombed and as you kill, you will be killed. And if you want to kill our women and children then the same thing will happen to you. This is not a joke."

Unable to refute the veracity of the tapes, the defense instead focused on their purpose. The defendants again insisted they wanted to make a documentary or a series of minidocumentaries to release online to shake up Britain; the videos shot within the Forest Road property would be interspersed with footage from Iraq, Afghanistan, and Palestine. Strangely, defense counsel did not introduce into evidence any raw footage from the Middle East or South Asia. Neither could defense counsel explain why the participants didn't cover their faces. After all, they were regular British citizens and starring in a pseudo-martyrdom video would harm their future professional prospects.

Questioned by his counsel Malcolm Bishop, Sarwar explained the purpose of the videos was to scare "the public and make them feel responsible of foreign policy and give them that—basically to make them stand up against their government and voice their opinions. Another purpose was also to scare the government and put basically pressure on them."

The witness was then asked to provide a reasonable explanation for threatening mass destruction. "The reason was because these were already shown and we knew that the government knew that these were already released," he said, "so we decided to use homegrown UK suicide bombers in the UK with British accents and basically homegrown individuals were ready to strike."[5]

Sarwar claimed his actions mirrored those of Greenpeace or of animal rights activists. He claimed his idea was that they'd set off a bomb, but nothing powerful enough to kill anyone. He'd call in a threat afterward claiming to be al Qaeda and that there were other bombs elsewhere. Sarwar, Ali, and the rest also insisted suicide attacks were forbidden in Islam and that they found the practice personally abhorrent.

Yet, when Sarwar was asked if he could think of any other al Qaeda plot involving a minor explosion preceded by a warning, he couldn't think of any. And when he was asked if he knew of any other al Qaeda plot that lacked a bona fide attempt to kill as many people as possible, he replied, "I'm not aware of any, no."[6]

◆

Even with so much evidence from the investigation, the prosecution began to run into serious trouble several weeks into the trial. As the Crown provided excruciatingly detailed scientific particulars about the explosive's possible chemical concentrations, the presiding Justice David Calvert-Smith exclaimed, "What is the purpose of all this? Why are we going into such detail?"

"My Lord—" the prosecutor began.

The judge cut him off. "There is no suggestion that any of these defendants had managed to create the 90 percent by weight volume, 75 to 25 percent HP to Tang mixture which caused all this."

"My Lord, there is not. The purpose—"

The judge cut the prosecutor off again, continuing his thought. "If they had, they would obviously have caused very considerable damage, but the jury and I no doubt are anxious to know what that actually would have amounted to rather than look at bits of plastic which would probably not have been in aeroplanes or anywhere else. By all means show us all this, but we have to deal with the fact that this is an allegation of conspiracy rather than the actual causing or explosion or murder."[7]

Sarwar's defense counsel later seized upon the judge's line of questioning during cross-examination. "Such a plot was unattainable, and really amounts to no more than prosecution fantasy."[8]

The Crown nevertheless asserted the conspirators had the ingredients for the bomb:

- The hydrogen peroxide that Sarwar would eventually boil down to an appropriate strength;
- The "Tang" powder to mask the chemical composition's color;
- The AA batteries, which would carry the HMTD charge;
- The bulb filament, in turn, connected via wiring; and
- The disposable camera, to serve as the detonator.

Prosecutors then articulated what the plotters planned to bring aboard an aircraft:

- Two sport drink bottles;
- The rigged AA batteries;
- The disposable camera; and
- A pornographic magazine and condoms to distract security if the bag was searched.

The prosecution painted the picture for judge and jury how the bombers might have gone to the lavatory during the flight, connected the charge (battery) to the detonator (camera), and joined them to the main explosive within the bottle via the wires already linked within the bulb's filament. After all this was completed, the bomb could be detonated.

The defense argued Ali and the rest had never actually constructed a working explosive device, nor tested anything anywhere. The defendants admitted they were involved in experiments, but there was a large gulf between theory and reality. Unlike the 7/7 and 7/21 bombers, the Overt conspirators never distilled the hydrogen peroxide to the concentration required to build a viable explosive. And they never put any chemicals into the plastic bottle or glass containers.

◆

The trial stretched on into the summer. The air conditioning inside the courtroom was unreliable, so the judge at one point advised counselors to remove their wigs. Everyone was sweating, and the trial was clearly taking a toll on the defendants. Family, friends, and coworkers eventually testified on the defendants' behalf. They were good fellows. Never in trouble. Helpful around the house. Kind to those in need.

Still, the defendants had admitted in court to building an explosive device. On July 14, Ali, Sarwar, and Tanvir Hussain entered a guilty plea to "conspiracy to cause an explosion likely to endanger life or cause serious damage to property." In addition, Ali, Sarwar, Hussain, Savant, and Islam pleaded guilty to "conspiracy to commit a public nuisance."[9]

Toward the close of the Crown's case, the main indictment—Count 1A—was amended to allege a conspiracy to murder without specifically asserting how the murder was to be carried out. The former "Count 2"—endangering a safety of an aircraft by blowing it up—had now become "Count 1." The prosecution felt confident, but just in case the jury believed there was a murder conspiracy afoot, but not one involving airplanes, the defendants could still be convicted of a serious crime.[10] The judge told the jury they could decide if the men wanted to murder but not specifically to place explosives on airplanes.[11]

The trial mercifully wound down by mid-July. On July 23, the judge gave the jury its instructions:

The burden of proving guilt on the charges the defendants face is upon the prosecution. A defendant does not have to prove his innocence. How does the prosecution achieve this? Answer: by making you sure of the defendant's guilt. Nothing less will do. If, when you have considered all the evidence, you are sure of guilt, you must convict. If you are not, you must acquit . . . The general principle is that this is not one trial but eight. The defendants are being tried together because much of the evidence is common to some or all the defendants. A verdict of guilty or not guilty in respect of one defendant on one count does not mean that the same verdict must be returned against him on another count, or against another defendant on any count.

Beyond the legal guidance, the judge told the jury:

Your verdict concerns these two questions, the two questions on the same page, and no others. You are not, for instance, deciding whether a defendant is or is not a fanatic. You are not deciding whether it was likely that any conspiracy would in the end have been successful. You are not deciding whether the interventions of British and US troops in either Afghanistan or Iraq were justified prospectively or in hindsight. You are not deciding the order, if any, of precedents between defendants, say, and you will know why I mention these two in particular, Sarwar and Ali. You are not deciding whether the plan was to be put in effect soon or in the medium or long-term. You are not deciding when, if a conspirator did join the conspiracy, he did so. You are not deciding what, if any, role other characters, either those named in the indictment, others, e.g., in Pakistan, or the Patels, father and son, and others for that matter, may have played. Only explore the roles of others to the extent you believe it necessary to help you answer the key questions: *was there a conspiracy to murder in either of the ways set out in Count 1 or Count 1A and was the defendant we are thinking about a party to it?* (emphasis added)

Following the final statements by the prosecution and the defense, the jury went into deliberation on July 29. The Crown felt confident it had shown, beyond a reasonable doubt, that the defendants were guilty. They had shown as much as they could of the plotters' meticulous planning—every invoice, every receipt, every speed trap the defendants ran, every movement caught by police mobile and static surveillance. But they were unable to include some of the most arresting documentation: emails back and forth to Rauf in Pakistan. That information was simply not allowed in this trial.

The judge informed the jury that they could even give a majority verdict, and not a unanimous one, to convict.[12] After fifty hours of deliberation, eleven days over a five-week period—remarkably, they were allowed to take a two-week break in August—the jurors came back with their verdict on September 8.

The jury concluded Ali, Sarwar, and Tanvir Hussain were guilty of conspiracy to murder (Count 1A). However, they deadlocked on the charge of conspiracy to commit an act of violence likely to endanger the safety of an aircraft (Count 1). The jury was simply unconvinced these men were going to bomb a series of airplanes.

With this limited evidence of actual intention, the jury also failed to reach a verdict on the charges against Ibrahim Savant, Umar Islam, Waheed Zaman, and Arafat Khan, despite watching their martyrdom videos at the beginning of the trial.

Most galling to the prosecutors was that Rashid Rauf's childhood friend Mohammed Gulzar was acquitted on all counts. He had held his ground and refused to plead guilty to even the public nuisance charge. Gulzar had not starred in any of the martyrdom videos, so he could credibly claim he had nothing to do with them.[13] He never bought any bombmaking chemicals or equipment, nor had he ever visited the Forest Road flat. Therefore, the jury did not find the Crown's arguments compelling enough to convict him of anything. The judge himself had indicated on July 23 the evidence against Gulzar was "purely circumstantial," based as it was on his strange arrival in Great Britain, his documented connections to other members of the conspiracy, and the unlikelihood of his rationale for both.[14]

◆

Where did the prosecution fail?

There were enough seeds of doubt in the jurors' minds to indicate that, perhaps, blowing up airplanes was not what the cell actually wanted to do. Despite reams of police surveillance information, there was no document or phrase used by Ali, Sarwar, or anyone else indicating hydrogen peroxide bombs would be used to strike airplanes to serve al Qaeda. They were careful enough to speak in code. While Ali's internet search of airlines leaving Heathrow was indeed suspicious, no one had purchased airline tickets yet. Umar Islam didn't even possess a valid passport.

There was also little evidence indicating the immediacy of the threat except for some crosstalk in the Forest Road safehouse. A possible attack was weeks, maybe even months, away. The bulk of the electronic surveillance that connected the London cell to Pakistan, and to one another, was not introduced into the court proceedings.

None of the defendants made any meaningful claim to innocence. Still, the case against Ibrahim Savant, Umar Islam, Arafat Khan, and Waheed Zaman rested upon the martyrdom videos, their contacts with Ali and Sarwar, and possession of materials deemed extremist by the prosecution. Khan had also bought beakers and cylinders at John Bell & Croyden, which were later hidden by Assad Sarwar. But they never touched a bomb, bought hydrogen peroxide, or researched flight timetables. Their counsel made the argument that they didn't know anything about the contours of the actual plot, which, per the voluminous evidence produced at trial, appeared to be accurate.

Perhaps if the conspiracy had been allowed to percolate a bit longer, as the British intelligence and police services had wished, there would have been more evidence to share. Whitehall was furious about the outcome of the trial, which had cost some £10 million, expended two years of work, and caused chaos in the global aviation system. The CPS tried to spin a partial success to the media: "The jury found there was a conspiracy to murder involving at least three men but failed to reach a verdict on whether the ambit of the conspiracy to murder included the allegation that they intended to detonate IEDs on transatlantic airliners in relation to seven of the men. It is therefore incorrect to say that the jury rejected the airline bomb plot."[15]

After the verdicts came in, Andy Hayman forlornly told the press, "This was one of our strongest cases."[16] Naturally, finger-pointing followed, mostly across the Atlantic at the Americans, for jump-starting the process before the men and women on the ground were ready to pull the trigger. An anonymous British official told the BBC the United States was to blame for pressing Pakistan into arresting Rauf before the evidence had been collected.[17]

The former shadow homeland security spokesman, Tory MP Patrick Mercer, went further. He told BBC's *Newsnight* that Rashid Rauf's arrest, without warning, had undercut the case: "A number of operations against our enemies inside this country were not executed to the level that we would have wished. There wasn't as much evidence gathered, for instance, as people wanted. And, as a result, I know for a fact that a number of military agencies felt that, with more consultation, they would have been able to get more evidence and that actually a number of their operations came close to being compromised."[18]

◆

Rashid Rauf had been prominently revealed in the press as Overt's mastermind, but his real name was never mentioned during the trial itself. Despite all the publicity, the defendants, the prosecution, and the judge conspicuously kept his name from entering court records.

Sarwar got the closest to mentioning Rauf's name. During his testimony, Sarwar had claimed a "Kashmiri freedom fighter" named "Jamil Shah" taught him how to build hydrogen peroxide explosives while he was in Pakistan.

"Who had taught you that 80 HP would make a bomb?"

"Jamil."

"Had it ever been demonstrated to you how it would go off?"

"Yes, yes, he did, yes."[19]

No name. No records of correspondence. Suspicious omissions in the transcript. This was all despite the prosecution and the police knowing about the electronic and telephone correspondence between multiple people in England and Rauf in Pakistan. He was the phantom haunting this trial.

◆

After the jury failed to reach a conclusion agreeable to the government, the CPS decided to retry each of the defendants again. Perhaps a different jury and a different judge would reach a more acceptable decision. Everyone was ready for round two, in February 2009—all except for one person.

Since Mohammed Gulzar was acquitted, he could not be retried. Still, his freedom was sharply curtailed. On September 8, 2008, the British government imposed a "control order" upon him, which severely restricted his freedom of movement and association. MI5 assessed he was a committed extremist and too dangerous to have roaming the streets freely. MI5 also asserted he had tried to contact the teenager, codenamed "AM" in the north, but was arrested before they could meet in person.[20] After examining two of Gulzar's telephones following his arrest, MI5 discovered mobile numbers under the name "Izzy"; after researching the number, MI5 believed it was for a person named "Ismail."[21] MI5 also noted Gulzar had filed Sarwar's number in his phone by subtracting by one digit the last four of his mobile number. "Izzy" was encoded in a similar fashion. He too was placed under control orders in June 2007.[22]

From the courthouse, Gulzar was forcibly brought to Tottenham, in London, to reside under the equivalent of house arrest. Over the years, he was relocated to two different places, along with his wife and soon, two young children.[23] After a change in government, control orders were phased out in 2012; like old wine in a new vessel, the protocols became known as the "Terrorism Prevention and Investigation Measures" (TPIMs), which functioned in much the same way. But an individual under TPIMs was subject to review every two years to determine if he had returned to terrorist activities; if not, then he was presumably allowed to return to normal life. Years following the trial, Gulzar's whereabouts became fuzzy, and he finally vanished from public view.

25

Rashid Rauf's Second Chance

About a month after Rauf's capture, Pakistan's Federal Interior Secretary Syed Kamal Shah was asked on the domestic channel GeoTV about extraditing him to Great Britain. He explained that before that happened, Pakistan wanted to first perform its own investigation.[1] This series of "investigations" then lasted for quite a while. For the next year and a half, Rauf was in and out of various courtrooms concerning his involvement in the Overt conspiracy. At almost every juncture, he emerged the victor.

First, the government of Pakistan charged Rauf in a high-security antiterrorism court with the crimes of "impersonation, cheating, forging documents, presenting those forged documents as real, and keeping explosives."[2] In December 2006, five months after his capture, a judge threw out many of the charges because they weren't specifically terrorism-related. He was therefore moved from the antiterrorism court system to the regular criminal one. Despite a push by the government to place Rauf back into the antiterror court, a high court in Lahore found in his favor and suspended this effort.

Compounding this issue was that the British government never formally charged Rauf in the Overt plot. This was probably due to the sensitivities of the signals and human intelligence gathered in the months beforehand. For London, protecting sources and methods was more important than nabbing the conspiracy's ringleader. Since

Rauf's emails were considered "top secret," and likely the "originator controlled" property of the Americans, the British would not have provided this evidence in an official extradition document.

Rauf's lawyer, Hashmat Habib, grandly declared that if the British Foreign and Commonwealth Office didn't proffer the grounds for his client's extradition, Rashid Rauf would sue the British government for £1 billion.[3] There were no teeth behind this threat, however. The Pakistani foreign ministry eventually claimed the CPS served an extradition request to the Pakistanis for Rauf, even though Britain and Pakistan did not have an extradition treaty. Supposedly Prime Minister Blair was willing to turn over several individuals in Great Britain who were wanted in Pakistan in exchange.[4] British authorities then referenced a "conspiracy to murder" charge to bring him home to face justice—at least, that's what the U.S. Department of Justice believed, according to a number of declassified emails.[5]

The British government considered another tactic: perhaps Pakistan would give up Rauf to help solve the unsolved murder of his uncle, a crime that had set off his flight from Birmingham to Pakistan in the first place. That gambit didn't make any headway either. Perhaps it didn't really matter; Rauf was in a maximum-security lockup. He was theoretically off the counterterrorism chessboard.

Following his capture at the railway junction, Rauf soon became an inmate at Adiala prison in the garrison city of Rawalpindi. Adiala, also known as the Central Jail Rawalpindi, was built in the late 1970s and early 1980s to house fifteen hundred inmates. By the time Rauf became one of its guests, the sprawling prison was officially home to over four thousand prisoners.[6] It was a rough, cruel, dangerous place. It was also a detention facility keenly attuned to social class divisions; inmates with status received certain generous perks. The "jihadi" class, and especially British nationals, generally received privileges in prison well above local inmates held for run-of-the-mill crimes.

In January 2007 Rauf's lawyer requested he be moved up from a "C" class facility to a "B" class, and a civil judge in Rawalpindi directed the jail's superintendent to move his inmate up the social ladder.[7] The upgrade meant he had a chair, a cot, a teapot, and a few other perks.

If he had opted to pay, he could even have a refrigerator, a television set, an air conditioner, and newspapers.[8]

By that May, there was little urgency to get Rauf's case processed. This al Qaeda leader had fingerprints on multiple terrorist plots abroad, but there seemed to be little movement to finalize his status. This was also past the point where Pakistan would secretly allow the Americans to take charge of an individual and ferry him to a U.S. holding facility, as they had done in the past.

The Americans tried to nudge things along. The assistant attorney general for national security, Kenneth Wainstein, advised that Department of Justice prosecutors fully pursue a case against Rauf. Wainstein also wanted to convene a federal grand jury to indict him. The FBI's Washington Field Office began the process of building an unclassified set of facts and associations between Rauf and other nefarious individuals for a possible extradition to the United States. "Significant urgency is being placed on this case by the Department of Justice due to the possibility of RAUF being released by the Pakistanis at any time," read an August 19, 2007 FBI internal memo.[9] "As such," it continued, "this lead has been given a PRIORITY precedence."[10]

It had been over a year since the plot had been thwarted. The FBI sent two special agents from the Washington Field Office to Pakistan on August 24 to interview Rashid Rauf, as well as examine the original evidence.[11] They also prepared a Miranda warning for Rauf in English and in Urdu. A few days later, on the twenty-seventh, FBI director Robert Mueller called a senior Pakistani official to see if his men could interrogate Rauf in Adiala prison. At that point, the special agents were cooling their heels at the embassy in Islamabad, waiting for the green light to proceed to the prison, which was less than an hour's drive away. Director Mueller emphasized Rauf could be released from custody in the coming days given the vagaries of the Pakistani criminal justice system, and it was urgent that the FBI interview him and review the evidence seized during his arrest.

The heavily redacted telephone call readout implied that not even personnel from another U.S. government agency—that is, the CIA— had been allowed to debrief Rauf at any point since his arrest a year beforehand. In response, the senior Pakistani official told Mueller that he "would take the director's request under consideration." Everyone thanked everyone else and, as he was hanging up the telephone, Mueller said "he personally looked forward" to his Pakistani interlocutor's next visit to Washington.[12] But it was obvious the FBI was getting the brush-off.

Two weeks later, on September 7, an FBI memo noted that, despite Rauf's continued incarceration, "requests of interviews of Rauf and access to associated items of evidence have gone unanswered."[13] Over a series of months, the FBI, CIA and MI6 remained eager to talk to Rauf.[14] But the Pakistanis never granted them permission to speak with him.

Indeed, Rashid Rauf might have been the only, or one of the only, captured people within the entire al Qaeda hierarchy with whom the ISI had refused to grant the CIA time in the interrogation room. Multiple intelligence officials could not recall another case in which the Pakistanis forbade the U.S. to interrogate an al Qaeda operative, especially one with direct links to a plot to strike America. This was especially galling since the CIA had played a direct, pivotal role in his capture.

For the Americans, this studied refusal by Pakistan to assist on this core counterterrorism concern was flabbergasting. It caused doubt to creep into many minds about the ISI's overall reliability on any issue. Given the organization's tacit support for the Taliban and other jihadist groups, some people at the agency began to wonder about whether al Qaeda itself was actually a secret ISI effort that had gotten out of hand.[15] Was the ISI working both sides or not, and if not, why was Rashid Rauf somebody they didn't want the United States to interrogate? Did he have more of a story to tell than the Americans and the British believed? What could they possibly be hiding?

Years later, Pakistani prime minister Imran Khan claimed in front of a Council on Foreign Relations audience in New York that the army and ISI had trained al Qaeda, and then maintained links after 9/11.[16]

◆

On November 15, 2007, now sixteen months after his capture, Rauf won again in the Pakistani legal system. The Federal Review Board, a legal body appointed by Pakistan's Supreme Court chief justice that reviews orders made for "preventative detention,"[17] acquitted him of all charges, including the ones pertaining to explosives.

Yet after being cleared, Rauf was immediately detained under Section Three of the Maintenance of Public Order Ordinance (3MPO), a catch-all British colonial-era law used to override due process and keep unwanted people in prison for up to six months.[18] Islamabad did not want to endure the embarrassment of Rauf going free or face the withering ire of the Americans and the British. They also presumed Rauf would resume his previous activities as soon as he walked out the jailhouse door.

3MPO was a lovely piece of authoritarian legalese permitting the government to jail anyone to prevent "any person from acting in any manner prejudicial to public safety or the maintenance of public order." Human Rights Watch noted this ordinance was frequently used against Pakistani journalists, lawyers, and human rights activists whom the government disliked.[19] Ironically this law, first constructed by the British and then strengthened under an independent Pakistan, was wielded against a British-Pakistani dual citizen wanted back in London.

But such critics need not have worried. Rauf wouldn't even have to wait six months to taste freedom.

◆

Here is the official story of what happened on December 15, 2007. The head of the Adiala jail knew exactly who Rauf was and the danger he represented. The operative was due to appear in court in Islamabad that day, driven there from the prison under guard. Five days in advance of his court appearance, the superintendent sent a "most urgent fax" to the police entitled "Provision of Special Police Guard for the production of detainee Rashid Rauf, son of Abdul Rauf, on Dec 15."[20] It stated, "The accused is a dangerous person and involved in international activities. Therefore, he needs strict security. If any mishap happens while he is travelling, the in-charge police will be responsible."[21]

Given Rauf's responsibility for at least three terror operations in the West, he had been initially transported to and from his court appearances in an armored personnel carrier surrounded by a throng of police officers. When he was first arrested and made his first appearances in public, he was also trailed by a crowd of curious onlookers and several journalists. It was well-known he had many friends in the country; the possibility his al Qaeda or JeM comrades might try to ambush the vehicles and free him while he traveled to court remained high. But by the winter, public interest in his comings and goings had dropped off significantly. On that December day, Rauf mysteriously took the hour-long trip to court in a regular thin-skinned police van guarded by only two constables, Nawabzada Khan and Mohammad Tufail Khan. These same constables had also escorted him to three previous hearings.[22]

Rauf arrived at court in Islamabad around midday. The perfunctory appointment was soon concluded, and he was about to return to prison when his uncle, Mohammed Rafiq, chatted up Rauf's two police escorts. Incredibly, Rauf's uncle convinced them to ride in his silver Mitsubishi station wagon instead of a police van back to prison. It was far better apportioned than the police-issued vehicle, and so the four men—Rauf, his uncle, and the two constables—left the courthouse, with Rauf's uncle behind the wheel. No one explained whatever happened to the abandoned police car.

They were on the road around 3 p.m., well past lunchtime, and everyone was hungry. Rauf asked his guards if they could stop at the McDonald's on the southern edge of Islamabad's Jinnah Park near the court buildings.[23] Rauf's uncle generously offered to pay for everyone's meal. The constables agreed. The uncle paid everyone's tab, as promised.

It was then rapidly approaching afternoon prayer time. Rauf and his uncle asked to make a further stop at a mosque in the Gulshan Abad section of Rawalpindi on the road to the prison. Rauf entered the mosque with his uncle, but the cops stayed by the car. According to the superintendent of Adiala prison, the two most gullible constables in history also removed Rauf's shackles so he could wash himself and pray.[24]

Then Rashid Rauf, one of al Qaeda's most accomplished terrorists, uncuffed and out of sight, strolled into the mosque complex and disappeared.

According to one version of the story, the uncle also initially dis-appeared but local authorities quickly apprehended him.[25] In another version, the uncle emerged from the mosque wondering where his nephew had gone, and with the constables, searched the property. After a fruitless effort to find him, the uncle gave the two hapless policemen a ride back to their station and then drove home.[26] A custodial report from Adiala issued at 4:30 p.m. neglected to mention Rauf's absence. By 6 p.m., the constables arrived at the Margalla police station and indicated Rauf had vanished.[27]

Depending on traffic and road construction, it takes about an hour to drive the twenty or so miles from the McDonald's at Jinnah Park in central Islamabad to the Gulshan Abad area in the southern part of Rawalpindi, and then another hour or so to drive back to the Margalla police station in Islamabad. To escape in that timeframe requires a plan, a fair number of moving parts, and several confederates. By 9 p.m., the jail formally notified police authorities that Rauf was missing.

A full-scale investigation kicked off that evening, including a police manhunt. Rauf's uncle was arrested, as were a number of other relatives. Rauf's house in Bahawalpur, 350 miles south of Rawalpindi, was raided the next day. Constables Nawabzada Khan and Mohammad Tufail Khan, along with seven other police officers, were sacked a month later.[28] Oddly, they couldn't provide any information whatsoever that could have led to the location and rearrest of Rashid Rauf.

The official story of Rashid Rauf's flight to freedom was, to put it mildly, utter baloney.

Yet the challenge with providing an alternative version of Rashid Rauf's escape from Pakistani custody has been complicated by an absence of hard facts. Rauf was definitely in court around midday on the fifteenth, then never showed up at the prison several hours later. Since these legal proceedings were an endless series of periodic, perfunctory court appearances, American and British diplomats in Islamabad didn't send anyone to monitor them anymore. Despite his high-profile case, Rauf's court dates didn't even make the local press. Everyone assumed Rauf would remain in custody. A subsequent inquiry discovered the constables transporting Rauf had detoured from previous court appearances and taken him to his uncle's home in the past, but no one had noticed.[29]

After he fled, the British High Commission in Islamabad took a particular interest in his rearrest, stating, "The High Commissioner spoke yesterday to the interim interior minister of Pakistan and was assured Rauf's recapture was a priority for them, and that they had set up an inquiry into how the escape had happened."[30] His name was placed on an Exit Control list, in the event Rauf would try to flee the country from an international airport under his own name. The Ministry of Interior also deployed teams to Rauf's family's town in Azad Kashmir. He wasn't there. Beyond Azad Kashmir, officials from the ministry alerted authorities in the North-West Frontier Province and were very well aware of his likely escape into Waziristan.[31] The government also established an official inquiry, comprised of Interior Secretary Imtiaz Qazi, Federal Investigation Agency deputy director-general Mirza Muhammad Yasin, Inspector-General of Prisons (Punjab) Mufti Sarfraz, and Islamabad's deputy commissioner Amer Ali.[32] Naturally, the Pakistanis told British diplomats that "the escape of Rashid Rauf was very unfortunate."[33]

In England, his father, Abdul Rauf, told the press, "I don't know anything. I'm shocked."[34]

Rauf's legal counsel, Hashmat Habib, shrugged his shoulders when asked about the escape and suggested darker forces were at play. "You could call it a 'mysterious disappearance' if you like, but not an escape," he said. "The Pakistanis [were] simply not interested in handing him over to the British."[35] Yet one unnamed source told the Pakistani newspaper *Dawn* that the Pakistani government, or at least one section of the government, had already decided to extradite him to Great Britain.[36]

Back in the U.S., when CIA director Hayden was told Rauf had escaped from custody during one of his meetings, he expressed the feeling felt by everyone around the conference room:

"He—*what*?"[37]

And then Hayden thought about it a bit more and said in a resigned tone, "They let him go? Sure, why not. They do a lot of things."[38] And by "they," he meant "the Pakistanis."

◆

It's unclear why Rauf escaped from prison when he did. He only had to wait five months before being theoretically released from jail. Perhaps he was concerned he'd be incarcerated indefinitely. Perhaps he thought the Americans would cut a deal and he would end up in a federal Supermax cell for the rest of his life. Perhaps the choice was not made by him. Still, the larger question remained: why was Rashid Rauf allowed to escape?

An official Pakistani inquiry subsequently determined Rauf's escape occurred in the area of Islamabad that encompassed the district court buildings and the McDonald's. It also noted Rauf's flight occurred right after the court hearing, not later in the afternoon as the original reporting claimed. Together, these facts undermined the story of his unbinding at the mosque. More damning, one of the constable's mobile phones pinged off of a cell tower a distance away from the route. It turns out he was chatting with the other constable on his phone that afternoon, an odd occurrence given they were supposedly together guarding their prisoner.[39]

A British diplomatic cable from Islamabad on December 11, 2008, indicated: "A high level probe ordered by the Pakistani authorities into the escape of Rashid Rauf from police custody on 15/12/2007 has concluded that he fled with the collusion of the police and some Jaish-e-Mohmmad [JeM] linked militants while he was being transported to Adiala jail, Rawalpindi, after a court appearance."[40]

Many fingers pointed toward an official hand in his escape. After all, who knows what Rauf might've told London and Washington about ongoing Pakistani complicity with various terrorist organizations. Despite the decades-old knowledge that the ISI founded, funded, trained, and deployed groups to cause mayhem in Kashmir and elsewhere, it remained a touchy subject in Islamabad. If Pakistani intelligence officials had trained Rauf, the man responsible for scores of deaths in Great Britain, the Americans and British would have gone ballistic and undoubtedly blamed them.

Therefore, a reasonably informed guess is that the Pakistani intelligence service somehow facilitated Rauf's escape and let a number of low-level police officers take the fall. As one former senior CIA official said, Pakistan's ISI was "a pain in the ass,"[41] and this latest bit of intrigue with Rauf was yet another irritant. They would say one thing and do something else. Pakistan would publicly rail against lethal efforts the United States made against militants and terrorists in the tribal areas, yet those same drones continued to operate for years from an air base near Quetta, even after the raid that killed Osama bin Laden in 2011.[42]

Perhaps the ISI hoped one problem could be solved by another. Rauf would run to safety in the tribal lands, the theory went, and would eventually die in an American airstrike. Everyone would win: the CIA would kill a dangerous al Qaeda operative, Britain would cease to be threatened by his activities, and Pakistan's dirty secrets would die with him. The local press reported the Pakistani foreign ministry claimed the British were not excessively concerned that Rauf was on the loose—a doubtful claim under the circumstances.[43]

Of course, Pakistan vehemently denied the theory Rauf was purposely allowed to escape. The CIA "leaned hard on Pakistan" to find him, and "we had all kinds of assurances" he would be caught, recalled Larry Pfeiffer.[44] Still, several weeks after Rauf disappeared, President Musharraf personally cleared the police, the army, and intelligence agencies of any wrongdoing. Speaking at the annual Davos conference in Switzerland early the next year, he said Pakistanis who blamed those institutions weren't patriotic because they unleashed accusations "only to promote their political objectives. But they must know how much damage they caused to the country."[45]

The Pakistani president was undoubtedly balancing competing political actors working at cross-purposes. As Bush's national security advisor Stephen Hadley later recalled, "We all got frustrated with the limitation of what Musharraf could do in terms of cooperating on the War on Terror, the unreliability of the Pakistani military, and the fact that they would leak the intelligence before we could do an operation. Somebody would leak intelligence before an operation so the bad guys would be gone before we got there."[46]

In other words, Hadley diplomatically noted, "There were frustrations."

◆

Following his escape from prison, the twenty-six-year-old Rashid Rauf evaded security, appearing only in rumor across Pakistan, like a ghost wandering the forest. Some claimed they saw him at a raucous JeM rally in Bahawalpur. Others saw him flitting around the tribal areas. A Muslim convert of Latin-American heritage from New York, Bryant Neal Vinas, claimed in the press he met with Rauf and other al Qaeda luminaries, such as military commander Abu Yayha al-Libi, at various training camps in Pakistan and Afghanistan in 2008.[47] In a subsequent court proceeding, though, Vinas retracted this comment, claiming he had never met Rauf.

Meanwhile, Pakistan continued to drag its feet on the investigation. Despite official requests dating back to 2007 to assist with the Overt trials, Pakistan only provided Rauf's belongings to British authorities in May 2008, after the first trial had already begun.[48]

Rashid Rauf remained up to his old bag of tricks, turning jihadi wannabes spoiling for a fight in Afghanistan back to their home counties to cause havoc. In August 2008, three high school buddies from Queens, New York—Adis Medunjanin, Zarein Ahmedzay, and Najibullah Zazi—arrived in Peshawar, Pakistan, in order to fight with the Taliban. These men were yet another group radicalized by Anwar al-Awlaqi's sermons. Once they showed up, Ahmedzay and Medunjanin tried to enter Afghanistan, but the Pakistani border guards stopped them, believing they were actually CIA case officers trying to enter through their checkpoint. Ahmedzay eventually convinced the authorities that they weren't intelligence officers since they were practicing Muslims—as if the CIA doesn't employ scores of Muslim officers—but they were nevertheless forbidden to cross the border. Disheartened, they returned to Peshawar, where they eventually connected with a facilitator, who rerouted them to a guesthouse in Miram Shah in North Waziristan. There, they eventually connected with al Qaeda's external operations commander Saleh al-Somali and an operative with a British accent named "Ibrahim"—Rauf's new identity.[49] From there, they traveled to South Waziristan for weapons training at an al Qaeda camp; a month later Zazi went to a similar camp for a week to learn how to build TATP detonators and concentrated hydrogen peroxide explosives. He was provided this training with the understanding the trio would strike targets in America.[50]

After returning to the United States, the three planned suicide attacks, most notably in the New York City subway system. Zazi visited beauty supply stores in Colorado and bought quantities of hydrogen peroxide and acetone to build bombs in a plot that would eventually be code-named High-Rise.[51] Eventually, the FBI caught up with Zazi and arrested him in September 2009. A few months later, his friend Medunjanin crashed his car into another vehicle on the Whitestone Freeway in New York, screaming at the 911 emergency operator the slogan, "We love death more than you love your life."[52] Ahmedzay was arrested as well.

Following their arrests, Zazi and Ahmedzay cut a deal with prosecutors and became witnesses for the government, testifying against their close friend Medunjanin.[53] By doing so, Zazi and Ahmedzay received much lighter sentences than they could have; they served only a handful of years. However, Medunjanin was unrepentant and was handed a life sentence. He is now in the ADX Florence prison in Colorado, the facility where America incarcerates terrible people and then throws away the key. Fellow inmates include terrorists Ramzi Yousef, shoe bomber Richard Reid, the 9/11 "twentieth hijacker" Zacarias Moussaoui, Unabomber Ted Kaczynski, and Russian asset Robert Hanssen.

Rauf also reportedly had a hand in a thwarted al Qaeda bombing against a mall in Manchester, UK. In foiling the plot, authorities arrested a twenty-two-year-old Pakistani national named Abid Naseer in northwest England in April 2009. Naseer was subsequently extradited to the United States, where Zazi and Ahmedzay both testified against him in court. He was convicted of multiple terrorism offenses and received a forty-year prison sentence in a medium-security federal lockup in Texas.[54]

Additionally, Rauf was somehow involved in an attempted suicide attack against EU leaders, including British prime minister Gordon Brown, in Brussels in December 2008.[55] And finally, Rauf, through Zazi and Saleh al-Somali, connected to three Norwegian residents building hydrogen peroxide bombs arrested in July 2010. The cell's leader, Mikael Davud, reportedly received training in hydrogen peroxide bombmaking while spending time in Waziristan.[56] It was never entirely clear what their targets were, and this cell received far lighter sentences than those convicted in the United States.

◆

Despite the malicious fellows circulating around Pakistan at this time, the Overt investigation was, in many ways, the highwater point in the comity between the American and the Pakistani intelligence services. The greatest level of cooperation occurred in the first few years following 9/11, when the Pakistanis and the United States hunted down many of the worst of the worst. But by 2006 onward, the shine was clearly off the relationship. The ISI "were unreliable partners with hidden agendas," recalled Tim Buch, a senior CIA analyst who led the Near East/South Asia Office.[57]

It was obvious the Pakistanis were, for their own reasons, withholding assistance to the Americans. CIA director Hayden recalled in his memoirs that when the United States went to Pakistan in 2007 with a plan to take out this or that al Qaeda operative, "the response was no, maddening delay, or our target suddenly and unexpectedly relocated."[58] Pakistan supported the "Kashmiri" jihadis whose remit spread far beyond Kashmir. There was certainly a reason why the Taliban's "Quetta Shura" met openly in Quetta.

Hayden recalled, "We got nothing [from the ISI]. So the next year we said, Mr. President, we aren't doing anything about this. We have to do it ourselves."[59] Thus, the CIA made the argument to aggressively pursue unilateral operations within Pakistan proper and cut out the ISI completely. Bit by bit, Bush saw the writing on the wall, that terrorists were operating in the open and that Pakistan was allowing the problem to fester. Finally, the president said, "Okay, I'll do it without the ISI."[60]

Soon, American intelligence officials knew a fair bit more about what was occurring in the tribal lands of Pakistan than the ISI did. One anonymous ISI major general sighed, "By 2007, CIA almost did not need the ISI's help. By that time, the CIA officers would rarely ask for any help; rather, they would inform us."[61] Absent the ISI's assistance, UAV strikes within Pakistan ramped up around this time. These unilateral operations caused the understandably paranoid Pakistani intelligence service to try to determine what the CIA knew about what was going on inside the country. By the middle of the decade, the CIA had many skilled debriefers and terrorist hunters operating both inside and out-side of Pakistan. Thus, the ISI's counterintelligence efforts against the Americans rose to become one of the organization's top priorities. Of course, this was several years before the May 2011 bin Laden raid, in which the United States inserted forces deep into Pakistan proper to kill the al Qaeda leader without the local intelligence service realizing what had happened until it was too late.

The year 2007 also saw the siege and assault of Islamabad's "Red Mosque," a hotbed of pro-Taliban thought and venue for speakers, including Masood Azhar, who openly called for President Musharraf's murder.[62] Members of the Red Mosque had clashed with government forces for many months, challenging their authority in the heart of the capital. Following a gun battle on July 3 between that left several people dead, the military laid siege to the compound. After a week-long stalemate, the Pakistani army's elite Special Service Group, whose commander was killed by small arms fire during the siege, eventually stormed the compound on July 10, touching off a brutal, take-no-prisoners battle. Over a hundred people died, including eight troops. The siege and assault infuriated many militants in the tribal areas, igniting a further round of deadly conflict in Waziristan in the north.

Pakistan's poisonous tree—its ongoing support for its so-called Kashmiri jihadists—continued to bear toxic fruit. America had long concluded that the ISI's fingerprints were all over the LeT November 2008 megaoperation in Mumbai, which struck a major train termi-nal, hotels, hospitals, and a Jewish community center. The terrorists killed 166 people over the course of four horrifying days.[63] "From the agency perspective," remembered the CIA's Steve Kappes, "the work continued. L[E]T was however one of the major issues between the US and Pakistan."[64] The Mumbai operation was indeed a meticulously planned mass murder spree in one of the biggest cities in the world, and the ISI had a hand in it. "Mumbai," recalled Juan Zarate, "is etched in my memory."[65]

The Americans and the Indians were furious. Did the ISI authorize this atrocity? And even if this massive attack wasn't explicitly authorized from the top, that must have meant command-and-control had broken down in Pakistan, or had barely existed in the first place. And if that were true, how could anyone in Washington really trust anyone in Islamabad?

The ISI chief, Lt. Gen. Ahmed Shuja Pasha, took over the intelligence agency a month before the attack in Mumbai. In his first trip as director-general to Washington shortly before Christmas 2008, he privately told Pakistan's ambassador in the United States that "these were our guys, but not our operation."[66] During the same trip, Pasha visited his counterparts at the CIA. Barack Obama had been elected president and would take office a month later, remaking the whole U.S. government; it was unclear who would lead the CIA. Still, Pasha came calling and gave his account of what happened in Mumbai. It was a rambling brief, since it was obvious to the Americans that an ISI-sponsored terrorist group had committed this massacre while its leadership lived comfortably and openly in Pakistan.

Following the ISI presentation, the Americans responded harshly. "Frankly," replied Director Hayden, who was leaving the post within a few months and had little time for spin, "that's all bullshit."[67] Later, he remarked about Pasha, "He was lying. He was lying about Mumbai. He was lying about a lot of things."[68]

◆

In 2008, during the waning months of the Bush administration, there were over thirty American airstrikes in Pakistani territory against al Qaeda and Taliban operatives, a threefold increase over the previous four years.[69] These operations usually, but not always, hit their target. The strikes were based not only upon America's fearsome technical capabilities but also upon information gleaned from the years-long effort to develop unilateral sources in the tribal areas. But each time something went "boom" and the Pakistanis didn't know why, it underscored the lack of control and insight the ISI had within their own borders. With Obama in the White House, the strikes would increase significantly, also without much local input.

The wheels were coming off the relationship.

◆

Here's the prime example of how sour the U.S.-Pakistani relationship had become within a few years of Overt.

Some weeks after Rashid Rauf vanished from custody and several months before the Mumbai massacre, Director of National Intelligence Michael McConnell and CIA director Michael Hayden, the two top men in American intelligence, flew secretly to Pakistan. They were on a mission to read Musharraf the riot act because the Americans felt Pakistan was providing al Qaeda and the Taliban space to regenerate their networks. Washington wanted Islamabad to be more aggressive about rooting out al Qaeda operatives in their country.[70] They were also coming on the heels of the tragic December 2007 murder of the charismatic once-and-likely-future PM, Benazir Bhutto. No one really knew who carried out the attack, since Pakistan quickly blamed the Tehrik-e-Taliban Pakistan organization for the assassination, then hosed down the crime scene, destroying all the evidence.

They met with President Musharraf, General Kayani (who had been since promoted to Chief of Army Staff), and the new ISI chief, Nadeem Taj. Taj was related to Musharraf's wife, cementing a close personal connection between the chief executive and his spy chief. The meeting was frosty, as the trust had broken down between the two countries. The two American intelligence chiefs were only supposed to be in South Asia for a single day, and they delivered their terse message. After the meeting, they went back to the ambassador's residence to wait for their plane to be refueled for the long flight home. As they killed time within the residence, their head of security arrived with some bad news.

Pakistan refused to refuel their plane.

The Air Force pilot had forgotten the government-issued credit card that the U.S. government would normally have used to pay for the fuel.[71] The pilot provided his personal credit card, but the Pakistanis said that wasn't good enough. Pakistan also declined to accept an IOU from the U.S. government. The two intelligence chiefs, senior staff, and security crews were now stuck in the country.

The pilots and the other crewmembers put their heads together and, after a few hours, devised a solution. The plane had just enough reserve fuel to fly to Afghanistan, where the United States could refuel the aircraft on a military base. However, the two senior American officials could not arrive unannounced in Afghanistan and forgo a formal meeting in the capital, as that would be a breach of diplomatic protocol. But they had no formal reason to be in the country.

So, in the dead of the night, the American military plane flew not to Kabul but to a remote part of the U.S.-controlled Bagram Air Base. Hayden and McConnell thus surreptitiously crossed an international border on a reserve tank into a warzone in order to pick up enough fuel to fly home—all because Pakistan decided to be stiff-necked.[72] It was early January and freezing outside as the Americans quietly refueled the plane. Tanks finally topped off, the plane made its long, clandestine journey back to America.[73]

Within the year, Musharraf was forced into exile. America's longtime authoritarian frenemy in Pakistan was gone. He resigned from office on August 18, 2008, twenty years to the day that President Zia ul-Haq, U.S. ambassador Arnold Raphel, and twenty-eight other people entered a plane that mysteriously exploded in the skies over Bahawalpur.

◆

Looking back on his tenure, Michael Hayden remarked, "I spent some three years as CIA Director, and I spent most of it on one problem: al Qaeda." There were other issues, "like what were the Chinese up to, that was important."[74] But during this time, there remained an overriding fixation for the American national security firmament: crushing al Qaeda everywhere.

But with this obsession came a great cost. With the benefit of hindsight, the NCTC's Andy Liepman commented, "We didn't fully appreciate or consider what the political consequences of Americans running drones for Pakistan and killing Pakistani citizens. We operated in this bubble—the attitude that every day was September twelfth. This motivated a ton of people to work unbelievably hard, but it also blinded us to everything else in the world."

"Would we have done anything differently? The vast majority of people in [the CIA] at the time would say 'no, I would've done everything the same.' I understand. They were operating under extremely clear guidelines which were, 'don't let it—another terrorist attack—happen.'"

But, he added, "For a lot of stuff, history will not judge us well."[75]

26

The Twisting Road

Half a year had passed since the end of the first trial. The Great Recession gripped America, Great Britain, and elsewhere, due to widespread failures of financial deregulation, toxic mortgages, corporate mismanagement, and institutional chicanery. In America, the keys to the White House passed from George Bush to Barack Obama, who was mostly preoccupied with rescuing the cratering economy. Most people on both sides of the Atlantic had long forgotten about the Overt case.

Except, of course, those in the British court system. Following the first trial, Ali's legal counsel applied for a stay of proceedings, arguing that a fair retrial was impossible for his client. He argued the press interest in the case had forever tainted the jury pool. A judge dismissed these concerns, noting, "There have been other terrorist trials in the meantime occupying crime correspondents and their readers. I am sure that the facts will have receded and faded, as will any possible prejudice."[1] Indeed, one of the jurors in her voir dire said she hadn't ever heard of the case, or of the plot, in the first place.[2]

The accused were still detained in Belmarsh prison, attached to the Woolwich Crown Court in the exurbs of London. The summer passed to freezing winter, and then again into spring. The heating systems of both Belmarsh and Woolwich had problems, forcing the prisoners to shower in icy water. The men shivered as they waited below the court building to be escorted into the courtroom. Due to a quirk in the building's architecture, Woolwich required forced air to be recirculated through the entire facility, lest any section became too cold.

The second trial of Ali and the others (minus Gulzar, who was under control orders) began on February 17, 2009, along with that of another defendant, Donald Stewart-Whyte. Stewart-Whyte was a recent convert to Islam picked up on the night of the roundup with a friend of Sarwar's, Waseem Kayani, who never faced charges. Stewart-Whyte had nothing to do with the safehouse at 386A Forest Road, but the police nonetheless found him suspicious and arrested him. Almost three years later, he was in the dock with the others for conspiracy to murder people on aircraft using liquid explosives (Count 1) and a more generalized conspiracy to murder (Count 1A).[3] This distinction was made since the "officers" (Ali, Sarwar, and Hussain) knew what the mechanism was to kill scores of people, but the "foot soldiers" (everyone else) probably did not.

While the charges remained the same, the emphasis had shifted to illustrate how the operation's roots led back in Pakistan. In the words of the prosecutor Peter Wright, "This was not something that had been devised merely by Ali and Sarwar, this was part of a much wider scheme of things. Acts of terrorism on an international scale, directed from abroad using home-grown terrorists, young, radicalized Muslims prepared to lose their lives in a global act of jihad."[4]

Yet only a day after the courtroom arguments began, Judge Richard Henriques dismissed the jury for vague "legal reasons" and postponed the trial to a later date.[5] As it turned out, one of the jurors was linked to a Belmarsh prison guard, which forced the judge to restart the retrial with a fresh group of twelve citizens.[6] Showing how much the world had moved on, this incident hardly made the papers or the evening news.

The retrial restarted in early March. A new jury was selected and the defendants returned to the dock, sitting in much the same row. Prosecutor Wright repeated his well-rehearsed opening speech as he had twice before, explaining the men had tried to inflict heavy casualties on innocent people by bombing trans-Atlantic aircraft. Almost word-for-word from his 2008 presentation, he explained, "They are men with the cold-eyed certainty of the fanatic, prepared to board a passenger aircraft with the materials required in order to construct and detonate a device that would bring about not only the loss of their own life but also all of those who happened, quite by chance, to be taking the same journey."

With new emphasis on foreign direction, he repeated his words from the previous month: "This was acts of terrorism on an international scale, directed from abroad, using home-grown terrorists, the young, the radicalized Muslims prepared to lose their lives in an act of jihad."

Ali was ill on the first day of the trial; he had a splitting headache and one of his eyes was dilated. His defense counsel noted his ability to read and write was "disintegrating." At some point, Ali was also involved in a fight with several prison guards, obliging three to receive medical care afterward.[7] It is not known what kind of injuries Ali suffered in return.

One major improvement for the prosecution from the last trial was the addition of the emails between the men in Britain and Rauf in Pakistan. While the intelligence and police services knew the contents of the emails, they had been unable to provide them in open court for the first go-around.[8] America reportedly refused to provide the data for the 2008 court case, preferring to keep Rauf's critical communications top secret. However, the U.S. government changed its tune for the second trial, and a subsequent court order in California obliged Yahoo! to turn over the emails to British prosecutors.[9] Yahoo! had access to any email available in any of its accounts as long as it hadn't been deleted. The firm also could access the IP address of the computer that was used for its emails.[10] Thus, these theoretical silver bullets allowed for "people convicting themselves out of their own mouths," as one former CPS chief noted.[11]

For something changed by early 2009, or at least those at the NSA thought something had changed.

Rashid Rauf was dead.

◆

The initial reports from the field were spotty: on a Saturday morning, November 22, 2008, a missile fired from an unmanned aircraft destroyed a mud-and-brick structure in North Waziristan. It was the compound of a Taliban commander, Maulvi Khaliq Noor.[12] Inside the targeted structure were Noor, his children, an al Qaeda bomb-maker named Abu Zubair al-Masri, and Rashid Rauf. Soon after the strike, anonymous Pakistani and American officials claimed Rauf, the mastermind of so much mayhem, was finally dead. However, no body was ever recovered and no forensic team could conclusively confirm this claim.

Still, the successful strike made the United States willing to let British prosecutors use the emails in court against the Overt plotters.

Except it turned out Rauf hadn't died.

After the airstrike and rumors of his killing, his longtime lawyer went to the press to say it was a "fake story." "We don't believe that this story is true . . . We still believe that my client, Rashid, is alive."[13] He advanced the idea that Rauf was instead in a deep, dark hole somewhere, being interrogated by the ISI, MI6, CIA, or Mossad.

By the next year, most in intelligence circles thought Rauf had escaped death that day in November. Almost a year later, even the local Pakistani papers claimed he was still alive.[14] In a communiqué from the Foreign and Commonwealth Office from September 14, 2009, entitled "Restricted: Top Ten Most Wanted Jihadis," Rauf remained "No. 5" on the most wanted list. It also helpfully noted, "Rashid was reportedly killed on November 22, 2008, after a missile fired from a CIA predator drone destroyed a mud-built bungalow in Alikhel village of North Waziristan. But it later transpired that he is alive and operating from the Waziristan region."[15]

He was still out there, somewhere. And the NSA had now given up his email communications for a public trial.

◆

The grueling retrial lasted for almost seven months, 114 days in all. Ali, Sarwar, Hussain, and the rest maintained that there had been no conspiracy to mass murder, but rather a political effort to protest British foreign policy. The videos were part of that protest. There was simply no plot to blow up airplanes over the Atlantic or anywhere else.

From the witness box, Sarwar told the jury about how he would calculate the concentration of hydrogen peroxide. He explained that his teacher in Pakistan, the "Kashmiri freedom fighter Jamil Shah," taught him how to boil it down without badly hurting himself. "You tend to place it in a large metal pot over a camping stove, keeping it at a low temperature," he said. "You need to monitor it constantly because if it gets too hot, it could catch fire . . . That's how they do it in Pakistan, in the outdoors."[16]

The jury took that comment and thousands of others into consideration.

On September 7, 2009, Abdulla Ahmed Ali, Assad Sarwar, and Tanvir Hussain were convicted on all charges, including conspiracy to murder using explosives on a plane (Count 1).

But this jury again rendered a decision that frustrated the Crown. Umar Islam was convicted of conspiracy to murder (Count 1A), but the jury deadlocked on whether to convict for the charge of conspiracy to murder on an aircraft (Count 1). The jury also acquitted Ibrahim Savant, Arafat Khan, and Waheed Zaman of the Count 1 charge—something had differentiated their behavior from that of Umar Islam—yet they remained hung on the general "conspiracy to murder" charge. Donald Stewart-Whyte was acquitted on all charges. He had admitted to possessing a firearm, a silencer, and ammunition, a serious charge, but not one linked to terrorism. He was sentenced to three years and six months in prison but was freed immediately on account of time served.

At sentencing, Justice Henriques addressed the convicted men before him: "Ali, Sarwar, and Hussain, you have been convicted of conspiracy to murder by planning to destroy seven trans-Atlantic aircraft in mid-flight. Umar Islam, you have been convicted of conspiracy to murder, being unaware of the intended targets. The plot to murder the passengers and crew of those seven airliners was the most grave and wicked conspiracy ever proven within this jurisdiction. The intention was to perpetrate a terrorist outrage which would stand alongside the events of September 11, 2001, in world history."

And, with that, he handed each of them their sentences:

Abdulla Ahmed Ali: life, with a minimum of forty years.

Assad Sarwar: life, with a minimum of thirty-six years.

Tanvir Hussain: life, with a minimum of thirty-two years.

Umar Islam: life, with a minimum term of twenty-two years.

The CPS immediately indicated it wanted a third trial of Savant, Khan, and Zaman on the conspiracy to murder charge. The remaining defendants claimed this was an abuse of the process, as they had already gone through two trials. These arguments were rejected.

Meanwhile, the other trial of Adam Khatib, Nabeel Hussain, and Mohammed Uddin ended a few months later, on December 10. Adam Khatib, who had traveled to Pakistan, connected with Rashid Rauf, and had been in the 386A Forest Road safehouse, was found guilty in his role in the Overt case, earning him a life sentence with the possibility of parole after eighteen years.

The twenty-two-year-old Nabeel Hussain was convicted for providing financial and logistical help to Ali. He received an eight-year sentence, minus the twenty months he had already spent in custody.[17] Hussain served only four years and was freed early from prison in 2012 under the condition that he surrender his passport. However, in September 2013, he was caught at Stansted Airport with an Istanbul-bound plane ticket and fake travel documents, likely en route to the conflict in Syria.[18]

Finally, Mohammed Uddin received a fifteen-month jail sentence for possessing a CD likely to be useful to terrorism and a five-year, nine-month jail sentence for possessing a firearm.[19]

As for the 386A Forest Road property, Ali's extended family decided to offload the former safehouse in the year after the international dragnet. The unit was sold in November 2007 for £205,000, generating a tidy £65,000 profit.[20]

Ali's now ex-wife Cossor was charged in August 2006 with failing to pass along information about a terrorist act. Following a three-week trial at the Inner London Crown Court in early 2010, a jury deliberated for a day, acquitting her of the charge. She exclaimed, "thank you, thank you, thank you." Following the conclusion of the trial, her father Mohammed Anwar told gathered reporters, "The truth has won and justice prevails. We are grateful to the jury for returning a unanimous verdict . . . We have suffered as a family over the last three and half years for the actions of some individuals with whom we have nothing in common."[21] Cossor went on to live quietly in Walthamstow with her son.

The third trial began on April 26, 2010. Once again, the Crown tried to convict Ibrahim Savant, Arafat Khan, and Waheed Zaman of conspiracy to murder. In an art-imitating-life situation, the wheels of justice turned so slowly that during this trial a satirical film about a group of bumbling suicide bombers entitled *Four Lions* was released across Britain. After forty-seven days, they were all convicted of the charge. Each was handed a sentence of life imprisonment with a minimum term of twenty years.

Thus, the largest, most expensive counterterrorism operation in British history, one rivaling 9/11 in scope and destruction, was finally over. By the end of the three trials, the authorities had compiled 26,000 exhibits, collected 9,710 statements, seized 800 electronic devices such as laptops, desktops, hard drives, and memory sticks, examined 14,000 GB of data, which included 15,000 CDs and DVDs and 500 floppy disks, and interviewed the suspects 142 times.[22]

◆

As of this writing, most of the main conspirators remain "Category A" guests of Her Majesty's Prison Service.[23] Abdulla Ahmed Ali is serving his sentence at the high-security HMP Frankland in County Durham, alongside Umar Islam.[24] Dhiren Barot is there. So is Omar Khyam, who tried to blow up a shopping center in Kent.[25] In prison, Ali has remained steadfast to his beliefs. In 2012 a *Sunday Times* investigation found Ali wrote a letter saying, "If the *mushriks* [nonbelievers] can leave their families and sacrifice their lives and limbs to occupy, enslave and oppress the ummah, then we too can sacrifice 100 times that to defend it."[26] Ali was also reportedly allowed to pray with extremist Islamist preacher Anjem Choudary while at Belmarsh; when Choudary was released following a prison stint, he said Ali and failed 7/21 suicide bomber Hussain Osman were "so strong in terms of their faith."[27]

Assad Sarwar and Tanvir Hussain are serving their sentences in the high-security HMP Full Sutton in Yorkshire.[28] Hussain was segregated from the other prisoners from April to October 2010 for reportedly bullying others over their faith; he eventually won a legal challenge over this separation and returned to the fold.[29] In 2013 the two played a "supportive" role in a plan to hold a prison guard hostage. According to the Ministry of Justice, three other inmates took the guard for several hours and threatened to kill him unless Islamist cleric Abu Qatada, who had been extradited to Jordan, and Roshonara Choudhry, who tried to assassinate Labour MP Stephen Timms in 2010, were both freed. Riot police eventually freed the guard.[30]

Ibrahim Savant appears to be in Her Majesty's Prison (HMP) Wakefield, in Yorkshire, alongside Waheed Zaman.[31] In a letter he sent during his first year, Savant told supporters being incarcerated gave him time to "cook his own food, attend the gym, gain some education and pray." Additionally, "within these prisons I can utilise my time to the best of my ability and make good of a bad situation."[32] He also said he could see his family from time to time.

Rashid Rauf's mentor and brother-in-law Masood Azhar remains at large. JeM remains a potent, wealthy, lethal jihadist force operating with Pakistan's acquiescence. The ISI likely views the group as an asset; during the Red Mosque siege in 2007, Islamabad reportedly flew in Masood's brother, Abdul Rauf Asghar, who the Indians thought masterminded the Indian Airlines hijacking in 1999, from Bahawalpur for negotiations. Pakistan reportedly requested his assistance again after Tehrik-e-Taliban Pakistan and Lashkar-e-Jhangvi struck the military's General Headquarters in 2009 and started taking hostages.[33] JeM continues to kill Indian soldiers, actions which supposedly benefit Pakistan's long-term strategic position in Kashmir. In February 2019 a JeM suicide bomber struck an Indian military convoy, killing forty-six troops in the worst attack there in decades.[34]

A year later, Pakistan declared Azhar and his family "missing," yet he still found time to record an audio message in March 2020 criticizing the United States and praising the Taliban.[35] China continues to block intermittent efforts to designate him a global terrorist at the United Nations on behalf of Pakistan, demonstrating Azhar's continued importance to Islamabad. Despite Azhar's decades of butchery, the ISI probably believes he and his jihadist organization can assist Pakistan in Afghanistan, Kashmir, and elsewhere.

As for Rashid Rauf, the instigator of so much madness, it's not clear how or where his curtain fell. Even now, the West Midlands Police have an open warrant out for his questioning in connection with his uncle's murder. That act of violence set the baker's boy out on his journey into Pakistan and into the history books. Until there is an official confirmation of his death, the warrant remains open.

In all likelihood, he was probably killed in one of the hundreds of CIA-led unmanned strikes or Pakistani airstrikes carried out in the tribal areas over the years. According to research from the New America think tank, Barack Obama significantly ramped up the UAV efforts against al Qaeda operatives in Pakistan—in the last full year Bush was in office, there were thirty-six strikes, but in Obama's first year, there were fifty-two. The next year the United States carried out 122 strikes; the year after that (2010), there were 70.[36] These numbers might be flawed, but they also indicate a strong preference for using lethal means to grind America's terrorist adversaries into dust.

It's also possible the Pakistani air force, rather than the CIA, killed Rauf. According to the Air Chief Marshal Rao Qamar Suleman at a conference in Dubai in November 2011, Pakistan's air force had over the previous two years pounded insurgents with over fifty-five hundred sorties by F-16s and C-130 gunships.[37] This kind of firepower is immensely destructive to anything underneath it—including Rauf, his al Qaeda colleagues, and any innocent civilians. The overall devastation caused by this airpower dwarfed whatever covert American efforts were occurring.

But the actual end of Rashid Rauf remains a question mark. Al Qaeda never acknowledged his death, and neither did the U.S. government. No one can conclusively say what happened, or when. As of this book's publication, his whereabouts remained unknown.

◆

Life ambles on. The sun continues to rise in the east and set in the west. Tens of millions still take to the skies in passenger aircraft, all under regulations stemming from the Overt operation.

But we all still feel the consequences of this stymied conspiracy. Following the crisis, as millions of people placed items that they would have normally carried into the cabin into the hold, passenger luggage began consuming more space in the cargo area. More bags meant significantly more wear-and-tear on airplane counter staff and baggage handlers, who had to physically move more luggage. With significantly more luggage, they began to get injured more often. The added weight also strained the conveyor belts taking the bags through security and then onto the planes themselves. These belts and the machines began to break down more frequently, costing the TSA, the airports, and the airlines.

Further, all these millions of new passenger bags in the hold displaced other cargo. This was problematic because the airlines generated a profitable stream of income by hauling cargo and mail on their planes. For the airline companies, nonpassenger freight aboard passenger aircraft generated about 9 percent of total revenue, more than twice that of first-class tickets.[38] That percentage will only increase as people continue to shop online in the $5 trillion global e-commerce market, as they will require more space for boxes in cargo holds.[39]

According to the TSA's Kip Hawley, because of this cargo situation and spiking oil prices in the late 2000s, the airline companies took decisive action: they started charging heretofore unknown luggage fees to generate revenue.[40] American Airlines was the first to impose baggage fees in May 2008—as Ali, Sarwar, and colleagues were sitting shackled in a high-security courtroom for their first trial—and many other carriers quickly followed suit. While fuel prices fell dramatically from their 2008 high and airlines returned to profitability after a series of business restructurings, baggage fees, which generated over five and a half billion dollars in 2019 for the top eleven U.S. carriers, remained.[41] Once a business "revenue enhancer" is in place, and its customers become used to it, it never really goes away.

So the next time you fly and wonder why you're carrying a tiny hand creamer or paying to stow your luggage, think about the contributions of Rashid Rauf, Abdulla Ahmed Ali, and the other Overt conspirators. While denied a big explosion, their efforts nonetheless found a small success in sticking it to you, personally.

27

A Fine Balance

In writing this book, I learned many things along the way. For example, after reading an early draft, my wife informed me most people already knew of William Morris's textiles and therefore there was no need to describe them. (I just quietly nodded.) The Overt conspiracy occurred some years in the past, but the lessons we can learn from them are ones that impact our world today: the pitfalls of racial profiling, the critical role of the police, the need for resilient societies and international cooperation, and finally, acknowledging the possibility of another mega–terror attack occurring again.

The sins of the few must not tar an entire community. Throughout this book, I've focused on a very small number of people who turned to mass murder to achieve personal or political goals. Most, but not all, of the plotters were British Muslim men of Kashmiri heritage. But there are hundreds of thousands of other people who fit that generalized profile who never turn to violence. This category includes the vast majority of the plotters' families, siblings, and friends, who were raised in the same communities and households and lead peaceful, upright lives.

Islamophobia and other religious and ethnic hatreds undermine both the security and the stability of free and open societies. About 850 Britons went to Syria in the last decade to fight for jihadist groups, including several who went on to shoot some of the most horrific videos from the conflict, but this was from a population of 2.7 million Muslims living in Great Britain.[1] That's about .03 percent of the community. Similarly, from a community of approximately 3.5 million Muslims living in the United States, only 250–300 people traveled to Syria to fight for the Islamic State or for the local al Qaeda affiliate as of 2018, or .008 percent.[2] The individuals are a fraction of a fraction of a larger group of otherwise peaceful citizens.

Why did these men commit to carrying out such a dastardly act? There's oftentimes an assumption that terrorists think long and hard about their actions before journeying down the dark path to martyrdom and oblivion. With the benefit of hindsight, they may blame an incident, tragedy, or grudge for pushing them in that direction. Yet billions of humans observe or experience personal, professional, or societal setbacks and refuse to commit mass murder.

It's impossible to truly peer into any person's heart, but allow me to offer a few possible answers. In Overt, some participants merely bumbled into the plot because someone charismatic, like Rashid Rauf or Ali, asked them to do so. They were willing to commit to mass murder without a great deal of thought. Umar Islam didn't bother to write out his martyrdom speech until the night before, although this act would have defined him forever. The other suicide bombers hadn't rehearsed their speeches before shooting them.

Thoughtlessness and a willingness to be swept along with the tide may be a stronger explanation for murderous behavior than one might think. Tell some people they're participating in a secret, global struggle against a great evil, and many will eagerly join the battle. Were they so different from the people they decried? These individuals might have also been caught up in a cause that gave meaning to their otherwise dreary, uninteresting lives. For a time, they were the subject of world leaders' conversations and, when caught, appeared on front pages of newspapers around the world. While the majority of people found this world vision abhorrent, some small percentage still answered the call. And while this is a gross oversimplification of the world around us, young men and women the world over are often convinced to take reckless, stupid, violent actions.[3]

A heavy hand against an ethnic or religious community suspected of political violence where the most granular intelligence into a plot often lies is often wildly counterproductive. When a democracy overreacts, it can simultaneously undermine its own freedoms and security. The ill-conceived Operation Demetrius in August 1971 saw the British Army detain hundreds of Catholics without trial in Northern Ireland in an effort to quell communal violence and fight the IRA. But, instead of tamping down the violence, the rough roundup of these British citizens into internment camps radicalized a large swath of the populace, leading to some of the worst Protestant-Catholic fighting in a century.[4] Indeed, detaining innocent individuals behind barbed wire spurred many political fence-sitters into the IRA's open arms, increasing republican support in areas where there previously had been little to none.[5] Dozens died in the subsequent clashes, hundreds of homes were burnt, and the Troubles soared to new heights. British paratroopers shot dead fourteen protesters at a march the following January 30 in what became known as Bloody Sunday; the march was protesting Britain's internments without trial policy. It took a generation of bloodshed before the 1998 Good Friday Agreement brought much of the violence to a halt.

Crushing the Overt conspiracy might've failed had it not been for local police. As the historian John Keegan artfully noted in his book *Intelligence in War*, "Foreknowledge is no protection against disaster. Even real-time intelligence is never real enough. Only force finally counts."[6] In stories like this, the national-level government agencies usually get the glory—the CIA, MI6, MI5, etc.—but there would've been little way to stop this plot had it not been for the Met and TVP performing much of the work. They were the ones who put hundreds of boots on the ground, eyes on the street, and fingers to computers to document every move the conspirators took. It also means higher-level organizations have to trust their police counterparts with sensitive information collected clandestinely and integrate them bureaucratically so everyone sings from the same sheet of music. The responsibility for taking down a great criminal conspiracy needs to not only occur horizontally across agencies but also vertically through the coercive instruments of the state.[7]

Societies must think critically about how to handle terrorists released from prison. Police and intelligence services cannot defend the realm alone. There need to be competent judicial and incarceration systems in place as well. But after those convicted of terrorism-related crimes serve their terms and pass from the prison walls, what then? What is an acceptable level of risk for these individuals to be reintegrated into society for the society's guardians?

Locking them all up indefinitely is simply not feasible, because not every terrorist activity rises to the level of life in prison. As the 7/21 and Overt sagas indicated, even the people caught in a major terror investigation can be paroled within a few years or decades. And most, if not all, of the peripheral individuals in these operations now walk the streets as free men.

While the United States takes a harder stance and hands down longer prison sentences than European nations, hundreds of individuals convicted of terrorism offenses have been released from jails across the United States since 9/11.[8] For those who are caught, convicted, incarcerated, and freed, what happens next? After all, there's a nonzero chance that people who have been caught up in jihadist activities will resume them once they leave the prison walls. The U.S. Office of the Director of National Intelligence (ODNI) in late 2019 recorded that of the released 729 detainees from Guantanamo Bay, 124 people (17 percent) had reengaged with terrorist activity, while another 102 (14 percent) were suspected of doing so.[9] Interestingly however, Gitmo detainees are actually less likely to reoffend compared to the run-of-the-mill American criminals. According to the U.S. Sentencing Commission, almost half of all offenders in the U.S. justice system will be rearrested. These rates are even more dramatic for violent offenders.[10]

What, then, if those convicted of terrorist acts are actually not as likely to commit further ones once they leave prison? Those who commit acts of terror once they leave prison tend to generate a great deal of media coverage, but one UK Parliamentary investigation in 2020 found that of the 196 individuals convicted of a terrorist offense released from prison between January 2013 and December 2019, only 6 were convicted again of a terrorism offense. This is a 3 percent recidivism rate, far lower than for any other crime.[11] The rest (97 percent) appear to have returned to their regular, unthreatening lives.

One London-based lawyer who represented many men accused of terrorism offenses, Tayab Ali, had an interesting take on this phenomenon of recidivism. There's a widely held assumption in the national security community that terrorists are difficult, if not impossible, to rehabilitate into society. But over the years, he noticed a trend in his clients: many quickly lose their fervor for jihadist violence after facing the very real consequences of their actions. "There seems to be this hysteria prior to them entering into the legal system," he said. "I find myself as soon as I meet with a client, they go very quickly from this 'jihadi' mindset to a 'Oh my God, what was I thinking?'" During their initial meeting, he'd sit down with his clients and ask basic questions. "I'd say to them, 'So why did you get yourself involved in this? Can we talk about your views on 7/7 and Osama bin Laden?' And many nowadays would respond, 'Who is Osama bin Laden?' and, 'I kind of know about 7/7, but what is it?'" For many, "this is history in a book to them."[12]

Hence, there may really be two discrete groups of terrorist offenders: a small core of individuals ideologically committed to their particular violent cause, and then everyone else who follows along without thinking through their actions. Once people in the latter group face real penalties, Tayab Ali remarked, "They wake up pretty sharpish. And the benefit to knowing this now is that there probably are mechanisms that can be deployed on those individuals which can break that before they commit a terrorist offense."[13]

Of course, terrorism is not just about committing acts of violence, but a phenomenon that encompasses a broader set of actions that serve a violent political agenda. The eternal worry is whether those who leave the prison walls remain secretly loyal to a terror group, becoming talent scouts, fundraisers, trainers, influencers, and quartermasters long after the authorities have moved on to more pressing topics. A prison sentence paradoxically provides a degree of gravitas to a subset of individuals, easing their way to recruit new people to the cause, even if they aren't breaking the law.[14] It's hard for a terror group to exist for very long without this human infrastructure.

Stemming the real and perceived generational threat from paroled terrorists, returnees from jihadist battlegrounds, and those who are neither but are brought to a boiling point by friends or the internet will remain a challenge for years to come. While many people mellow out from the fires of their youth, some retain the fervor of their warped beliefs. Separating these individuals from the rest of society will be difficult, costly, and time-consuming and requires continual attention from lawmakers and law-enforcers alike. ODNI in 2019 glumly opined, "Homegrown violent extremist activity almost certainly will have societal effects disproportionate to the casualties and damage it causes."[15]

There is no one-size-fits-all solution to this challenge. Resources are always finite. There are only so many cops and spooks and social workers the state can deploy. And, of course, they won't have perfect information or the discernment required to always make the correct decision. And there are legitimate civil liberties concerns about excessive surveillance. But the countries affected may be obliged to keep a close eye on these individuals, or a certain subset of them, for decades to come.

Our societies must become more resilient to shock and terror. Terrorism is political theater performed for an audience on and in screens, smartphones, and newspapers. The resulting devastation of an attack is intended not just to harm its direct recipients but to make the broader audience shudder as well. That's why Rauf, Ali, and Abu Ubaydah were so insistent on taping suicide videos for the "media brothers": they knew the propaganda value of these attacks would have a durable shelf life, long after the physical wreckage from the operation was cleared and its victims buried.

Al Qaeda hoped the 9/11 attack would cause the United States to overreact and eventually harm itself. In many ways, their hopes proved true. In the early twenty-first century, as the United States overcompensated in the counterterrorism space, it left other long-term challenges unattended. America's global counterterrorism efforts over the last few decades have metastasized to such an extent that the country is engaged in lethal combat through large swaths of the Middle East, Asia, and Africa. This fundamental reorientation of America's national security posture simply would not have occurred but for the 9/11 attacks. There are now men and women serving in combat zones today who have no personal recollection of the attacks that fundamentally altered American society—because they were children at the time, or not even born yet.

Localized attacks like 7/7 are horrific. For the families and friends of the fifty-two victims who died and the hundreds who were injured, the impact will be everlasting. However, it's actually quite difficult to pull off a spectacular operation that moves the needle in terms of fundamentally altering society. As 7/7 showed, the general public in London accepted the risk of riding public transit the very next day. But the Overt conspiracy, had it been successfully executed, would have had a massive global impact on par with the 9/11 attack. Beyond the death and destruction, the operation would have profoundly altered society. We would continue to feel its ripples decades later.

There remains a fine balance between the requirement to protect people from violent groups and the need to preserve the blessings of a free and open society. Complicating matters, in a free society, some people and institutions espouse noxious opinions. Can governments maintain an aggressive national security posture with increasingly sophisticated, intrusive surveillance mechanisms while making sure society doesn't tip over into a police state? Where should the line be drawn—legally, ethically, morally, logistically—when the state has to step in and enforce its monopoly on violence? For once a country takes away certain liberties in the name of protection, it's hard to reverse course once the threat has passed.

Democracies may very well be at the outer limit of what our societies are willing to tolerate in terms of intrusive surveillance and police violence. Heavy-handed operations routinely boomerang and degrade the willingness for those living in our societies to work with authorities to fight mayhem on the streets. Treating people with respect and justice, on the other hand, builds those intangible relationships, which often come into play during a crisis.

There are hard limits in free and open societies that we rightly place upon intelligence organizations and law enforcement. Paradoxically, maximum-surveillance police states are fundamentally unstable entities. For example, perhaps one out of a hundred East German citizens informed on his or her neighbors for the Ministry of State Security, better known as the Stasi, during the late 1980s.[16] Many more worked for decades with other East German government organizations to denounce their colleagues, classmates, and neighbors. Yet even with all those eyes watching, the whole enterprise collapsed along with its symbol of brutality—the Berlin Wall—within weeks. They, and we, never saw it coming.

But here's the good news: people and societies are more resilient than one thinks. Further, states with competent civilian institutions and law enforcement can withstand a fairly high level of strife without completely coming undone. London was able to endure waves of Irish Republican terrorism for over a century. Israel has stood strong despite terrorism during its entire existence.

And even the United States has dealt with serious domestic terrorism issues and survived. At one point in America, bombings and other violence we would classify nowadays as "terrorism" were just accepted as a fact of life. In the not-too-distant past, at least one airplane over American skies was hijacked a week. Between 1971 and 1972, some twenty-five hundred bombs, or about five a day, went off across America, according to the FBI.[17] Bomb threats and the mass evacuation of skyscrapers in New York City and San Francisco became a fairly regular occurrence. In 1970 the Weather Underground bombed NYPD's headquarters.[18] The following year, the group placed another bomb in a restroom in the U.S. Senate, in-between the Capitol Rotunda and Senate chambers, causing "extensive damage," according to Capitol Police.[19] The Pentagon was hit in 1972 and the State Department in 1975. Eleven people died several days after Christmas 1975 when a baggage carousel at La Guardia Airport in New York City was blown up in what remains an unsolved crime. This mayhem, mostly forgotten nowadays, seems very much at odds with a post-9/11 security mindset, now two-plus decades old.

Intelligence is a team sport, and not even the United States can play it alone. The Overt bombings might have succeeded had it not been for three countries working together to thwart it. The global security community came together, albeit with somewhat differing objectives, to take decisive actions in Pakistan, Great Britain, and the United States. And global transportation agencies acted relatively quickly to unify their policies, with some feather-ruffling, to ensure public safety. There remains a shared pride at the success of spotting and stopping the Overt conspiracy. At the most reductionist level, a dastardly plot was stopped, and the majority of the plotters were convicted in court.

So much of history can turn on a few quick decisions. Overt's hinge point was the American decision to greenlight Rashid Rauf's seizure from a bus in Pakistan, overriding the British desire to collect more intelligence for a future trial. But what would have happened had the Crown's commands held, or if Rauf hadn't slipped up by not turning off his cellphones for the bus trip? What if he had just stayed in the tribal lands of Pakistan, far from the grasp of anyone, instead of passing through Pakistan proper in early August 2006?

The answer is unknowable, but had it not been for Rauf's takedown, the British could have likely built a more solid case against the Overt conspirators, saved themselves three agonizing public trials, and avoided several years of effort. There could have been stronger evidence, including admissible correspondence, or even a working bomb. Perhaps there would've been a more comprehensive takedown of suspects. Maybe others who knew about the conspiracy who destroyed evidence before the trial—for example, bottles of hydrogen peroxide dumped on the side of the motorway following the arrests—would have been implicated as well. Some people given scant notice in this book were picked up in the original dragnet but were never charged with a crime due to lack of involvement or lack of evidence. Others may have gotten away completely.

On the other hand, from the perspective of the White House and CIA, each day Rashid Rauf was a free man, the United States was decidedly less safe. The Americans understood the seriousness of the crisis and believed the United States would take the brunt of the attack. The U.S.

intelligence community considered this plot to be the biggest operation since 9/11 and treated it as such. The choice to strike a crushing blow was thus not really a hard decision at all. The strong Anglo-American alliance notwithstanding, America was confident in the decision to "go it alone" to protect its people and its assets. The needs of the British legal system remained secondary to saving lives.

But no one country controls all the pieces of the national security chessboard. To fight terrorism on a global scale across far-flung battlefields, nations must rely on allies. These bonds must be more than just transactional and temporary; they have to be based on mutual trust. Alas, no partnership is forever. As Lord Palmerston famously told Parliament in 1848, "We have no eternal allies, and we have no perpetual enemies. Our interests are eternal and perpetual, and those interests it is our duty to follow."

I hope, in spite of disagreements, that the strong Anglo-American partnership continues. There is too much at stake. The U.S., UK, and other allied intelligence communities must continue to work and operate as a single entity to stop these lethal organizations from carrying out attacks. As Hayden remarked a year after the conspiracy was thwarted, "Nothing less than intensive cooperation with our overseas colleagues could have achieved such a complete success."[20]

It could happen again. Despite all the advances made by our counterterrorism professionals, airports and airplanes remain top targets. Overt could have changed the face of global aviation and travel forever. But it was certainly not the first, nor the last, complex operations against airplanes, airports, and our interconnected world.

Terrorists from al Qaeda and the Islamic State over the last decade have struck airports and airplanes in Brussels, Istanbul, Moscow, and Sharm El-Sheikh in their quest to advance the narrative of crippling the West. In a devious plot that should have garnered more media attention, in mid-2017 Islamic State operatives mailed explosive substances and other devices via international air cargo from Turkey to Australia *without* being detected. This bomb kit astonishingly managed to evade global security measures in at least two major airports, and the cell would have likely struck a Dubai-bound Etihad flight had the explosive not reportedly exceeded the plane's weight limit. Eventually a "foreign intelligence partner" caught wind of the plot and alerted Australian authorities, who swept up the cell a few days later.[21]

It's likely only a matter of time before a group again tries to carry out a large terrorist operation. Al Qaeda has faded somewhat in overall importance, but others have picked up the flag. In 2019 the U.S. intelligence community assessed that "ISIS still commands thousands of fighters in Iraq and Syria, and it maintains eight branches, more than a dozen networks, and thousands of dispersed supporters around the world, despite significant leadership and territorial losses . . . ISIS very likely will continue to pursue external attacks from Iraq and Syria against regional and Western adversaries, including the United States."[22]

Some counterterrorism professionals I've spoken with assert it's harder to execute a terrorist strike in the sky than ever before. Not only are those dedicated to keeping us safe more vigilant but 9/11 also changed the mindset of the passengers on the flights themselves. More than a few determined people have evaded security and boarded a plane ready to do catastrophic damage only to be subdued by other passengers. Anonymous flyers and a female steward tackled Richard Reid after they noticed him trying to light a bomb in his shoe in late 2001. Similarly, his fellow passengers restrained the thwarted 2009 Christmas Day "Underwear" bomber Umar Farouk Abdulmutallab aboard a Detroit-bound Northwest Airlines flight. A fortunate intervention, as DHS Under Secretary for Intelligence Todd Rosenblum admitted everyone in the U.S. intelligence community "was caught flat-footed" in that attack.[23]

Sometimes, we get lucky and basic operational errors save the day. In the Reid and Abdulmutallab cases, both knew they wanted to blow up the plane. So why didn't these suicide attackers detonate their explosives in the airplane bathroom instead of in front of their fellow passengers? The FBI had even gamed this scenario out as far back as 2003: the bureau drafted a bulletin entitled "Possible Hijacking Tactic for Using Aircraft as Weapons" and forwarded it to its international partners. It noted, "Components of improvised explosive devices can be smuggled onto an aircraft, concealed in either clothing or personal carry-on items such as shampoo and medicine bottles, and assembled on board. In many cases of suspicious passenger activity, incidents have taken place in the aircraft's forward lavatory."[24]

Had they followed the scenario forecast by the FBI, Reid and Abdulmutallab might have succeeded and killed hundreds of people.

More ominously, the Overt plotters might have been successful had they carried forth their conspiracy a few years beforehand, when governments and global aviation firms were still laboriously putting into place new security mechanisms. Even with the advances made by 2006, the combined efforts of the world's intelligence services missed the Madrid 2004 train bombings and the 7/7 attacks. Had Rashid Rauf dared to dream bigger, he might have diverted Mohammad Sidique Khan and his cell from the Underground and onto airplanes. No one would have seen them coming.

The United States spends billions of dollars annually on devices at the airport dedicated to finding weapons and explosives, such as walk-through metal detectors, handheld devices, explosive trace detectors, explosive trace portals, whole body scanners, and backscatter x-ray scanners. We also employ tens of thousands of personnel like TSA officials, local and state police, behavior specialists, and trained K-9 officers. All these people and machines complement a whole host of other physical security protocols.[25] But most readers likely have an anecdote of cracks in the system: some contraband they forgot was in their bag or a bottle of water a kind agent allowed them to bring through for their kid. And, in response to the 2020 global coronavirus pandemic, the TSA in March 2020 began to allow up to twelve ounces of hand sanitizer in carry-on bags.[26]

The adversary is a nimble, adaptable foe. The difference between the older groups like al Qaeda and relatively newer organizations like the Islamic State is that the latter generally avoids the megaconspiracy, even though it carried out the assault on Paris in November 2015 and the simultaneous bombings of Easter services in Sri Lanka in 2019. But their modus operandi now relies on individuals acting out in their own countries with the weapons they can source on their own. In this "war of the flea," it might be a vehicle ramming a group of people or using a completely legal firearm in a crowded, enclosed space. It could be a wild knife attack or pipe bombs in mailboxes. It doesn't really matter whether you have bought into the murderous ideology in any great way, or are a particularly sophisticated person. As long as you are willing to commit violence in your home country, that's good enough.

There are other threats against aviation that remain legitimate menaces. The soft underbelly to global aviation is, and likely forever will be, the "insider threat"—a person in the aviation business or who otherwise has access to aircraft through their work. These people are far more dangerous than those on the outside. Some one million people work in nearly 440 airports under federal jurisdiction around the United States; not just pilots and stewards, but TSA officials, fast food workers, mechanics, security personnel, cleaners, airline employees, you name it. Even now, it's unclear how thoroughly checked each and every one of these people are despite a three-part vetting program.[27] The hostile insider is better equipped to subvert airport security protocols.

On the other hand, airport operations would grind to a halt if every one of these employees were subject to the same daily scrutiny as regular passengers. In 2015 the TSA inspector general found seventy-three people out of over nine hundred thousand individuals employed by airlines, airport vendors, and other firms cleared to access secure airport areas were flagged with "terrorism-related category codes."[28] They don't even have to have particularly nefarious connections: In the last several years, determined insider threats have tried to smuggle a van packed full of explosives onto airport grounds in Kansas,[29] run hundreds of guns through Hartsfield-Jackson International Airport in Atlanta,[30] and sabotage critical navigation systems in Miami.[31] The suicidal first officer of GermanWings flight 9525 deliberately crashed the jet into the side of a mountain in March 2015, killing 150, while an Alaska Airlines ground-services worker in August 2018 stole a turboprop to commit suicide outside of Seattle.

Terrorist groups and narcotraffickers have also long known about the widespread legal availability of high-powered firearms such as .50 cal rifles in the United States that can be used to down planes. Al Qaeda's Abu Azzam al-Amriki (a.k.a. Adam Gadahn) opined at length in 2011 about this uniquely American phenomenon, calling at one point on supporters to buy guns in America to use against Americans. Bin Laden himself reportedly bought two dozen .50 caliber Barrett sniper rifles in the United States in 1989, according to the sworn testimony of a government witness who transacted the deal and shipped the weapons to Afghanistan.[32] More recently, Islamic State supporters in 2015 in San Bernardino, California, gunned down sixteen people at a Christmas party with pistols and an AR-15, while another Islamic State killer murdered forty-nine people in Orlando, Florida, in 2016 using a SIG Sauer MCX.

Beyond complex gun-and-bomb attacks, there is the still-unrealized challenge of devastating cyberattacks on aviation infrastructure. Reservation systems could melt down. Computer viruses could spread through air traffic control systems. Hostile individuals could deliberately install malware on passenger planes, causing "death by firmware." A weaponized drone—or a weaponized drone swarm—could overwhelm a plane as it lands or takes off. These scenarios remain in the realm of cinema, but in the not-too-distant future, they could very well occur.

◆

Around 3.5 percent of the global GDP is based on civilian aviation. An easily spooked populace could spell doom for much of the world economy. Al Qaeda in the Arabian Peninsula made great strides in building sophisticated explosives to put onto planes in the first decade of the 2000s, which were mostly thwarted due to aggressive intelligence work and a fair amount of luck. One way to mitigate this endemic problem is to create resilient cities and resilient populations.

Indeed, London might serve as the model for American cities. Not only does London have competent security forces—it also has a resilient population that knows terrorist atrocities will occur and life will continue. Terrorist groups remain clever, adaptable, and continuously probing for weaknesses at the security perimeter. And yes: terrorism can cause grave damage and mass death, but only a panicky population and shaky leadership at the top can take an attack and turn it into an existential crisis.

The work continues. The world's safety and the benefits of globalization depend on professionals' expertise to keep our airports and airplanes safe. And again, excellent intelligence won't always save us—like one might say of men and horses, you can never know enough.

◆

Years after the events described in this book, CIA director Hayden shared with me a coda of sorts to the white-knuckle summer of 2006. I visited him in his modern office in downtown Washington DC; he had suffered a serious stroke the year prior, and he had a frailty about him that I had never previously noticed. Still, his mind was sharp as ever. He told me that sometime after the conspiracy was brought to a conclusion, a CIA employee called the front office to ask to see him.

At the appointed time, the officer arrived and told General Hayden that his brother worked as a pilot for United Airlines and frequently flew the transatlantic route. He had been caught up in the wake of the global air lockdown that August and only found out about the plot's particulars from the media. The officer then said, "He said he doesn't know what we did, but he figured we did a lot. And he wanted you to have this." He then handed the CIA director a model of a United Airlines passenger jet.

All these years later, this model has remained in General Hayden's possession, even after his retirement from government service. At one point during our conversation, the general's eyes wandered up to the top of his office bookshelf. Frozen in permanent flight, the model jet was perched atop his belongings, a winged reminder of how very close the world came to disaster.

ACKNOWLEDGMENTS

This book was originally supposed to be a very short one about a very big plot. But the more I pulled on the various strands of this story, the more there was to know.

I'm indebted to the many people who generously shared their time, recollections, and advice about how to proceed with this book. These include: Raffaello Pantucci, Amardeep Bassey, Mitch Silber, Jose Rodriguez Jr., Stephen Kappes, Larry Pfeiffer, Nigel Inkster, Patrick Smith, James Hutton, Liz Thomas, Brett Holmgren, Andy Liepman, Josh Shiffrin, Shimon Taylor, Robin Simcox, Paul Cruickshank, Chris Phillips, Syl Tang, Adrian Levy, Paul Coletti, Fran Townsend, Tim Buch, Shuja Nawaz, Rich Davis, Shaun Greenough, Volodymyr Bilotkach, Margaret Gilmore, Todd Rosenblum, Steve Dryden, Seth Goldman, Yassin Musharbash, Chad Wolf, Tom Blank, Juan Zarate, Ira Greenberg, Tayab Ali, Andrew Cummings, Admiral Scott Redd, and General Michael Hayden.

Along the way, many people offered constructive suggestions and edits to the manuscript. Your help has made this a far better book. Many thanks to: Darren Brooks, Connie Min, Max Wachtel, Bobby Smith, Liz S., Alex Finley, Faris Alikhan, and Stephen Dyer.

There were many who helped me along this journey to better understand what occurred during many clandestine meetings and top-secret conversations. Many of these individuals wished to remain anonymous. Thank you very much for your insights and your kind assistance in nudging this book to its conclusion.

This book would not have seen the light of day without the dogged determination of my agent Joshua Bilmes and Jabberwocky Literary Agency, Inc. Thank you. I also want to thank the University of Nebraska Press/Potomac Books team—Tom Swanson, Taylor Rothgeb, Irina du Quenoy, Rosemary Sekora, and Tish Fobben—for bringing this story to life. Thanks also to Erin Greb, who constructed the maps in this book.

Collecting the documents and researching this plot consumed my life for several years, with the final manuscript coming together during a global pandemic. My beloved wife, Dana, would see me late at night plunking away at my computer and understand why I couldn't come to bed until the wee hours until I had found that one last citation. She remains my favorite editor. I am grateful for everything she does.

Finally, my thanks to the thousands of honest, hard-working women and men who earn a government salary to keep all of us safe, secure, and free. Despite its occasional shortcomings, public service remains an honorable calling. May you all get a raise soon.

APPENDIX 1

The Overt plotters had numerous codenames and nicknames, given by both the authorities and by themselves. Police codenames are in italics.

Rashid Rauf	Khalid, Jamil, Joseph, Ishmael
Abdulla Ahmed Ali	*Lion Roar*, AAA, AAK (U.S. intelligence used this exclusively), Ahmed, Armadillo, Dillo, Abu Talhah & Big D (in Ibrahim Savant's phone), Imran (in Assad Sarwar's phone), Amjad, PPDillos (in Tanvir Hussain's phone), Abu A & Amjid (in Nabeel Hussain's phone), Joseph, Tall Imi, Chatcha
Assad Sarwar	*Rich Food*, Nabs, Jona Lewis, Nabsy, Nabs, Nabeel, Victor Orlando, Fati
Tanvir Hussain	*Top Drawer*, T, Half Guji
Mohammed Yasar Gulzar	*Pie Chart*, Yaq, Yaks, Altaf Ravat (or Rabat), Arif
Umar Islam	*Polar Mist*, Brian Young (his original name), Omar B, Kala
Waheed Zaman	*Sweet Bowl*
Waheed Arafat Khan	*Goody Bag*, Arro, Ardam (in Hussain's phone)
Ibrahim Savant	Ibo, Oliver Savant, Irish

APPENDIX 2

Here are the operations (in chronological order) mentioned in the book. Of note, there were multiple investigations into various terrorist plots in Great Britain and the United States during this era, but they fell outside the narrative of this book.

Demetrius (1971)	A British Army effort to detain suspected IRA members in Northern Ireland, which involved rounding up hundreds of people and interning them without trial.
Kratos (post 9/11)	A Metropolitan Police strategy to kill suspected suicide bombers prior to an attack.
Crevice (2003 to 2004)	An al Qaeda-linked plot to strike shopping centers, nightclubs, and pubs throughout Britain with a series of large fertilizer bombs. This was the largest counterterrorism operation carried out by MI5 and the police prior to Overt.
Rhyme (2004)	A plot concocted by KSM and Dhiren Barot to attack underground carparks and the London Underground. Barot wanted to explode a "dirty bomb" but was unable to secure the right precursor materials.

Theseus (2005)   Better known as the 7/7 attack, wherein
                                   al Qaeda suicide bombers struck London
                                   transportation, killing fifty-two people.

Vivace (2005)   Better known as the 7/21 or the 21/7 attack,
                                   this bungled attack led by Muktar Said
                                   Ibrahim tried to strike public transport in
                                   London, but the bombs failed.

Volga (2006)   A police raid on a private home in the
                                   Forest Gate neighborhood of East London,
                                   where authorities believed terrorists
                                   were keeping a chemical weapon on the
                                   premises. Police shot one man in the raid
                                   but found no evidence of explosives or
                                   terrorist activity.

Overt (2006)   The plot to destroy several North
                                   America–bound passenger jets over the
                                   Atlantic Ocean using liquid explosives.
                                   MI5 believed this was the most dangerous
                                   terrorist conspiracy in British history.

High-Rise (2009)   An al Qaeda plot to bomb New York City's
                                   subway system.

NOTES

1. THE KILLER BESIDE YOU

1. Mahanty, "Physics of Explosion Hazards."
2. Author interview with Tom Blank, February 1, 2012.
3. Vermette, "General Protocols," 88–89.
4. Garstang, "Aircraft Explosive Sabotage," 199.
5. Garstang, "Aircraft Explosive Sabotage," 210.
6. Marquise, *Scotbom*, 17.
7. "Flight 103 Souvenir Hunters Fined," Associated Press, March 8, 1989; "Souvenir Hunters Hurt Probe of Plane Crash," Associated Press, December 22, 1992; "Red Arrows Crash: 'Souvenir Hunter in EBay Sale Claim,'" BBC, August 31, 2011.
8. Miguel Lo Bianco, "Brazilian Crews Gather First Air France Wreckage," Reuters, June 4, 2009.
9. "Investigators Recover Second Air France Black Box," Agence France-Presse, May 3, 2011.
10. Epstein and Wang, "'Beliefs about Beliefs' without Probabilities," 1343–73.
11. Goldin and Mariathasan, *Butterfly Defect*.
12. Federal Aviation Administration, *Air Traffic by the Numbers*.
13. Association for Safe International Road Travel, *Road Safety Facts*.
14. Bilotkach, *Economics of Airlines*.
15. Bilotkach, *Economics of Airlines*.
16. Hartwig and Wilkinson, *Terrorism Risk*, 3.
17. Blunk, Clark, and McGibany, "Evaluating the Long-Run Impacts," 363–70.
18. "Remarks of Alexandre de Juniac."
19. Author interview with Chad Wolf, February 1, 2012.
20. Duty Free World Council, *Global Travel Retail History*.

2. BAKER'S BOY

1. Federal Bureau of Investigation, "Rashid Rauf; IT-AL-QAEDA OO:WFO."
2. "Mystery of Dad Murder," *Birmingham Mail*, April 26, 2002.
3. Shaw, *Kinship and Continuity*, 30.
4. UK Department for Communities and Local Government, with the Change Institute, *Pakistani Muslim Community in England*.
5. Schehrezade Faramarzi, "British Suspects Described as Ordinary," Associated Press, August 15, 2006.
6. Mshari Al-Zaydi, "European Islam and Islam from the Subcontinent," *Asharq Al-Awsat*, August 22, 2006.
7. Al-Zayadi, "European Islam."
8. BBC Panorama Team, "Operation Overt—Panorama."
9. Author interview with Raffaello Pantucci, July 12, 2019.
10. Steven Brocklehurst, "Top Terror Suspect Urged Jihad in Glasgow," BBC, January 9, 2018.
11. "The Man Who Brought Jihad to Britain," BBC, April 5, 2016.
12. Levy and Scott-Clark, *The Meadow*, 38.
13. Levy and Scott-Clark, *The Meadow*, 36–37.
14. Emma Brockes, "British Man Named as Bomber Who Killed 10," *Guardian*, December 28, 2000.
15. Brockes, "British Man Named as Bomber."
16. Interview with Raffaello Pantucci.
17. Levy and Scott-Clark, *The Meadow*, 296.
18. Federal Bureau of Investigation, "Rashid Rauf; IT-AL-QAEDA OO:WFO."
19. Goldby, "Special Investigation."
20. Duncan Gardham, "Airliner Bomb Trial: The Electronics Expert Cleared of Blame," *Telegraph*, September 8, 2008; Secretary of State for the Home Department v. AY [2012] EWHC 2054 (Admin), 2012, England and Wales High Court (Administrative Court) Decisions.
21. Pantucci, "Biography of Rashid Rauf."
22. These institutions are now called Washwood Heath Academy and Saltley Academy, respectively.
23. "Muslim Teacher in Carol Concert Tirade Is Made Ofsted Inspector," *Evening Standard* (London), September 30, 2006.
24. Author interview with Amardeep Bassey, July 23, 2019.
25. Pantucci, "Biography of Rashid Rauf."
26. Silber, *Al Qaeda Factor*, 42.
27. Silber, *Al Qaeda Factor*, 42.
28. Goldby, "Special Investigation."

29. *Secretary of State for the Home Department v. AY*; BBC Panorama Team, "Operation Overt—Panorama."

30. Mark Cowan, "Mosque Visit in Murder Probe—Unveiled: Our Face of the Future," *Birmingham Mail*, May 6, 2002.

31. This assertion is based on two confidential interviews independently conducted by the author.

32. BBC Panorama Team, "Operation Overt—Panorama."

33. Author interview with Shuja Nawaz, January 7, 2020.

34. Nawaz, *Crossed Swords*, 385.

35. Nawaz, *Crossed Swords*, 539; interview with Shuja Nawaz.

36. Regina v. Abdulla Ahmed Ali et al., Woolwich Crown Court, June 18, 2008.

37. Kim Barker, "In Pakistani Village, Disbelief over Allegations of Terror Plot," *Chicago Tribune*, August 20, 2006.

38. Asif Farooqi, Carol Gristanti, and Robert Windrem, "Sources: U.K. Terror Plot Suspects Forced to Talk," *NBC News*, August 18, 2006.

39. Sageman, *London Bombings*, 137.

40. Riedel, "Pakistan and Terror," 31–45.

41. Kim Sengupta, "Exclusive: Army is Fighting British Jihadists in Afghanistan," *Independent*, February 25, 2009.

42. Aguilar et al., "An Introduction to Pakistan's Military."

43. JeM has changed its name several times over its existence, while maintaining its mission, headquarters, and leadership structure. As of September 2019, the group was known as "Majlis Wurasa-e-Shuhuda Jammu wa Kashmir," partially to ward off international opprobrium. See Shishir Gupta, "Terror Group Jaish Gets A New Name, Preps 30 Suicide Attackers to Hit India," *Hindustan Times*, September 24, 2019.

44. Riedel, "Pakistan and Terror." In response to the U.S. Department of State's designation of HUA as a foreign terrorist organization in 1997, the group devolved into its two major factions: HUM and Harakat ul-Jihad Islami.

45. All-India Radio, New Delhi, in English, at 0245 GMT, February 22, 1994.

46. Sidhartha Barua, "Somalian Link Seen to Al Qaeda," *Los Angeles Times*, February 22, 2002.

47. Text of report by Indian Doordarshan TV on December 26, 1999.

48. "JeM Chief Masood Azhar Son, Brother, Among 44 Detained in Pakistan," *BusinessTodayIn.*, March 5, 2019.

49. Singh and Talbott, *In Service of Emergent India*, 203.

50. Muzamil Jaleel, "After Kandahar Swap, India Offered Taliban Cash to Get Me: JeM Chief," *Indian Express*, June 6, 2016. Mullah Mansur would

eventually die when the United States struck his convoy on the N-40 highway in Pakistan in 2016.

51. Riedel, "Pakistan and Terror."

52. "Kashmiri, Freed after Hijacking, Is Still Militant," *New York Times*, January 6, 2000.

53. Rashid, *Descent into Chaos*, 114.

54. Sanaullah Khan, "Punjab Govt Takes Administrative Control of Bahawal-pur Seminary," *Dawn* (Pakistan), February 22, 2009.

55. "It's All Lies, Protests Suspected Air Bomber," *Evening Standard*, December 22, 2006.

56. Tanveer Khalid, "Schools for Extremists Thrive in Pakistan," MSNBC.com, March 23, 2009.

3. TRIPLE A

1. Diamond, *People's History of Walthamstow*.

2. Abdulla Ahmed Ali was known by many names but will be referred to as "Ali" through the rest of the book.

3. *Regina v. Abdulla Ahmed Ali et al.*, April 2, 2008. There are some variations to his name. As he later related, "My family, they don't have a tradition of a family name. We have a tradition when you call your child whatever you want to call your child, not by family name that goes back generations and my Dad just thought Abdulla Ali was good enough and didn't need a Khan to it." He would later be nicknamed "AAK" by American authorities due to a misunderstanding that his formal last name was "Khan."

4. *Regina v. Abdulla Ahmed Ali et al.*, June 2, 2008.

5. *Regina v. Abdulla Ahmed Ali et al.*, June 3, 2008.

6. David Harrison and Adam Lusher, "Investigation; A Terrorist in the Making at the Age of 14; Last Week a Court Found Abdulla Ahmed Ali Guilty of Plotting Murder," *Sunday Telegraph* (London), September 14, 2008.

7. *Regina v. Abdulla Ahmed Ali et al.*, June 2, 2008.

8. "Blunkett Rebuts Terror Criticism," BBC, December 21, 2003.

9. *Regina v. Abdulla Ahmed Ali et al.*, June 2, 2008.

10. That structure was torn down in June 2002 and a new structure was completed in October 2003.

11. Martin Evans and Ben Farmer, "How Anjem Choudary, the Firebrand Cleric Linked to a String of Terror Plots, Reveled in Role of Sharia Law's Agent Provocateur," *Telegraph*, August 16, 2016.

12. *Regina v. Abdulla Ahmed Ali et al.*, June 2, 2008.

13. *Regina v. Abdulla Ahmed Ali et al.*, June 2, 2008.

14. *Regina v. Abdulla Ahmed Ali et al.*, June 6, 2008.
15. *Regina v. Abdulla Ahmed Ali et al.*, June 16, 2008, and June 17, 2008.
16. *Regina v. Abdulla Ahmed Ali et al.*, June 30, 2008.
17. *Regina v. Abdulla Ahmed Ali et al.*, June 26, 2008.
18. Regina v. Abdulla Ahmed Ali et al. (Retrial), Woolwich Crown Court, May 5, 2009.
19. *Regina v. Abdulla Ahmed Ali et al.*, June 16, 2008.
20. *Regina v. Abdulla Ahmed Ali et al.*, June 2, 2008.
21. Silber, *Al Qaeda Factor*, 42.
22. BBC Panorama Team, "Operation Overt—Panorama."
23. *Regina v. Abdulla Ahmed Ali et al.*, June 2, 2008.
24. *Regina v. Abdulla Ahmed Ali et al.*, June 2, 2008.
25. Médecins Sans Frontières, "Waiting in the 'Green Fields.'"
26. Cue, "New Influx of Afghan Refugees."
27. *Regina v. Abdulla Ahmed Ali et al.*, June 2, 2008.
28. *Regina v. Abdulla Ahmed Ali et al.*, June 2, 2008.
29. "'Truth Has Won' as Terror Plotter's Wife Cleared," *Independent*, March 5, 2010.
30. Sageman, *London Bombings*, 199.
31. *Regina v. Abdulla Ahmed Ali et al.*, June 2, 2008.
32. *Regina v. Abdulla Ahmed Ali et al.*, June 2, 2008.
33. Sageman, *London Bombings*, 199–200.
34. *Regina v. Abdulla Ahmed Ali et al.*, June 2, 2008.

4. RECRUITS

1. This airport was renamed O. R. Tambo International Airport in October 2006, in honor of an ANC political activist.
2. BBC Panorama Team, "Operation Overt—Panorama."
3. Secretary of State for the Home Department v AP [2008] EWHC 2001 (Admin), 2008, England and Wales High Court (Administrative Court) Decisions.
4. Silber, *Al Qaeda Factor*, 135.
5. Silber, *Al Qaeda Factor*, 140.
6. United Nations Security Council, "Mohamed al Ghabra."
7. Al-Ghabra v. Commission (Judgment [Third Chamber]) [2016] EUECJ T-248/13, December 13, 2016, Court of Justice of the European Union.
8. Nic Robertson, Paul Cruickshank, and Tim Lister, "Documents Give New Details on al Qaeda's London Bombings," CNN, April 30, 2012.
9. The compound's description was taken from the testimony of two other British citizens who were subsequently captured before they could com-

mit an attack in the United Kingdom. See Regina v. Mohammed Shakil et al., Woolwich Crown Court, 2008.

10. Sageman, *London Bombings*, 171.
11. Sageman, *London Bombings*, 171.

5. ALI'S EVOLUTION

1. Nic Robertson, Paul Cruickshank, and Tim Lister, "Document Shows Origins of 2006 Plot for Liquid Bombs on Planes," CNN, April 30, 2012, https://www.cnn.com/2012/04/30/world/al-qaeda-documents/index.html.
2. Robertson, Cruickshank, and Lister, "Document Shows Origins."
3. Robertson, Cruickshank, and Lister, "Document Shows Origins."
4. Robertson, Cruickshank, and Lister, "Document Shows Origins."
5. Bergen, *Holy War, Inc.*, 4.
6. Michael R. Gordon, "Chechen Rebels Say Leader Died in Russian Air Attack," *New York Times*, April 25, 1996.
7. Holbrook, "The Spread of Its Message," 93.
8. Wright, *Looming Tower*.
9. *Regina v. Abdulla Ahmed Ali et al.*, June 2, 2008.
10. *Regina v. Abdulla Ahmed Ali et al.*, June 2, 2008.
11. Robertson, Cruickshank, and Lister, "Document Shows Origins."

6. INCIDENT ON THE TUBE

1. Blair, *A Journey*, 547.
2. Blair, *A Journey*, 543.
3. Gerson, *Heroic Conservatism*, 120.
4. Blair, *A Journey*, 556.
5. "Bush 'Waving When Fell Off Bike,'" BBC, February 27, 2006.
6. White House Office of the Press Secretary, "President and Prime Minister Blair Discuss."
7. Blair, *A Journey*, 559.
8. Blair, *A Journey*, 559.
9. Author interview with Fran Townsend, November 7, 2019.
10. Author interview with Juan Zarate, February 10, 2020, and March 28, 2020.
11. Author interview with Steve Dryden, January 30, 2020.
12. Andrew, *Defend the Realm*, 821–22.
13. "7/7 Attacks: The Victims," BBC News, July 3, 2015.
14. Arifa Akbar, "Ateeque Sharifi: The Final Victim," *Independent*, July 21, 2005.
15. "7/7 Attacks: The Victims."

16. "Voices of 7/7: The Survivors' Testimonies Form a Searing but Inspiring Memorial to the 52 Victims," *Independent*, March 4, 2011.

17. Tulloch, *One Day in July*; Caroline Gammell, "July 7: Professor John Tulloch Tells How He Moved Closer to Edgware Road Bomber," *Telegraph*, November 11, 2010.

18. Author interview with Shimon Taylor, September 20, 2019.

19. London Assembly, *Report of the 7 July Review Committee*.

20. Andrew, *Defend the Realm*, 822.

21. London Assembly, *Report of the 7 July Review Committee*.

22. Interview with Steve Dryden.

23. Parliament, *Report into the London Terrorist Attacks*.

24. Parliament, *Could 7/7 Have Been Prevented?*

25. Parliament, *Could 7/7 Have Been Prevented?*

26. "Transcript from Secretary Michael Chertoff Press Briefing on London Bombings," States News Service, July 7, 2005.

27. Eric Roston, "President Bush Responds to London Attacks," *Time*, June 7, 2005.

28. Central Intelligence Agency, "A Day in the Life."

29. The new U.S. embassy in Nine Elms, Battersea, London, was formally opened on January 16, 2018.

30. Author interview with Fran Townsend, April 2, 2020.

31. Allister Heath, "The Day of Reckoning—In the Aftermath of the Bombing Outrage, the Cost in Human Terms Is Appalling. The Economic Consequences May Be Negligible, but It Could All Have Been Much, Much Worse," *Business*, July 10, 2005.

32. Musharraf, *In the Line of Fire*, 242.

33. Musharraf, *In the Line of Fire*, 242.

34. Pantucci, *We Love Death*, 39.

35. Briggs et al., "Anatomy of a Terrorist Attack."

36. Silber, *Al Qaeda Factor*, 117.

37. Silber, *Al Qaeda Factor*, 117.

38. "Bomb-Plot Accused's 'Bid to Join Taliban,'" *Yorkshire Post*, May 21, 2008.

39. Dean, Cruickshank, and Lister, *Nine Lives*, 290–92.

40. Dean, Cruickshank, and Lister, *Nine Lives*, 290–92.

41. Parliament, *Could 7/7 Have Been Prevented?*; Dean, Cruickshank, and Lister, *Nine Lives*.

42. Parliament, *Could 7/7 Have Been Prevented?*

43. Parliament, *Could 7/7 Have Been Prevented?*

44. "7/7 Bomber's Farewell Video Shown," BBC, April 24, 2008.

45. Pantucci, *We Love Death*, 195.

46. Pantucci, *We Love Death*, 196.
47. "Profile: Mohammad Sidique Khan," bbc *News*, March 2, 2011.
48. Pantucci, *We Love Death*, 196–97.
49. Mohammed Khan and Carlotta Gall, "A Qaeda Bomb Expert Killed in Pakistan Was a Paymaster," *New York Times*, April 22, 2006.
50. Parliament, *Could 7/7 Have Been Prevented?*
51. Parliament, *Could 7/7 Have Been Prevented?*
52. Parliament, *Could 7/7 Have Been Prevented?*
53. Confidential document from an undated German government assessment.
54. Pantucci, *We Love Death*, 197.
55. U.S. Senate, *The Impact of isis*.
56. Parliament, "Report of the Official Account."
57. Pantucci, *We Love Death*, 199.
58. Parliament, *Report of the Official Account*.
59. Robertson, Cruickshank, and Lister, "Documents Give New Details."
60. Robertson, Cruickshank, and Lister, "Documents Give New Details."
61. Hayman and Gilmore, *Terrorist Hunters*, 84.
62. "London Bomber: Text in Full," bbc, September 1, 2005, http://news.bbc .co.uk/2/hi/uk/4206800.stm.
63. Reinares, "Evidence of al-Qa'ida's Role." It is possible Zawahiri was alluding to another operation in the works, although it is unclear how much of a hand he had in external operations planning. Tantalizingly, in December 2005, the United States killed Hamza Rabi'a, who was considering a 7/7-style strike on public transport within the United States. It remains unclear if this operation had progressed much beyond the planning stages.

7. BANG/FIZZ

1. Rauf commentary from a confidential German government assessment.
2. Dulat and Sinha, *Spy Chronicles*, 57.
3. Confidential interview with a former Met police officer.
4. Metropolitan Police Authority, "Re: Counter Suicide Terrorism."
5. Author interview with Ira Greenberg, July 17, 2020.
6. Hayman and Gilmore, *Terrorist Hunters*, 98.
7. Hayman and Gilmore, *Terrorist Hunters*, 100.
8. Interview with Juan Zarate, February 10, 2020.
9. Interview with Steve Dryden.
10. Sewell Chan and Kareem Fahim, "New York Starts to Inspect Bags on the Subways," *New York Times*, July 22, 2005.
11. John Doyle, "City Pays Man $25G Over Subway Terror Searches," *New York Post* (blog), July 2, 2009.

12. Hayman and Gilmore, *Terrorist Hunters*, 181.
13. Dale Fuchs, "Bomb Is Found on Spanish Rail Line," *New York Times*, April 2, 2004.
14. Confidential German assessment.
15. Regina v. Muktar Said Ibrahim et al., January 15, 2007, Woolwich Crown Court.
16. *Regina v. Muktar Said Ibrahim et al.*, January 15, 2007.
17. Pantucci, *We Love Death*, 215.
18. Sageman, *London Bombings*, 183.
19. *Regina v. Muktar Said Ibrahim et al.*, January 15, 2007.
20. *Regina v. Muktar Said Ibrahim et al.*, January 15, 2007.
21. James Button, "London's Second Wave of Terror," *Sydney Morning Herald* (Australia), July 22, 2005.
22. *Regina v. Muktar Said Ibrahim et al.*, January 15, 2007.
23. Case of Ibrahim and Others v. The United Kingdom (Applications Nos. 50541/08, 50571/08, 50573/08 and 40351/09), December 16, 2014, European Court Of Human Rights.
24. Hayman and Gilmore, *Terrorist Hunters*, 185.
25. There is now a new station between Latimer Road and Shepherd's Bush named Wood Lane, which opened in 2008. A similar station with the same name closed in 1959. Furthermore, the Shepherd's Bush station that was targeted was renamed "Shepherd's Bush Market" station in October 2008 in order to avoid confusion between two other similarly named "Shepherd's Bush" stations on the London Overground and the Central Line. As of this writing, one cannot freely interchange between Central Line's Shepherd's Bush and the Hammersmith & City's Shepherd's Bush Market stations, despite being about a third of a mile from each other.
26. *Regina v. Muktar Said Ibrahim et al.*, January 15, 2007.
27. Hayman and Gilmore, *Terrorist Hunters*.
28. ANPRs are called License Plate Readers or Automatic License Plate Readers in the United States. On the difficulty of determing which vehicles were relevant to the hunt, see Transport for London, *Roads Task Force*.
29. Interview with Ira Greenberg.
30. Michael Howie, "Police Arrest Downing Street Man at Gunpoint," *Scotsman*, July 22, 2005.
31. Catherine MacLeod, "Business Goes on at No 10 as Armed Police Arrest Suspect Nearby," *Herald* (Glasgow), July 22, 2005.
32. Author interview with James Hutton, October 18, 2019.
33. Haroon Siddique, "Who Was Jean Charles de Menezes?," *Guardian*, March 30, 2016.

34. Arifa Akbar, "Attacks in London: Muslims in London: 'This Is the Backlash. We Are Not Safe Because We Are Muslims,'" *Independent*, July 23, 2005; Patrick Barkham, "'The Main Thing We Feel Is Fear, 24/7': Muslim Communities Sense of Danger at Mosques Subjected to Smashed Windows, Abuse, and Hoax Bomb Warnings," *Guardian*, July 23, 2005.

35. Robert Verkaik, "Attacks in London: Arson Attacks Raise Muslim Fears," *Independent*, July 23, 2005.

36. Andrew, *Defend the Realm*, 823.

37. Andrew, *Defend the Realm*, 823.

38. *Regina v. Muktar Said Ibrahim et al.*, January 15, 2007.

39. *Regina v. Sherif & Ors*, England and Wales Court of Appeal (Criminal Division), November 21, 2008.

40. *Case of Ibrahim and Others v. The United Kingdom*, December 16, 2014.

41. *Case of Ibrahim and Others v. The United Kingdom*, December 16, 2014.

42. *Case of Ibrahim and Others v. The United Kingdom*, December 16, 2014.

43. *Regina v. Muktar Said Ibrahim et al.*, January 15, 2007.

44. *Case of Ibrahim and Others v. The United Kingdom*, December 16, 2014.

45. *Case of Ibrahim and Others v. The United Kingdom*, December 16, 2014.

46. *Regina v. Muktar Said Ibrahim et al.*, January 15, 2007.

47. *Regina v. Sherif & Ors*, November 21, 2008.

48. *Case of Ibrahim and Others v. The United Kingdom*, December 16, 2014.

49. *Regina v. Sherif & Ors*, November 21, 2008.

50. *Regina v. Muktar Said Ibrahim et al.*, January 15, 2007.

51. *Regina v. Muktar Said Ibrahim et al.*, January 15, 2007.

52. *Regina v. Sherif & Ors*, November 21, 2008.

53. Isambard Wilkinson and Anton La Guardia, "Bombers Blow Themselves Up as Police Raid Their Madrid Hideout," *Telegraph*, April 4, 2004.

54. "Spanish Officer's Grave Attacked," BBC, April 19, 2004.

55. "The Attacks on London, Part One: The Arrests," *Independent*, July 31, 2005.

56. *Regina v. Muktar Said Ibrahim et al.*, January 15, 2007.

57. *Regina v. Muktar Said Ibrahim et al.*, January 15, 2007.

58. Rose, "Discussion."

8. THE ROSEWATER SOLUTION

1. These comments are drawn from Rauf's recollections conveyed by a confidential German government assessment.

2. Robertson, Cruickshank, and Lister, "Document Shows Origins."

3. Duncan Gardham, "Rashid Rauf's Connections to Terror," *Telegraph*, September 8, 2009.

4. Gardham, "Rashid Rauf's Connections to Terror."

5. Robertson, Cruickshank, and Lister, "Document Shows Origins."

6. Zaidi, "Response," 54.

7. Ikram Junaidi, "Release of Probe Report on Margalla Towers' Collapse Demanded," *Dawn* (Pakistan), October 9, 2017.

8. Harp and Crone, *Landslides Triggered.*

9. Sudmeier-Rieux et al., "The 2005 Pakistan Earthquake Revisited," 112–21.

10. Human Rights Watch, "*With Friends Like These . . .*"

11. Paul, *Environmental Hazards and Disasters*, 248.

12. Kronenfeld and Margesson, *Earthquake in South Asia.*

13. Tankel, *Storming the World Stage.*

14. U.S. Department of Defense, "When the Earth Shook"; United Nations Security Council, "Al Rashid Trust"; Isambard Wilkinson, "Islamist Groups Win Support for Pakistan Quake Aid," *Daily Telegraph* (UK), November 2, 2005; U.S. Department of the Treasury, "Typologies."

15. Tankel, *Storming the World Stage.*

16. Puri, *Across the LoC*; Rassler et al., "Fighters of Lashkar-e-Taiba."

17. Jamal, *Shadow War*, 170–71.

18. *Regina v. Abdulla Ahmed Ali et al.*, June 2, 2008.

9. GLIMMERS

1. "Full Text of the Bin Laden Tape," *New York Times*, January 19, 2006.

2. Jones, *Hunting in the Shadows*, 183.

3. Craig Whitlock and Kamran Khan, "Blast in Pakistan Kills Al Qaeda Commander," *Washington Post*, December 4, 2005.

4. Barton Gellman and Dafna Linzer, "Top Counterterrorism Officer Removed Amid Turmoil at CIA," *Washington Post*, February 7, 2006.

5. Confidential author interview with a former CIA officer.

6. *Regina v. Abdulla Ahmed Ali et al.*, (Retrial), July 15, 2009.

7. *Regina v. Abdulla Ahmed Ali et al.*, April 23, 2008.

8. *Regina v. Abdulla Ahmed Ali et al.*, April 23, 2008.

9. Federal Bureau of Investigation, *11 September Hijacker Model*, 29.

10. *Regina v. Abdulla Ahmed Ali et al.*, June 16, 2008.

11. Robertson, Cruickshank, and Lister, "Document Shows Origins."

12. Duncan Gardham, "Teenager Sentenced to 18 Years after Being Groomed as Suicide Bomber in Trans-Atlantic Airlines Plot," *Telegraph*, December 10, 2009.

13. *Regina v. Abdulla Ahmed Ali et al.*, July 1, 2008.

14. *Regina v. Ibrahim Savant, Arafat Khan, and Waheed Zaman*, Woolwich Crown Court, June 28, 2010.

15. *Regina v. Ibrahim Savant, Arafat Khan, and Waheed Zaman*, June 23, 2010.

16. *Regina v. Ibrahim Savant, Arafat Khan, and Waheed Zaman*, June 23, 2010.

17. McChrystal, *My Share of the Task*, 172.

18. Khan, "A Letter from Sister Fatima."

19. U.S. Department of Defense, *Article 15-6 Investigation*.

20. *Regina v. Abdulla Ahmed Ali et al.*, July 1, 2008.

21. *Regina v. Abdulla Ahmed Ali et al.*, July 1, 2008.

22. Fiona Hudson, "Baby Used as Terror Bomb—22/8 Apocalypse: Parents' Plan to Sacrifice Child," *Daily Telegraph* (Australia), August 14, 2006.

23. Robertson, Cruickshank, and Lister, "Document Shows Origins."

24. Robertson, Cruickshank, and Lister, "Document Shows Origins."

25. Confidential author interview with a former CIA officer.

26. Henry Chu and Zulfiqar Ali, "Al Qaeda Operative Is Targeted," *Los Angeles Times*, April 14, 2006.

27. Hawley and Means, *Permanent Emergency*, 136.

28. *Regina v. Abdulla Ahmed Ali et al.* (Retrial), July 15, 2009.

29. *Regina v. Abdulla Ahmed Ali et al.* (Retrial), July 15, 2009.

30. Independent Police Complaints Commission, *IPCC Independent Investigations*.

31. Hayman and Gilmore, *Terrorist Hunters*, 321–23.

32. Peter Walker and David Fickling, "Police Apologise to East London Raid Family," *Guardian*, June 13, 2006.

33. Independent Police Complaints Commission, *IPCC Independent Investigations*.

34. Hayman and Gilmore, *Terrorist Hunters*, 324.

35. "In Full: Police Raid Statement," BBC, June 13, 2006.

36. BBC Panorama Team, "Operation Overt—Panorama."

37. BBC Panorama Team, "Operation Overt—Panorama."

38. BBC Panorama Team, "Operation Overt—Panorama."

39. BBC Panorama Team, "Operation Overt—Panorama."

40. Sean O'Neill, "Key Conspirator 'Took on New Identity to Join in Transatlantic Bomb Plot,'" *Times* (London), April 8, 2008.

10. THE DILEMMA

1. *Regina v. Abdulla Ahmed Ali et al.* (Retrial), July 15, 2009.

2. Interview with Steve Dryden.

3. Rodriguez and Harlow, *Hard Measures*.

4. Anderson, "Report of the Bulk Power."

5. *Regina v. Abdulla Ahmed Ali et al.* (Retrial), July 15, 2009.

6. *Regina v. Abdulla Ahmed Ali et al.* (Retrial), July 15, 2009.

7. "Airlines Bomb Plot: The E-Mails," BBC, September 7, 2009.

8. *Regina v. Abdulla Ahmed Ali et al.* (Retrial), May 5, 2009.

9. *Regina v. Ibrahim Savant, Arafat Khan, and Waheed Zaman,* June 25, 2010.

10. *Regina v. Ibrahim Savant, Arafat Khan, and Waheed Zaman,* April 28, 2010.

11. *Regina v. Ibrahim Savant, Arafat Khan, and Waheed Zaman,* April 28, 2010.

12. *Regina v. Ibrahim Savant, Arafat Khan, and Waheed Zaman,* April 28, 2010.

13. *Regina v. Abdulla Ahmed Ali et al.*, April 16, 2008.

14. *Regina v. Abdulla Ahmed Ali et al.*, May 13, 2008.

15. *Regina v. Abdulla Ahmed Ali et al.*, May 13, 2008.

16. *Regina v. Abdulla Ahmed Ali et al.*, May 13, 2008.

17. Confidential interview conducted by the author.

18. *Regina v. Abdulla Ahmed Ali et al.*, April 16, 2008.

19. *Regina v. Abdulla Ahmed Ali et al.*, April 16, 2008.

11. RENDEZVOUS IN LLOYD PARK

1. *Regina v. Abdulla Ahmed Ali et al.* (Retrial), July 15, 2009.

2. *Regina v. Abdulla Ahmed Ali et al.* (Retrial), July 15, 2009.

3. *Regina v. Abdulla Ahmed Ali et al.* (Retrial), July 15, 2009.

4. *Regina v. Abdulla Ahmed Ali et al.* (Retrial), July 15, 2009.

5. *Regina v. Abdulla Ahmed Ali et al.* (Retrial), July 15, 2009.

6. *Regina v. Abdulla Ahmed Ali et al.*, April 16, 2008.

7. In Great Britain these are known as "bum-bags."

8. *Regina v. Abdulla Ahmed Ali et al.*, April 16, 2008.

9. *Regina v. Ibrahim Savant, Arafat Khan, and Waheed Zaman,* April 28, 2010.

10. *Regina v. Ibrahim Savant, Arafat Khan, and Waheed Zaman,* April 28, 2010.

11. *Regina v. Abdulla Ahmed Ali et al.* (Retrial), July 15, 2009.

12. Author interview with Shaun Greenough, January 14, 2020.

13. Interview with Shaun Greenough.

14. Interview with Shaun Greenough.

15. *Regina v. Ibrahim Savant, Arafat Khan, and Waheed Zaman,* April 28, 2010.

16. BBC Panorama Team, "Operation Overt—Panorama."

17. BBC Panorama Team, "Operation Overt—Panorama."

18. BBC Panorama Team, "Operation Overt—Panorama."

19. *Secretary of State for the Home Department v. AY.*

20. *Regina v. Abdulla Ahmed Ali et al.*, April 16, 2008; BBC Panorama Team, "Operation Overt—Panorama."

21. *Regina v. Abdulla Ahmed Ali et al.* (Retrial), May 6, 2009.

22. *Regina v. Abdulla Ahmed Ali et al.*, April 16, 2008; BBC Panorama Team, "Operation Overt—Panorama."

23. *Regina v. Abdulla Ahmed Ali et al.*, June 24, 2008.

24. *Regina v. Ibrahim Savant, Arafat Khan, and Waheed Zaman*, June 25, 2010.
25. Federal Bureau of Investigation, *11 September Hijacker Model.*
26. *Regina v. Ibrahim Savant, Arafat Khan, and Waheed Zaman*, June 24, 2010.
27. *Regina v. Abdulla Ahmed Ali et al.* (Retrial), July 15, 2009.
28. *Regina v. Abdulla Ahmed Ali et al.*, May 6, 2008.
29. *Regina v. Abdulla Ahmed Ali et al.*, May 6, 2008.
30. "Airlines Bomb Plot."
31. *Regina v. Ibrahim Savant, Arafat Khan, and Waheed Zaman*, June 24, 2010.
32. *Regina v. Abdulla Ahmed Ali et al.* (Retrial), July 15, 2009.
33. *Regina v. Ibrahim Savant, Arafat Khan, and Waheed Zaman*, June 24, 2010.

12. PATTERN OF LIFE

1. Robertson, Cruickshank, and Lister, "Document Shows Origins."
2. *Regina v. Abdulla Ahmed Ali et al.*, April 16, 2008.
3. *Regina v. Abdulla Ahmed Ali et al.*, April 16, 2008.
4. *Regina v. Abdulla Ahmed Ali et al.*, April 16, 2008.
5. *Regina v. Ibrahim Savant, Arafat Khan, and Waheed Zaman*, June 26, 2010.
6. *Regina v. Ibrahim Savant, Arafat Khan, and Waheed Zaman*, June 24, 2010.
7. *Regina v. Abdulla Ahmed Ali et al.*, April 17, 2008.
8. *Regina v. Abdulla Ahmed Ali et al.* (Retrial), July 15, 2009.
9. *Regina v. Abdulla Ahmed Ali et al.* (Retrial), July 15, 2009.
10. *Regina v. Abdulla Ahmed Ali et al.* (Retrial), July 15, 2009.
11. *Regina v. Abdulla Ahmed Ali et al.* (Retrial), July 15, 2009.
12. *Regina v. Abdulla Ahmed Ali et al.* (Retrial), July 15, 2009.
13. *Regina v. Ibrahim Savant, Arafat Khan, and Waheed Zaman*, June 25, 2010.
14. *Regina v. Abdulla Ahmed Ali et al.* (Retrial), July 15, 2009.
15. *Regina v. Abdulla Ahmed Ali et al.* (Retrial), July 15, 2009.
16. *Regina v. Abdulla Ahmed Ali et al.*, April 17, 2008.
17. *Regina v. Abdulla Ahmed Ali et al.*, April 17, 2008.
18. *Regina v. Abdulla Ahmed Ali et al.*, April 17, 2008.
19. *Regina v. Abdulla Ahmed Ali et al.*, April 17, 2008.
20. *Regina v. Abdulla Ahmed Ali et al.*, April 17, 2008.
21. *Regina v. Ibrahim Savant, Arafat Khan, and Waheed Zaman*, April 28, 2010.
22. *Regina v. Abdulla Ahmed Ali et al.*, April 17, 2008.
23. Graff, *Threat Matrix.*

13. WEDDING VIDEOS

1. *Regina v. Abdulla Ahmed Ali et al.*, July 1, 2008.
2. Transcription by the author.
3. "'Suicide Videos': What They Said," BBC, April 4, 2008.

4. *Regina v. Ibrahim Savant, Arafat Khan, and Waheed Zaman*, June 24, 2010.
5. *Regina v. Abdulla Ahmed Ali et al.*, July 1, 2008.
6. *Regina v. Abdulla Ahmed Ali et al.* (Retrial), July 15, 2009.
7. *Regina v. Abdulla Ahmed Ali et al.*, July 1, 2008.
8. *Regina v. Abdulla Ahmed Ali et al.* (Retrial), August 11, 2009.
9. *Regina v. Ibrahim Savant, Arafat Khan, and Waheed Zaman*, April 28, 2010.
10. *Regina v. Ibrahim Savant, Arafat Khan, and Waheed Zaman*, April 28, 2010.
11. *Regina v. Ibrahim Savant, Arafat Khan, and Waheed Zaman*, July 12, 2010.

14. PROBE

1. *Regina v. Abdulla Ahmed Ali et al.* (Retrial), July 15, 2009.
2. *Regina v. Abdulla Ahmed Ali et al.* June 11, 2008.
3. *Regina v. Abdulla Ahmed Ali et al.*, June 10, 2008.
4. *Secretary of State for the Home Department v. AY.*
5. *Regina v. Abdulla Ahmed Ali et al.*, June 10, 2008.
6. Author interview with Nigel Inkster, February 10, 2012.
7. UK Home Office, *Covert Surveillance.*
8. Chanan, *Liquid Bomb Plot.*
9. Justin Davenport, "The Walthamstow Flat Where Bomb Plot Was Hatched," *Evening Standard*, September 8, 2009.
10. "Jon" is a pseudonym.
11. *Regina v. Abdulla Ahmed Ali et al.*, June 3, 2008.

15. SEPTEMBER 12, 2001

1. Hayden, *Playing to the Edge*, 195.
2. Interview with Fran Townsend, November 7, 2019. Muir's employment with the CIA was described in Mike Conklin, "Students Are Stirred, Not Shaken, by Thought of Working for the CIA," *Chicago Tribune*, November 23, 2001.
3. Interview with Juan Zarate, March 28, 2020.
4. Parliament, *Rendition*, 11.
5. Author interview with Jose Rodriguez, January 30, 2013.
6. A reference to CE Division and an explanation of its acronym can be found in U.S. Senate, *Investigation of Illegal*, 2917; Tenet and Harlow, *At the Center*, 287–97. Also author interview with Steve Kappes, January 8, 2020.
7. Coll, *Directorate S*, 246.
8. Confidential author interview with a former CIA officer.
9. Nawaz, *Battle for Pakistan*, 81.
10. Confidential author interview with a former CIA officer.
11. Parliament, "Home Office's Response to Terrorist Attacks."

12. Author interview with Larry Pfeiffer, January 16, 2020.

13. *Damian Lewis: Spy Wars*, "Bombs in the Sky."

14. Coll, *Directorate S*, 248.

15. Gantt, *Irish-American Terrorism*, 325–57.

16. Hwang, *London's Underground Spaces*, 159–97.

17. Federal Emergency Management Agency, *FEMA 430*. The iconic "Gherkin" building in London now stands where this IRA attack occurred, at 30 St. Mary Axe.

18. Teague, "Double Blind."

19. Author interview with Adm. Scott Redd, November 14, 2012.

20. Interview with Jose Rodriguez, January 30, 2013.

21. *Damian Lewis: Spy Wars*, "Bombs in the Sky."

22. Interview with Larry Pfeiffer.

23. Interview with Steve Kappes, January 16, 2020.

24. Interview with Larry Pfeiffer.

16. SARWAR'S HOLE

1. *Regina v. Ibrahim Savant, Arafat Khan, and Waheed Zaman*, June 25, 2010. Also *Regina v. Abdulla Ahmed Ali et al.*, June 11, 2008.

2. *Regina v. Abdulla Ahmed Ali et al.*, June 11, 2008.

3. In the trial transcript and in subsequent documents, British authorities believed "TH" was code for "Telehouse," but this makes little sense since Sarwar was researching gas and oil terminals, and Telehouse is a data center provider. It is far more likely that "TH" was shorthand for the former "Theddlethorpe Gas Terminal" on the Lincolnshire coast.

4. *Regina v. Abdulla Ahmed Ali et al.*, June 11, 2008.

5. Chiltern Rangers, "Kings Wood."

6. *Regina v. Abdulla Ahmed Ali et al.*, April 18, 2008.

7. *Regina v. Abdulla Ahmed Ali et al.*, June 10, 2008.

8. *Regina v. Abdulla Ahmed Ali et al.* (Retrial), March 4, 2009.

9. *Regina v. Abdulla Ahmed Ali et al.*, June 10, 2008.

10. *Regina v. Abdulla Ahmed Ali et al.*, June 10, 2008.

11. *Regina v. Abdulla Ahmed Ali et al.*, June 10, 2008.

12. Interview with Shaun Greenough.

13. *Regina v. Abdulla Ahmed Ali et al.* (Retrial), July 15, 2009.

14. *Regina v. Abdulla Ahmed Ali et al.*, June 30, 2008.

15. *Regina v. Abdulla Ahmed Ali et al.* (Retrial), May 6, 2009.

16. *Regina v. Abdulla Ahmed Ali et al.*, June 30, 2008.

17. *Regina v. Abdulla Ahmed Ali et al.*, June 3, 2008.

18. *Regina v. Abdulla Ahmed Ali et al.*, June 3, 2008.
19. *Regina v. Abdulla Ahmed Ali et al.*, June 3, 2008.
20. *Regina v. Abdulla Ahmed Ali et al.* (Retrial), March 4, 2009.
21. *Regina v. Abdulla Ahmed Ali et al.* (Retrial), March 4, 2009.
22. *Regina v. Abdulla Ahmed Ali et al.*, May 6, 2008.
23. Interview with Steve Dryden.
24. *Damian Lewis: Spy Wars*, "Bombs in the Sky."
25. Interview with Steve Dryden.
26. *Damian Lewis: Spy Wars*, "Bombs in the Sky."
27. *Damian Lewis: Spy Wars*, "Bombs in the Sky."
28. Interview with Shaun Greenough.
29. Cruickshank, "View from the CT Foxhole."

17. TRANSATLANTIC TENSIONS

1. Suskind, *One Percent Doctrine*, 194.
2. Suskind, *One Percent Doctrine*, 194.
3. Dean, *Nine Lives*.
4. Hawley and Means, *Permanent Emergency*, 139.
5. Tom Hays, "NYPD Reveals Details of London Attack," Associated Press, August 3, 2005.
6. While the early version of this story indicated British authorities allowed the NYPD to provide this information publicly, an updated version published on August 4 explicitly noted UK officials had not authorized this briefing.
7. Richard Norton-Taylor and Nick Hopkins, "How the Shock of 9/11 Made MI5 Stronger," *Guardian*, September 7, 2011.
8. Davies, *Intelligence and Government*, 304.
9. BBC *Reith Lectures 2011*.
10. Greg Miller and Julie Tate, "CIA Shifts Focus to Killing Targets," *Washington Post*, September 1, 2011.
11. Mueller, "Statement."
12. Interview with Nigel Inkster.
13. Interview with Nigel Inkster.
14. Interview with Steve Kappes, January 8, 2020.
15. Interview with Fran Townsend, November 7, 2019.
16. Interview with Fran Townsend, November 7, 2019.
17. Author interview with Michael Hayden, March 2, 2020.
18. Interview with Michael Hayden.
19. *Damian Lewis: Spy Wars*, "Bombs in the Sky."

20. Author interview with Fran Townsend, November 7, 2019.
21. Author interview with Fran Townsend, November 7, 2019.
22. Robertson, Cruickshank, and Lister, "Document Shows Origins."

18. SKIN INFECTION

1. *Regina v. Abdulla Ahmed Ali et al.*, April 18, 2008.
2. *Regina v. Ibrahim Savant, Arafat Khan, and Waheed Zaman*, June 25, 2010.
3. *Regina v. Abdulla Ahmed Ali et al.*, May13, 2008.
4. *Regina v. Abdulla Ahmed Ali et al.*, April 14, 2008.
5. *Regina v. Abdulla Ahmed Ali et al.*, April 14, 2008.
6. Interview with Steve Dryden.
7. *Regina v. Ibrahim Savant, Arafat Khan, and Waheed Zaman*, June 25, 2010; "Airlines Bomb Plot."
8. *Regina v. Ibrahim Savant, Arafat Khan, and Waheed Zaman*, June 25, 2010.
9. *Regina v. Ibrahim Savant, Arafat Khan, and Waheed Zaman*, June 25, 2010.
10. BBC Panorama Team, "Operation Overt—Panorama."
11. *Regina v. Abdulla Ahmed Ali et al.*, June 10, 2008.
12. *Regina v. Abdulla Ahmed Ali et al.*, April 14, 2008.
13. *Regina v. Abdulla Ahmed Ali et al.*, April 14, 2008.
14. *Regina v. Abdulla Ahmed Ali et al.*, June 10, 2008.
15. *Regina v. Abdulla Ahmed Ali et al.*, April 14, 2008.
16. *Regina v. Abdulla Ahmed Ali et al.*, April 14, 2008.
17. *Regina v. Abdulla Ahmed Ali et al.*, April 14, 2008.
18. *Regina v. Abdulla Ahmed Ali et al.*, April 18, 2008.
19. *Regina v. Abdulla Ahmed Ali et al.*, June 10, 2008.
20. *Regina v. Ibrahim Savant, Arafat Khan, and Waheed Zaman*, June 25, 2010.
21. *Regina v. Abdulla Ahmed Ali et al.*, June 10, 2008.
22. *Regina v. Abdulla Ahmed Ali et al.* (Retrial), August 3, 2009.
23. *Regina v. Abdulla Ahmed Ali et al.* (Retrial), August 3, 2009.

19. OUR CITIZENS, OUR PLANES

1. *Damian Lewis: Spy Wars*, "Bombs in the Sky."
2. *Regina v. Ibrahim Savant, Arafat Khan, and Waheed Zaman*, June 25, 2010.
3. *Regina v. Abdulla Ahmed Ali et al.*, April 21, 2008.
4. *Regina v. Ibrahim Savant, Arafat Khan, and Waheed Zaman*, April 28, 2010.
5. "Airlines Bomb Plot."
6. *Regina v. Abdulla Ahmed Ali et al.*, April 21, 2008.
7. *Regina v. Abdulla Ahmed Ali et al.*, April 21, 2008.
8. *Regina v. Abdulla Ahmed Ali et al.*, June 10, 2008.
9. Interview with Fran Townsend, November 7, 2019.

10. Hawley and Means, *Permanent Emergency*, 145.

11. Hawley and Means, *Permanent Emergency*, 145.

12. Graff, *Threat Matrix*.

13. Blair, *A Journey*.

14. Bush, *Decision Points*, 140.

15. Interview with Juan Zarate, February 10, 2020.

16. Interview with Adm. Scott Redd, November 14, 2012.

17. Interview with Fran Townsend, November 7, 2019.

18. Interview with Juan Zarate, February 10, 2020.

19. Interview with Fran Townsend, November 7, 2019.

20. Interview with Fran Townsend, November 7, 2019.

21. Interview with Fran Townsend, November 7, 2019.

22. Interview with Adm. Scott Redd.

23. Author interview with Andy Liepman, May 14, 2019.

24. Interview with Andy Liepman.

25. Interview with Andy Liepman.

26. Graff, *Threat Matrix*, 501.

27. Hawley and Means, *Permanent Emergency*, 141.

28. TSA is a DHS component.

29. Hawley and Means, *Permanent Emergency*, 146.

30. Hawley and Means, *Permanent Emergency*, 146.

31. National Commission on Terrorist Attacks upon the United States, *9/11 Commission Report*, 11.

32. Central Intelligence Agency, "Khalid Shaykh Muhammad."

33. National Commission on Terrorist Attacks upon the United States, "Memorandum for the Record."

34. Interview with Steve Dryden.

35. Confidential author interview with a former CIA officer.

36. Confidential author interview with a former CIA officer.

37. Interview with Larry Pfeiffer.

38. Interview with Larry Pfeiffer.

39. Interview with Larry Pfeiffer.

40. Interview with Larry Pfeiffer.

41. *Damian Lewis: Spy Wars*, "Bombs in the Sky."

42. Interview with Michael Hayden.

43. Interview with Juan Zarate, February 10, 2020.

44. Interview with Steve Kappes, January 8, 2020.

45. Interview with Fran Townsend, November 7, 2019.

46. Interview with Fran Townsend, November 7, 2019.

47. Interview with Fran Townsend, November 7, 2019.

48. Interview with Fran Townsend, November 7, 2019.

20. IT FELL OUT OF MY POCKET

1. *Regina v. Ibrahim Savant, Arafat Khan, and Waheed Zaman*, June 25, 2010.
2. *Regina v. Ibrahim Savant, Arafat Khan, and Waheed Zaman*, June 25, 2010.
3. *Regina v. Abdulla Ahmed Ali et al.*, April 21, 2008.
4. *Regina v. Abdulla Ahmed Ali et al.*, July 7, 2008.
5. *Regina v. Abdulla Ahmed Ali et al.* (Retrial), March 5, 2009.
6. This dialogue comes directly from the MI5 audio probe. Also *Regina v. Abdulla Ahmed Ali et al.*, July 7, 2008.
7. *Regina v. Abdulla Ahmed Ali et al.*, July 7, 2008.
8. *Regina v. Abdulla Ahmed Ali et al.*, July 7, 2008.
9. *Regina v. Abdulla Ahmed Ali et al.*, April 4, 2008.
10. "Bug Records 'Posh Instruction' to Terror Suspect," *Bucks Free Press*, May 7, 2008.
11. Sean O'Neill, "Terror Cell Tried to Blow up Seven Planes," *Times* (London), February 18, 2009.
12. Chris Greenwood and Margaret Davis, "Gang Planned to Bomb Transatlantic Jets—Court Told," *Press Association Mediapoint*, February 17, 2009.
13. Simon Hughes, "Be Aggressive on Your Martyrdom Video . . . and Don't Speak Too Posh," *Sun*, May 8, 2008.
14. Mandy Sauer, "Chilling Martyrdom Video Shown in Court," ABC News, April 10, 2008.
15. Confidential author interview with a former NCTC officer.

21. THE RAILWAY CROSSING

1. "Ancestral Village of British Suspected Terror Plotter Rashid Rauf," AP Television, August 16, 2006.
2. Hayden, *Playing to the Edge*, 203–4.
3. Hayden, *Playing to the Edge*, 206.
4. Rodriguez and Harlow, *Hard Measures*, 3.
5. Interview with Larry Pfeiffer.
6. Author interview with Jose Rodriguez, February 11, 2020.
7. Interview with Jose Rodriguez, January 30, 2013.
8. "President Confers 192 Civilian Awards," *Dawn* (Pakistan), August 14, 2005.
9. Interview with Larry Pfeiffer.
10. Interview with Jose Rodriguez, January 30, 2013.
11. Interview with Shuja Nawaz.
12. Interview with Michael Hayden.

13. Interview with Jose Rodriguez, January 30, 2013.
14. German authorities' assessment.
15. Rodriguez and Harlow, *Hard Measures*, 8.
16. Interview with Jose Rodriguez, January 30, 2013.
17. "Terrorism Close Calls," *Netflix*.
18. German authorities' assessment.
19. Rodriguez and Harlow, *Hard Measures*, 8.
20. Interview with Steve Kappes, January 8, 2020.
21. Interview with Jose Rodriguez, January 30, 2013.
22. Interview with Fran Townsend, November 7, 2019.
23. Interview with Fran Townsend, November 7, 2019.
24. Interview with Steve Dryden.
25. Author interview with Margaret Gilmore, January 22, 2020.
26. David Leppard et al., "Terror in the Skies," *Sunday Times* (London), August 13, 2006.
27. Chanan, *Liquid Bomb Plot*.
28. Hayman and Gilmore, *Terrorist Hunters*, 333–34.
29. Reid, "Security, Freedom."
30. Patrick Hennessy, "It Was the Best of Timing, It Was the Worst of Timing," *Sunday Telegraph*, August 13, 2006.
31. David Leigh, "Phone-Hacking Documents 'Confirm That Labour Government Was Briefed,'" *Guardian*, March 5, 2012.
32. Catherine MacLeod, "After His Toughest Week Yet, He's Tipped to Go Far. But First He's Got a Lobster to Enjoy," *Herald* (Glasgow), August 16, 2006.
33. Hennessy, "It Was the Best of Timing."
34. Raymond Whitaker et al., "Apocalyptic: Bigger than 7/7? Worse than 9/11? Piece by Piece, the Plot Unravels," *Independent*, August 13, 2006.
35. Interview with Shaun Greenough.
36. Interview with Shaun Greenough.

22. FELLOWSHIP IS LIFE

1. *Regina v. Abdulla Ahmed Ali et al.*, April 21, 2008.
2. *Regina v. Abdulla Ahmed Ali et al.*, April 21, 2008.
3. *Regina v. Abdulla Ahmed Ali et al.*, April 21, 2008.
4. Chanan, *Liquid Bomb Plot*.
5. *Regina v. Abdulla Ahmed Ali et al.*, April 8, 2008.
6. *Regina v. Abdulla Ahmed Ali et al.*, April 3, 2008.
7. *Regina v. Abdulla Ahmed Ali et al.*, June 3, 2008.
8. *Regina v. Abdulla Ahmed Ali et al.*, April 10, 2008.
9. *Regina v. Abdulla Ahmed Ali et al.*, April 8, 2008.

10. *Regina v. Ibrahim Savant, Arafat Khan, and Waheed Zaman*, June 24, 2010.
11. *Regina v. Abdulla Ahmed Ali et al.*, July 7, 2008.
12. *Regina v. Abdulla Ahmed Ali et al.*, April 5, 2008.
13. *Regina v. Abdulla Ahmed Ali et al.*, April 5, 2008.
14. *Regina v. Abdulla Ahmed Ali et al.*, June 25, 2008.
15. *Regina v. Abdulla Ahmed Ali et al.*, April 28, 2008.
16. *Regina v. Abdulla Ahmed Ali et al.* (Retrial), August 3, 2009 and August 11, 2009.
17. Caroline Mallan, "Suspects Led 'Fish and Chip' Lives," *Toronto Star*, August 12, 2006.
18. Chris Tryhorn, "Newspaper Groups Pay Out over 'Bomb' Story," *Guardian*, May 16, 2007.
19. *Regina v. Ibrahim Savant, Arafat Khan, and Waheed Zaman*, June 24, 2010.
20. *Regina v. Abdulla Ahmed Ali et al.*, April 4, 2008.
21. *Regina v. Ibrahim Savant, Arafat Khan, and Waheed Zaman*, June 25, 2010.
22. *Regina v. Abdulla Ahmed Ali et al.* (Retrial), March 6, 2009.
23. Robertson, Cruickshank, and Lister, "Document Shows Origins."
24. Secretary of State for the Home Department v. AM [2009] EWHC 3053 (Admin), 2009, England and Wales High Court (Administrative Court) Decisions.

23. SCRAMBLE

1. Hawley and Means, *Permanent Emergency*, 150–51.
2. Author interview with Rich Davis, December 10, 2019.
3. Interview with Rich Davis.
4. Hawley and Means, *Permanent Emergency*, 152.
5. Dan Simon et al., "British Authorities Thwart Alleged Sky Terror Plot; Airports on Alert; Terror in a Bottle," CNN, August 10, 2006.
6. Annabel Crabb, "Plane Bomb Plot Foiled; 21 People Arrested, Airports across Europe in Chaos," *Sydney Morning Herald*, August 11, 2006.
7. "Travel Chaos Grips UK's Airports," BBC, August 10, 2006.
8. "BA Back to Normal 'in 48 Hours,'" BBC, August 16, 2006.
9. Geoff Earle, "Schumer Caught in Heathrow Travel Hell," *New York Post*, August 11, 2006.
10. Jonathan Prynn and Dick Murray, "Heathrow Mayhem as Planes Are Grounded; Thousands of Passengers Turned Away," *Evening Standard*, August 10, 2006.
11. Author interview with Syl Tang, December 17, 2019.
12. Soledad O'Brien et al., "British Police Disrupt Terror Plot; Near Chaos at Heathrow Airport," CNN, August 10, 2006.

13. Hawley and Means, *Permanent Emergency*, 153–54.
14. Hawley and Means, *Permanent Emergency*, 168.
15. U.S. Government Accountability Office, *Aviation Security*.
16. U.S. House of Representatives, *Oversight of the Transportation Security Administration*.
17. Department of Homeland Security, TSA *Needs to Improve*.
18. White House Office of the Press Secretary, "President Bush Discusses Terror Plot."
19. White House Office of the Press Secretary, "President Bush Meets."
20. Confidential author interview with a former NCTC officer, July 21, 2012.
21. "Our Terror Nightmare: Britain Acts under UN Powers to Freeze Suspects' Assets; Britain on Alert," *Birmingham Post*, August 12, 2006.
22. Author interview with Andrew Cummings, July 17, 2020.
23. Interview with Andrew Cummings.
24. "Britain Lowers Terrorist Threat Level," *Voice of America News*, August 14, 2006.
25. "Report: Suitcase with Bomb Parts Discovered," Associated Press, August 17, 2006.
26. Tom Zeller Jr., "Times Withholds Web Article in Britain," *New York Times*, August 29, 2006.
27. Author interview with Mitch Silber, June 29, 2019.
28. Sam Jones, "Terror Plot: Claims of Bomb Kit Find in Wood," *Guardian*, August 18, 2006.
29. Interview with Shaun Greenough.
30. Mark Hughes, "490,000 to Make Paddington Green Habitable," *Independent*, May 26, 2009.
31. Beth Gardiner, "British Terror Plot Suspects Interrogated in High-Security Police Station," Associated Press, August 18, 2006.
32. European Committee for the Prevention of Torture and Inhuman or Degrading Treatment or Punishment, *Report to the United Kingdom Government*.
33. *Regina v. Abdulla Ahmed Ali et al.*, June 3, 2008.
34. *Regina v. Abdulla Ahmed Ali et al.*, April 22, 2008.
35. *Regina v. Abdulla Ahmed Ali et al.*, June 11, 2008.
36. *Regina v. Abdulla Ahmed Ali et al.*, April 23, 2008.
37. *Regina v. Abdulla Ahmed Ali et al.*, June 16, 2008.
38. *Regina v. Abdulla Ahmed Ali et al.*, June 25, 2008.
39. *Regina v. Abdulla Ahmed Ali et al.*, July 7, 2008.
40. *Regina v. Abdulla Ahmed Ali et al.*, July 23, 2008.
41. *Regina v. Abdulla Ahmed Ali et al.*, May 1, 2008.

42. Parliament, House of Commons Debate.

43. UK Foreign & Commonwealth Office, eGram 35309/06, Islamabad.

44. German authorities' assessment.

45. "Sources: U.K. Terror Plot Suspects Forced to Talk."

46. Robertson, Cruickshank, and Lister, "Document Shows Origins."

24. THE SYSTEM WORKED?

1. "Belmarsh: A 'Complex' Jail," BBC, March 8, 2006, http://news.bbc.co.uk/2/hi/uk_news/4785268.stm.

2. *Regina v. Abdulla Ahmed Ali et al.*, June 3, 2008.

3. *Regina v. Abdulla Ahmed Ali et al.*, June 3, 2008.

4. *Regina v. Abdulla Ahmed Ali et al.*, June 3, 2008.

5. *Regina v. Abdulla Ahmed Ali et al.*, June 11, 2008.

6. *Regina v. Abdulla Ahmed Ali et al.*, June 11, 2008.

7. *Regina v. Abdulla Ahmed Ali et al.*, May 13, 2008.

8. Elaine Sciolino et al., "In '06 Bomb Plot Trial, a Question of Imminence," *New York Times*, July 15, 2008.

9. They would all, except Mohammed Gulzar, eventually plead guilty to this lesser charge.

10. Judgment: Case of Abdulla Ali v. The United Kingdom (Application No. 30971/12), December 14, 2015, European Court of Human Rights, Fourth Section, Strasbourg.

11. *Regina v. Abdulla Ahmed Ali et al.*, July 14, 2008.

12. Tom Pochciol, "Terror Trial Jury Can Give Majority Verdict," *Bucks Free Press*, August 28, 2008.

13. Elizabeth Barrett, "Airline Plot Jury Out for 12th Day," *Press Association Mediapoint*, September 4, 2008.

14. *Regina v. Abdulla Ahmed Ali et al.*, July 23, 2008.

15. Sean O'Neill, "Police in Crisis after Jury Rejects £10m Terror Case," *Times* (London), September 9, 2008.

16. "Police in Crisis."

17. "'Astonishment' at Terror Verdicts," BBC, September 9, 2008, http://news.bbc.co.uk/2/hi/uk_news/7605583.stm.

18. "Experts: U.S. Hindered 'Jet Bomb Plot' Probe," CNN, September 9, 2008.

19. *Regina v. Abdulla Ahmed Ali et al.*, June 12, 2008.

20. *Secretary of State for the Home Department v. AY.*

21. *Secretary of State for the Home Department v. AY.*

22. *AM v. Secretary of State for the Home Department*, [2011] EWHC 2486 (Admin), 2011, High Court of Justice.

23. *Secretary of State for the Home Department v. AY.*

25. RASHID RAUF'S SECOND CHANCE

1. "Pakistani Official: No Decision 'Yet' on Handing Over Terror Plot Suspect to UK," GeoTV, September 9, 2006.
2. Salman Masood, "Pakistan Court Drops Charge in London Plot Case," *New York Times*, December 13, 2006.
3. "Airliner Plot Suspect Weighs 'Billion-Pound' Suit against Britain," Deutsche Presse-Agentur, January 12, 2007.
4. Saulino, "Strategic Choices."
5. U.S. Department of Justice, Emails from [redacted] to Laura Ingersoll.
6. "Central Jail, Rawalpindi."
7. "Court Directs Adiala Jail Supdt to Provide Jail Facilities to Rashid Rauf As Per Jail Manual," *Pak Tribune*, January 6, 2007.
8. "Cot, Chair, Lantern: Nawaz Sharif, Daughter Maryam Get 'B' Grade Cells in Rawalpindi Jail in Pakistan," *Hindustan Times*, July 14, 2018.
9. The FBI refers to these internal memos as "Electronic Correspondence," or ECs.
10. Federal Bureau of Investigation, Washington Field Squad CT-3.
11. Federal Bureau of Investigation, Redacted sender.
12. Federal Bureau of Investigation, Counterterrorism to Director's Office.
13. Federal Bureau of Investigation, Washington Field CT-3 to Directorate of Intelligence.
14. Interview with Andy Liepman.
15. Interview with Larry Pfeiffer.
16. Council on Foreign Relations, "Conversation with Prime Minister Imran Khan."
17. Supreme Court of Pakistan, *Annual Report*.
18. "Nine Police Officials: Rashid Rauf's Escape," *Dawn* (Pakistan), February 3, 2008.
19. Human Rights Watch, "IV. Laws Used to Detain Protestors."
20. "Pakistan Investigative Agencies Find 'Clue' to UK Suspect's Escape—Paper," BBC *Monitoring South Asia; London*, December 18, 2007.
21. "Terror Plots and Conspiracy Theories: The Hunt for Rashid Rauf," *Independent*, September 27, 2008.
22. Mohammed Asghar, "Pakistan Report Terms UK Suspect's Escape 'Criminal Collusion,'" *Dawn*, December 20, 2007.
23. "Pakistan Investigative Agencies Find 'Clue.'"
24. "Rashid Rauf Escaped with His Uncle," *Dawn*, December 18, 2007.
25. "Rashid Rauf Escaped with His Uncle."
26. "Terror Plots and Conspiracy Theories."
27. "Pakistan Investigative Agencies Find 'Clue.'"

28. "Nine Police Officials."
29. Asghar, "Pakistan Report."
30. "Pakistan Security Agencies 'Arranged' UK Suspect's Escape—Family," *Dawn*, December 17, 2007.
31. UK Foreign & Commonwealth Office, From: [redacted].
32. "Pakistan Security Agencies 'Arranged' UK Suspect's Escape."
33. UK Foreign & Commonwealth Office, From: [redacted].
34. Massoud Ansari and Miles Erwin, "London Airline Bomb Plot Suspect Escapes," *Telegraph*, December 16, 2007.
35. "Terror Plots and Conspiracy Theories."
36. "Pakistan Security Agencies Find 'Clue.'"
37. Interview with Larry Pfeiffer.
38. Interview with Michael Hayden.
39. Asghar, "Pakistan Report.'"
40. UK Foreign & Commonwealth Office, eGram 49040/08, Islamabad.
41. Confidential author interview with a former CIA officer.
42. Salman Masood, "C.I.A. Leaves Pakistan Base Used for Drone Strikes," *New York Times*, December 11, 2011.
43. "No Explanation Sought by UK on Suspect's Escape—Pakistan Foreign Office," *Nawa-i-Waq*, December 18, 2007.
44. Interview with Larry Pfeiffer.
45. Salim Bokhari, "Musharraf Assures Pakistanis in UK of Holding Fair, Free Polls," *News* (Pakistan), January 26, 2008.
46. "Stephen J. Hadley Oral History."
47. Sebastian Rotella and Josh Meyer, "A Young American's Journey into Al Qaeda," *Los Angeles Times*, July 24, 2009. After U.S. and Pakistani forces captured Vinas, he became a star cooperator for the United States in tracking down and smiting this terror group. Adam Goldman, "He Turned on Al Qaeda and Aided the U.S. Now He's on Food Stamps and Needs a Job," *New York Times*, March 6, 2018.
48. UK Foreign & Commonwealth Office, eGram 33050/08, Islamabad.
49. U.S. Department of Justice, "Al Qaeda Operative Convicted"; United States v. Najibullah Zazi, U.S. Attorney, Eastern District of New York, Criminal Docket No. 09-663 (S-1) (RJD), redacted for public filing, Case 1:09-cr-00663-RJD-SMG, document 71, February 15, 2019, filed May 1, 2019.
50. *United States v. Najibullah Zazi.*
51. U.S. Department of Justice, "Government's Proffer and Memorandum of Law in Support of Motion for Detention," Criminal Case No. 09-mj-03001-CBS United States of America, Plaintiff, v. 1. Najibullah Zazi,

Defendant, Filed September 24, 2009, https://www.justice.gov/archive /usao/co/news/2009/September09/Zazi_Detention_Motion.pdf.

52. U.S. Department of Justice, "Al Qaeda Operative Convicted."

53. United States v. Zarein Ahmedzay, U.S. Attorney, Eastern District of New York, Criminal Docket No. 10-019 (s-1) (rjd), redacted for public filing, Case 1:10-cr-00019-rjd, document 480, December 6, 2018, filed December 14, 2018.

54. U.S. Department of Justice, "Al-Qaeda Operative Sentenced."

55. David Leppard, "Rauf, the Ghost in the Terror Machine; Last Week's British Raids Followed the Investigation of an Al-Qaeda Chief's Europe-Wide Campaign," *Sunday Times* (London), April 12, 2009.

56. Lia and Nesser, "Lessons Learned."

57. Author interview with Tim Buch, December 11, 2019.

58. Hayden, *Playing to the Edge*, 346.

59. Interview with Michael Hayden.

60. Interview with Michael Hayden.

61. Syed, *Secrets of Pakistan's War*, 143.

62. "Profile: Islamabad's Red Mosque," bbc, July 27, 2007, http://news.bbc.co .uk/2/hi/south_asia/6503477.stm.

63. Eric Schmitt and Somini Sengupta, "Ex-US Official Cites Pakistani Training for India Attackers," *New York Times*, December 3, 2008; Sebastian Rotella, "Four Alleged Masterminds of 2008 Mumbai Attacks Are Indicted in Chicago," *ProPublica*, April 25, 2011.

64. Interview with Steve Kappes, March 13, 2020.

65. Interview with Juan Zarate, February 10, 2020.

66. Ḥaqqānī, *India vs Pakistan*.

67. Interview with Michael Hayden.

68. Interview with Michael Hayden.

69. Hayden, *Playing to the Edge*, 336–37.

70. Eric Schmitt and David E. Sanger, "Pakistan Shuns C.I.A. Buildup Sought by U.S.," *New York Times*, January 27, 2008.

71. Hayden, *Playing to the Edge*, 348.

72. Interview with Larry Pfeiffer.

73. Interview with Larry Pfeiffer.

74. Interview with Michael Hayden.

75. Interview with Andy Liepman.

26. THE TWISTING ROAD

1. *Judgment: Case of Abdulla Ali v. The United Kingdom.*

2. *Regina v. Abdulla Ahmed Ali et al.* (Retrial), March 4, 2009.

3. *Regina v. Abdulla Ahmed Ali et al.* (Retrial), March 5, 2009.

4. Paul Cheston, "Jet Bombing Plot Was Directed From Pakistan, Jury Told," *Evening Standard.* February 17, 2009.

5. "Bomb Plot Case Jury Dismissed; Britain in Brief," *Independent*, February 19, 2009.

6. *Regina v. Abdulla Ahmed Ali et al.* (Retrial), March 4, 2009.

7. *Regina v. Abdulla Ahmed Ali et al.* (Retrial), March 4, 2009.

8. Robert Mackey, "E-Mail Read by N.S.A. Helped Convict Liquid Bomb Plotters," *Lede* (*New York Times* blog), September 8, 2009.

9. Mackey, "E-Mail Read by N.S.A."

10. Electronic Frontier Foundation, *Yahoo! Compliance Guide.*

11. "'Allow Intercept Evidence,'" BBC, September 8, 2009.

12. Ismail Khan and Jane Perlez, "Airstrike Kills Qaeda-Linked Militant in Pakistan," *New York Times*, November 22, 2008.

13. "British-Pakistani Terror Suspect Still Alive: Lawyer," Agence France Presse, November 24, 2008.

14. "Pakistan: UK Bombing Mastermind Rashid Alive in Pakistan," *Nawa-e Waqt (Urdu)*, September 11, 2009.

15. UK Foreign & Commonwealth Office, Redacted to Redacted.

16. Vikram Dodd, "Airline Bomb Plotters' Links to Al-Qaida and Other Convicted Terrorists," *Guardian*, September 7, 2009.

17. Ahmed Ali & Ors, R. v. [2011] EWCA Crim 1260, 2011, England and Wales Court of Appeal (Criminal Division).

18. John Simpson, "Terrorist Bound for Syria Was Freed Early from Jail," *Times* (London), March 15, 2014.

19. Felix Allen, "Terror Foot Soldier Jailed for Life over Heathrow Liquid Bomb Plot," *Evening Standard*, December 10, 2009.

20. HM Land Registry, Wales Office, "386A Forest Road."

21. "Truth Has Won' as Terror Plotter's Wife Cleared," *Independent*, March 5, 2010.

22. UK Crown Prosecution Service, "Three Men Linked."

23. A Category "A" status indicates the prisoner poses a continuing danger to the public. For the conviction, see Ali and Others v. The United Kingdom—30971/12—Communicated Case [2013] 1028, October 1, 2013, European Court of Human Rights.

24. *Ali and Others v. The United Kingdom.*

25. "Extremist Prisoners to Be Separated at Durham Jail," *ITV News*, March 31, 2017.

26. Dipesh Gadher, "'Lie, Say You Have Reformed, Be Set Free and Strike Again'; Some of Britain's Most Dangerous Islamists Are Flouting Prison

Rules to Spread Their Hate and Inspire New Followers, Says Dipesh Gadher," *Sunday Times* (London), February 19, 2012.

27. Nick Parker, "Terror Cells Freed Hate Preacher Anjem Choudary's Sick Boast about 'Amazing' Convicted Terrorists He Met in Belmarsh Prison; Choudary Prayed with Failed 21/7 Bomber Hussain Osman and Jet Plot Mastermind Abdulla Ahmed Ali," *Sun*, October 24, 2018.

28. *Ali and Others v. The United Kingdom.*

29. "Liquid Bomb Plot Terrorist Tanvir Hussain Wins Legal Challenge over Segregation at Durham Prison," *Northern Echo (Newsquest Regional Press)*, July 29, 2015.

30. Richard Kerbaj, "Jailed Jihadists 'Aided' Capture of Warder," *Times* (London), October 16, 2016.

31. *Ali and Others v. The United Kingdom.*

32. "Bomber Having a Blast in Prison," *Daily Star Sunday*, August 7, 2011.

33. Abhinandan Mishra, "'Masood Azhar Not Missing, Pak Lied to FATF,'" *Sunday Guardian Live* (India), February 22, 2020.

34. "Pulwama Attack: India Will 'Completely Isolate' Pakistan," BBC, February 15, 2019.

35. Rohan Dua, "In New Audio, Masood Azhar Calls US Deal with Taliban a Bid to 'Escape Afghanistan,'" *Times of India*, March 8, 2020.

36. New America, "Drone Strikes: Pakistan."

37. Stephen Trimble, "Dubai: F-16s Powered Up Pakistan's Counter-Insurgency Strikes," *Flight Global*, November 13, 2011.

38. International Air Transport Association, "Air Cargo."

39. International Air Transport Association, "Air Cargo and E-Commerce."

40. Hawley and Means, *Permanent Emergency*, 158.

41. U.S. Department of Transportation, "Baggage Fees by Airline 2019."

27. A FINE BALANCE

1. Dan Sabbagh, "Thirty Britons Believed to Be among Isis Fighters Held in Syria," *Guardian*, December 6, 2019; and "British Muslims in Numbers."

2. Meleagrou-Hitchens, Hughes, and Clifford, *Travelers*; and Besheer Mohamed, "New Estimates Show U.S. Muslim Population Continues to Grow," *Pew Research Center*, January 3, 2018.

3. Tamás et al., "Young Male Syndrome," 366; Rogers et al., "Social, Behavioral, and Biological Factors," 555–78.

4. Coogan, *The Troubles*, 150.

5. Coogan, *The Troubles*, 150.

6. Keegan, *Intelligence in War*, 349.

7. Waxman, "Police and National Security," 387.

8. Trevor Aaronson, "The Released," *Intercept*, April 20, 2017.
9. U.S. Office of the Director of National Intelligence, *Summary*.
10. Hunt, Iaconetti, and Maas, *Recidivism among Federal Violent Offenders*.
11. Parliament, "Terrorism."
12. Interview with Tayab Ali, July 8, 2020.
13. Interview with Tayab Ali, July 8, 2020.
14. Simcox and Stuart, "Threat."
15. Coats, *Worldwide Threat Assessment*.
16. "East German Stasi Had 189,000 Informers, Study Says," *Deutsche Welle*, March 11, 2008.
17. Burrough, *Days of Rage*.
18. Frank J. Prial, "Bomb at Police Headquarters Injures 7 and Damages Offices," *New York Times*, June 10, 1970.
19. "Bomb Rocks U.S. Capital: Extensive Damage Is Done to Senate," *Chicago Tribune*, March 1, 1971.
20. "Remarks by CIA Director at DNI Headquarters."
21. Zammit, "New Developments."
22. Coats, *Worldwide Threat Assessment*.
23. Author interview with Todd Rosenblum, February 19, 2019.
24. Jones, *Hunting in the Shadows*.
25. Ashford, Stanton, and Moore, *Airport Operations*.
26. Terry Gardner, "Coronavirus: Large Hand Sanitizer Bottles, Wipes Allowed in Carry-On Bags, TSA Says," *Los Angeles Times*, March 14, 2020.
27. Koenig, "How US Is Attempting to Manage Risk from 'Insider' Terrorist Threat in Aviation."
28. U.S. Department of Homeland Security, *TSA Can Improve*.
29. U.S. Department of Justice, "Kansas Man Charged."
30. U.S. Department of Justice, "Former Baggage Handler Sentenced."
31. Jay Weaver, "American Airlines Mechanic Pleads Guilty to Sabotaging Plane at Miami International," *Miami Herald*, December 18, 2019.
32. United States of America v. Usama bin Laden et al., U.S. District Court, Southern District of New York, S(7)98 Cr. 1023, February 14, 2001, 556–59.

BIBLIOGRAPHY

Aguilar, Francisco, Randy Bell, Natalie Black, Sayce Falk, Sasha Rogers, and
  Aki Peritz. *An Introduction to Pakistan's Military*. Harvard Kennedy
  School Belfer Center for Science and International Affairs, July 2011.
  https://www.belfercenter.org/sites/default/files/legacy/files/Pakistan
  -Military-final-B.pdf.

Anderson, David. *Report of the Bulk Powers Review*. Report for Parliament,
  August 2016. https://assets.publishing.service.gov.uk/government
  /uploads/system/uploads/attachment_data/file/546925/56730_Cm9326
  _WEB.PDF.

Andrew, Christopher. *Defend the Realm: The Authorized History of* MI5. New
  York: Alfred A. Knopf, 2009.

Ashford, Norman, H. P. Martin Stanton, and Clifton A. Moore. *Airport
  Operations*. 3rd ed. New York: McGraw-Hill, 2013.

Association for Safe International Road Travel. *Road Safety Facts*. Accessed
  April 9, 2021. https://www.asirt.org/safe-travel/road-safety-facts/.

BBC Panorama Team. "Operation Overt—Panorama." Unpublished notes
  from the 2008 trial.

BBC *Reith Lectures 2011: Securing Freedom*. Lecture 1, "Terror First." Presented
  by Baroness Eliza Manningham-Buller. Aired September 6, 2011, on BBC
  Radio 4.

Bergen, Peter L. *Holy War, Inc: Inside the Secret World of Osama Bin Laden*.
  New York: Simon & Schuster, 2002.

Beveridge, Alexander, ed. *Forensic Investigation of Explosions*. Boca Raton FL:
  CRC Press, 2012.

Bilotkach, Volodymyr. *The Economics of Airlines*. Newcastle upon Tyne:
  Agenda, 2017.

Blair, Tony. *A Journey: My Political Life*. New York: Alfred A. Knopf, 2010.

Blunk, Scott, David Clark, and James McGibany. "Evaluating the Long-Run Impacts of the 9/11 Terrorist Attacks on US Domestic Airline Travel." *Applied Economics* 38, no. 4 (2006): 363–70.

Briggs, Rachel, Jennifer Cole, Margaret Gilmore, and Valentina Soria. "Anatomy of a Terrorist Attack: What the Coroner's Inquests Revealed about the London Bombings." Occasional paper, Royal United Services Institute, April 2011. https://rusi.org/sites/default/files/201104_op_anatomy _of_a_terrorist_attack.pdf.

"British Muslims in Numbers." Muslim Council of Britain, January 2015. http://www.mcb.org.uk/wp-content/uploads/2015/02/MCB-Muslims-in -Numbers-infographic-final.jpg.

Burrough, Bryan. *Days of Rage: America's Radical Underground, the FBI, and the Forgotten Age of Revolutionary Violence.* New York: Penguin, 2016.

Bush, George W. *Decision Points.* New York: Crown, 2010.

Central Intelligence Agency. "A Day in the Life of a CIA Operations Center Officer." Press release, January 23, 2014.

——— . "Khalid Shaykh Muhammad: Preeminent Source on Al-Qa'ida." Intelligence assessment, July 13, 2004. Declassified August 24, 2009.

Chanan, Ben, dir. *The Liquid Bomb Plot.* Documentary, National Geographic, DVD. 2012.

Chiltern Rangers, "Kings Wood." Accessed November 23, 2019. https:// chilternrangers.co.uk/where-we-work/kings-wood/.

Coats, Daniel R. *Worldwide Threat Assessment of the US Intelligence Community.* January 29, 2019. https://www.dni.gov/files/ODNI/documents/2019 -ATA-SFR---SSCI.pdf.

Coll, Steve. *Directorate S: The C.I.A. and America's Secret Wars in Afghanistan and Pakistan.* New York: Penguin, 2018.

Coogan, Tim Pat. *The Troubles: Ireland's Ordeal and the Search for Peace.* New York: St. Martin's, 2002.

Council on Foreign Relations. "A Conversation with Prime Minister Imran Khan of Pakistan." September 23, 2019. https://www.cfr.org/event /conversation-prime-minister-imran-khan-pakistan-0.

Cruickshank, Paul. "A View from the CT Foxhole: Shaun Greenough, Case Strategy and Mentor Supervisor, The Unity Initiative." *CTC Sentinel* 12, no. 2 (February 2019): 7–11. https://ctc.usma.edu/view-ct-foxhole-shaun -greenough-case-strategy-mentor-supervisor-unity-initiative/.

Cue, Eduardo. "New Influx of Afghan Refugees Arrives at Chaman Border Crossing in Pakistan." UNHCR, January 29, 2002. https://www.unhcr.org /en-us/news/latest/2002/1/3c56c9a44/new-influx-afghan-refugees-arrives -chaman-border-crossing-pakistan.html.

Damian Lewis: Spy Wars. Season 1, episode 2, "Bombs in the Sky." Aired October 14, 2019, on History Channel UK.

Davies, Philip H. J. *Intelligence and Government in Britain and the United States: A Comparative Perspective.* Vol 2. Santa Barbara CA: Praeger, 2012.

Dean, Aimen, Paul Cruickshank, and Tim Lister. *Nine Lives: My Time as MI6's Top Spy inside Al-Qaeda.* London: Oneworld, 2018.

Diamond, James. *A People's History of Walthamstow.* Gloucestershire: History Press, 2018.

Dulat, A. S., and Aditya Sinha. *The Spy Chronicles: RAW, ISI and the Illusion of Peace.* Noida, Uttar Pradesh: HarperCollins Publishers India, 2018.

Duty Free World Council. *Global Travel Retail History—Trends—Forecast.* Accessed April 6, 2021. http://dfworldcouncil.com/wp-content/uploads /2019/02/DFWC-Website-market-update-first-half-2018.pdf.

Electronic Frontier Foundation. *Yahoo! Compliance Guide for Law Enforcement.* Accessed August 1, 2020. https://www.eff.org/files/filenode/social _network/yahoo_sn_leg-doj.pdf.

Epstein, Larry G., and Tan Wang. "'Beliefs about Beliefs' without Probabilities." *Econometrica* 64, no. 6 (November 1996): 1343–73.

European Committee for the Prevention of Torture and Inhuman or Degrading Treatment or Punishment. *Report to the United Kingdom Government on the Visit to the United Kingdom Carried Out by the European Committee for the Prevention of Torture and Inhuman or Degrading Treatment or Punishment (CPT) from 11 to 15 July 2005.* August 10, 2006.

Federal Aviation Administration. *Air Traffic by the Numbers.* August 2020. https://www.faa.gov/air_traffic/by_the_numbers/media/Air_Traffic_by _the_Numbers_2020.pdf.

Federal Bureau of Investigation. Counterterrorism to Director's Office. "Director Mueller Telephone Call [redacted] Rashid Rauf." Case ID 315N-WF-234463. August 27, 2007. Declassified July 17, 2012.

———. *The 11 September Hijacker Model.* February 2003. Declassified April 26, 2006.

———. "Rashid Rauf; IT-AL-QAEDA OO:WFO." Case ID 315M-HQ-C1424550. Washington Field Squad CT-3. August 8, 2007. Page 2.

———. Redacted sender. "Rashid Rauf; IT—Al Qaeda OO: WFO." Case ID 315N-WF-234463. August 27, 2007. Pages 2–3. Declassified July 17, 2012.

———. Washington Field CT-3 to Directorate of Intelligence. "Rashid Rauf; IT—Al Qaeda OO: WFO." Case ID 315N-WF-234463. September 7, 2007. Declassified July 17, 2012.

———. Washington Field Squad CT-3. "Rashid Rauf; IT—Al Qaeda" To:

Counterterrorism. Case ID 315N-WF-234463. July 19, 2007. Pages 2–3. Declassified August 11, 2012.

Federal Emergency Management Agency. FEMA 430, *Site and Urban Design for Security: Guidance against Potential Terrorist Attacks.* 2007. https:// www.fema.gov/sites/default/files/2020-08/fema430.pdf.

Gantt, Jonathan W. "Irish-American Terrorism and Anglo-American Relations, 1881–1885." *Journal of the Gilded Age and Progressive Era* 5, no. 4 (October 2006): 325–57.

Garstang, John H. "Aircraft Explosive Sabotage Investigation." In Beveridge, *Forensic Investigation,* 197–288.

Gerson, Michael J. *Heroic Conservatism: Why Republicans Need to Embrace America's Ideals (And Why They Deserve to Fail If They Don't).* 2007. Reprint, New York: HarperOne, 2008.

Goldby, Ben. "Special Investigation into Mohammed Gulzar for *Sunday Mercury* (Birmingham)." Unpublished, author's archive.

Goldin, Ian, and Mike Mariathasan. *The Butterfly Defect: How Globalization Creates Systemic Risks, and What to Do about It.* Princeton NJ: Princeton University Press, 2014.

Graff, Garrett M. *The Threat Matrix: The FBI at War in the Age of Terror.* New York: Little, Brown, 2011.

Ḥaqqānī, Ḥusain. *India vs Pakistan: Why Can't We Just Be Friends?* New Delhi, India: Juggernaut, 2016.

Harp, Edwin L., and Anthony J. Crone. *Landslides Triggered by the October 8, 2005, Pakistan Earthquake and Associated Landslide-Dammed Reservoir.* U.S. Geological Survey, 2006. https://pubs.usgs.gov/of/2006/1052/pdf/ofr -2006-1052.pdf.

Hartwig, Robert, and Claire Wilkinson. *Terrorism Risk: A Reemergent Threat.* Insurance Information Institute, April 2011. http://docplayer.net/13901712 -Terrorism-risk-a-reemergent-threat.html.

Hawley, Edmund S., and Nathan Means. *Permanent Emergency: Inside the TSA and the Fight for the Future of American Security.* New York: Palgrave Macmillan, 2012.

Hayden, Michael Vincent. *Playing to the Edge: American Intelligence in the Age of Terror.* New York: Penguin, 2016.

Hayman, Andy, and Margaret Gilmore. *The Terrorist Hunters.* London: Corgi, 2010.

HM Land Registry, Wales Office. "386A Forest Road, Walthamstow, London (E17 5JF)." Title Number EGL149009. https://www.gov.uk/government /publications/hm-land-registry-office-addresses.

Holbrook, Donald. "The Spread of Its Message: Studying the Prominence of Al-Qaida Materials in UK Terrorism Investigations." *Perspectives on Terrorism* 11, no. 6 (2017): 89–100.

Human Rights Watch. "IV. Laws Used to Detain Protestors." In *Destroying Legality: Pakistan's Crackdown on Lawyers and Judges,* December 2007. https://www.hrw.org/reports/2007/pakistan1207/4.htm.

———. *"With Friends Like These . . .": Human Rights Violations in Azad Kashmir.* September 20, 2006. https://www.hrw.org/reports/2006 /pakistan0906/.

Hunt, Kim Steven, Matthew J. Iaconetti, and Kevin T. Maas. *Recidivism among Federal Violent Offenders.* U.S. Sentencing Commission, January 2019. https://www.ussc.gov/sites/default/files/pdf/research-and -publications/research-publications/2019/20190124_Recidivism _Violence.pdf.

Hwang, Haewon. *London's Underground Spaces: Representing the Victorian City, 1840–1915.* Edinburgh: Edinburgh University Press, 2013.

Independent Police Complaints Commission. *IPCC Independent Investiga- tions into Complaints Made Following the Forest Gate Counter-Terrorist Operation on 2 June 2006.* February 2007.

International Air Transport Association. "Air Cargo." Accessed August 1, 2020. https://www.iata.org/en/programs/cargo/.

———. "Air Cargo and E-Commerce Enabling Global Trade." White paper, March 2019. https://www.iata.org/contentassets /d22340c37e0c4cfd8fc05ca6ebf6cc9f/stb-cargo-white-paper-e -commerce.pdf.

Jamal, Arif. *Shadow War: The Untold Story of Jihad in Kashmir.* London: Melville House, 2009.

Jones, Seth G. *Hunting in the Shadows: The Pursuit of Al Qa'ida since 9/11.* New York: Norton, 2012.

Keegan, John. *Intelligence in War.* New York: Vintage, 2004.

Khan, Hamrad. "A Letter from Sister Fatima from Abu Ghraib Prison in Iraq." Facebook, October 25, 2010. https://www.facebook.com/notes /youth-awareness-project-yap/a-letter-from-sister-fatima-from -abu-ghraib-prison-in-iraq/106941049372347/.

Koenig, David. "How US Is Attempting to Manage Risk from 'Insider' Ter- rorist Threat in Aviation." *Insurance Journal,* September 25, 2019. https:/ /www.insurancejournal.com/news/national/2019/09/25/540751.htm.

Kronenfeld, Daniel, and Rhoda Margesson. *The Earthquake in South Asia: Humanitarian Assistance and Relief Operations.* Congressional Research Service, December 12, 2005.

Levy, Adrian, and Cathy Scott-Clark. *The Meadow: Kashmir 1995– Where the Terror Began*. London: Harper, 2012.

Lia, Brynjar, and Petter Nesser. "Lessons Learned from the July 2010 Norwegian Terrorist Plot." *CTC Sentinel* 3, no. 8 (August 2010): 13–17. https://ctc .usma.edu/lessons-learned-from-the-july-2010-norwegian-terrorist-plot/.

London Assembly. *Report of the 7 July Review Committee*. June 2006. https:// www.london.gov.uk/sites/default/files/gla_migrate_files_destination /archives/assembly-reports-7july-report.pdf.

Mahanty, Bibhu. "Physics of Explosion Hazards." In Beveridge, *Forensic Investigation*, 19–52.

Marquise, Richard. *Scotbom: Evidence and the Lockerbie Investigation*. New York: Algora, 2006.

McChrystal, Stanley A. *My Share of the Task: A Memoir*. New York: Penguin, 2013.

Médecins Sans Frontières. "Waiting in the 'Green Fields' of Chaman." November 15, 2004. https://www.msf.org/waiting-green-fields-chaman -pakistan.

Meleagrou-Hitchens, Alexander, Seamus Hughes, and Bennett Clifford. *The Travelers: American Jihadists in Syria and Iraq*. Program on Extremism, George Washington University, February 2018. https://extremism.gwu .edu/sites/g/files/zaxdzs2191/f/TravelersAmericanJihadistsinSyriaandIraq .pdf.

Metropolitan Police Authority. "Re: Counter Suicide Terrorism." Memo, August 8, 2005. http://policeauthority.org/metropolitan/downloads/foi /log/kratos-attach.pdf.

Mueller, Robert S., III. "Statement Before the House Permanent Select Committee on Intelligence." U.S. House of Representatives, October 6, 2011. https://archives.fbi.gov/archives/news/testimony/the-state-of-intelligence -reform-10-years-after-911.

Musharraf, Pervez. *In the Line of Fire: A Memoir*. New York: Free Press, 2006.

National Commission on Terrorist Attacks upon the United States, ed. "Memorandum for the Record (MFR) of the Interview of Winston Wiley of the Central Intelligence Agency Conducted by Team 2." Series: Memorandums for the Record, 2003–2004. Record Group 148: Records of Commissions of the Legislative Branch, 1928–2007.

——. *The 9/11 Commission Report: Final Report of the National Commission on Terrorist Attacks upon the United States*. New York: Norton, 2004.

Nawaz, Shuja. *The Battle for Pakistan: The Bitter US Friendship and a Tough Neighbourhood*. New Delhi: Vintage Penguin Random House India, 2019.

———. *Crossed Swords: Pakistan, Its Army, and the Wars Within*. Karachi: Oxford University Press, 2008.

New America. "Drone Strikes: Pakistan." Accessed April 10, 2021. https:/ /www.newamerica.org/in-depth/americas-counterterrorism-wars /pakistan/.

Pantucci, Raffaello. "A Biography of Rashid Rauf: Al-Qa`ida's British Operative." CTC *Sentinel* 5, no. 7 (July 2012): 12–16.

———. *We Love Death as You Love Life: Britain's Suburban Terrorists*. London: Hurst, 2015.

Parliament (UK). *Could 7/7 Have Been Prevented? Review of the Intelligence on the London Terrorist Attacks on 7 July 2005*. Intelligence and Security Committee, May 2009.

———. "The Home Office's Response to Terrorist Attacks—Home Affairs Committee." Examination of Witness Lord West of Spithead, Parliament, October 13, 2009. https://publications.parliament.uk/pa/cm200910 /cmselect/cmhaff/117-ii/9101303.htm.

———. House of Commons Debate: Written Comments. November 8, 2006: Column 1703w. https://publications.parliament.uk/pa/cm200506 /cmhansrd/vo061108/text/61108w0041.htm#0611134013775.

———. *Rendition*. Intelligence and Security Committee, June 28, 2007. https://fas.org/irp/world/uk/rendition.pdf.

———. *Report into the London Terrorist Attacks on 7 July 2005*. Intelligence and Security Committee, May 2006. https://fas.org/irp/world/uk/isc _7july_report.pdf.

———. *Report of the Official Account of the Bombings in London on 7th July 2005*. House of Commons, May 11, 2006. https://fas.org/irp/world/uk/7 -july-report.pdf.

———. "Terrorism: Prisoners' Release: Written Question—HL782." February 11, 2020. https://www.parliament.uk/business/publications/written -questions-answers-statements/written-question/Lords/2020-01-27 /HL782/.

Paul, Bimal Kanti. *Environmental Hazards and Disasters: Contexts, Perspectives and Management*. Hoboken: John Wiley & Sons, 2011.

Punjab Prisons, Government of the Punjab. "Central Jail, Rawalpindi." Accessed August 1, 2020. https://prisons.punjab.gov.pk/central_jail _rawalpindi.

Puri, Luv. *Across the LoC: Inside Pakistan-Administered Jammu and Kashmir*. New Delhi: Penguin 2010.

Rashid, Ahmed. *Descent into Chaos: The US and the Failure of Nation Building in Pakistan, Afghanistan, and Central Asia*. New York: Viking, 2008.

Rassler, Don, C. C. Fair, Anirban Ghosh, Arif Jamal, and Nadia Shoeb. "The Fighters of Lashkar-e-Taiba: Recruitment, Training, Deployment and Death." Occasional Paper Series, Combatting Terrorism Center at West Point. Fort Belvoir VA: Defense Technical Information Center, April 1, 2013. https://ctc.usma.edu/app/uploads/2014/07/Fighters-of-LeT_Final .pdf.

Reid, John. "Security, Freedom and the Protection of our Values." *Demos*, August 9, 2006. http://www.demos.co.uk/files /johnreidsecurityandfreedom.pdf.

Reinares, Fernando. "The Evidence of al-Qa'ida's Role in the 2004 Madrid Attacks." *CTC Sentinel* 5, no. 3 (March 2012): 1–6. https://ctc.usma.edu /the-evidence-of-al-qaidas-role-in-the-2004-madrid-attack/.

"Remarks by CIA Director at DNI Headquarters." January 19, 2007.

"Remarks of Alexandre de Juniac at the IATA Media Briefing on COVID-19, 09 June." International Air Transport Association, June 9, 2020.

Riedel, Bruce. "Pakistan and Terror: The Eye of the Storm." *Annals of the American Academy of Political and Social Science* 618, no. 1 (July 2008): 31–45.

Rodriguez, Jose A., and Bill Harlow. *Hard Measures: How Aggressive CIA Actions after 9/11 Saved American Lives*. New York: Threshold, 2012.

Rogers, R. G., B. G. Everett, J. M. Onge, and P. M. Krueger. "Social, Behavioral, and Biological Factors, and Sex Differences in Mortality." *Demography* 47, no. 3 (August 2010): 555–78.

Rose, Charlie. "Discussion with the Home Secretary of the United Kingdom; A Discussion With the Foreign Minister of Hungary." *Charlie Rose Show*. Aired October 5, 2005, on PBS.

Sageman, Marc. *The London Bombings*. Philadelphia: University of Pennsylvania Press, 2019.

Saulino, James J. "Strategic Choices: Four Legal Models for Counterterrorism in Pakistan." *Harvard National Security Journal* 2 (2011): 247–82.

Shaw, Alison. *Kinship and Continuity: Pakistani Families in Britain*. London: Routledge, 2000.

Silber, Mitchell D. *The Al Qaeda Factor: Plots against the West*. Philadelphia: University of Pennsylvania Press, 2012.

Simcox, Robin, and Hannah Stuart. "The Threat from Europe's Jihadi Prisoners and Prison Leavers." *CTC Sentinel* 13, no. 7 (July 2020): 22–36.

Singh, Jaswant, and Strobe Talbott. *In Service of Emergent India: A Call to Honor*. Indianapolis: Indiana University Press, 2007.

"Stephen J. Hadley Oral History: Transcript." Presidential Oral Histories, University of Virginia Miller Center. Accessed April 12, 2021. https:/

/millercenter.org/the-presidency/presidential-oral-histories/stephen-j
-hadley-oral-history.

Sudmeier-Rieux, Karen, Michel Jaboyedoff, Alain Breguet, and Jérôme
Dubois. "The 2005 Pakistan Earthquake Revisited: Methods for Integrated Landslide Assessment." *Mountain Research and Development* 31,
no. 2 (May 2011): 112–21.

Supreme Court of Pakistan. *Annual Report*. March 9, 2010.

Suskind, Ron. *The One Percent Doctrine: Deep inside America's Pursuit of Its
Enemies since 9/11*. New York: Simon & Schuster, 2006.

Syed, Azaz. *The Secrets of Pakistan's War on Al-Qaeda*. Islamabad: Narratives,
2015.

Tamás, V., F. Kocsor, P. Gyuris, N. Kovács, E. Czeiter, and A. Büki. "The
Young Male Syndrome—An Analysis of Sex, Age, Risk Taking and
Mortality in Patients with Severe Traumatic Brain Injuries." *Frontiers in
Neurology* 10 (April 2019): 1–13.

Tankel, Stephen. *Storming the World Stage: The Story of Lashkar-e-Taiba*.
London: Hurst, 2011.

Teague, Matthew. "Double Blind." *Atlantic*. April 2006.

Tenet, George, and Bill Harlow. *At the Center of the Storm: My Years at the
CIA*. New York: HarperCollins, 2007.

Terrorism Close Calls. Season 1, episode 5, "Operation Overt: The Transatlantic Liquid Bomb Plot." Aired October 26, 2018, on Netflix. https://www
.netflix.com/title/80185048.

Transport for London. *Roads Task Force—Technical Note 12. How Many
Cars Are There in London and Who Owns Them?* Accessed April 9, 2021.
http://content.tfl.gov.uk/technical-note-12-how-many-cars-are-there-in
-london.pdf.

Tulloch, John. *One Day in July: Experiencing 7/7*. London: Little, Brown,
2006.

UK Crown Prosecution Service. July 8, 2010. "Three Men Linked to Liquid
Bomb Plot Guilty of Conspiracy to Murder." https://web.archive.org/web
/20101122031625/https://www.cps.gov.uk/news/press_releases/125_10/.

UK Department for Communities and Local Government, with the Change
Institute. *The Pakistani Muslim Community in England: Understanding
Muslim Ethnic Communities*. London: Communities and Local Government, 2009. http://www.communities.gov.uk/documents/communities
/pdf/1170952.pdf.

UK Foreign & Commonwealth Office. eGram 49040/08, Islamabad. December 11, 2008.

———. eGram 35309/06, Islamabad. August 12, 2006.

———. eGram 33050/08, Islamabad. August 25, 2008.

———. From: [redacted] to FCO Response Centre. "Subject: The Escape of Rashid Rauf in Pakistan (16.12.07, 1525 Pakistan time)." December 16, 2007. 11:19:24 GMT.

———. Redacted to Redacted. September 14, 2009.

UK Home Office. *Covert Surveillance and Property Interference: Revised Code of Practice*, 2018. https://assets.publishing.service.gov.uk/government /uploads/system/uploads/attachment_data/file/742041/201800802_CSPI _code.pdf.

United Nations Security Council. "Al Rashid Trust." https://www.un.org /securitycouncil/sanctions/1267/aq_sanctions_list/summaries/entity/al -rashid-trust.

———. "Mohamed al Ghabra." Al Qaeda Sanctions Committee, October 30, 2009. https://www.un.org/securitycouncil/sanctions/1267/aq_sanctions _list/summaries/individual/mohammed-al-ghabra.

U.S. Department of Defense. *Article 15-6 Investigation of the 800th Military Police Brigade*. Accessed April 10, 2021. https://fas.org/irp/agency/dod /taguba.pdf.

———. "When the Earth Shook: US Responds to Magnitude 7.6 Earthquake in Pakistan." August 4, 2015. https://archive.defense.gov/home/features /2006/2005yearinreview/article4.html.

U.S. Department of Homeland Security. *TSA Can Improve Aviation Worker Vetting (Redacted)*. Department of Homeland Security Office of the Inspector General, June 4, 2015. https://www.oig.dhs.gov/assets/Mgmt /2015/OIG_15-98_Jun15.pdf.

———. *TSA Needs to Improve Monitoring of the Deployed Advanced Imaging Technology System*. Department of Homeland Security Office of the Inspector General, May 8, 2020. https://www.oig.dhs.gov/sites/default /files/assets/2020-05/OIG-20-33-May20.pdf.

U.S. Department of Justice. "Al Qaeda Operative Convicted by Jury in One of the Most Serious Terrorist Plots against America since 9/11." Office of Public Affairs, May 1, 2012. https://www.justice.gov/opa/pr/al-qaeda -operative-convicted-jury-one-most-serious-terrorist-plots-against -america-911.

———. "Al-Qaeda Operative Sentenced to 40 Years in Prison for Role in International Terrorism Plot That Targeted the United States and Europe." Office of Public Affairs, November 24, 2015. https://www.justice .gov/opa/pr/al-qaeda-operative-sentenced-40-years-prison-role -international-terrorism-plot-targeted.

———. Emails from [redacted] to Laura Ingersoll. October 16, 2006.

———. "Former Baggage Handler Sentenced for Smuggling Loaded Firearms onto Aircraft." U.S. Attorney's Office Northern District of Georgia,
July 19, 2018. https://www.justice.gov/usao-ndga/pr/former-baggage
-handler-sentenced-smuggling-loaded-firearms-aircraft.

———. "Kansas Man Charged in Plot to Explode Car Bomb at Airport."
Office of Public Affairs, December 13, 2013. https://archives.fbi.gov
/archives/kansascity/press-releases/2013/kansas-man-charged-in-plot-to
-explode-car-bomb-at-airport.

U.S. Department of Transportation. "Baggage Fees by Airline 2019." Bureau
of Transportation Statistics. Accessed August 1, 2020. https://www.bts.gov
/content/baggage-fees-airline-2019.

U.S. Department of the Treasury. "Typologies and Open Source Reporting on Terrorist Abuse of Charitable Operations in Post-Earthquake
Pakistan and India." Accessed April 10, 2021. https://www.treasury.gov/
resource-center/terrorist-illicit-finance/Documents/charities_post
-earthquake.pdf.

U.S. Government Accountability Office. *Aviation Security: Vulnerabilities
Exposed through Covert Testing of TSA's Passenger Screening Process.*
Testimony before the Committee on Oversight and Government Reform,
House of Representatives, November 15, 2007. https://www.gao.gov/assets
/120/118618.pdf.

———. *TSA Should Ensure Screening Technologies Continue to Meet Detection
Requirements after Deployment.* December 2019. https://www.gao.gov
/assets/710/703019.pdf.

U.S. House of Representatives. *Oversight of the Transportation Security
Administration: First Hand and Government Watchdog Accounts of
Agency Challenges.* Committee on Oversight and Government Reform,
114th Cong., 1st sess., June 9, 2015.

U.S. Office of the Director of National Intelligence. *Summary of the Reengage-
ment of Detainees Formerly Held at Guantanamo Bay, Cuba.* Declassified
by Joseph Maguire, acting DNI, on November 25, 2019. https://www.dni
.gov/files/documents/Newsroom/Reports%20and%20Pubs/Final
_Version_11-26-19_ATTACH_Declassified_Summary_Reengagement
_of_GTMO_Detainees_19-1392_A-DNI_Approved.pd.pdf.

U.S. Senate. *The Impact of ISIS on the Homeland and Refugee Resettlement.*
Committee on Homeland Security and Governmental Affairs, 114th
Cong., 1st sess., November 19, 2015.

———. *Investigation of Illegal or Improper Activities in Connection with
1996 Federal Election Campaign: Final Report, Volume 2.* Committee on
Governmental Affairs, 105th Cong., 2nd sess., March 10, 1998.

Vermette, Jean-Yves. "General Protocols at the Scene of an Explosion." In Beveridge, *Forensic Investigation*, 79–95.

Waxman, Matthew. "Police and National Security: American Local Law Enforcement and Counterterrorism after 9/11." *Journal of National Security Law and Policy* 3 (2009): 377–407.

White House Office of the Press Secretary. "President and Prime Minister Blair Discuss Africa, Trade, Climate Change." July 7, 2005. https://georgewbush-whitehouse.archives.gov/news/releases/2005/07/20050707.html.

———. "President Bush Discusses Terror Plot Upon Arrival in Wisconsin." August 10, 2006. https://georgewbush-whitehouse.archives.gov/news/releases/2006/08/20060810-3.html.

———. "President Bush Meets with Counterterrorism Team." August 15, 2006. https://georgewbush-whitehouse.archives.gov/news/releases/2006/08/20060815.html.

Wright, Lawrence. *The Looming Tower: Al-Qaeda and the Road to 9/11*. New York: Vintage, 2007.

Zaidi, S. H. "Response of Government and Society to the October Earthquake." *Pakistan Horizon* 59, no. 4 (October 2006): 39–54.

Zammit, Andrew. "New Developments in the Islamic State's External Operations: The 2017 Sydney Plane Plot." *CTC Sentinel* 10, no. 9 (October 2017): 13–17. https://ctc.usma.edu/new-developments-in-the-islamic-states-external-operations-the-2017-sydney-plane-plot/.

INDEX

Page locators in italics refer to maps.